While Father Is Away

While Father Is Away

The Civil War Letters of William H. Bradbury

Edited by
JENNIFER CAIN BOHRNSTEDT

Compiled by
KASSANDRA R. CHANEY

UNIVERSITY PRESS OF KENTUCKY

Publication of this volume was made possible in part by a grant from the National Endowment for the Humanities.

Scholarly publisher for the Commonwealth,
serving Bellarmine University, Berea College, Centre College of Kentucky, Eastern Kentucky University, The Filson Historical Society, Georgetown College, Kentucky Historical Society, Kentucky State University, Morehead State University, Murray State University, Northern Kentucky University, Transylvania University, University of Kentucky, University of Louisville, and Western Kentucky University.

Editorial and Sales Offices: The University Press of Kentucky
663 South Limestone Street, Lexington, Kentucky 40508-4008

Frontispiece: Mary Bradbury with daughter Jane. Courtesy of the Spencer Research Library, University of Kansas.

07 06 05 04 03 5 4 3 2 1

Library of Congress Cataloging-in-Publication Data

Bradbury, William H., 1829-1900.
While father is away : the Civil War letters of William H. Bradbury / edited by Jennifer Cain Bohrnstedt ; compiled by Kassandra R. Chaney.
p. cm.
Includes bibliographical references (p.) and index.
ISBN 0-8131-2259-7 (acid-free paper)
1. Bradbury, William H., 1829-1900—Correspondence. 2. United States. Army. Illinois Infantry Regiment, 129th (1862-1865) 3. United States—History—Civil War, 1861-1865—Personal narratives. 4. British Americans—United States—Correspondence. 5. Soldiers—United States—Correspondence. 6. Fathers—United States—Correspondence. 7. Journalists—United States—Correspondence. 8. United States. Army—Staffs—Correspondence. 9. Businessmen—Illinois—Livingston County—Correspondence. 10. Livingston County (Ill.)—Biography.
I. Bohrnstedt, Jennifer Cain. II. Chaney, Kassandra R. III. Title.
E505.5 129th .B73 2002
973.7'4773'092—dc21 2002010905

Contents

Acknowledgments

There are many people to acknowledge for their special efforts in making it possibly for me to bring the Civil War story of William H. Bradbury and his family to readers.

Had I not found Bradbury's Civil War letter collection years ago while researching another soldier in the same brigade, I would have missed an extraordinary story in its own right. I am very grateful to the staff of the Manuscript Division of the Library of Congress for their assistance.[1]

The task of identifying additional information pertinent to Bradbury's experience in the Civil Was was challenging. Through years of searching, I was fortunate to discover very useful information at the Filson Historical Society, the Indiana Historical Society, the Illinois State Historical Library, Western Kentucky University, the Tennessee State Library and Archives, and the Topika Cemetery Association. However, nothing during this long research process could compare with the treasure trove I found in Kansas. I learned about the Grant-Bradbury Collection of the Spencer Research Library at the University of Kansas and found that their vast array of materials would fuel a myriad of researcher's epiphanies while providing concrete answers to puzzling questions about the war years and rich insight to human behavior and complex relationships. The library staff provided me with excellent assistance during my research of these invaluable records.

Those of us who love history and are intrigued by the Civil War era are fortunate that Bradbury's female descendants were such great preservationists. The voluminous collection of additional letters and other materials were kept and passed from Bradbury's wife, Mary Brown Bradbury, to their only daughter, Jane Bradbury Grant, and finally to one of their granddaughters, Mary Amelia Grant. Miss Grant contributed the "Grant-Bradbury Collection" to her alma mater, the University of Kansas, where she was also a professor of classics for forty years. I am also grateful for interviews granted by James Seaver, Virginia Seaver, and Oliver Phillips, former university colleagues of Miss Grant. Other friends, G. Baley Price and Cora Lee Beers Price provided helpful context for understanding Miss Grant's sense of responsibility to her academic discipline as well as delightful memories of her life and character. Because of her provision of the Grant-Bradbuy collection and my personal contact with her friends and associates, the gulf that first separated me from the subject of my investigation felt greatly reduced.

Private William H. Bradbury's military records and those of his closest comrades were researched at the National Archives, and the assistance of the staff there is much appreciated. I was fortunate that other members of his assigned regiment, the 129th Illinois Infantry, also wrote letters that would later be published as well.[2] In particular were the letters of Lt. Joseph F. Culver, a friend of Private Bradbury's. It was especially worthwhile to compare Bradbury's perspectives of camp life before the regiment faced combat with Culver's letter collection, published many years ago.[3] I appreciated the willingness of Lt. Culver's great-grandson, former U.S. Senator John C. Culver, to talk with me about his ancestor's Civil War experiences.

A fortuitous excursion with fine traveling companions, my grandson José Bohrnstedt Cabezas and his father Wilmer Cabezas, through Eastern Tennessee helped illuminate another aspect of Bradbury's Civil War career. Little did we know then that our own journey from a family dinner in Burkesville, Kentucky, would lead us through the same mountain pass to Jamestown, Tennessee, that Private Bradbury would describe in great detail in his letters dating from 1863. Traveling through Fentress County, Tennessee, we were close to the stomping grounds of guerrilla raider Champ Ferguson, whose life would intersect with Private Bradbury's. At Loudon, Tennessee, we gazed where Private Bradbury likely sat while writing letters home on the riverbank.

In Knoxville, we felt Bradbury's spirit was with us as we toured the historic Mabry-Hazen house that sits above the city. Later I learned that Private Bradbury apparently spent time in work or in residence at this fine home, known as the Mabry House at that time. The Mabry-Hazen House is today an outstanding historical site. Thanks to Bradbury's writings and the help of archives, museums, visitor centers, and historical societies, the majestic yet volatile Eastern Tennessee region of 1863 and 1864 became alive again.

But of all of the help, kindnesses, and encouragement I received, none meant more to me than the support of a British friend and researcher with an abiding love for U.S. Civil War history. Through the powerful capacity of the Internet, I met William L. McDonald of Droylsden, England, who lives near the native home of William H. Bradbury. After writing him electronically, Bill McDonald supported my inquiries enthusiastically and extended himself beyond the call of a volunteer's duty. He provided me with information that helped clarify Bradbury's background and the legacy of his family throughout the Saddleworth region in particular and in Yorkshire and Lancashire more generally.

Finally, many family members, friends, colleagues, and Civil War enthusiasts were helpful in encouraging me and actively listening through the long years of research and writing. I value their support, comfort, lodging, computer assistance, and fine meals. To all of you—Allen Grimshaw, Polly Swift Grimshaw, Janet Nicely, Rhonda Bohrnstedt, Matthew M. Bohrnstedt, Systa Arnadottir Bohrnstedt, Brian R. Bohrnstedt, Donald Lloyd Smith, Bettye Glover, Jack Cato, Ruth Cato, A.J. Cain, Juanita Willis Cain, Roxann Stephens, Patricia Collins, Mary Ann Gorski, and Patricia McCarthy—my most sincere thanks.

The feedback of volunteer (or enlisted) readers was especially valuable in bringing this book to its present form. My sincere thanks to Pamela K. Roe, Stephen Bohrer, Nikki Schofield, Roger E. Bohn, Ruth E. Bohn, Mary Anita Willis, Kristin Higgins, Brochton Elliott Shipley, James C. Gardner, James Ferguson, Irene Martinez Audet, Meghan Flanagan, J. C. Tumblin, Angela Brown, and Jack Leathers.

I thank Rich Vaupel for his cartographic assistance, Vonnie Zullo of the Horse Soldier Research Service for her fine help, Jim Enos for assistance with photographs, and Kathleen Manning for continuing support and access to Prints Old and Rare's extensive resources.

Professional staff, organizations, and other individuals who must be recognized for their contributions to this work include: Kathleen Neeley, Sheryl Williams, Kristin Eshelman, and Barry Bunch, Kenneth Spencer Research Library, the University of Kansas; John Scarffe, Kansas University Endowment Association; the Manuscript Division of the Library of Congress; Cynthia Cook, the Geography and Map Division of the Library of Congress; Patricia Hodges and Sara McCaslin, Manuscript and Folklife Archives, Kentucky Library, Western Kentucky University; Nancy Baird, Western Kentucky University; Vanderbilt University Library; Connie Menninger and Nancy Sherbert, Kansas History Center, Kansas State Historical Society; Watkins Community Museum of History, Lawrence, Kansas; the Illinois State Historical Library; the Cumberland Valley Civil War Heritage Association, Portland, Tennessee; Highland Rim Historical Society; Marylin Bell Hughes, Tennessee State Library and Archives; Yolanda Reid, Archives of Robertson County, Tennessee; the U.S. Army Military History Institute; the Peninsula Civil

War Round Table, San Carlos, California; Eric L. Mundell, the Indiana Historical Library, Indianapolis; Shirley Harmon and James Holmberg, the Filson Historical Society, Louisville, Kentucky; Pontiac, Illinois Public Library; Dwight, Illinois Public Library; Tony Thorsen, Dwight, Illinois Historical Society; Lillian Linebeck and Sarah McNieve, Topeka Cemetery Association; Topeka Genealogical Society; Warren Taylor, Topeka-Shawnee County Public Library; Bill Riphahn and Rogers Brazier, Parks and Recreation Department, City of Topeka, Kansas; Elizabeth Gaudi, Mabry-Hazen House; Patricia G. Bresee; James R. Allison, Botanist, Georgia Natural Heritage Program; Carmichael Inn, Loudon, Tennessee; David McCartney, Special Collections, University of Iowa Library; Kentucky State Historical Society; Vanderbilt University Library; Sutro Library, California State Library System; Mary Waters, South San Francisco Public Library; Rancho Mirage, California Public Library; Ann Toplovich of the Tennessee Historical Society; Ivan Hannibal, Wisconsin Veteran's Museum; Steve Cotham, McClung Historical Collection, East Tennessee Historical Center; John Beatty, Allen County, Indiana Public Library; Green Library, Stanford University; Jackie Clare Wood; Scott Wood; Lyle Rausch; Nigel Salway; Joan Lowrey; Kay Townsend; and Walter T. Durham.

I appreciated the opportunity to integrate some of the story of William and Mary Bradbury into the curriculum of a seminar, on the "Human side of the Civil War," at the College of the Desert, Palm Desert, California, at the Del Webb Sun City's community campus site. I had the fine and rewarding experience of "pupils,"—many veterans of World War II and the Korean War, their wives, and their widows—who probed and challenged Private Bradbury during the seminar.

My sincere thanks to individuals and organizations in England who contributed to my research: Mike McDonald; Mike Buckley; Maurice Dennett, Saddleworth Museum and Art Gallery, Oldham; Rod Lockwood; Droylsden Public Library; John Rylands University Library of Manchester; Local Studies Unit of the Manchester City Archives; Greater Manchester County Records Office; Manchester Registry Office; Oldham Local Studies Department, Oldham Archives; Neil Barrow, Saddleworth Historical Society Archives; Alice Locke, Tameside Local Studies Library, Stalybridge Library; and Griffith Institute, Oxford University.

Finally, William H. Bradbury's Civil War story was possible to undertake only through the contributions by my assistant and compiler, Kassandra Chaney, and with the unwavering support of George W. Bohrnstedt.

For George William Bohrnstedt

"Not wars and conquests mark a century . . .
but the thoughts of men, their attitude toward
their environment, their struggles toward duty—
these are the things which endure."

David Starr Jordan, 1903
The Call of the Twentieth Century

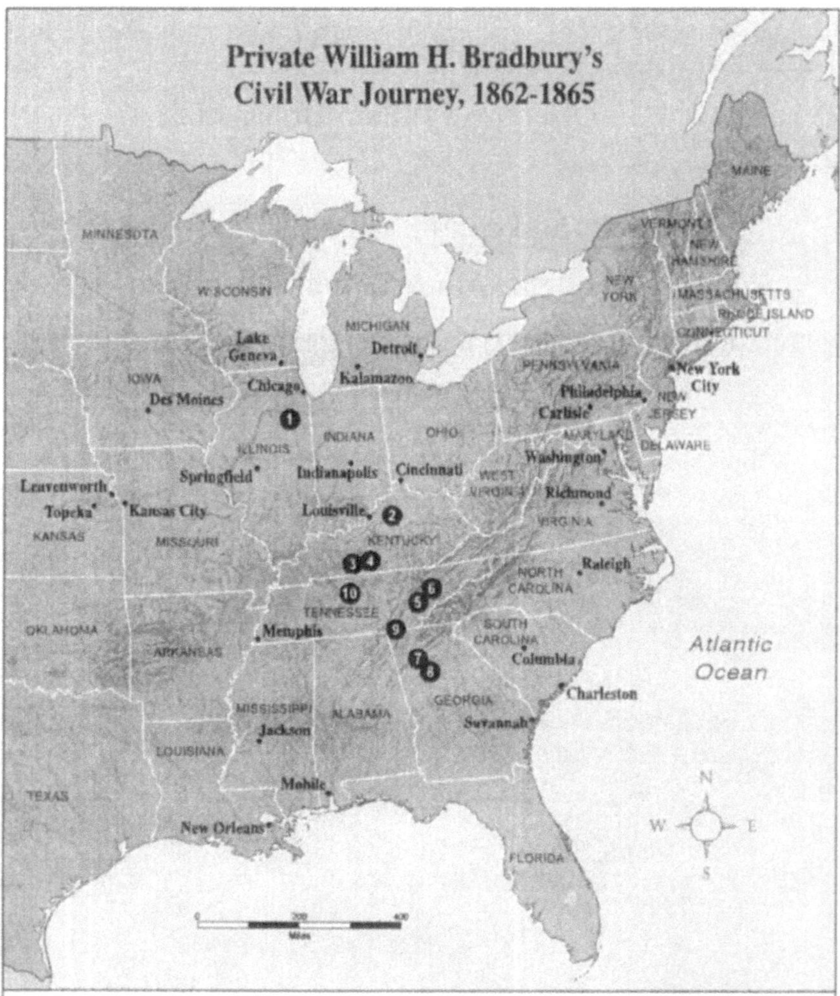

❶ ***Dwight, Illinois:*** Bradbury's home upon enlistment in the 129th Ill. Inf. during the Civil War.

❷ ***Frankfort, Kentucky:*** The countryside reminded him of home, of England.

❸ ***Bowling Green, Kentucky:*** Access to key information increased while he worked directly for Union generals.

❹ ***Glasgow, Kentucky:*** Bradbury's letters were rife with rumors of Confederate John Hunt Morgan's expected attacks.

❺ ***Loudon, Tennessee:*** Camped on the river bank.

❻ ***Knoxville, Tennessee:*** Bradbury reported the siege of Knoxville for the *Chicago Tribune*.

❼ ***Northern Georgia:*** Assigned to General Butterfield & Colonel Benjamin Harrison.

❽ ***Atlanta, Georgia:*** From the piazza of a fine home on Peach Tree Street, Bradbury watched the Union-forced exodus of Atlanta's citizens.

❾ ***Chattanooga, Tennessee:*** Joined the staff of the Judge Advocate of the Department of the Cumberland.

❿ ***Nashville, Tennessee:*** As a court reporter, Bradbury chronicled the trials of the notorious Champ Ferguson, debated his future life, and awaited a "little stranger."

Introduction

Why does Private William H. Bradbury matter? What value can yet another soldier's letters offer about the U.S. Civil War to those of us in the 21st century and beyond?

The writings of a British immigrant living in Illinois, Private William H. Bradbury of the 129th Illinois Infantry, contribute to many aspects of history, over and above his own legacy as a prolific writer and recorder of the Civil War: immigration history; land speculation and prairie settlement in the mid-19th century; the roles of women left to run domestic and business affairs at home; the effect of the U.S. Civil War on foreign affairs and conditions abroad, particularly in Britain; and long-distance family relations by husbands and fathers in the Union army.

His was not a typical Civil War story; this soldier probably never fired a gun. As an attorney-turned-soldier/clerk, Bradbury's story mirrors the very peaks, valleys, strengths, and foibles of what is often called the human condition. Through Bradbury's letters, we know considerably more about business, social, and familial responsibilities carried into war and how they unfolded during a time of a prolonged and fearful absence. While styles and mannerisms were of the era, Bradbury's experience of coping with the complete palette of life during war bears a striking and timeless comparison to that of soldiers of any war.

Bradbury's is not the only letter collection of an immigrant to the U.S. who found himself in the thick of our conflict. Thirty-three years of age at the time of his enlistment, Bradbury never rose above the rank of private, although he referred to himself, most tellingly, as a "high private."[1]

He was not the only father who went to war and pined for his absent family, although few collections of letters to children exist for comparison. He was also not the only well-educated soldier in the Union army, and there were likely other attorneys who became military clerks.

Traveling from his home in Livingston County, Illinois, to Frankfort, Crab Orchard, Bowling Green, Glasgow, Columbia, Lebanon, Loudon, Knoxville, Chattanooga, Atlanta, and Nashville, Bradbury's Civil War was spent as a member of the 129th Illinois Infantry detached to corps and division headquarters for most of the war. His access to key individuals was unique, and his letters home as well as those written for newspapers were full of informative details. With a brother back in England vested in the lucrative business of milling Southern cotton before the war, Bradbury wrote as liberally for the readers back in Manchester, England, during the war as he did for those in Chicago. He was not a partisan politico as were many well-educated men of his day; Bradbury was a pragmatic private in the Union army.

His letters contain a behind-the-scenes look at some of the major leaders of the western campaigns of the war and the character of their leadership. Private Bradbury's associations with Generals Granger, Dumont, Judah, Manson, Boyle, Burnside, Butterfield, White, Thomas, Fisk, Colonel Benjamin Harrison, and Judge Advocate Thruston help explain the characters of U.S. history from 1862 to 1865 and beyond.

Bradbury wrote extensively for these leaders—from discharge papers and "Official Operations in Virginia" to the minutes of the trial and execution of guerrilla raider Champ Ferguson and an assessment of the Freedmen Bureau's schools in the postwar South. These were not trivial tasks. It took an astute character like Private Bradbury to insinuate himself into the various entrepreneurial opportunities and then to accomplish the careful documentation the tasks warranted.

Reading about Bradbury's activities as a clerk almost permanently detailed to Union generals, we understand the lengths to which a soldier will go to avoid the routine demands of a soldier's life. At the time of his enlistment, Bradbury was not a strapping nineteen-year-old farmboy but a thirty-three-year-old businessman. At times he revealed the frail side of his health and constitution.

What is clear is that Bradbury was accustomed to taking care of himself; while it was often difficult, he made certain that he would continue to be taken care of during a war that didn't cater to the needs of individual soldiers. Shrewd, calculating, manipulative, and scheming are all appropriate words to describe him, as are passionate, humorous, philosophical, and paternal. He was not all saint, neither was he all sinner—Bradbury was an unabashedly complex individual in a complex war.

Most of all, though, Bradbury's writings reveal the long reach and power of the pen to enable him to participate in the process of parenting his children during the war. That is, he influenced the education and upbringing of his children in spite of the war and their distance it imposed on them. (Bradbury's letters to his children are also included in this volume.) His expectations for his children, especially for his only daughter, Jane, were high, firm, yet always articulated lovingly. Simply put, William H. Bradbury provides a striking example of how one father wanted and needed to participate in his children's lives in spite of war. Others may have found that the war eliminated them from the family entirely; *this* father made sure that he mattered.

Bradbury's convoluted business affairs reveal the entrepreneurial challenges a soldier faced by not being able to manage the family business affairs as he normally would. For a man like Bradbury, with his need for control, this may have been even more frightening than the prospect of facing the enemy in war. Bradbury knew he had to groom someone who could, with his confidence, act on his behalf.

Some men in 1862 might have turned to other male family members, or perhaps an attorney or pastor. Bradbury, however, turned to his partner-in-life, Mary Brown Bradbury. As he coached and cajoled Mary to represent him in business affairs—sometimes very firmly—the fact remains that during the fragile financial years of the Civil War, the Bradburys succeeded in not only maintaining their wealth, but in increasing it. As reticent as Mary may have been in undertaking some of these assignments, she rose to the occasion at a time in history when nearly no wife was expected to perform in such a wide-sweeping capacity. The unusual relationship between William H. Bradbury and Mary Brown Bradbury was both excruciatingly demanding and painfully egalitarian.

Collaborative work aside, the story of the Bradburys is also a love story. While theirs was a mature relationship—they had been married for nine years when William enlisted—his 130 war-era letters to Mary reveal that the coals of passion had not cooled over the years. What occurs behind the closed doors of any couple, let alone those of a nineteenth-century couple whose relationship is available to us only in letters, can never be known for certain. However, the intimacy of their relationship may have been enhanced by the long distances that separated them and the anticipation of mail and hopeful reunions.

While not newlyweds, romantic desire and written longings for "one more embrace" were intermingled with pragmatic requests to "collect the rent." All told, the letters provide a rich insight to their virtues, vices, and a fairly typical nineteenth-century marriage. They needed each other. They pined for each other, and they were sufficiently comfortable with each other to put intimate thoughts on paper, teasing each other when their longing gave way to passion, eventually resulting in fertile furloughs.

Leaving multiple, highly complex, and unsettled business affairs with his wife (who had not benefited from extensive education as he had) and the existence of three, five, then six children meant that Bradbury was highly motivated to stay alive. Assuring their survival meant that he was intent on avoiding the typical risks a soldier faces. While unsuccessful in his pursuit of the commission of his choosing—and he intended to have some choice in the matter—his letters also reveal controversial schemes that would help perpetuate the comforts that a mere private would not normally receive.

A Victorian-era Englishman from a privileged background recently living on the American prairie, Bradbury necessarily had a different perspective on the events occurring around him. Furthermore, the Civil War and the new experience of soldiering created an opportunity for Bradbury to discover another side of himself, as a different type of soldier, immigrant, and pioneer on American soil. Without Bradbury's enlistment and tenure in the Union Army, we would know far less about the Western campaigns and the evolution of the postwar West.

The history of place, an important but underemphasized aspect to the Civil War, is elevated in importance by Bradbury's writings. Rich in detail with comparisons to the Lancashire and Yorkshire towns back home in England, Bradbury adds a great deal of information to our impressions of communities in Kentucky, Tennessee, and Georgia during the war. His was a story of the settling of the United States, an immigrant's history, which informs the trend that continues today, as other immigrant groups negotiate a path similar to Bradbury's.

A key element of Bradbury's Civil War story is the role of his own native soil. Yorkshire-born, Bradbury was the second of three sons to Timothy and Jane Buckley Bradbury, who were originally of Delph, in the Saddleworth region to the west of the Pennine Range and east of County Lancashire.[2] William H. Bradbury was educated and spent his early adult years in Ashton-under-Lyne and Droylsden, towns near Manchester and not far from his place of birth.

Bradbury is an example of the mid–nineteenth-century entrepreneur, one who was inspired to conquer some section of the new West in America; in this aim he was resoundingly successful, owning land in multiple states at different times. The American land system at that time provided the unique and lucrative opportunity for individuals both to hold land and to sell it. One nineteenth-century writer described the prevalent spirit behind the "American land question" in the following terms:

> The whole public mind, for a couple of centuries, had been drunk or diseased on the subject. . . . There was not one who did not think he had a right to sell the plains, the valleys, even the rivers and the everlasting hills and mountains, just as much as the King of Persia had a right to sell all the winds that ever blew over Cashmere [*sic*].[3]

Bradbury must have felt confident and motivated, if not rebellious, to sever his past life and take on this new project, away from his family's long and prosperous heritage in the woolen and cotton textile mill industry, in which his older brother Charles T. Bradbury excelled and which he expanded. In fact, William's father, Timothy, had early ties to the U.S. Knowing a little more about Bradbury's family helps to explain his letters and some of the references.

During the 1830's, Timothy Bradbury commissioned his brother James W. Bradbury[4] and other agents[5] to study the mills that were taking hold in the American East. In 1821, just nine years earlier, when James W. Bradbury was eager to go to America, it was a source of contention as brother Timothy wrote to their parents, Benjamin and Sarah Bradbury, already established cloth manufacturers in Germantown near Philadelphia:

> James is now learning the dying business in Scotland . . . engaged for a year . . . and his master and him mean to go back to America next summer. . . . What are your hopes and fears? What prospects, wishes, and anxieties have you all three together respecting this world and the things that are in it? If you feel inclined to come to England, come if you can. . . .[6]

However, by 1835 James Bradbury would position himself in the mill industry of Millbury, Massachusetts; it was from there he would write his observations home to brother Timothy.[7]

An associate's reports from New York back to Timothy and Jane Buckley Bradbury in 1835 addressed the condition of both cotton and woollen manufacturing—he did not shy away from sharing observations of the people he encountered:

> Of the characteristics of the Americans, the first that an English-

> man discovers is their inveterate hatred of England; the next their unequalled national vanity. . . . I have been in several cotton mills in Paterson where I was much surprised to find that the work people are neither better paid nor worked shorter time than they are in Lancashire. This appears more astonishing when it is contrasted by the exhorbitant prices that are paid for labour in this city. . . . New York, a pleasant lively place and I am well pleased with the country as far as I have seen of it but I do not like the people, I mean as a body; some of them are well enough. Mrs. [Bradbury] always smiled when I talked of getting married. Tell her I shall not marry an American lady.[8]

Timothy's last known reply to this friend and associate indicated that he believed he was nearing his own journey's end. Further, he predicted that a certain six-year-old member of his household, his middle son, desperately wanted to join the old friend across the ocean in spite of admonitions about the advantages and disadvantages of life in the States. "And my son, Wm., I verily believe would any day set out with a stranger for New York to come to you."[9]

Timothy and Jane Bradbury's sons, Charles, William, and Frederic, would each integrate U.S. commerce and culture into their lives, as had their grandparents and uncles. Their sons' advantage of early education in a private half-year boarding school, the Sunderland Terrace Academy, may have been financially aided through an inheritance from Timothy, who died in 1839.[10]

Years later, when William wrote about the Sunderland Academy, he provided insight about the skills that would later spare him from duty on the front lines during the Civil War. He learned handwriting, calligraphy, dictation, spelling, rapid arithmetic, mechanical drawing, geography, and cartography.[11] All of these skills would be highly valued by Union Generals in preparing official reports in the years to come. Beyond expertise and skills, William H. Bradbury's education helped shape the ease, facility, and refinement of a man who was very comfortable among those who held power.

Perhaps the most telling lesson learned from the academy was the demeanor that Bradbury would incorporate into his personal interactions with authority figures throughout the rest of his life. While a good student and a favorite with the principal, it seems that there was a pivotal incident that shaped Bradbury forever. One day, young William had a fight with another student, and upon being scolded he shouted in reply to the vice-principal, "I don't care!" Writing for an education journal at the age of sixty-seven, Bradbury reflected on the lesson that he subsequently learned:

> This was the unpardonable sin. He [I] was at once taken before Mr. Sunderland and received a severe caning and much reproof. 'Boys who did not care were not fit for the company of decent boys.' I was degraded, disgraced before the whole school, humiliated, demoralized, and did not get over it for a long time; all not because of the turbulence or quarreling, but because I had dared to assert a little independence. . . . Towards the close I was treated very well indeed; but self-assertion was frowned down in every case and modesty and deference to the verge of obsequiousness commended."[12]

We see from this revealing vignette the beginning of Bradbury's passive-aggressive conduct with senior-ranking officials who held his future in their hands. He tended not to directly confront authority figures; yet he wrote to Mary with his complaints. This autobiographical insight may help explain his dispassionate interest in practiced religion; the academy's headmaster usually served as the church pastor as well. Rebellion was part of who Bradbury was, and this quality may have had its origins from those early schoolboy days.

Bradbury's extracurricular education included a skill, phonography (a precursor to shorthand), that also had much to do with positioning his term as a soldier out of harm's way. As a graduate of Sir Isaac Pitman's instruction in phonography,[13] Bradbury excelled at this skill and taught it to many others during the war and later in life. Had Pitman not traveled on his own from his home in Bath to instruct pupils like Bradbury in the Manchester vicinity in this then-controversial technique, Bradbury's fate in the war could have been quite different.[14]

Bradbury was also provided a post-academy education under the auspices of his guardian, James Smith Buckley of Ryecroft Hall near Ashton-under-Lyne.[15] While living in the mansion-like Ryecroft Hall, William was placed in the charge of Henry Gartside,[16] in order to learn the practice of an attorney and solicitor. Bradbury completed his apprenticeship and became an attorney of "her Majesty's Courts of Queen's Bench and Common Pleas at Westminster," in 1850.[17]

The estate of Timothy and Jane Buckley Bradbury took years to settle. By all accounts, youngest brother Frederic Bradbury never reaped his fair share of the inheritance.[18] William, the attorney in the family, complained loudly about the excessive time brother Charles took as executor to resolve their parents' estates, as reflected in an 1852 letter demanding payment. William's move to Illinois was based upon Charles's promise to settle the accounts, and he also identified favorable land investment opportunities that he would have acted on if he only had the funds coming from Charles to support them:

> I am surprized that you have sent me no Debit & Credit account of money matters between us. You ought to know that the longer it is delayed the more difficulty & disagreeable will be the task. Charles Tomlins[19] is by this time left for Australia & you will now have no excuse about the books. I really must insist on having it sent immediately.[20]

Three months later, in 1853, writing from Chicago, William provided brother Charles with a clearer picture of land speculation as a means of profitable investment. He was hardly alone. A prominent New Yorker described the feverish excitement as "mania" when he traveled West to acquire land.[21] William joined the emerging class of professional land agents who helped facilitate the land purchases of others for a commission or a share in the transaction. He would often help rent the land for absentee owners back East, sometimes in exchange for a percentage of the rent or of the produce grown and sold from it.

However, in spite of William's thorough and careful explanation, persuading wealthy Charles[22] to part with some of the funds that William thought were rightfully his was a constant challenge:

> The prices of grain & other produce of every kind are so high that land is in great request & now farms are making in places which 5 years ago seemed out of the world. Land adjoining Morris [Illinois] which 3 yrs ago might have been bought for 3 or 4 $$ an acre is now bought at 20 times the amount for building purposes. . . . Railroads are building & projecting in every direction. Western railroads pay well as an investment. . . . The Rock Island Road is now complete to Morris from which place I can go to New York or Boston without getting off the track in 45 hours!!! Chicago—20 years ago not marked on the map—will soon be one of the greatest commercial cities in the Union. . . . In 50 years this state will be one of the wealthiest & most important in the Union.[23]

The soil on prairie land of central and northern Illinois was very good and there was an added benefit in supplies of coal and limestone.[24] Yet other British immigrants took a far different view of the virtues of Chicago, including one woman who described the city as "a rough, ragged town, built on a swamp with everything rudimentary and unclean." It seemed to her to be the "end of all things, the veritable jumping off place."[25]

Many around the world shared Bradbury's curiosity about the U.S. and the quest for land ownership. According to records, between 1856 and 1860 an estimated half a million immigrants came to Illinois, many attracted by the lure of the new Illinois Central Railroad.[26] During this period, more than sixty-five million acres of public land were disposed of to land speculators, many of whom were new immigrants.[27] Huge numbers of people from the mill towns of Lancashire, England, were settling throughout Grundy, Kendall, and Livingston Counties in Illinois in the 1840's.[28]

Members of another British family, the Browns, were among them. John Brown[29] of Thursington County in Leicester, England, was apprenticed in the pharmacy trade in Ashton, when an opportunity arose. From there, Brown, an active Methodist, bought his own store in Droylsden and also became the town Postmaster. Times were so good that John sent for his brother, James, to join him in business. John then married Ann[30] and sent for his older sister Mary to help run their prospering businesses.

Judging from their correspondence as young adults in England, John and Mary Brown were close siblings. Always a doting brother, John wrote to her with passionate, religious fervor, challenging her to examine her life:

> Mary, are you keeping your heart with all diligence (I am afraid not), do you hold such sweet communion with God as you have done in your closet? Now Mary, when ever you are idle, the Devil will be busy, be upon your watch, and when ever you perceive him coming, resist him with all the force you can and he will flee from you, do not give vent to any light talk that will be of no profit to you. . . . If you are a child of God, distinguish yourself from the ungodly.[31]

John Brown might have left an even longer legacy in Droylsden, but his acquaintance, William H. Bradbury, had traveled to America, and the correspondence encouraged John to go see America for himself. Brown followed Bradbury's advice, crossing the Atlantic in the Fall of 1851. Upon arriving in Illinois, John was so pleased with what he found that he immediately bought several acres near Morris. From John Brown's "Last Will and Testament," we learn more of his motivation in moving his family to the U.S.:

> When I look back to that time and think of my decision, I suppose it was due to my constant reading about the New World—but being deeply imbibed with religious sentiments, I thought I was under guidance of the Almighty, and that he was directing my path. . . . We left the following Spring for a life on the Prairie of Illinois.[32]

Mary Brown joined her brother, his wife, and their new baby in the move to Illinois, taking the last segment of the long trip by a canal boat bound for Morris. Women of the era were instructed to "develop any talent we might possess or at least learn how to do some one thing which the world needed."[33] Mary Brown ended up choosing a life for which she was particularly well-suited—becoming the life partner of William H. Bradbury.

After weathering a rough year on the prairie in primitive conditions, Mary Brown married her brother's friend, William Henry Bradbury, six years her junior, on August 17, 1853.[34] A marriage on the American prairie of these two British immigrants, of diverse backgrounds, regions, and social class, was also a marriage of two entirely different motives for being in the New World. William and Mary answered to two diverse callings—to the aspirations of financial success and to the fulfillment of God's beckon, respectively.

During the 1850's in Illinois, William H. Bradbury worked as an attorney, a teacher, and, most importantly, as a land agent for various railroad companies. He bought land whenever he could, especially those that the federal government put up for sale—territorial lands in need of future settlers.

By all accounts, Bradbury bought land in Kansas for different reasons than did those of Amos Lawrence's New England followers in the emigrant aid societies, who aimed to ensure the end of slavery in new western states.[35] Instead, Bradbury bet on the emerging importance of lands in Kansas and Nebraska for the burgeoning railroads and gambled on land acquisition as a route to developing future wealth. His ability to acquire and hold onto these lands—as economic times tightened—would become the real challenge. And the upcoming times certainly gripped the financial heart of the nation as the Civil War ensued.

William H. Bradbury's younger brother Frederic followed in the footsteps of his Uncle James, emigrating to New York during the late 1840's and becoming involved in the textile business. Frederic, a lifelong bachelor, felt a strong sense of kinship with William's children—especially the oldest, Jane—which would last for decades. Three Civil War–era letters from kindly Uncle Frederic to Jane and his sister-in-law, Mary Brown Bradbury (included in this volume), must have been a comfort to them during the Civil War years.

What did Bradbury sacrifice by leaving his native home in the years before the transatlantic telegraph and telephone? Of course, communication with England continued in spite of limitations, yet there were worries and speculations about business affairs that remained unsettled when the Civil War erupted. When William H. Bradbury enlisted, Mary was left to act on his behalf, a role in which she did not seem as skilled nor as comfortable as her husband.

His excellent British education placed him in visible community leadership roles in various Lyceum and literary associations, the Cornet Band, and the church choir. His extensive writing was widely respected as well. At one point, Bradbury was called, to his apparent pleasure, the "Poet Laureate of Dwight, Illinois."[36] Mary B. Bradbury, by contrast, was more retiring, if not shy, and was less comfortable being in the public eye.

Life looked very promising indeed for families like the Bradburys who found nearly endless opportunities for personal growth and attainment—until the Civil War came along. Livingston County's men readily answered President Lincoln's call for more Union troops in the Summer of 1862.[37] While they organized and bivouacked in Pontiac, Illinois, they enjoyed bountiful picnic spreads provided by patriotic women. But of course Pontiac was not the end of the line; rather it was a mere beginning on their road to soldiering.

Why then did Bradbury enlist? It would have been very difficult to continue living in a small village after failing to volunteer with neighbors and colleagues. Peer pressure was one of the most compelling reasons that men who might otherwise have had legitimate excuses from serving enlisted. Not enlisting, not going to war, was plainly not a viable alternative for a member of society, or anyone who strived to become one.

Restoring the Union would have been a likely factor in his decision to enlist; it is unlikely, though, that fighting slavery was his personal priority. Bradbury's own words indicate that he wasn't pro-slavery either. He observed slaves he encountered and again when they became freedmen. His remarks about slaves and freedmen were much like those he sent home along with botanical specimens during the war—analytical observations, not personal beliefs. Private Bradbury's most extensive set of thoughts about the issue of slavery and the fight for restoration of the Union were not articulated in letters home; instead, he wrote directly to the readers of the *Chicago Tribune* and the *Manchester Guardian* with these opinions.

William H. Bradbury is listed on Company B's roster of the 129th Illinois Infantry. But unlike other regimental comrades whose published accounts depict more typical soldiering, camp life and front-line duties, Bradbury's is quite different. His experience was as a clerk detached to top commanding officers, a veritable "Who's Who of Union Leaders in the Western Campaigns." When Bradbury did witness the action during the siege of Knoxville and later rejoined his regiment near Atlanta, his observations seem distant compared with other soldiers who wrote home.

Private Bradbury's reluctance to discuss the up-close look at the passionate frenzy of bloody war reflects either his decision to spare his family worry or his lack of firsthand knowledge of the fighting. Instead, he wrote rhymes and fashioned blue silk stars for the children to represent the symbol of his assignment, the 20th Army Corps. What is clear is this—he did not think of himself as a typical soldier, nor did he pretend to be so with his wife and comrades.

Yet his letters to his children expressed great longing. At a level appropriate for children under nine years of age, Bradbury tried to explain aspects of the war in ways that they could understand. The attention most soldiers put into caring for their weapons and knapsacks, Bradbury applied to the orderliness of his desk, papers, pen, and ink. To appreciate the contributions of soldiers like Bradbury who clerked their way through the war is to understand that they also served who scribed.

Bradbury's characteristics were a mixture of the analytical mind and the poetic soul. Bradbury strove to ensure a legacy on American soil, one dug deeply in the tracks that he figuratively helped to lay—the railway tracks heading West, specifically the Atchison Topeka Santa Fe Railway. Illinois was his home for two decades, but Bradbury was perhaps always headed for what the advertising broadsheets across Europe declared—"The Boundless West." To the West, the wild, the untamable, and a further prairie he would eventually seek and find—the unbridled Kansas.

Bradbury's letters to his wife, children, brothers, and comrades; his published and unpublished poetry; articles he wrote for newspapers; journals he kept; family photographs; and scrapbooks he made were liberally used in setting the context of his Civil War experiences in this book. Two Civil War–era letters from Mary Bradbury, one to William and another to her sister-in-law, were included because they help explain the circumstances on the home front. Three letters from his brother Frederic and two from his brother Charles were also edited and included to add more insight to their family relationships. A letter from Bradbury to Captain Bailhache was included to explain the politicking behind the scenes. Sixteen of Private Bradbury's war-era published newspaper letters were edited and included to help amplify his view of the war to a very different readership—the folks back home.

While punctuation was added and paragraphing standardized throughout for greater ease in reading, I have endeavored to preserve the spelling, whether British or archaic, as found in the original text. In addition, an editorial decision was made to sacrifice remarks about his numerous business affairs in the notes in favor of ones about the family's livelihood, for which there was adequate supplemental documentation for corroboration.

"While Father is away. . ." was a frequent refrain in his letters. Throughout their long lives together, William and Mary would address each other as "Father" and "Mother," as was often the custom at the time, especially when simultaneously addressing the issues of several children. The use of "Father" in the title is not intended to disparage Mary, nor to suggest that he treated her like a child. However, it is true that William did scold, reprimand, and find fault with Mary—although he generally apologized for this. Perhaps the most that we can know for certain is that theirs was a mature relationship in which the familiarity and comfort of "Father" and "Mother" flowed easily in their correspondence.

And as in any partnership, understanding the perspective or voice of the other partner can be very enlightening. What was William, after all, without his "dear Mary" back in Dwight, holding his family and business together? Mary Brown Bradbury's two war-era letters and one postwar letter, while shorter and less verbose than William's in style, contain the characteristics of someone who spoke simply and from the heart.

Her spelling and syntax errors were many and were left as found in the text, although punctuation was added for ease in reading.

Mary Brown Bradbury's Civil War years were not those of a solider, but she certainly *soldiered* in service to her "captain." A wife's role during this era was to be sympathetic, self-sacrificing, subservient, and to provide the domestic strength in the home that would help guide him, in theory, to success.[38] Yet to keep up with William's extensive requests would have tested the best of wives in any era. William requested more than 150 challenging tasks of Mary, well beyond those passing suggestions about caring for the children.

Was he relentless? Yes, but there was a lot at stake during the years of the war, and Mary's capacity to execute directives would help determine the future success of this new American family. For Mary, the front lines of battle were fought every day from the uncertainty of their home in Dwight, Illinois.

The U.S. Civil War turned out to be a remarkable educational opportunity for many women, including Mary. True, the war was also a great burden, but as was said, "Educate a man and you have educated one person; educate a mother and you have educated the whole family."[39] Mary's education in this way would be reflected in the future lives of their children, especially Jane. Thanks to Mary, her intelligence, tolerance, flexibility, perseverance, and ability to perform multiple tasks (even while pregnant) including killing hogs, raising children and gardens, and collecting back rents and debts, we have a broader view of an entire family's experience of the Civil War. In the absence of a dominant, if not domineering, husband and father, a man possessed to make a go of it on the prairie, Mary Brown Bradbury carried on.

Bradbury's capacity for success in his plans resided in the promising help of his partner Mary. Turning back was not his style. Instead, Bradbury focused on surviving the war. His eyes surely danced with thoughts of lands that he continued to acquire parcel by parcel, as he sat at a military desk in Bowling Green, Knoxville or Atlanta.

A complex man, prairie pioneer, entrepreneur, poet, always a doting father, and sometimes a passionate husband, Private William H. Bradbury marched methodically in 1862 into the heart of the U.S. Civil War. Marching to uncertainty, he wrote home frequently, not imagining that others would one day read of his experiences, thoughts, and dreams.

Among his extensive letters, he sometimes included messages for the children which were written in rhyme. Through the expression of his longing, we have a rare look at the heart of a father who sorely missed his children while he served as a Union soldier in the Civil War:

Lines for the Children[40]
One little girl—two little boys—
Too little room to play
Two little twins to make a noise,
and teaze mamma all day.
Two little jackets on the chairs—
Two little boys in bed.
Too little money father spared;
because he don't get paid.
Two little babies in a cradle,
that go to sleep so snug.
Too little care upsets the table
and throws things on the rug.
Too little wood to light the fire,
Two little boys fetch cobs—
And Mamma's arms would often tire
if nobody did her jobs.
One little girl that father loves
helps Mother with her work.
Two little boys whose hunger proves
that they like bread & pork.
They hold the babies on their laps
and dare not let them fall,
and often ask for "dear old Pop,"
who loves his children all.
And Mother cooks & mends & makes
and thinks of one that's far away
and father, every time he wakes
would like to see his children play.
The joys of home—domestic ties
are solid, sweet & never pale.
A gentle daughter, roguish boys
Mamma & the little twins & all!

1

"My Dear Wife and Children"

September 8, 1862–November 14, 1862

Dwight, Illinois, was just a few miles from the county seat of Pontiac, close enough for Private William H. Bradbury, who immigrated from Yorkshire, England, in 1851, to be familiar with many of his fellow comrades in the 129th Illinois Infantry. However, most of the regimental officers were from Pontiac.

Dwight was a town of just 550 people in 1860, and it was located some 75 miles from Chicago, yet it was strategically important for its railway linkages, namely the Chicago, Alton & St. Louis Railroad. In spite of Dwight's remoteness, it was treasured for its hunting by a member of the royal family of England, the nineteen-year-old Prince of Wales, Albert Edward, who later would become King Edward VII. Prince Albert Edward visited Dwight in 1860, and he was warmly welcomed by its residents, including British expatriates like Bradbury, who sang at church services on his behalf. The prince was reported to have said about Dwight after his successful game shooting: "I would like to stay here shooting for a month longer; it's the only real fun I have had in America."[1]

When the 129th Illinois Infantry Volunteer Regiment was formed, Companies A, B, C, E, and G consisted of Livingston County men. Scott County contributed troops to Companies D, F, H, and I, and Rock Island sent men to Company K. As some soldiers vied for regimental positions of rank, prestige, and increased pay, Bradbury, in Company B, was more concerned about his safety and was wary of accepting any position that might place him on the front lines.

After he left his growing family in the late summer of 1862, Bradbury actively promoted his wide array of scholarly talents to the brigade and division officers. This was sensible, as the army needed competent clerks, and he was intent on avoiding the life of a typical rank-and-file soldier.

Because of his maturity, he was often mistaken for the regimental adjutant[2] or other senior ranking officers. And although he tried to gain a commission as an officer during those early months, he did not get one he wanted. As a compromise to himself, he remained what he termed a "privileged private" by concentrating on learning the operations of headquarters. By making himself invaluable to the army bureaucracy, he garnered significant status de facto.

Bradbury adeptly assumed the deferential role of a "scribe-in-waiting," a role that would spare him exposure from bullets for many months. But as a gentleman-scholar, he was uncomfortable with the undignified officers and the disobedient soldiers of the volunteer army. He described what he felt was the gross impropriety of this strange new environment in his letters home to his dear Mary.

As wife and mother, Mary Brown Bradbury's adjustments to life on the prairie during the Civil War without her husband are largely unknown. When William went off to war, she was left in Dwight with three children, pregnant, and responsible for her husband's business activities. A business affair with a man named Keyt began to unravel and agitated her husband constantly in the months ahead.

Mary's brother, John Brown, and her sister-in-law, Ann, with whom she was especially close, lived twenty miles away in Morris, Illinois. The Bradburys had moved from Morris to Dwight just a few years before the war began.

While Mary's adaptation to this new situation is largely unknown, there are some clues in Bradbury's letters to her. Women of the middle class often found this kind of transition very difficult. There were few opportunities for cultivating friendships with other women in these sparsely settled regions, notorious for deadly grass-fires and blizzards, and they worried constantly about finances.[3]

Propriety, pride, and dignity were often on Private Bradbury's mind, rather than the threat of being killed in action, as so many other soldiers feared. Socializing as he did with Mrs. Garrard, the wife of Kentucky's state treasurer, and officers like "Major" Samuel Starling, Bradbury's first years of soldiering were atypical. While Bradbury sought the administrative side of war as a means of distancing himself from combat, *Lieutenant* Starling[4] (as Bradbury called him) shunned such duty and instead wrote to his daughters:

I shall be a Major or an Adjutant Genl. soon. I believe I prefer Major, the adjutant is a man of papers. . . . Now if there ever was a thing on earth I did despise, it was taking care of papers. . . . Some men have a taste for [it], but I have *none.*[5]

Wednesday afternoon
Pontiac, Ill.
Sept. '62

I write in great haste to catch the mail. I have been very busy. Plattenburg is Adjutant[6] & I am clerk. Dwight Co. did not get any regimental officers. Pontiac was well represented. We have now 10 companies, about 850 men which makes the camp look very lively. Plattenburg was nominated by Colonel Smith who had promised him the office.[7]

I have plenty to do in the office, not much time for exercise but I think of what I am doing for you & the children. The pay will be about $25 a month. We expect our pay next Friday—$40 down. I can get the county order whenever I wish.

We were mustered in on Monday. Rearick was the only man who stepped out & said he had an injury which would disable him for service. The officer examined & mustered us in, in about 3 hours. He thought I was really the Adjutant; as Plattenburg was not on hand, he proposed to swear me in! I told him I was not the man or we might have had a good joke on Plattenburg.

I mean to be as careful as I can & save all my money. I shall have a good chance for promotion as I am constantly in contact with the regimental officers.

John McWilliams is now at Dwight. He is after the Quartermastership. Brother David[8] is going to help him. There are about three men for every vacant office. Cropsey is Major.[9] Smith is Colonel. Captain Case[10] of the new companies is Lieut. Colonel. The surgeon, chaplain, quarter master, etc. are not appointed yet.

The weather has been fine & pleasant. I will get you some nuts in a short time. They are getting ripe. I have not time to say much more now. I will write again in a day or two.

Give my love to the children & accept the same yourself.
Yours affectionately
WmHBradbury

We shall be very busy this week. The rebels have crossed into Maryland & not far from Pennsylvania.

Pontiac, Camp Livingston
Sept. 13th 1862
My dearest wife,

Last night & this morning were very cold. I have just opened the Adjutant's office. It is about ½ past 5 o'clock.

The quarter master is now appointed to the disgust of the candidates who accuse Colonel Smith of breaking his promise & lying.

I have been very busy in the adjutant's office & the only time I have to write to you is late & at night or early in the morning. I shall not neglect to write to you at least once a week & frequently oftener. I thought it was Thursday yesterday or I would have written.

There was concert in town last night for the benefit of sick soldiers. I did not go. They are very strict now with regard to passes. The concert realized $14.

I have sold my county order for a mortgage on 160 acres of land for $85 payable in a year at 10 per cent or if the man can raise the money in a few days (of which he has a good prospect), I am to take $80 in cash—$50 or $60 is the usual price. Mr. Caldwell—Smith's brother-in-law—is the man. I did some little business for him the other day for which he will pay me a dollar.

I have worn out the seat of my pants in the service; sitting so much on the rough benches has done it. I wish you would send me the next best pair of pants as soon as you can.

There is somebody from Dwight here nearly every day. We had men in the guard house for drunkenness.

I have not had time to get any more plums yet. I will try to get some & some nuts today. We had some sweet potatoes late last night roasted & boiled. They were very good.

I have had my shawl taken by somebody. You give me a description of it— if [you would] jot [a description of] what color it was almost. There have been many articles missed here.

We expect our uniforms & arms in a few days. The officers begin to complain of the expense they are out. There is considerable jealousy & dissatisfaction with regard to many things.

We had some bad beef a few days ago & the next time the butcher arrived in camp he was greeted with bellowings wherever he went, only very glad to get away. There will be no more bad beef yet awhile.

We expect to receive our bounty money & month's advance pay on Monday. In which case I shall send you all I can possibly spare. I must go & wash now. The orderly who waits upon us at headquarters has just brought in my shawl. I have marked it in several places. I shall keep it at the headquarters & take good care of it.

Manning Smith[11] & several others are going home today. I send the shirt by him. He will bring the pants back. Some turpentine will take out the ink on my pants. I spilt it accidentally.

I shall come home next Saturday if possible. We are just dividing into messes, 17 to a mess. I am along with Stevens, Judd,[12] etc. They go fishing at the river & we have fish sometimes.

Some ladies living near Pontiac took compassion on us on learning that we had had no pic nic parties with cake, chickens, etc. & accordingly brought us a very handsome spread. I think I mentioned this in my last letter.

I will write Freddy & Jane a letter tomorrow & you probably [will] get it next Wednesday.

The officers here treat me very well. Major Cropsey thinks I ought to have this position till I can get something better.

Send me a little good butter & some tomato preserves when you have a chance.

With my love to you & the children.

I am yours forever,

WmHBradbury

129 Regt Illinois Volunteers
Louisville, KY
Sept 26 1862, Friday
My dearest wife,

I wrote you on Wednesday from Jeffersonville.[13] We arrived safe at Louisville the same night. We are now stationed here but without any tents or shelter & with only very short rations. Owing to the vast number of men here & the regiments & officers being mostly green, everything is rather confused. There is a good deal of grumbling & confusion.

An attack by Bragg[14] was thought not unlikely last night. The regiments are all roused up & placed in battle array every morning at 3 o'clock. I have not had more than 4 hours sleep the last two nights. I can sleep very well on the ground.

I am very busy here. We have had to do the work of others, but now we are relieved of some of it.

The boys have confiscated both geese & hogs & the way the feathers fly & the pigs squeal is a caution.

There is a great deal of strictness here. Nobody is allowed out of camp unless for special reasons. Our regiment is considered the finest in the Brigade, but we have now a great many sick. Our headquarters consists of a few poles with blankets thrown over them. The regiments & officers are parading about & I snatch this time to write to you.

Buell's army is here. Themselves & horses are weary looking objects.

I had coffee, ham & dry crackers for breakfast this morning. We shall have a change after awhile.

Col. Smith is not here yet. We are under Lieut. Col. Case. Some of the soldiers have their wives here. The post master goes with the mail to town at 10.20 a.m. We are about a mile from the city which is quite a large place. This is no place to write a private letter.

I understand that some of the people here are secesh,[15] but they are quiet over it. We are encamped in a dry sandy place which must be healthy. Many of the sick are in a sort of blanket tent just behind my desk. There is no system about anything yet.

The weather today looks like Indian Summer. We are placed on the outside, in the post of danger, as we had the best armed [men]. It is thought by many that the enemy will not attack Louisville at all as we have so many here.

The most of the women & children & some valuables, &c were moved over to the Indiana side of the river.

I have not time to add any more. I will write again the next opportunity. Accept my best love for yourself & children.

Yours in haste to catch the mail,

WmHBradbury

Frankfort, Kentucky
October 10, 1862
My dearest wife,

We are now encamped on a high mound overlooking the capital of Kentucky. We arrived here from Shelbyville at 4 o'clock on the morning of the ninth. The rebels had burned the railroad bridge & had removed some plank & were preparing to burn the regular bridge across the Kentucky River. Our advance guard stopped this proceeding & after some little fighting the rebels fled. This was on the evening of our arrival. We stayed in the city a short time & several of us were well entertained by the Union ladies.

Mr. Judd & myself were fortunate enough to be received by Major Starling & the wife of the State Treasurer,[16] who had fled to Louisville with the state funds.

We have left at Louisville & at Shelbyville & on the road many sick & stragglers. The Adjutant, W. Plattenburg & Capt. Walkley[17] are very sick at Shelbyville. I am the only person to represent the office. I rode the adjutant's horse into Frankfort. My baggage is always carried in the wagons.

Frankfort is situated in a woody bend of the river. The banks on our side are very high & steep & covered with beautiful cedars & maples. From the heights on which our camp is situated we have a splendid view of the city. Until today the weather has been very warm & the sky clear. But today it is quite the reverse. It is quite cold & rainy.

The rebels are supposed to be near us in small parties & we send out scouts & skirmishers. The men are now cutting limbs from the beautiful cedars & maples & using them for shelter. A team has just been sent after some tents which were left behind by one of our generals & are only about a mile off.

The quartermaster has not yet arrived & there is a perpetual growling & complaint about not having enough to eat. I have fared very well lately. I have friends who always bring me something when I am busy.

I don't think much of the system & management of the army. It is *volunteer* all round. The officers have no dignity & the men no subordination.

The pins, which hold our tent down, are driven in only a little owing to the soil being so shallow. Limestone underlies the whole of this part of the state. The roads are most excellent & the fields are often fenced in with stone walls. The country is full of ravines & gorges & high wooded slopes & is very romantic. If I had time I would make a sketch of the view.

We have got a comfortable tent for headquarters & Mr. Judd & I sleep in our corner. We got some hay in today. Last night we slept without hay & the night before which was very warm, without shelter.

I am sorry to say that many of the men behave very badly & commit depredations & insults without any cause. In our present circumstances it is almost impossible to punish these offences. We gave up our tent last night for the sick and have now a smaller one. Mr. Judd, myself, the Sergeant Major & John sleep in it. It is now ½ past 4 Saturday morning. We are awakened by the firing of a cannon every morning at 4.

The adjutant Plattenburg has not come along yet. It is thought that he cannot stand the hardships of camp life. I may get the office but I have no money to keep up appearances.[18] Most of the officers have spent already nearly all their money. I have only but a dollar left. I bought a pair of laces at 75¢.

Our greatest trouble is for water which has to be fetched at least half a mile from the river below. The road is winding on account of the steep precipice on which we are camped.

General Dumont[19] commands our division [12th] which consists of three brigades. Our brigade [38th] consists of the 129 Ill. Vols., the 23rd Michigan Volunteers, the 111th Ohio Vols. & another regt [102 Ohio Vols.]. It is commanded by Colonel Chapin[20] who is acting as Brigadier Genl. Our Quarter Master has not yet arrived; if he does not come today, hard crackers like that I sent you in the trunk will be our fare. I can live on crackers as well as anybody.

I find that I can stand this kind of life pretty well but I can't say that I like it. There is too much responsibility & excitement. The brigade adjutant still wants me but I cannot leave at present. The orderlies are coming in with their morning reports & I must close. It is now about 6 o'clock. You should put on your letters to me, 38th Brig. 12th Div. AG

I remain your most affectionate husband
WmHBradbury
Write as soon as you can.

DEAR LITTLE CHILDREN

There are two big guns as long as across our kitchen. They shoot a ball as big as a cup. The ball weighs 6 pounds. I have seen lots of Negroes which are black people and little Negroe children. A Negroe woman got me some water to wash my feet. Their skin is dark brown and their hair is short and black and curly. We have plenty of music every day. Be good children and Father will write to you again.

Wednesday afternoon
Oct. 15, 1862
My dearest wife,

I received your welcome letter last Wednesday just as we had left Frankfort on our way to Lawrenceburg.[21] I wrote to you from Frankfort. I sent you a *Harper's Weekly* from Louisville which contains a map of Kentucky. Jane will find the places for you. We left Lawrenceburg on Monday and passed on southeasterly direction thro' Harrisburg & Danville.

The bugle has just sounded, I must make haste. The country is very like some parts of England. The roads are like coach roads and there are spacious brick mansions with beautiful grounds & handsome fences & gates all along our route. Timber abounds & covers the high swelling land & the deep ravines & gorges.

I am now sitting on the edge of a small hill overlooking the road. A wagon train has just gone along not belonging to our brigade. I counted nearly one hundred of them. They are each drawn by 6 mules & stretch more than a mile. I am watching for our brigade. They are getting into the road again. We are expecting the mail along today with news from sweet home!

We have just encamped near a small place called Stanford & I have another opportunity to write. We traveled only 13 miles today. Many in our company are quite foot sore. I am all right & very well. The rebels are only one day's march ahead & are reported to be marching their army forward to Cumberland Gap.

We are accompanied by Cavalry & Artillery. Our Infantry consists of 129th Illinois, the 23rd Michigan, the 111th Ohio & the 102nd Ohio. These four Regiments with the Artillery (Board of Trade Battery—6 guns) & several hundred small cavalry go together & form part of the 12th Division under General Dumont. Our brigade—the 38th consists only of the before-named regiments.

General Crittenden's[22] forces are just before us pressing close on Bragg who is making all hard with his provision train out of Kentucky thru Cumberland Gap which is 90 miles from this place.

I have a good desk on which to write but we don't take it out of the wagon when we stop, only for the night.

The battery is gone forward & we may have to march very early. Plattenburg is still sick.

The colonel has appointed a lieutenant as adjutant. I do not care much for the office. I have no suitable clothes & could not maintain the dignity of the office. If the war was to stop in three or four months most of the officers would be out of pocket. They have to board themselves & have already spent considerable for their outfit.

I understand that Captain Walkley & Plattenburg are getting well & will soon overtake us. While I am writing, the tent is full of officers, telling incidents of the march—how General Granger[23] swore at the men for not carrying their knapsacks.

There is a good deal of fever. Culver is sick.[24] We allow him to sleep in our tent tonight.

Several Negroes accompany the regiment & the citizens try almost in vain to get them back. Some come along willingly, there required a little coaxing. Some won't come at all. I don't see how the Negroes' condition will be improved by the change.

We start at 3 in the morning. Judd & I & several others sleep in a small tent. A drove of cattle came with us today. We shall have beef tomorrow.

I must now close—it is getting late and we are fixing the straw for our bed—nearly all the men sleep in the open air. My duties now are very light as we are on the march & and don't do much writing.

I think of my dear wife & children every day & look forward to the time when we shall meet again. I think next Spring at the furthest will see the end of the war.

I hope the children are good & that you keep in good health yourself. Goodbye dearest wife, I expect a letter from you now every day. I have not written to Walkley yet.

Your most affectionate husband,
WmHBradbury

Saturday morning Oct. 25/ 62
On the march near Lebanon Kentucky—
My dearest wife,

I received your letter a few days ago. Since writing it you must have acquired another from me. We are now traveling over the forest-covered hills of Kentucky. Our regiment with the Board of Trade Battery & some few other troops are (as we think) going to Bowling Green which places [us] you will find near the Tennessee line.

This morning is quite cold & cloudy. Yesterday was clear & very warm—my health continues pretty good—tho' I have colics & bowel complaints occasionally. We have more than 100 sick out of the Rgt.—at Louisville, Shelbyville, & Danville—they have diarrhea, flux, rheumatism, sore feet etc.

The small blanket in the trunk belongs to us—our Dutchman got it somewhere; you will keep it. Judd will no doubtedly pay his share of the freight if I ask him. Don't know what would become of some of us in our present condition. The country is almost destitute of water except along some of the streams where there are springs. To obtain water we have to follow these streams which is very tedious.

It is now Sunday morning. It was very cold & rainy & snowy last night & this morning & the men had a very hard time. I always sleep in a tent but my feet were cold all night.

Many of the shoes are giving out & the naked feet will come in . . .
[missing section]

He is now in Louisville on business. We expect soon to be supplied with tents—the men have suffered for want of them. We have not wagons enough. There is a good deal of hardship, confusion & want of discipline. If it should rain for any length of time, I . . .

[missing section]

I am glad you have got the stove. I hope the wet weather will not prevent your getting a supply of coal.

It is surprising that you have heard nothing from Keyt[25]—I think you had better write to him. I have not yet written to L.N. Walkley. I would like to know what he would give for the land.

[missing section]

Munfordsville, Kentucky
Oct. 27, 1862
My dearest wife,

After a long weary march we have arrived at this town which is on the Railroad about 60 miles south or southwest of Louisville.

I have made notes of every day's march & have material for a very long communication to the Pontiac paper but I have no opportunity to copy it—we have left sick & disabled men behind at nearly every town.

I always sleep in a tent but most of the men sleep in the open air—we have severe frosts in these forest-clad fields & one morning we found the ground covered with snow fully two inches deep—I have suffered somewhat from colics & diarrhea & cold feet. Captain Walkley and the adjutant are still ailing. Col. Smith is sick at Bradfordsville.

I enclose you part of a letter I had written in my pocket book. I hope you will be able to make it out—we are pretty well situated tonight—have had a good supper & Mr. Plattenburg & myself are sitting & writing at a table before a good log-fire which we have made in the timber. The camp fires shine all around us through the trees.

Our brigade consists of the 111th Ohio Regiment, the 102nd Ohio Regt. & the 23rd Michigan Regt. & the Board of Trade Battery of 6 guns commanded by Capt. Stokes[26]—I think the weather is fully as severe as it is at Dwight at this time of year. Perhaps it will be milder when we get out of the mountains. I was in hopes that we should have staid here a few days so that I could have written you a long letter & one to *Pontiac Sentinel.*[27]

I think of you every day & shall send you some money when we get our pay which will not be yet I am afraid. We have crossed Green River twice—we cross again tomorrow—we shall push on to Bowling Green which is 4 miles further—we average nearly 15 miles a day. Our Brigade is traveling alone at present.

We should have had our tents tonight but we have heard nothing of them. Our quarter master is looking after them. When we go into winter quarters I will get you to send me something by express—some potted beef or something of that kind would be good. All sorts of food are very dear here.

I think of you & the children every day & wonder how you are & what you are doing. I shall try to get a furlough at Christmas—I am in hopes there will be peace before next Spring. It is getting quite cold & I am writing in the open air.

I expect a letter from you tomorrow (Tuesday). I send my best love to you & the dear little children.

I will write again first chance.

Your affectionate husband,

WHB

HeadQrts. 38 Brigade 10 Div. A.G.
Bowling Green, Ky
Nov. 3, 1862
My dearest wife,

I received your letter dated Oct. 18th last Saturday the 1st Nov. I think I have received all your letters. Your last letter was a very long one for you. I don't see how you wrote it all.

I am now Secretary or Clerk for the Brigade Head Quarters. The Brigade Adjutant would not rest till he had me over.[28] Plattenburg did not really wish me to go unless it was to my own interest. I was quite undecided about it. I finally told the Brigade Adjutant I would come over & try how I liked it. I have no reason to repent. It is considered a sort of promotion tho' the pay is just the same. I have plenty of room, as I occupy the same tent with the Adjutant & his son.

I take my meals from the same table as the General & his staff—only after theirs along with the adjutant's son & the servants. The food is just as good. We have wheat bread, cornbread, ham, beef, coffee with milk, butter, etc. I have not trouble cooking or doing any dirty work—I have charge of everything during the Adjutant's absence & do the whole business except the outside work.

I lent Gagan my rug.[29] I thought he was only going to Louisville, but he went home. I wish I had it now as the nights are very cold. I do not find that the weather is any milder than in Illinois. I sleep in all my clothes, over-coat & all & frequently have to get up on account of the cold tho' I always sleep in a tent which only keeps off the dew.

Bowling Green is situated on Green River on the Louisville & Nashville Railroad which is now in running order so that we shall receive letters from home in less time than before.

I am without money but I do not wish you to send me any. You have little enough yourself & we expect to receive our pay in a few days. If we don't you might send me a little if you get any from Keyt or from Washington on account of the claims.

I wrote a long letter to the *Pontiac Sentinel* yesterday. I told Gagan to be sure & send it to you regularly.

I thought Morgan's trial was not going to be.[30] I should like to hear how it goes.

The County Recorder ought to send you Caldwell's mortgage. If you know of any body going down—send by them. I paid a dollar for the copy of the mill mortgage.

You should write to Keyt & get him to come over. He ought to have sent you the money long since. I hope he will not back out. If he shows any disposition to do so you might acquaint Mr. Kenyon with the facts & hold him to the agreement. He was to have delivered us 800 bus[hels] corn or to have paid us the money the corn fetched. You will see by the agreement.

I will get a furlough about Christmas if I possibly can. It cannot be more than 20 days. Mr. Judd is now back from Louisville. He is sorry I have left & so is the Dutch orderly & several others. I propose that the Regiment go into mourning. . .

[missing section]

Head Quarters 38th B. 10 D.
Nov. 6, 1862
Bowling Green, KY
My dearest wife,

I received your letter of the 24th & another of the 29th October within a day of each other. The latter enclosed a letter from Charles which I have answered as you will see.[31] You will seal it & send it as soon as you can.

I am glad your health is so much better. I hope it will continue. I slept warm last night & feel better today.

I can get along without money if we get paid soon. You might send me a few postage stamps.

I am sorry poor Jane dreams so much.[32] But I dreamt that I was wading thro' deep water the night before I got the letter. You must keep her in good health & cheerful before going to bed.

I always feel glad to hear from you. The letters will now come in much less time.

You *must* see Keyt & find out what he means.

Send me the Pontiac papers when you have read them. I see there are several correspondents from the 129th. You can tell my composition.

We had a grand review yesterday. Three Regiments & the Battery were reviewed by Genl. Rosecrans[33] & the other Generals. They were well pleased with the troops.

I have a good deal of work here as the papers have not been copied for more than six weeks. The other clerk did not do much.

I have got a comfortable bed in my tent—I only require some more covering.

We had a cold rain last night. It is very pleasant today, I do not know what else to say as I wrote to you a few days ago & to the *Sentinel*.

I send off my documents on mounted orderlies who carry the orders to the different regiments. I send round the countersign & other dispatches in the absence of the Adjutant.

Judd will pay me something for his things being carried in the trunk.

You must think over Mr. Gartside's proposal & help me to arrive at some conclusion.[34]

Mrs. Reed's sister's husband, Richardson Hicks, writes from Topeka, Kansas to the *Pontiac Sentinel*. I will write to L.N. Walkley about the Kansas land & ask him what he will give for it.

I will write you a long letter next time—I shall have matters of more interest to communicate.

Give my love to the dear little chuckies[35] & accept my best love yourself.

I remain,

Your affectionate & devoted husband,

WmHBradbury

I shall look for another letter from you in 6 or 7 days.

Head Quarters 38th Brigade
Bowling Green Kentucky
Nov. 14/ 62
My dearest wife,

I duly received your letter enclosing one from Charles & wrote an answer to it which you have received long since I suppose. I have been waiting to hear from you again hoping that you might have heard something from the farm. I ought to have written before this as I know that you don't like writing & that you have not much to communicate.

We shall stay here all winter. General Granger has charge of the Post & the defenses of Bowling Green. The Regiments composing this Brigade will be placed in different positions around & in the town.

Our mess has received an addition of a Captain in a Michigan Regt. who looks after good things to eat. We now have everything in reason that any body can expect. Besides the Capt. brought his cook with him who knows *how.*

We take care to get plenty of wood these cold nights. If I had another blanket I should have no cause of complaining as far as creature comforts are concerned. I have not exercise enough to keep in good health. The adjutant has so much confidence in me that he wishes me in the tent all the time, more especially as our acting Brigadier, Colonel Chapin, is quite sick in the city. I don't know much about the Regiment now as I go to see them only 3 or 4 times a week.

Col. Smith & Capt. Walkley are still sick. Mr. Borin, whom I saw this morning, is looking very well indeed. His rheumatism is much better.[36]

The weather is dry & fine with occasional small rains. It is frosty every night. We have had *I think* two deaths in the regiment—thirteen from the whole forces stationed here were buried yesterday.

You need not send me anything from home except the rug which Mr. Gagan has. Perhaps he will bring it when comes around again. Some good tea would be acceptable but we can exchange coffee for it. The Government has complete control of the road & it is difficult to get anything thro.' Everything is consequently very high. Tea is $3 a pound—at Nashville it is $5 a pound. Our Capt. Sheldon has just priced some turkeys—75¢ each—*cheap enough.* Butter is 30 to 50¢ a pound. We have some now that is first rate. "Head Quarters" always get the best of everything.

We shall probably move into the city & occupy a house. If Col. Chapin should die (which is not unlikely) my place is gone; but I have looked out for a place as Postmaster which will give me as much pay & more exercise.

The rails, hay, straw, firewood, etc are rapidly being consumed round this place. In a few weeks more there will be nothing to be seen scarcely in the shape of forage. Hay has to be fetched 8 miles. Firewood is becoming equally scarce & the boys *will* take rails in spite of all orders to the contrary. No rooster has been heard to crow within 20 miles of Nashville.

All the troops except our Brigade, Board of Trade Battery & some Cavalry have gone forward in the direction of Nashville. They are under different Division Generals, but all under Rosecrans. Part of our Brigade guards the RR. bridge & part is Provost Guard of the city. The Battery is planted on an eminence overlooking the town.

I have not written anything lately to the *Sentinel.* I am not *now* conversant with the condition of the regiment & do not know anything particularly interesting about the different members of it.[37]

I think it will be very difficult to get a furlough, as nearly every application has been refused even in case of sickness. The sick have to go into Hospitals at different places. I will do my best.

I hope you have heard something by this time from Keyt & that you have received the mortgage from Pontiac. I feel uneasy as to where your money will come from. I will write to L.N. Walkley this week about the Kansas land.[38] I feel inclined to sell it, if he will give a fair price for it. The taxes will be due next June & the interest next January.

I mended my pants & coat today in pretty good shape. The needle case comes in very useful.

I think of you & the children every day & long to see you at home again. I hope the war will end this Winter. Our colonel has telegraphed for his wife. It will be a sad thing if he should die as he is well liked & has many friends.

The days pass away quickly & we scarcely know when it is Sunday. We expect to receive our pay every day now. The rolls are made out. Some Regts. have been paid but not in our Brigade.

I enclose a letter to Jane & Freddy—

I expect a letter from you tomorrow. They will now come in about 4 days.

Hoping you keep in good health & spirits, I send my best love to you & the dear children & remain

Your ever affectionate & devoted husband,

WmHBradbury

2

"If We Go to England . . ."

November 20, 1862–January 23, 1863

While Bradbury's thoughts about Illinois as a permanent residence are not known, he did dream of his native England as he explored the gardens, homes, and trails of Kentucky. Perhaps he felt such homesickness for England while in Kentucky because his thoughts were full of speculations of how he might honorably get out of the war and return with Mary and the family to his native land. Interestingly, the handsome grounds of the once-elegant estate where Bradbury camped likely belonged to former Congressman Warner Lewis Underwood, who only a few months before had been appointed by President Lincoln as Consul to Glasgow, Scotland.[1]

Resigned to his fate of service, Bradbury represented his office with discretion and aplomb. However, in his free time he was consumed with trying to settle, untangle, litigate, and mitigate a number of complex business affairs through the mail, with his wife serving as his representative. Managing these long-distance business affairs proved to be an endless source of frustration for him and illustrated a common complaint—that those who stayed behind on the homefront often took advantage of soldiers unable to manage their business affairs effectively from the front lines.

No matter how business matters might unfold, there was one thing Bradbury refused to leave to chance—the care of his wife and children. However, the friends and neighbors surely observed Mary's ordeal that winter as she raised three children and tended to their business affairs during the last trimester of her pregnancy at age forty. Bradbury's pride, though, refused his friends' and neighbors' charitable efforts to help them.

Neither did he leave the parenting of Jane, Willie, and Freddie to chance. He kept a rigorous schedule of correspondence to each of them with explicit instructions and evaluations of compositions and mathematical assignments. While most soldiers eagerly awaited loving letters from sweethearts, at age thirty-three Bradbury was interested in improving Jane's penmanship and her grasp of the botanical specimens that he often mailed to her and her brothers.

Contrary to the notion that everything back home fell to the wives and mothers, Bradbury involved himself as much as possible in the pragmatic, emotional, and financial support of his loved ones.

Even Mary, or "Mother" as he called her, was occasionally advised and sometimes chided on her parenting skills. He recommended that she closely monitor the children to ensure that they had fresh air, fresh fruit, physical exercise, and the proper respect for their teachers.

Like many soldiers who thought the war would play itself out in just a few months, Bradbury eventually began to realize how wrong this estimate was. Reckoning with that reality, he became preoccupied with entrepreneurial ways to generate extra income for his family beyond his soldier pay. And as was the case in most of his endeavors, Bradbury's perseverance in this mission paid off handsomely.

Head Quarters 38th Brigade
Bowling Green, Kentucky
Nov. 20, 1862
My dearest wife,

I received your long letter dated Nov. 11th last Sunday morning. It is now Thursday morning. I was very glad to hear from you, tho' the news about the farm was discouraging.

I suppose you received my *two* letters since you sent off your last to me. I wrote in answer to your letter containing the one from Charles, & again about 5 or 6 days ago.

I told you what to do with Keyt. You have the agreement. You will show it to Strong or Kenyon & endeavor to make Keyt fulfill his part. We sold him the land for a fair price & must make him stick to the bargain if possible.[2]

You will see what I wrote to Charles. I sometimes think it would be pleasant to live at Droylsden [England] & take care of your mother.[3] But I am afraid it will be impossible to realize any money by selling out the land. I have written to L.N. Walkley but have had no reply yet.

I don't think much of Lindsays—I suppose it was the other brother who came to see you. I think I would just as soon take a small cash rent from McDonald.[4] He talked as if he would pay a cash rent. By the time I hear from you again, you will probably have seen Keyt. I wish I had sold the place to John Brown.[5]

I hope you are better this time than you were. You can dispose of that mortgage to Eldredge or McWilliams & take it out in goods I should think. It will be due next August & calls for $85 & interest at 10 percent. That is, if you are hard up, which you must be. I suppose Corey's hopes are all boiled over by this time.

I wrote Jane & Freddy a short letter last time. I couldn't read Jane's letter very well.

I have made a sketch of the inside of our tent for the Adjutant. I will send it next time I write. We get plenty of good things to eat. My washing is done by a Negro. It is only done occasionally. I only require my shirts washed.

We have been expecting our pay every day; but it has not arrived yet. When it does I will send you all but what little I shall require. I am afraid I shall not get any extra pay. Nobody seems to know how it will be done. There are many more in the same position. We shall try our best.

I wrote a long letter to the *Pontiac Sentinel* on Sunday which you might see on Wednesday next—I suppose you saw my letter dated Bowling Green.

We have moved our quarters to the place lately occupied by Genl. Granger among the shrubbery of what has been a very handsome residence. It is now burnt down, all but the Negro quarters.

I hope you will excuse this short letter. I will write again next Sunday.

I am in a hurry for the mail—You have this to read on Sunday.

Give my love to the children. Mr. Walkley is just saying that Mrs. Walkley does not receive as many letters as Mrs. Bradbury. He says he won't allow me to write so often. He is getting better. I am writing this in Plattenburg's tent.

Accept my best love from your affectionate husband,
WmHBradbury

Head Quarters 38th Brigade
Bowling Green, Ky
Nov. 21st 1862
My dearest wife,

I have been thinking about you all day & I thought you would like to have another letter from me tho' I wrote you a short one last Wednesday. It is now Friday night.

I was in a hurry when I wrote then & I omitted to answer some parts of your last letter. Dr. Hagerty should not have given those papers to Kenyon as I paid K. what he had given me & I was to have the *whole.* If you hear from Washington send the letter to me & I will answer it. Perhaps Strong will take it for *two* months rent. I was to have $5 for each claim.

I hope you will get your coal. You did not say how you liked the stove. We have not received any pay yet, so that I cannot send you anything. I wish I could.

I wish you would not say anything about being extravagant. You know I never accused you of anything of the kind. I wish you to live well & keep warm this winter & I shall feel sorry someday if I think you want for the ordinary comforts of life. I only wish I could provide you with the luxuries.

If we go to England, I will try hard for it; & if we don't, we will go on the farm & make the best of it.[6] Things *must* change soon.

I hope to hear from you again next Sunday or Monday. I shall count the days.

The 129th Regt. moved away today from our Brigade. They are gone to Mitchellville,[7] 27 miles south of Bowling Green. I hope you will use one of the envelopes I sent you as my address is not with the Regiment anymore.

I am very well in health. I never felt much better. My work is all straight up to today. But for appearances I would leave & go to Capt. Granger's Head Quarters. They want a clerk very much & would make the *extra pay* sure. I don't feel quite sure of it now tho' the adjutant says it will be "all right."

You need not trouble about sending me any money—I don't really require it. We get plenty to eat & my clothes are all good. I only require to pay for my washing. I got another pair of shoes today. Gagan of Pontiac has arrived. He brought my rug. I am now well provided with covering.

Our Head Quarters is now on a high bluff from which we can see the town, river & a good deal of the country. The whole camp is (or was) on a large farm belonging to a Gentleman who has a Government appointment in Europe. We occupy the garden & grounds round the remnants of a splendid house. It was supposed to have been set on fire by some enemy of the owner when the rebels were here. It has been a very beautiful place. Our tents are pitched among the gravel-walks & ornamental bushes & evergreens.

I was not much disappointed in not getting much rent. I don't feel like letting the place again to Lindsays. They might have done better. Stevens says Corey is quite rich—having property down East.

Had not you better sell the pigs or at least some of them?

I saw Eli Lower yesterday.[8] He looks very well. Many are sick in Co. "B." Gilchrist[9] tells me they cannot muster many more than 30 for duty.

Chilcott has not lost his office.[10] Riggs laid us a small brick fireplace in our tent yesterday.[11] He wonders what you would think if you were to receive a letter from him. I told him to write. He said he could not spell well enough. He says he receives one or two letters from home every week. Sometimes his little girl writes.

I had made a sketch of the inside of our tent for the adjutant. I will send it to you when I can find it again.

The adjutant is still out tho' it is past 10 o'clock at night. He got lost in the bushes near the river last night. He drinks too much whiskey. His son is gone to sleep. They are not so rich as many suppose. The adjutant has just arrived.

My firewood is nearly burnt out & my paper & ideas are about finished. We have nothing but an old dull axe to chop with.

I should like to see you & the children this Winter, but I think I can't get away. They are very strict even with the high officers—I shall hear from you again.

I must now say good bye & kiss the dear little chuckies for Father.

Your ever faithful & affec.

WHB

PS. The adjutant is tight.

[Written across last page]

You sent me by mistake the enclosed ticket. I don't approve of such dodges to make money.[12]

Bowling Green, KY
Dec. 2, 1862
My dearest wife,

I have just received your letter dated Nov 16th tho' the postmark on the envelope is the 20th. From the 26th till now is 12 days. Five days is long enough.

I have been to the Post Office every day for the last week. And it appears that the letter must have gone thro' Bowling Green to the 129th Reg. at Mitchellville—27 miles from here. Capt. Perry[13] brought it up this morning. He came to see about the body of Lieut. S.H. Kyle who died yesterday morning. His death was sudden & unexpected by the Regt.[14] He was left here at a farmer's house. John McW. & Capt. Perry are endeavoring to raise money enough to send home the corpse.

I think I have written lately *two* letters to your *one.* I was afraid you were so unwell that you could not write, but I am very glad to hear from you at last.

I sent you news in my reply to Frederick's[15] letters. Our brigade Adjutant is now Aide de Camp to Gen. Granger & I have scarcely anything to do. Capt. Patterson of the Division Quarter Master wants a clerk—I think of going to him. Smith has left McWilliams' and is with Patterson. I handed Smith two letters that Capt. Perry brought from the Regt. Smith is first rate in health. I presume Eldredge's folks hear from him regularly now.

Col. Chapin has gone home sick. Capt. Shelden has joined his Regt. & we are not very well provided with food. Scarce any of the officers have a cent of money.

I don't know how soon we may leave here. We shall not stay much longer I think. If you had sent the box of things to me at Bowling Green, I could have taken out my things & forwarded the rest to Eli Lower.

I wrote to L.N. Walkley about the Kansas land & have had no reply. Hicks is perhaps merely traveling thro' Kansas, & could not attend to the Land.

I received the rug from Gagan & have enjoyed its warmth for some time. Still I feel cold at nights, especially my feet. I slept in a hay pile last night.

I don't think there is any chance at all for me to come home this Christmas unless I am extremely unwell. The Rules are very strict.

We shall have to wait patiently till there is a truce or till the war is over.

Nothing in the world would please me better than to come home & see you & the dear children. You have friends—Mrs. Eldredge & Mrs. Lower.

I feel sorry often that I left you. I will never leave you alone again. I should have to pay my own expenses. I did not receive any newspaper from you. I should like to see my last letter in print.

I remember very well the night we were alarmed at the firing of a gun. Mrs. Jones stayed with you round the house. I should like to read the details of the trial when it comes off. If I could go to Poughkeepsie as a witness it would be a good chance to get home.[16]

Any package we may receive will come thro' Louisville. I think the whole charges would be about $4 for a package of 50 lbs. or thereabout.

You must really find out what Keyt intends to do. Send Kenyon or Mr. Young over.

I am glad you visit Mrs. Eldredge. She will be company for you.[17] I don't think you will require a Doctor unless something goes wrong.

Mr. Young knows where Keyt lives & would go over willingly. Give him the agreement & send him off.

I received the stamps. I suppose you received the 25¢ ticket back. I think I shall not write any more for the *Sentinel.*

I am not now & not likely to be with the Regt. Money would be very acceptable to me. But it is not really necessary. I think I shall go to the Division Q. Master. They have a warm, comfortable place. I am going to see him this afternoon. Our pay day is not yet come nor do we know when it will come. I understand Capt. Patterson pays his extra duty men every month—that is the *extra pay.*

I shall mail this letter tomorrow morning & will not send it by Chicago. You will see how soon it arrives.

I have thought a good deal about Mr. Gartside's proposition—if we could sell out everything, I should feel like going. We could live near Droylsden & take care of your mother.[18] But it will be some time before we can think of starting. I went to see Capt. Patterson this afternoon. He was not in.

I am writing this in Gen. Granger's Head Quarters. The chief clerk tells me that the Genl. will probably stay here all winter. I should like to get into some warm place this winter.

The Chicago Battery moves towards Nashville tomorrow. I think you might safely send the box of articles to Bowling Green. I think I shall be here. Send me a vest, one of those Frederick sent.

Don't send the things at all unless you can spare the express charges. I don't really *need* anything. I hope you & the children keep in health. I should like photographs of you all. Some of the soldiers have got them.

I send my best love to you & the children. I will write again when anything of interest happens & in any case in a week from now.

Your most affectionate,
WHB

Head Quarters U.S. Forces,
Bowling Green, Ky
Dec. 7th Sunday 1862
My dearest wife,

I have now got a position in the office of Brig. General Granger which is likely to continue thro' the winter. We have a large, comfortable, warm room in which to write. The General & his staff occupy the same room with us. The house is spacious & elegant & one of the best in the city. It was formerly occupied by a secessionist. We have a very comfortable place in which to sleep.

The only trouble is about board. The Adjutant Genl. whom I served last did not seem well pleased at my leaving. I said I was going to Capt. Patterson's but he thought Capt. Patterson's would not be a good place. I told him that I was doing nothing with him & must look out. He was very reserved.

Capt. Patterson set me to work to make some copies of documents & then left without saying anything more. I made the copies & then *left* myself. I then found a vacancy at Genl. Granger's & I am here now.

I am sure of my extra pay from the time I left the Regt. but not before as Adjutant Plattenburg was not entitled to a clerk. Perhaps he will pay me something. He certainly ought to do.

The other two clerks in the office are boarding at a private house. I can't afford this. If I draw money instead of rations I only get 15 cents a day. I tried to join a mess & help pay a cook but the mess did not want any more members.

I have been boarding with John McWilliams & Stevens who have plenty of provisions. They will leave tomorrow. I think that we clerks shall probably make a mess. At all events I shall arrange it somehow.

The Inspector Genl.—a jolly old Captain—finds me in Blacking.[19] He perceived I had been well educated & thought I ought to appear as well as I could. He gave me some words to spell & I gave him some. I beat him all to pieces. He treats us to a drink of liquor sometimes.

I said in my last letter that I would write again in few days if anything of moment happens. I have been promoted from the Regt. to the Brigade & from the Brigade to the Division.

I go to John McW's every night a distance of two miles & walk down every morning to the office. We commence work about 8 o'clock & sometimes do a letter by candle—or kerosene light.

I finished all of Adjutant Montgomery's work before I left him. I did all his back work & posted his books & arranged his papers in good order.

The 129th Illinois Regt. is still at Mitchellville. They have received orders today to fortify themselves. We hear many reports of guerillas being around. We had 500 men under arms one night. It is supposed that the rebels mean to attack the railroad at some point.[20]

Last night it froze very hard—in fact as hard as it ever does in this part of the country as I was informed this morning. The milk was frozen & the ground was quite hard as I walked down the hill about 7 o'clock. The sun is now warm & pleasant & the frost is thawing on the sunny side of the streets. But the Summer will be very hot. I was told this morning that it has been known to be 93 degrees in the early part of April.

I don't know what will result from the proposed mediation of the European powers, but I have an idea that the war will soon close.

Smith has got a good place under the Division Commissary. He is quite fat & lively.[21]

I have been expecting another letter from you every day. I may get one this afternoon.[22]

My health is pretty good & will improve if I get a regular place to board. A Negro woman washes a few things for me. She charges 5¢ a shirt.

We are discharging sick soldiers here very fast. There are 19 hospitals in this town besides many at Louisville, Danville & other parts of Kentucky. This clear bracing weather will thin out some of them. The churches & large buildings are used as hospitals. The Commissary stores for these hospitals comprize—besides the usual kinds of food—fresh meats, eggs, chickens, dried fruit, apples, &c. I saw in Smith's Department about 100 live chickens. They were growing as if in their wanted yards.

I think the sick are as well attended to as the circumstances will admit—there are many parents here getting discharges for their sick children, wives for their husbands.

Nearly all those discharged ought never to have entered the army. They will not get any Government bounty & ought to refund the County bounty. I see the medical certificates in every case & know all about it.

The post office is open only one hour after the arrival of the mail on Sunday afternoon. There is a tremendous rush every day. I hope the letter I am expecting has not gone to Mitchellville.

I will write again latter end of this week after I have received yours.

I send my best love to you & the children.

Your affectionate husband,

WmHBradbury

Head Quarters US Forces
Bowling Green Ky
Dec. 12th 1862
My dearest wife,

I received your letter dated Dec. 2 1862, enclosing 50 cents in postage stamps & not a dollar as you stated, last night. I was very glad to get it as I had been to the Post office nearly every day for a week. I don't really need any money. I have never received the socks, gloves & Keyt's letter.

Capt. Walkley, who was here from Mitchellville a few days ago, said the parcels had arrived & that he had sent it by Mr. Reeder of Dwight, who had been visiting the army at Mitchellville & Bowling Green. I saw Mr. Reeder & talked with him, but he did [not] give me any parcel. There must be some mistake about it. I told Capt. Walkley that Reeder had not given it me. Perhaps in his hurry & excitement he took it along with him back to Dwight. I told him to call & see you.

I must write Capt. Walkley again about it. The socks would have been acceptable, & without Keyt's letter I cannot tell you much respecting the farm.

You must have had a hard time taking down the stove pipe & helping kill pigs. I feel very sorry to think of what you have to do. I hope you will get sufficient coal. You did not say how much the pigs weigh. I hope you will have enough meat left. I feel sometimes as if I had neglected you & the dear children.

With regard to the farm & Keyt, the object is to have the farm worked by some *body even by Lindsay.* If there is no better application for it, you had better let Lindsay have it without delay. Many farms must go unworked next year & we should endeavor to make as much as we can from ours.

The next object is get the amount of the interest which is $152—about $8 has been paid for which you will find a receipt somewhere. The whole interest is $160. I expect Van Dusen will call or write for it. You ought to get it if possible in green backs or government money. I should not feel sorry if the money was not paid at the time under the peculiar circumstances. I wrote some time since to Van Dusen on the subject. I cannot advise anymore. You will let me know how you make out & I will write again.

I did not think of Mrs. Caldwell having to sign the note. I don't think it is absolutely necessary.

Whatever you do *don't fret or trouble about anything.* Nobody will take any advantage of us under these peculiar circumstances.

I received a few dollars in place of rations while I was with the 38th Brigade but I shall have to refund it when I get my pay.

There are two Paymasters now in the neighborhood paying some of the troops; but I have not yet found out when the 129th is going to be paid. I think it will be in a few weeks at the farthest. I shall then take the greatest pleasure in sending you every cent I can possibly spare. I don't require much here. I am not so well dressed as either of the other clerks. I will try to get a new cap & a neck tie—a flannel shirt buttoned up in front without any vest does not look well in a large parlor hung with maps & mirrors & occupied by gentlemen in bright uniforms.

I don't think you can dispose of Caldwell's mortgage for *cash* unless at a sacrifice. You ought not to sell it for less than $80.

I have a good place to get my board at now. I have had an attack of diarrhea but am much better & tho' quite thin I am gaining. I don't suppose I weigh more than 140 pounds, 20 less than I once weighed. I mean to take all the exercise I can. I always feel best at home with my dear wife & children.

I engaged in making out discharges for disabled soldiers—We discharge a number every day.

I suppose you heard of the 39th Brigade being surprised & captured by the enemy at Nashville.[23] It is considered by many as a disgraceful surrender & the Colonel in command will be punished when caught.

The Inspector of the Troops has been here tonight. His business is to examine into everything & punish all negligent or remove all negligent or incapable officers. The 129th have room for improvement. Their turn will come soon.[24]

John McW & Stevens have gone back to their Regt. Smith is still here—Colonel Smith has sent back for me, but I am required here.[25]

I shall give my washerwoman some coffee tomorrow for her work. She charges me 5¢ a piece. She is a darky—I understand they have Negroe dances in town sometimes. I never attended any.

I hope you will require nothing from the county. It is not exactly like taking charity, but I would not make any application till compelled.

I suppose you received the letter I sent to Frederic. I have not heard from him or Charles since. If you have not sent any package to me, you need not—I do not really require anything; & the regulations are now so strict that it would take too much time & expense to get it through.

The advance has begun in Virginia & our troops have crossed the river & shelled the city of Fredericksburg. A battle is expected near Nashville—the 129th & the troops stationed here may be ordered forward. We can't tell—telegrams & dispatches are constantly received here & sometimes things look lively.

I find that other letters are as long coming thro' as ours. The mails seem very irregular. We had no passenger train for two days this week. I shall mail this tomorrow (Dec. 13) & you will see how soon you get it. I suppose another letter from you is now on its way here. I hope to get it about the 15th.

I have heard nothing from Walkley's brother about the Kansas Land. I suppose you got the sketch of the inside of the tent.

Why don't you use the envelopes I sent you? If you don't write often I will excuse you because I know how disagreeable it is to you in your present position. I will write myself *at least* once a week.

I don't write any more to the Pontiac paper. I understand Billy Gagan's sutler's shop is played out. The boys have no money & he can't get any goods, scarcely.

I am glad to see that there are indications of peace propositions. I really think the war will not be protracted much longer. I should like to get home to you & the children; tho' I am now earning more than I did by school-teaching last winter. I don't suppose we shall receive more than two months pay & some of that will be retained for our clothing. We are allowed \$3½ a month for clothes or \$42 a year. I shall have been in the service 5 months on the 11th January, 1863 which will give \$17½ for clothing. I have had more than that in clothing.

In conclusion, I must urge you not to trouble or fret. I think of you & the children every day. I dreamt the other night I was kissing little Willie.

Goodbye dearest wife. Kiss the children for me.

Your affectionate husband,

WmHBradbury

Head Quarters, Bowling Green, Ky
Dec. 18th 1862
My dearest wife,

I duly received your letter of Dec. 7th a few days ago. I also received yours of the 2nd Dec. I received one about 2 days after the other. Yesterday I got Kenyon's letter, which ought not to have been sent to the Regt. at Mitchellville as it had to come back here.

I sent the bond back to Kenyon by yesterday's mail with a letter of instructions. I sent him today a power of attorney and more instructions which will render it unnecessary for me to say anything more to you about the Farm.[26]

I don't feel uneasy about it. Van Dusen will never exact the interest at the time. Money is very cheap in New York & his security is as good as any paper money now circulating.

I don't think the war will last much longer. Both sides seem weary of it & disposed to a peace. I never received the socks &

gloves yet. Reeder must have brought them back with him. I understand Patrick Fuge has some parcels for the boys—perhaps I may get something from you.[27] I shall see him tomorrow.

I am very comfortably situated now. Our Head Quarters is a large handsome mansion belonging to a Gentleman now in the rebel army. We occupy a large & lofty room downstairs & a similar room upstairs. The grounds in front are ornamented with evergreens & other choice trees & shrubs. The family occupy the rest of the house & the Negro quarters are in the outhouses at the back. It is a very elegant residence—I generally sleep on the floor upstairs where we have a fire as well as below. It is much more comfortable than in Adjutant Montgomery's tent. I can get my rations at 40¢ a day—$2.80 a week which will nearly pay my board at $3 a week. I am trying it a week at a private boarding house where they keep a very good table.

I have no doubt I live much better than you. But I could not get anything satisfactory with the orderlies & escort as a rainstorm spoiled all their cooking and arrangements & they live in a very rude manner. The other clerks do the same thing as regards board. I think this is much better than being with the Regt. while the weather is cold. We are just as comfortable as if we were living in a private house.

I have made out my papers for extra duty while with Adjutant Montgomery—4 days at 40¢ = $13.60. I expect to get this money at Christmas *positively.* It is promised me by the Quarter Master. I shall then send you every cent I can spare. I think I can send you $10. You may certainly expect $5 on New Year's Day. I shall now get my extra duty every month from the Quarter Master ***$12 a month.*** I came to Genl. Granger's on the 4th of this month—I shall consequently claim 26 days at 40¢, $10.40 on first January. I am afraid I shall get nothing from Adjutant Plattenburg unless he should pay me out of his own pocket. We shall see.

I received a summons today from Capt. Walkley's sergeant, Mr. Henyon,[28] to report to my company or be considered a *deserter.* I showed it to Genl. Granger. He scolded the Adjutant for not sending notice of my detail to the Regt.

Company B numbers only a few men & Walkley wants to get all he can together. They can't scare me. A comfortable place & 40 cents a day is not to be despised.

I am still making out discharge papers. I leave the office & take a walk downtown & see Smith twice a day. Capt. Patterson, Smith's *boss* was relieved, but the new Commissary is a *Free Mason* & so is Smith. He was tickled to death at his good luck. They draw rations from the Hospital Stores & live first rate. Eggs, chickens, apples, butter &c are provided for the use of the Hospitals of which there are 19.

The sick & disabled of all the transitory hosps. are left here & all the churches & very large private houses are converted into Hospitals. Our office is besieged every day with invalid soldiers wanting their papers. They are sadly disappointed if the General has not signed them.

All kinds & classes of people come to our Head Quarters: Disloyal men wanting to return to their allegiance & take the oath; men of questionable loyalty wanting passes; ladies wanting to get to their husbands; cotton speculators who have been arrested & their goods confiscated, prisoners who have to be sent to the Guard houses & secesh soldiers who have or pretend to have deserted & wish to return to the Union—all come here & state their cases—some of which are pitiful enough. Scarce a day passes but some crying scene occurs. One woman today wanted permission to go & fetch home her husband's body.

The regulations are very strict. A Patrol guard walks the streets night & day & arrests every person without a pass. The Railroad Depot & the trains are constantly watched & a pass signed by the highest authorities are required when any one gets aboard.

I expect a letter from you about the 20th—two more days—& then I will write more than I have this time. I am well & in good spirits. I hope you & the children are. Receive my best & dearest love, & believe me.

PS. I will write again to the children.

Yours ever affectionate,

WmHBradbury

I forgot to put this letter along with the other for Kenyon.

Head Quarters U.S. Forces
Bowling Green, Ky
Dec. 23rd, 1862
My dearest wife,

I have been waiting for a letter from you for the last few days, but have concluded that perhaps you are not able to write. I last wrote to you about the farm & sent you a letter to Kenyon. I wrote to Van Dusen & requested him to come to Dwight & see Keyt & Kenyon together. I have no doubt they will arrange it among themselves.

I enclose a printed letter for the children. I suppose Willie can pick out the capital letters, & Freddy & Janie will understand about the boats.

I find the Post Commissary will only commute our rations at 30¢ instead of 40¢ which leaves me deficient 90¢ a week—I can't afford that. He also refuses to commute any more at all at present. I shall have to mess with somebody & take my turn cooking.

General Granger is now relieved from this Post. He goes to Nashville to command a division under Genl. Rosecrans. The new Commander here retains the old clerks. Consequently I shall still remain here at present. I think it quite likely that Smith will be retained here also.

We have had serious apprehensions lately of an attack at this place & have made extensive preparations to receive the enemy. The Railroad is guarded all along, & the bridges are well defended. The 129th Ill. have moved a short distance from Mitchellville. Col. Smith commands the Post. Lt. Col. Case commands the Regt. I see a stray Capt. or Lieut. here occasionally from the Regt.

I received a note from Capt. Walkley requiring me to return to the company or be considered a deserter. I think I told you about this before. I have scarcely anything to do in the office this afternoon.

The new Commander with his Adjutant are in & just being introduced to the other "shoulder straps." Our extra duty, pay roll is made out, & we expect to get our money up to the 23rd this evening.

Brig. General Manson is the new Commander.[29] His insignia of office is a strap on the shoulder with a star in the center. A Colonel's strap has an Eagle in the center. A Major has a leaf at each end of the strap. A Captain has a strap with two bars. A 1st Lieutenant only one bar & a Second Lieut.—plain. A Lieutenant Colonel has a silver leaf instead of a gold leaf like the Major's.

No liquor is allowed to be sold to soldiers. The consequence [is] that the officers drink the whiskey & the Privates get only Lager Beer—a very small glass for 5¢—I scarcely ever drink any at all. Many of the officers had a jolly drunk last night. They played cards

& had a good time. The clerks in this office play cards & drink a little sometimes.[30]

The weather here is more like May than December. We heard the birds chirping every morning & the blue grass is still quite green. I go out without drawers or overcoat & never wear a vest. I get my clothes—shirt & drawers—washed pretty regularly. I air my blankets every day on the balcony upstairs & make myself as comfortable as I can.

I think of you & the children every day & frequently dream of you at night. There is of course no female society. We hear the girls playing the piano in the next room & singing *awfully.* They are *secesh* and play Rebel pieces.

Our life is sometimes tedious & monotonous & if it were not for the extra pay I think I should go to the Regiment.

I shall conclude this letter tomorrow morning. I received a friendly letter from Adjutant Plattenburg yesterday. I desired him to get me 25¢ a day as extra pay if he could.

I don't think any forward movement will be made till the rivers rise. The season has been uncommonly dry. I have just received my extra duty pay $21.20—this includes the pay due to me as clerk in the 38th Brigade. I enclose to you $5. I will send you another $5 when you have received this.

I was quite disappointed in not receiving a letter from you tonight. I think there must be one on the road.

The other clerks got their pay also. I left two of them playing cards for money. They were gambling all night last night.

I feel anxious when I think of your position & wish I could be with you at the time. I feel confident however that you will get thro' & then the baby will be a great comfort to you.

I send my best & sweetest & kindest love to you. I think of your goodness every day & frequently reproach myself that I have not provided for you better. I do think that when the war is over (which I hope will be soon) we shall have better times & live happily & prosperously with the dear little children.

I am expecting a letter from you every mail. But if you do not write I shall attribute it to the right cause.

I remain,
Your devoted & affectionate husband,
WmHBradbury

Head Quarters U.S. Forces
Bowling Green, Ky
December 30, 1862
My dearest wife,

I wrote to you several days ago enclosing $5, but as the Rebels burnt a bridge & tore up a track for two miles near Munfordsville, I suppose you have not received it. This goes by the steamboat & I hope will reach you. Since then they have committed other attacks on the Railroad which renders travel toward the north impracticable by the cars.

I received the letter you sent, enclosed to Smith, after I received the one addressed direct to me. I am afraid our communications hereafter will be sometimes quite irregular.

I now hold the most responsible position in the office. One of the clerks is discharged from the service & another above me is ordered to his Regiment.

An order was received here today from our Lieut. Col. for me to report to the Regt., but Genl. Manson replied that it should not be complied as I was regularly detailed & was required here.

I feel quite anxious on your account & would like to hear from you as often as you can write. Some mode of transporting the mail will be discovered soon—I have hopes that the Rebels who have given us so much trouble lately will be taken.

Our new General is a very humorous man & we have some rich scenes in the office occasionally. I have done a great deal of writing today. Matters at the office are quite lively as we have to concert measures & prepare against attacks at different points. Bowling Green is considered quite safe, but our supplies are cut off by rail. I enclosed a letter to Janey & Freddy in my last.

You must be mistaken about the price of the washing. I said 5 cents a piece & I have never had my stockings washed. That is quite cheap as anybody North or South would wash a shirt or drawers.[31]

I received my money as I told you before. I had to stick hard for it. I have now $15 in cash. I will send you $10 by the first safe mode of conveyance. I have not heard anything about the box for the Dwight Co. that was to come by *express.* I suppose you had news of the interception in travel before you sent it off. It is quite uncertain about its getting here at all for some time.

I have been thinking about trying to get a discharge. One of our clerks has been successful & I think I could persuade the Medical Director that I was unfit for duty as a soldier. I have not felt well till just lately & I do think I have done the Government good service while I have been here. If I were to refund the County bounty I think no one could say a word against it.[32]

If I were ordered back to my Regiment & made to undergo exposure & great excitement, I should certainly suffer. What do you think about it? The 129th Regt. is removed 8 miles down the Railroad from Mitchellville & are pleasantly encamped in the woods. McWilliams & Stevens are not in the ranks but aching to take care of the provisions.

General Granger is still with us. Our post here is so important that we have 2 Generals, 2 adjutants and 4 clerks.

I generally take a walk about a mile before breakfast every fine morning. I don't often have a chance in the day time. I have quit boarding in town & now mess with the orderlies in a very rough and dirty manner but my health is pretty good. I enjoy my bread & beef & coffee very well.

There are many Christmas dances & festivities but the shoulder straps are the "elite." They also are the first to drink all the liquors. There is a dance tonight, many of the staff are going. Whiskey, cigars & cards. Are all quite military.

I send my best love to you & the children. I will write again as soon as possible.

Your devotedly & affectionate,
WmHBradbury.

Head Quarters United States Forces
Bowling Green, Jany. 1st 1863
My dearest wife,

I have an opportunity to send this by a Captain going to Louisville. I send you $5 in bills which I hope you have got by this time. I wrote once since that by a boat which was going along the Big Barren River.

The Rebels have been destroying the Railroad bridges & giving us fits all over. It will be a long time before communications is open, perhaps 3 or 4 weeks. I am very sorry that it is so, but we cannot help it. There will probably be another mode by which letters will come.

A battle is still going on at Murfeesborough beyond Nashville. Many of our best Generals have been killed. Our cause is certainly not prosperous at present.

I am now Chief Clerk in the office at General Manson's Head Quarters. There are four clerks altogether. I have the most responsibility. Another summons came from the Regt. but it was no go.[33] Genl. Manson would not let me leave.

I understand from last night's dispatches that there was a long & severe fight yesterday closely contested on both sides. The loss was very heavy. But we finally gained some advantage & it will probably result in a glorious victory. Nashville is full of the wounded.

I dare not enclose any money in this letter for fear it might miscarry.

You will get *what you want* at the stores—I am in a position to pay for it as soon as communication is established. Nobody will refuse you credit unless it is John Hetzel[34] who is by nature timid & on a *small scale.*

Genl. Sill & Genl. Negley are reported killed. Colonel Garesche Adjt. Genl. had his head shot off—General Rousseau is wounded. There will be no contest here. We are too well prepared. The only disasters to be apprehended in Kentucky are sudden attacks on unguarded points & destruction of the Louisville & Nashville RR. bridges & the tearing of the track.

I have spoken to the Post Surgeon about my discharge. I may *perhaps* get out at the end of this month.

One of our clerks got a discharge & is now hired as a citizen at big wages in the Quarter Master's department!

I am writing this letter on the second of January. We know no holidays or Sundays here even tho' the Genl. threatens to "dry up this Sunday business," we have as much work as on any other day.[35]

I feel very anxious about you & hope you may have a good time. You have some friends who will sympathize with you & a husband who thinks of you every day & is doing his best to save something for your benefit. I would have sent $10 if it would have been quite safe.

The days are fine & pleasant & the nights frosty—I have no

time to say more. You kiss the children for me & accept my best & warmest love.

Your most affectly,

WmHBradbury

We have had no news from the North for more than a week.

Jany 7th 1863
My dearest wife,

I received your welcome letter yesterday. I duly received yours that was enclosed in one to Smith. I handed Smith *two* letters today—one, I suppose contained a photograph from Dwight—perhaps Miss. P. At least there was a stiff card or a plate inside. Of course I received Keyt's letter enclosed.

I have paid Smith $8. He has written to Eldredge stating the fact; so that you can get the $8 from Eldredge.

I am very glad to hear that you feel pretty well & that the neighbors are kind. I have no doubt but you will have a good time tho' it may be over before this reaches you. The full moon is just over. There will be a new moon on about 12 days.[36]

I board with the orderlies in a very rough way but it suits me very well. I am much confined in the office, owing to the great amount of business doing. I have much annoyance & responsibility. Poor fellows come crowding in every day after their discharge papers begging that their turn may come next. I have one clerk & sometimes two clerks to help me. I also make out the morning reports which properly belongs to another clerk; but as he can't do it, devolves upon me.

At first when I came, the two older clerks were exclusive & thought themselves above me & one tried to get me away. But now my abilities are recognized & a clerk who was placed above me has to come under. Those two clerks are now gone.

If I were to leave, I think they would have some difficulty to find a man to do my work. It is too confining & sedentary for my health. I contrive to take a walk down town in the forenoon & afternoon & call on Smith & steal an apple from the Hospital Stores.

Genl. Manson is a big rough vulgar looking man & is keeping a sharp eye on discharged soldiers. I do not think I could get through if he was to know of it. I really don't look sickly & have never been in hospital. I shall present myself for examination sometime this month if nothing happens.

The Union cause is now very prosperous. You have heard of the victories in Tennessee & Arkansas & the rumor of the taking of Vicksburg on the Mississippi. I hope this Spring will decide it. Steam boats come up here regularly from the Ohio River—up the Green River & the Big Barren River, which is a very winding stream. Janey will find it on the map. The Green River empties into the Ohio near Evansville between Louisville & Cairo. The Louisville & Nashville RR which runs thro' this place have refused to carry the mail anymore at the Government price. The track is still torn up & some bridges not repaired. Many of the discharged soldiers go by the boats.

The Generals are not austere, but they have plenty of shoulder straps to converse with, without condescending to talk to "high privates." The Adjutant Generals are much more familiar. We got some egg-nog on Christmas day, but no dinner except our ordinary fare.

You do not say anything about the box for the Dwight Co. I have heard nothing of it. We are on three quarter rations now, owing to the condition of the RR—I get quite enough myself.

Our new clerk is a Polish soldier related to the nobility. He can talk French & Dutch & English. He understands Latin & drawing & carving figures. He is also a good soldier & can drill troops & cook. He's an excellent clerk & tho' a little man & 46 years old, he is as active & tough as many young men, but this Polish man is dirty *rather.*

I have heard nothing whatever from Frederic or Charles, nor from Luthur N. Walkley.

The children must have been quite pleased with their presents. I should have liked to have seen them.

We have had very dry weather so far. The showers have been scarce & the river is still low for the season. It seems strange that you have so much rain at Dwight. The Ohio River is rising. If the Cumberland & Tennessee rise, it will be of great advantage to us in getting supplies into Tennessee.

I know I did not date the letter to Jane. I suppose she did not find it out herself. I will write another next time I write to you.

I sent you a letter a few days ago by an officer going to

Louisville. You ought to have got it about the 3rd Jany. Probably you have answered it by this time. I am expecting one tomorrow or next day.

The 129th Ill. is still near Buck Lodge at a place called Fountainhead. We have discharged several from that Regiment.

I will write again in a few days. Give my love to the children & accept the same from your ever affectionate & faithful,

WmHBradbury

Bowling Green, Kentucky
Jany. 13, 1863
My dearest wife,

I answered your last letter three or four days ago. I hope you have received it by this time. I have received nothing from you since your dated Dec. 30, 1862.

The mails will now be more regular. I understand that the RR Co. & the Government have arranged matters. In the meantime, until the Railroad is repaired, a messenger will start every morning from Nashville with the mail calling at Bowling Green.

I am still in the office here & am likely to remain. I occasionally see officers from the 129th from whom I inquire about the Regt. I understand there has been some ill feeling among the officers, particularly the Regimental officers.

We have now 4 clerks in the office besides myself & we all keep busy. We have discharged nearly 100 men this month.

I told you in my last that Eldredge would pay you $8 which I had paid to Smith. Our extra pay will be due again at the end of this month. We expect to receive our regular pay this month if there is money enough in Louisville to do it. I don't think we shall receive more than 2 or 3 months pay for the Paymaster always leaves some back.

I have heard nothing whatever of the box for the Dwight Co. I presume it has not been sent at all. There is only a short length of the Railroad out of repair.

We sent down a number of prisoners the other day to Evansville. They are going to Vicksburg to be exchanged. Two of them tried to escape & were shot by our guards.

It must seem strange to you that the rivers are open & that there is no snow. The weather is very mild & pleasant. It freezes very little at night & the days are very pleasant.

While I am writing Genl. Manson is examining a Deserter from the Rebels. He pretends to be surprised that these men never owned any Negroes as *that* is what they pretend to be fighting for. This man is a member of Morgan's Band & the Genl. is putting him thro' the small sieve. We generally make these men take the oath of allegiance & give bonds that they will behave themselves & be loyal in future. The security ranges from $1500 & upwards.

My washerwoman has cleared out lately. I went to the house yesterday; but it was vacated & going to be used as a *hospital!* The person living in it was a Schoolmaster & an Episcopalian Preacher. That was "pretty rugged" on the parson as our old Genl. says. It certainly seems hard for a man to be turned out with his wife & family & his house taken for the uses of a lot of sick soldiers. But such is the case with many large fine houses in this town.

We have more spare time on Sunday now than before. Last Sunday I had a pleasant walk with Capt. Anderson of our Regt. down to the Steamboat Landing.

I have just got ready the discharge papers of a member of our Regt.—he offered me his watch this morning if I would put them thro' for him. I could not take anything from him.[37] We have now about 70 discharges in the office for which the poor fellows are anxiously waiting.

My health is pretty good tho' I have a very bad cold just now. I think I caught with putting on a shirt which was not quite dry.

I think of you & the children every day. I hope Jane will take good care of the baby. I wish I could just see you & Jane & Freddy & Willie. I can imagine what a noise there would be. I must send you my Photograph next pay day so that the children will not forget me. My face is all prickly now.

I have not yet presented myself for examination but it would do no harm to try. If I should be ordered to rejoin the Regiment I should have to go into the ranks at $13 a month or loaf round Head Quarters on some pretense or other.

I have written again to L.N. Walkley & have inquired his present address from Capt. Walkley.

There is no war news here at present. In fact there seems to be a lull in Military matters all over.

Newspapers sell for 10¢ each. The blue grass is springing in the garden & roadsides, & the birds sing & chirp in the morning. The evergreen look very green & fresh. We have had no snow at all. In another month we shall have spring. And in April it will be hot here as it with you in June.

I frequently sleep in the landing or lobby upstairs where there is more & purer air. My clothes are all in good condition, but they don't begin with those of the *shoulder strap* gentlemen—"Fine feathers make fine birds."

I expect a letter from you tomorrow. A mail is coming from Louisville.

I will now conclude by sending my best & kindest love to you & the children.

Yours affectionately,
WmHBradbury

Head Quarters
Bowling Green, Kentucky
January 16, 1863

I wrote you a letter the other day, which owing to the state of the weather, has not yet left this town. You will receive that letter & this both at once.

We have had a very heavy rain storm followed by a deep snow which is quite unusual for this part of the state. The snow is about five inches deep & considerably deeper at Louisville. When this melts we shall have a great flood. One Railroad bridge between here & Nashville is already gone. The Railroad Co. now refuses to carry the mail at all. We have to carry it ourselves as Baggage. A messenger leaves this place tomorrow morning.

The weather is very severe on the soldiers. It is quite cold for this climate. The rivers are now rising fast. I am comfortably sheltered; but the cooking does not progress very well in wet, snowy weather.

I have had 2 or 3 meals down town for which I shall paint a small sign. I have three clerks under me & discharge about 15 soldiers every day.

Military operations are suspended by the weather. The Rebels were coming again into Kentucky but this rain & snow will prevent them.

Major Cropsey has applied for leave of absence on account of death in his family. He can get leave for 10 days if he can hunt up any deserters from his Regiment. This is only an excuse.

We have sent for the Paymaster & expect a mail by a messenger from Louisville. There is quite enough snow to make good sleighing.

We are going to move our Head Quarters into the City. We are now a little on one side of the place.

Complaints are frequently made of robberies & outrages by the soldiers & there are strange tales & complaints every day. My cold is getting better but I suffer from chilliness & cold feet. I hope to be better in awhile—I shall certainly get a letter from you when the mail comes. It seems a long time since I heard from you—I hope this weather will not interfere with your comfort at home.

If we get paid off next month I will send you $25 or $30. I feel pretty sure that we shall get our money about the 31st January.

I do hope you will be comfortable & be well taken care of during your trial.[38] I think of you every day & wish I was with you. The neighbors will be kind & you always have an easy time compared to some.

I am glad Morgan was successful at the trial. I wonder if Mr. Jones was there.

I have nothing more to say at present—I send you my best & sweetest love & may God bless you & the children.

The other clerks are playing cards & yelling like mad to my intense disgust.

Your ever affectionate & devoted husband,
WmHBradbury

Bowling Green
Friday eve.
January 23, 1863
My dearest wife,

I have received no letter from you since one dated December 30th, 1862. The Railroad Co. refused to carry any mail at all & the consequence is that all communication between us & the rest of the world has to be carried on by private means or by military authority.

We sent a Messenger with the mail several days ago. We expect that he will bring a mail back with him which will bring me news of you & the children. I send this letter by a discharged soldier of our Regiment who leaves this place in the morning for Ancona, Livingston Co.

I suppose the expected event has taken place by this time. You have my warmest sympathies and dearest love. I do hope you feel pretty well & that the child is well. It will occupy your thoughts & be a source of comfort to you during my absence. You must take the best care of yourself that you can.

I should like to be with you, but I don't see how I can. On reflection I don't think it would be very honorable to try to get a discharge. I feel sure they will retain me in my present position unless our Regiment moves out of this Brigade.

I still think the war will be concluded this spring or summer. The distress in France & England & the fact that both contending parties are becoming weary of the struggling indicates that it cannot continue much longer.[39]

My health is good—tho' the employment is too sedentary. The weather is too wet & the roads too muddy to take any walks. The snow is nearly all gone & the sky is cloudy & showery.

I sent you *two* letters since I received your last. I hope you got them both.

My life here is very monotonous. One day is just like another except Sunday which gives a half holiday in the afternoon. We get up about 7 o'clock & take breakfast of bread, bacon, & coffee about 8—I then sit at the desk till noon. Sometimes I take dinner & sometimes go without as I have not much appetite. The afternoon passes like the forenoon. We have supper at 5 o'clock & sometimes work an hour or two afterwards when we are behind. I take a run downtown sometimes & exchange compliments with Smith who still serves out the provisions in the brick building at the corner.

We have discovered that a key belonging to some desk would open a large cupboard in the bedroom upstairs of this *secesh.* house & there we found a lot of "Harper's monthlies" which affords us very good reading.[40] This is a great mitigation.

The dry & frequently vulgar jokes of Genl. Manson are source of much merriment. The language made use of by shoulder straps is sometimes quite obscene & disgusting tho' it is much relished on that account.

The officers at this post have a good time. They board down town & sit in the offices 6 or 7 hours a day & get $120 to $200 &

$300 a month for their *arduous* services. They never express a wish that the war should stop—they are doing too well.[41]

The other clerks are chiefly young harem scarems. They have just been dancing & singing & "cutting up." They are now playing cards. I scarcely ever go out at nights. There is nothing to see & nothing to do & nowhere to go. The officers get up entertainments but of course privates are excluded. Sometimes there is a Negroe dance, but I have never been to any yet.

When I am alone & have nothing to do, I always think of my dear wife & children who are working & waiting & thinking of me. My emotions are sometimes sad & sometimes pleasant according to the mood I may be in. My mind wanders homeward when I should be thinking of my duties in the office. Your next letter will relieve my apprehensions & stop my conjectures.

It is now positively stated that the Paymaster will be here next week when I shall send you all the money I can spare. We shall probably receive four months pay with our clothing deducted from it. I expect that I can send you at least $40.

But I have not got my descriptives roll. I have written for it several times but I have not yet received it. I don't know whether that is the fault of Capt. Walkley or not. He does not regard me with any favor. If he still refuses to sent it Genl. Manson will pitch into him pretty "rugged." I cannot draw my pay without it.

We are still discharging disabled soldiers. The number already amounts to upwards of 500 at this post alone.

We never see any women except occasionally in the street or when they come to the office to coax a pass or urge some petition or other for their husbands or sons who have got into trouble. Nothing but shoulder straps & uniforms & blue coats & brass buttons are to be seen anywhere except of course in the boarding houses where the officers play cards & drink whiskey with their friends male & female.

There are Negroe women always to be seen in the streets. They dressed in all their finery in New Year's week & put on a great deal of "style." It was quite amusing to me. The time from Christmas day to New Year's day is all their own & the swarms of "Ladies & genmen" of color was a caution. I have kept entirely clear of them except Joe, our cook, when I was with Adjutant Montgomery. He left unexpectedly & cleared out to his old master in the north part of the state.

The River is now in good boating condition & steamers frequently come from the Ohio River, laden with army stores. Many things are contraband & much watching is required to prevent illicit traffic.

There is scarcely any news from Nashville. I suppose the two armies are watching each other & preparing for another conflict. I do not see much glory in civil war where men kill their friends & neighbors & relations.

A battle is now raging on the Rappahannock in Virginia. I hope it will be decisive. I have no doubt the privates are tired of the war. With officers, the case may be different as they are getting more now than most of them made before.

My clothes begin to require some mending. I must attend to them on Sunday. I got a good wash all over this evening which makes me feel first rate. Smith is quite well. He seems anxious to have the war stop.

I will now conclude by sending my warmest & best love to you & the children. Keep up your spirits. The war will soon be over & then we shall love each other all the more if possible.

I hope you get plenty of coal.

Your faithful & affectionate husband,

WmHBradbury

3

"*Stand on Your Dignity!*"

February 5, 1863–March 26, 1863

By early February 1863, Bradbury's former comrades of the 129th Illinois Infantry were positioned in the border states, where the strongly held feelings for both Union allegiance and secessionist defiance were much in evidence.[1] Some of the regiment was detached to guard the Louisville & Nashville Railroad at South Tunnel, in north central Tennessee, where conditions in the forests and hills were quite difficult. Their task was to prevent Morgan's raiders from again destroying the railroad at this important position in the high elevation of the Highland Rim range.

The regiment's Colonel Smith grew steadily unpopular among his men when, at Fountain Head, Tennessee, he issued General Order No. 3, which threatened severe punishment if misbehavior continued:

> The commander is pained in being compelled to believe that large quantities of spiritous liquors are used by officers and privates of this regiment even to intoxication.[2]

However, courts-martial for drunkenness, leaving one's post, insubordination, intimidating local citizens, and threatening comrades continued during the months away from headquarters in north central Tennessee.

Colonel Smith also increased in unpopularity among local residents, as he threatened his own brand of enslavement. Issuing Special Order No. 34, Colonel Smith made his presence clear among local citizens:

> You will also notify the disloyal citizens living in the vicinity of the

> railroad between Buck Lodge and Mitchellville to take their teams and Negroes and furnish wood for the use of the railroad to the nearest station. If enough wood already chopped cannot be found, they will chop and furnish it. Notify them that should they fail promptly to comply with this order, their teams, wagons, axes, and Negroes will be taken possession of and used for this purpose.[3]

In addition to harnessing the participation and resources of local citizens, if not enslaving them (many were already impoverished by the steady encroachment of troops from both sides), Colonel Smith targeted the home of Confederate Captain Petticord for close observation. Smith believed it was a depot of sorts for goods heading south to Confederate troops. Upon visiting, he found "his [Capt. Petticord's] bed still warm."[4] In retaliation, Smith confiscated barrels of meat and other provisions from his home, while Mrs. Petticord defiantly cursed him and his men. To Colonel Smith's dismay, when Mrs. Petticord protested to General Paine, she was permitted to "take the oath," make a sworn statement that she would become a willing subject of the occupying Union troops and not engage in support of the Confederacy. Colonel Smith became so angry when she was permitted return to her home along with the confiscated provisions that he protested directly to General Manson at Bowling Green: "I do not relish the kid gloves treatment of robbers disguised in the garb of federal soldiers."[5] Strong accusations against one general, Paine, to a higher-ranking general, Manson, was, at the least, a dangerous career strategy. Smith, impolitic to the end of his colonelcy,[6] became an unenviable leader with waning power.

At a time when officers were recruited for newly formed regiments, why Bradbury was not given a commission is unclear. Yet by not following his comrades in the 129th Illinois Infantry and by not receiving a commission to his liking, or of any kind, he was likely spared the many dissatisfactions of a leadership role. Bradbury, though, remained frustrated and bitter about being overlooked, and his capacity to have taken charge of a company or a regiment in action as well as he implied he would have in his letters will forever remain an uncertainty. All we can know is that his wartime experience would have been radically different as an officer in a command role during the war than it was as a clerk. Bradbury's untapped reservoir of high regard for his own abilities would only play out in his letters home, in which his descriptive and sometimes snide observations of the changing cast of characters at headquarters were always rich.

Perhaps had Bradbury been commissioned, he would have had less time to criticize Mary's performance as a businesswoman. Her performance as a mother, delivered once again—this time with twin boys—was surely put to the test in 1863. A rare letter from Mary to her sister-in-law Ann Brown, the last letter of this chapter, reflects the rough times she was having, fearful of losing one or more of the children to sickness. Bradbury's letters, however, sharply critiqued her management of business affairs. He seemed oblivious or at worst unsympathetic to the dire conditions Mary was facing on the home front.

William's pride cost his family dearly, as his compulsive concern for the appearance of financial independence to others was of paramount concern. The family he left behind struggled enormously with the sheer absence of a parent, over and above the extraneous business affairs that loomed around Mary's crowded life. Since William was not accustomed to receiving charity, however it might be defined, he did not think Mary should accept it either.

Yet, a battle of life and death was fought on the prairies of Illinois as well as in the field of combat. Mary, in this respect, saw far more "action"—sheer struggle for survival—than her husband had witnessed at this time from the relative comforts of Bowling Green. Had he understood how bleak and frightening the times were for Mary, he might have offered more loving words of support instead of criticism.

Bowling Green, Ky
February 5th 1863
My dearest wife,

I received your last letter of the 30th of January on the 3rd of this month. I sent you a letter by Leander Morgan.[7] He would tell you how he found me &c.

I am glad to hear that the neighbors are so very kind; but you should quietly reject anything like charity. If R.P. Morgan intends it as compensation for your attendance as witness, it is all right. I received my extra duty money today & enclose you $10.

While I am writing this there is quite an excitement & mounted orderlies are carrying dispatches warning all the troops round this post to stand at arms all night & a cold snowy night it is.

Upon second consideration, I will pay Smith the $10 & you will get it from Eldredge as before. If the Railroad should be again destroyed the mail might be seized. It will be much safer to do so.

The Report which sets us all on the move is a Telegraphic dispatch that the Rebels are in large force 31 miles south of us on the Railroad. They have cut the wires & taken possession of the road there.[8] The 129th Ill. are stationed about that point & it *is possible* that they may have been captured.

I don't wish to alarm anybody but these two facts taken together make it quite probable that the 129th have *seen something of the enemy.* I will leave this subject till morning.

I wrote to Kenyon by Leander Morgan & I hope we shall not be troubled about the interest till next year. I think I shall offer the Kansas land for $1000 & pay off some of the mortgage if I can sell it to Walkley.

I imagine Kenyon will do the fair thing about Bunker's claim & hand you the money. It is quite time Gantzert's claim was settled. I am glad the whole farm is let. Many farms will go idle this year unless the war closes immediately.

I am glad to hear the babies are doing well, but I am sorry for your sake that there are two as it makes you so much work, but if they are fine healthy children you will get along with them as well as others have done before.[9] I hope you will not exert yourself too much for the sake of the children.

We expect the Paymaster every day & then I will send you all I can possibly spare. If the farm had produced anything we should have been better able to stand it.

I will write an encouraging letter to Jane. She is a good girl & I think of her & Freddy every day & Willie too.

I think that events transpiring around us point to a speedy termination of the war. I feel tolerably confident that next Summer will see the end of it. I am in no danger here at all & I shall most likely continue here so that you may certainly expect me to be with you again before long.

I received the socks & vest all right. They are very useful. I do not get exercise enough to keep in good health & the weather is still such that I cannot take any walks.

This morning all seems quiet, but I have not made any inquiries yet about the affairs of yesterday.

I will write again in a few days. I have not time to send anything more before the train leaves—I enclose $5 at a venture.[10]

The weather is very cold & there is good sleighing which is quite uncommon here.

With my best love to you & the children.

I remain,

Your affectionate husband,

WmHBradbury

Head Quarters
Bowling Green, Ky
February 12th 1863
My dearest wife,

I have just received your letter dated February 9th, 1863.

I feel quite indignant to hear that Eaton & Armstrong have offered you money. I shall write to Armstrong immediately & enclose him the dollar. I shall also write to Eaton & decline his offer. When I am not able to support you & the children, I will apply to the county & obtain relief in the proper way. So long as we can get credit at the stores, we ought not to apply to anybody not even to the county.[11] An offer of a little milk or kindling wood is not so objectionable.

I am earning now $25 a month & I can easily spare you $20 at least—I shall receive $10 *every month* for extra duty which I can send you *nearly all.*

I received $10 from an unexpected source today.[12] I will send you $50 as soon as I can find some safe method of sending it. The Paymasters are here, and we expect to receive our pay almost every day. Several regiments have been paid. Our Roll is made out & approved all complete.

You need not say anything to Eaton & Armstrong; I will attend to their case.

There will be some little I think from the farm after paying Van Dusen's claim. I am glad you got Bunker's money.

I sent you $5 in a letter about a week ago & also $5 through Smith to Eldredge.

If Hetzel shows any disposition not to credit you, trade with Eldredge. He will trust us.[13] I can settle that with Smith.

I do hope you will not strict yourself of any thing that is necessary. I think you ought to have some ale. I sure it would do you good. You had better get a gallon & try it. If you do not keep up your strength *now*, you will sink under the trial of two babies & never recover.[14]

I have the promise from our Adjutant of something that will be agreeable. I don't know what it is. They find me very useful & almost indispensable. My spirits are low only when my bodily health is not good. I have felt first rate lately.

We had a great deal of fun in the office today. The General was [im]personating a soldier pretending to be deaf for the sake of getting discharged; an officer who wanted a furlough to see his wife who was sick; showing a dispatch from Kalamazoo, Michigan; a Kentucky volunteer who wanted to go to Regiment & a sick soldier who pretended not to be able to join his regiment. Col. Hanson was the "General" for the time being, & both did their parts first rate. It was very rich.

We had a couple of "fancy women" today who wanted to go to Nashville. This of course produced some facetious remarks.[15]

Can't you get a girl to help you, I mean a small girl. I wish I was at home to make a fire for Jane in the morning.

One of my fellow clerks has received a commission as second Lieut. & has gone home to Michigan. One of Smith's fellow clerks has had the same good luck.

One of our Adjutants is gone home to Michigan. I am expecting to hear from Kenyon again soon.

Your dreams about me joining the regiment may come true; but I don't think Gen'l. Manson will let me go if he can help it.

The 129th are not now in our command, & I am liable to be called away any day. All I care for is the extra pay, which comes every month.

I am writing this letter in Smith's room. I stay with him every night. He wants me for company as the other clerk is going away.

You don't say how the babies are. I suppose they look like all other babies.

I never received any letter from Mr. Hetzel. I will write again when I receive the money. I expect to hear again from you as to whether you got the $5.

With love & kisses to the children, *twins & all,* I remain,

Your affectionate & devoted husband,

WmHBradbury

Head Qtrs.
Bowling Green, Ky
February 23, 1863
My dearest wife,

I received yours of the 17th Feby on the 20th inst. & yours of the 19th and the 22nd.

Perhaps I was more indignant at Armstrong & Eaton than I need to have been. Any little acts of kindness that may be shown to you are all right; but when *money* is offered, the case is quite different.

I forwarded Eli Lower's letter. I never received the letter from you or from Kenyon enclosing one from Van Dusen nor did I receive one from John Hetzel all of which were sent soon after the babies were born.

I am very glad that you have Ann with you.[16] She will be company for you. I hope you enjoy yourselves together & I wish I was with you. I mean to try for leave of absence & make the government pay my way home & back.

If you go or send to Eldredge's, you will find the five dollars all right. It is not likely they will send it to you. Perhaps they wish it applied on the old account, but I don't think they do. You can trade it out there.

I do not expect anything from Leander Morgan except that he will see that you are not without coal.[17] You will pay for the coal & he will haul it from the depot or any place where it can be got. You know it is sometimes difficult to get a little hauling done.

I sent you last Monday $50 which you should have received by this time. I should not like you to receive any money from the County unless you are without money; but if you really need it you ought to have it by all means. We pay taxes on a large quantity of land & are entitled to some share of the benefits arising from taxes.[18] I shall send you a few more dollars at the end of this month.

With regard to Mr. Morgan's donations, I don't think you ought to take more than the usual fee for your attendance at the examination.[19] Where does Mr. Morgan live now?

I have heard nothing from Kenyon relative to his paying Van Dusen's claim.

I am glad to hear that the babies are fine & healthy. They will be quite interesting by the time I shall be able to see them. I think I can get leave of absence this Spring.

The 129th Regt. has not yet been paid off. The men are greatly in need of money. An order has been issued requiring all men on extra duty belonging to that Regiment to proceed to it without delay. The General has made an exception as regards Smith & me.

I got the five dollars I spoke about for making out a set of discharge papers in advance of their regular turns so that the man got off a few days earlier.

I really don't know what name to give the little innocents. You & Ann must fix on something & submit it to me. I will write a few more rhymes for Jane & send them next time I write.

I expect soon to hear from you that you have received the money by express. I shall send you about six dollars this month. I received pay up to the 6th Feby. & shall have only 22 days to draw for. Afterwards I can send you at least $9 every month as long as I stay here. I hope you will use the money with a wise liberality, so that you may have some benefit & enjoyment from it. I think Nelly has served her day & Geneva too.[20] It won't pay to winter her anymore after this.

We had a review & speech making today. It was rather a tame demonstration. The weather has been very severe yesterday & today. It seems likely to be pleasant & Spring-like tomorrow. The days are now getting longer & I shall walk out into the country every day. I am not obliged to work more than 6 or 8 hours a day. I sleep with Smith at nights. He talks of going to the regiment but I think he will stay here on second consideration.

I think of Willie & Freddy & Jane everyday & dreamt last night of the twins.

I send my love to you & Ann & the children. The secesh girls are torturing the piano & screaming "Southern rights Hurrah!" in the next room.

Your affectionate husband,
WmHBradbury

Head Qtrs.
Bowling Green, Ky
March 3, 1863
My dearest wife,

I wrote to you last Friday saying I should probably start on

Sunday to pay you a visit. Gen. Manson wrote to Colonel Smith for permission to retain me here & not having received a reply, he did not like to take the responsibility of sending me anywhere, unless I was fairly under his jurisdiction. Today we are all astonished that Gen. Manson is relieved; and we suddenly find ourselves under a "new boss."[21] How this will affect my promised leave of absence I do not know. But I am sure that the Adjutant will do all he can to redeem his pledge. I was quite disappointed chiefly because I thought you would be expecting me on Wednesday or Thursday.

I will take the first opportunity to press the matter again, & I hope to succeed; but I cannot tell how soon I shall be able to leave.

With regard to receiving money from friends in Dwight, I have nearly dismissed the subject from my mind. If the money had been raised by a general subscription & divided, it would not have seemed quite so bad, but I could not help feeling as bad as I did about it. I do not doubt for a moment the kind intentions of the donors. If I come home soon I will explain the matter, if not, it will gradually wear out.

You need not hold any conversation with Kenyon about it. Stand on your dignity & let the matter drop! You can accept with propriety any little offers of kindness or any milk &c. but an offer of money seems rather too much. Mrs. Young would be a fit person to consult on such matters.

The rebels have been troublesome in this immediate neighborhood. We bring in prisoners every day. The Guerilla bands are quite numerous & active & our cavalry scouts are in constant employment. The turning slaves out of camp is a subject of much dispute & some officers will get into trouble if they don't turn out the Negroes according to orders from Louisville.

I would not move away from Dwight in the winter & not at all until we know how the war is likely to go. I still think this Summer will bring it to a close. Let the rent go till next pay day. They can afford to wait. Kenyon does not say what he did with the Caldwell mortgage. I will write to him on the subject.

I have not written Jane any more rhymes yet. I have been expecting to visit you & had dismissed the subject from my mind. I write this letter in the presence of both old & new generals & old & new Adjutants. Genl. Manson said I should have got my leave of absence before he was relieved. He seems to think it a good joke.

There have been many changes at this post lately. I have not time to write any more before the mail goes out. I will write you again more fully this week.

I send my best & kindest & most sympathizing love to you & the children.

Your affect. husband,
WmHBradbury

Head Quarters US Forces
Bowling Green, Ky
March 6, 1863
My dearest wife,

I have just received your letter of the 28th February.

Your last letters have made me feel quite uneasy. I have not got your letter in which you mentioned Armstrong paying you money & Eaton offering to pay you $3½ a month. That is I destroyed it. My blood boiled the moment I read it.[22]

Tho' I have no doubt it was meant in a proper kindly spirit yet it did seem improper at the time to me. I have not been in the habit of receiving anything in the shape of charity. I wish you could see the difference between an offer of money & an offering of kindness &c. which cost the donors nothing. If a fund had been collected & divided around it would have seemed some what different. I could not bear the thoughts of my wife & family receiving money or its equivalent in provisions. But I stated to you before that it would be proper to receive such little things as kindling wood, milk, &c.

I am earning $25 a month of which you will get $23 leaving me $2 a month to pay for my washing &c. $5 a month from the County will make $28 a month. I only wish it was $50 for my heart melts when I think of you & the dear little ones. How it would sound—"Bradbury was so poor when he went into the army that his wife & family had to be supported by the contributions of the citizens!"

Now you know best what is the sentiment in Dwight & I have written to Kenyon in answer to the enclosed one I send you explaining & modifying the one I sent to John Eaton; & if you feel like receiving anything from any body you can use your own sense of propriety & do so. And here let the matter rest for ever. It was a natural impulse with me, & I wrote as I felt at the time. If nobody will do any little chores for you I will try to get home & do them myself. Now let it rest.

I am sorry the children are sick because I know the trouble & anxiety it will cause you. I hope they will get better.

We should have sold Nellie last fall. She is getting old & feeble. If you cannot take care of her ask Kenyon to dispose of her this winter & with so much mud even if you had no little babies. I do feel very much for you & think of all schemes for your benefit. I think I shall get home to see you this month yet.

I went yesterday to the Regt. about 40 miles down the Railroad toward Nashville. Smith went with me. He has now joined his Regt. & left Bowling Green. Col. Smith had not recd. Capt. Kise's[23] letter asking to retain me here. I brought back a favorable answer & a request on Col. Smith's part that they would send me to Illinois to *look after deserters* (which of course is chiefly a *pretense* & you must say nothing about it till I come). If I get an *order* to go on *business,* Gov't furnishes transportation; otherwise I go at my own expense. Capt. Kise will write for the necessary instructions tomorrow & if our new General is willing I shall get the order.

I took another letter to Col. Smith & the ride cost me nothing. I was mentioned in both letters in a very flattering manner & my services were spoken of as being almost indispensable. The non-receipt of the first letter caused the delay. Now I shall know my fate in this respect in a few days more. But, in any event, I shall soon get leave of absence, as Genl. Rosecrans intends to let the soldiers go home, in turns, for a short time.

Col. Smith is in great trouble. Nearly *all* the officers have requested him to resign on account of unfitness or incompetency. I heard both sides, but being an outsider I give no opinion. It appears Col. Smith had promised to resign, but afterwards changed his mind & arrested Adjutant Plattenburg. They charge him, the Col., with gross negligence, partiality, & incompetency. He charges them with failure to carry out his orders & calls it a conspiracy of a few men whom he had reprimanded deservedly.

I spent the evening in the Col's. tent & Capt. Walkley's & slept with Stevens & John McW. who is quartermaster now. All the officers & men were very glad to see me & wished me to come again. It seemed something like home. I saw Eli Lower. He was fat & healthy & so were all the men. The Regt. seems in good condition. Co. "B" is now pretty well filled up & doing well.

The scouting party caught Capt. Petticord[24] a notorious rebel Capt. of Guerillas last night at about 12 o'clock. It is a great feather in their cap. Capt. Perry slept with him last night. I saw them both under the same blankets this morning. It looked very funny but the Capt (Perry) was bound to stick to his prisoner.

I now board very comfortably with Dr. Welch, the Medical Director, & his clerks. It will not cost but a little extra & is much pleasanter than standing up to a dirty bench out of doors this rainy weather. Besides, we have eatables and butter & dried fruit. I bought 2 lbs butter today for the mess at 30¢ a pound. I come home I take back a few pounds.

I have got a couch or cot from the doctor which I brought up this evening to sleep upon. You see I am a sort of privileged character.

I composed a testimonial to Genl Manson when he left. I got it signed by all the men round headquarters. The testimonial was truthful and complimentary and the general was highly pleased with it.

If I knew that you & the children were comfortable and well provided for, I should have no cause of complaints. Kiss the dear little twins & the other children for me and accept my best and kindest love.

Your affectionate husband,

WmHBradbury.

I write to Jane next time without fail. I have today recd John Hetzel's letter dated Jan. 9. I enclose you $10 which I hope you will employ in promoting your comfort and enjoyment. I shall have another $100 to send at the end of the month.

Head Quarters
Bowling Green, Ky
March 22, 1863
My dearest wife,

I received your letter of the 17th inst. in due course.

I was glad to hear that the baby was better. Mrs. Hetzel & Mrs. Lower must have a good time with their babies. Mrs. Lower must take care of hers or else Mrs. Hetzel's will be ahead. They must be a great trouble as well as pleasure to you. I am sure you must have your hands full without doing any sewing or anything else. I suppose Jane helps you cheerfully.

As I started in my last I see no prospect of coming home. I have asked so many times without result that I do not feel like asking any more. The new General Judah is very stiff & does not wish to do anything irregularly.[25] I do not properly belong to his Department & I stay here only on sufferance & am liable to be called away to my Regiment any day. Smith & many others have been sent back & others are going every day. There is a little jealousy between the two Departments & they are determined to keep their men to themselves.

Capt. Little—Genl. Manson's Adjutant—took my recommendations & applications to Louisville to get the signature of Genl. Manson. He will then forward them to the Governor of Illinois. I shall probably hear what the result is by the end of this month. As my hope is rather small, I shall not be disappointed at an unfavorable issue.

You must have had a disagreeable winter if the roads have not been fit to haul anything. The interest should have been paid, if possible. As I have not heard from Charles or Frederick, I have not written to them.

I am rather surprised to hear that Mrs. Jones[26] is coming back. I should like to see her.

I make out the countersign for every night. I send it to you for tonight. You must keep it a secret as it is "confidential." If you get near "our lines" tonight, you will find it of service as the pickets will be sure to stop you. But you must keep in mind that this countersign is not good for tomorrow, or any future night.[27]

You should not send the neck ties by Mrs. Mott unless she will stop at Bowling Green. If I knew the time when she would come thro,' I would have some one take it from her at the station. Mrs. Mott is nearly 40 miles from here and she would have to send it to me by someone who might be coming to Bowling Green which occasions trouble & delay.

Capt. Little gave me a sword worth $6 or $7—I don't know what to do with it.

If I succeed in getting a commission. I shall certainly come home after I have got my positions on the General's staff.

I suppose I could get leave of absence by paying my own expenses home. It would cost not less than $16 or $18 going & coming.

We expect to be paid again in a short time. I rather think the 129th have not been paid yet. There was a little excitement about an attack on the Railroad below this place. We sent out 200 men about 30 miles down the road & a detachment of the 129th came up behind & made the rebels clear out without doing any damage.[28]

I must now hurry up for the mail—I am going to church this morning. I send Freddy a bird.

With my best love to you & all.

I am,

Your affectionate husband,

WHB

Dwight Livingston County
[from Mary Brown Bradbury to Ann Brown][29]
March 26, 1863
My dearest Ann,[30]

I cannot tell you what a relief it was to my mind to receive your letter. I was so glad to hear you got home safe and that babys journey did not make him sick. I would have answered sooner but I realy had not time.

The day you left Jane appeared quite sick with a high fever.[31] I gave them some senna tea the next day. They all appeared better except the babies. I got them some syrup from the dockters but it did no good and one night in the middle of the week the bigest was taken worse. Mrs. Lower came in, applied some simple remedies but to no effect.

On Friday I sent for the dockter but he would not come. I never thought he would live but on the Saturday we thought him some better. Sunday night he was taken worse. We both sat and watched him all nights. In the morning I went again for the dockter. I tried his medicine for one day and night without any good effect.

During that time Mrs. Hetzel had sent another dockter in as soon as I tried the remedies. In less than an hour I could perceive a change for the better. The complaint was spasmodic croop. Was afraid of a false membrane forming in the throat.[32] We sat and watched him night and day untill the end of the week. He was out of danger.

You must immagine how thankfull I was and how a nights rest

would feel to me. At the end of three weeks baby was no biger than when you left. The other had a bad cough but nothing like so bad still I gave him the same medicien as the other.

The same week I had a letter from William saying I might expect him home on a firlo in a few days and hoped you was still with me. He failed to come at the time mentioned and the next letter came saying they were surprised to find General Manson relieved and General Judah in his stead. For that reason he could not leave. I was much disapointed but had to make the best of it.

Since you left I have received sixty dollars and expect ten more at the end of the month. 20 I paid for rent and 20 I sent to Van Dusen as part payment of the intrest. The rest I get every thing I want.

With that particular letter caused so much talk.[33] I supose there was not a house in town but had something to say. I have seen the letter. It was mearly polite refusal of the donation. The same week you left Eaton sent and took away the loan of wood. I began to think if he could retailiate in that way his kindness did not ammount to much. It seems now to have pretty much died away. I shall feel more independent without their gifts.

William is very kind in sending me all the money he can posssiablly spare. In my last letter he says he has nothing to complain of there. All the trouble he feels is on our account. His superiors think very highly of him. He has a good many favoures shewed him. He got up a testimonial for General Manson which gave great satisfaction. He has a comfortable place to board at with the post sergeant also a good bed to sleep on.

It is well enough to enjoy the small blessings as they come for I have found out there is nothing certain in war and we know not how soon the little comforts may remove. I should have been glad to have rented Millers house so I could have been nearer you but the uncertainty as to how long I might remain there and the awful state of the roads would be an objection to my leaving Dwight this Spring. The house I now live in could be bought at a very low rate for cash.

I get about 2 quarts of milk from Nellie. Her calf died. I am now feeding her well.

Mrs. Jones returned to America this Spring. I have not written home yet.

I find the babies a constant care. I cannot say that I feel well but hope to improve when fine weather comes.

The older children are well. Jane shall write to her cousins next time. They all send their love.

Remember me kindly to all inquiring friends.

The babies are very succeptable of colds. They each of them have a slight cough now.

Be sure to write again soon.

Sister Mary Bradbury

4

"Chief of the Topographical Engineers"

March 31, 1863–May 31, 1863

As bleak as things were for the Bradburys, their dreams of a better life back home in England were not being realized, in fact, by many British citizens. In the years leading up to the secession of the Confederate States of America in 1861, the British cotton-textile trade had grown enormously. The county of Lancashire, with roughly 2,200 factories containing more than 30 million spindles and 350,000 looms, employed nearly a half million workers, of whom more than half were females.[1] England imported 2 million bales of cotton in 1860, twice U.S. consumption overall. By the outbreak of the war, Britain was responsible for more than half of all cotton consumption.[2]

Back in England, statesmen were suspicious of U.S. motives to acquire Canada.[3] Foreign Secretary Lord John Russell wrote in 1862: "The great majority [of the British] are in favor of the South & nearly all [of] our people are of [the] opinion that separation [secession] would be a benefit both to North & South."[4]

While Manchester's mill workers may have supported the sentiments of Harriet Beecher Stowe's book *Uncle Tom's Cabin,* widely read in that region of England in 1863,[5] mill owners—among them Charles T. Bradbury, William's brother—were primarily interested in the flow of a single commodity—high-quality cotton from the American South. The imperative to feed the British economy's huge appetite for cotton made businessmen like Charles support the Confederacy. The two brothers found themselves on opposite sides of the conflict.

As President Lincoln called for 300,000 more volunteer soldiers, the British *Saturday Review* also wrote, in the summer of 1862, "The cotton famine is the saddest thing that has befallen our country for many a year."[6] As early as January 1863, nearly one-third of English cotton mills had shut down for lack of cotton, leaving 500,000 factory workers out of work.[7]

John Bright, a Quaker and a member of Parliament, may have promoted one of the greatest tactical maneuvers to keep England from further intervention in the U.S. Civil War. Based on Bright's suggestion, the North sent cargo ships of meat, flour, and other goods from New York to Liverpool on behalf of destitute, out-of-work textile families throughout the region.[8] After reading Lincoln's Emancipation Proclamation, Manchester workers met and wrote to him declaring their support: "For your own honor and welfare, not to faint in your providential mission. While your enthusiasm is aflame, and the tide of events runs high, let the work be finished effectually. . . . We are truly one people, though, locally separate."[9]

When British Conservatives wrote about the U.S. Civil War, their mixed and halting opinions to articulate commitment more publicly were obvious: "I should be sorry if in taking up a Southern line, we were to alienate the Manchester party. . . . In fact, it seems that there is nothing good to be got out of this American question, at present. . . .[10] Numerous U.S. publications, most of them inexpensive tracts, helped keep England out of the war by agitating the British with inflammatory comparisons to conditions in their own backyard: "We have the South and Slavery. You have Ireland. . . . All [Ireland] wants is separation from England, and independence—that is all! Would you counsel the queen to let Ireland go?"[11] While William and Mary Bradbury's children were born Americans, William's ties to British mill owners, his loyalty, and at times his behavior during the war seemed muddled, if not suspect.

Mapping one's course, both figuratively and literally, was of the utmost importance. Not surprisingly, Bradbury tried his hand at cartography, on General Judah's request. He created a map that was well accepted—it was even supposed to be lithographed in Cincinnati. However, such plans often fell through, and no map bearing his name could be located. However, a map fitting its description was printed at that time by the Chief of Topographical Engineers in Cincinnati—a title that Bradbury had facetiously bestowed upon himself in his letters.[12]

Head Quarters
Bowling Green, Ky
March 31st, 1863
My dearest wife,

I received your letter of the 24th of March on the 28th. You need not apologize for I think you do very well considering the work & trouble you have with the children.

With regards to the dollar you got from Ketcham,[13] I know all about *that* but I want to know *what taxes* you paid with it. We ought not to pay the taxes on the house.

With regards to Keyt's matters which Kenyon is managing—the corn which Keyt has to deliver together with a sum to be paid by him next Summer (which is secured by the mortgage of stock) will make the payment which ought to have been made last Fall. The other payments will have to be made as agreed upon. The corn ought to have been delivered by the first of February, but the state of the roads prevented it.

I think Rutgers will have a good time getting anything out of Mr. Morgan. I don't suppose the man is worth anything. He does not own the lot you speak of. You can find out by inquiring from Jim Strong.[14] I understood that all his building lots were gone.

I wrote to Mr. Morgan, Mr. Gardner & Hon. Wash. Bushwell wishing them to send recommendations to Springfield (to the Governor) in support of my application for a Commission which I mentioned in my last letter. I received a very satisfactory letter from Friend "Bush"—as he calls himself—stating that he had sent to Governor Yates "a very strong private recommend" that he would attend to my "best interests."

I also just received a letter from General Manson's Adjutant General stating that General M. had endorsed my application in a very complimentary manner & that it was a recommendation that I "ought to be proud of." I am waiting particularly, if not hopefully. If I get the commission I shall come home if possible.

I am now engaged making a plan of the town & the fortifications & prominent objects in the vicinity at the request of General Judah. I have a horse at my disposal when I wish to ride. I was out yesterday & caught a severe cold. There was a high wind & it was very chilly. I tell the other clerks &c that I am "Chief of the

Topographical Engineers." The map is nearly completed. Everybody that sees it thinks it quite correct.[15]

John McWilliams was here yesterday. He has got a commission as Quarter Master which is the same as 1st Lieutenant. Col. Smith is sick again. The Reg't is reported as not doing very well—several companies having dwindled considerably—Company "B" is all right & flourishing.

You must teach Jane to be self reliant & endeavor to counteract her sensitiveness. I sent Freddy a bird in my last letter. I send one for Willie in this.

I can imagine what Dwight must look like with so much rain. We have had considerable rain here & the river is still very high but the roads are dry & quite solid. The peach trees & shrubs of various kinds are in bloom. Yellow lilies (I believe) & crocuses have been in flower some time but the present cold weather is keeping them back. Tonight it is snowing. We have a fire in our bedroom.

A friend belonging to the Hospital Department procured me a straw tick upon which I sleep very well. I get very good board & feel very comfortable. I always think of you at these times & wonder if you & the dear little chuckies are well supplied with comforts.

I shall not get my monthly extra pay till next week when I will send you all I can spare which will be about $8. I sent you every cent & a little more twice last time. We did expect the paymaster but we hear nothing of him now.

According to the extracts from Rebel papers the Secesh are getting pretty "hard up." They are suffering in many instances for the necessaries of life & begin to talk of making concessions in order to put an end to the war.

I can't think of any names for the twins. I will try & suggest something. In the meantime you can notify the two claimants, Mrs. H & Mrs. L, by adopting their names—Edwin & what?[16]

I should like to see Willie "from big boys down." I suppose Freddy is quite active & climbs up the posts. Let them run about just as much as they can conveniently.

Our new Quarters are very comfortable, but our coal is nearly gone & we have none to last all day tomorrow. The weather is quite changeable. It may be very warm in a few days.

I write this about 9½ o'clock at night by the light of a kerosene lamp in a spacious room of the "Green River House" which is occupied by the different departments. General Burnside[17] is our "new boss" tho' Gen'l. Boyle[18] at Louisville is in *immediate* command over us.

We expected some trouble a few days ago in the centre of the state & sent our Regiment to Gen'l. Manson at Lebanon & another at Louisville. Kentucky is safe once more. The "*Hon* Member" gave me a *very* good recommend on my application.

Accept my warmest & most sympathizing love & give the same to the children.

I remain,
Your affectionate husband,
WmHBradbury

Head Quarters, US Forces
Bowling Green, Ky
April 7, 1863
My dearest wife,

I received your last letter on the fourth of April—only three days from the day on which it was posted. You must by this time have received my last containing a bird for Willie.

I have just completed my "Map of Bowling Green & vicinity showing the hills, fortifications, and defences." It is executed pretty well considering that I had no instruments to work with except a pair of compasses and a common ruler. I copied the main features from a small sketch which I borrowed in town & made the rest from personal observation which afforded me good opportunities of making rambles in the country & climbing the rugged hills of old Kentucky.

The General thinks a good deal of it & everybody that has seen it has complimented me on its accuracy & finish. It may be the means yet of enabling me to obtain a leave of absence yet. The Adjutant General has promised to try again for me but I consider it quite uncertain.

All extra duty & men detached from their Regiments who, belonging to the "Army of the Cumberland," have been ordered to clear out to their respective regiments. None are allowed to stay in the Department if the Ohio who belong out of it & the Tennessee state line separates the two departments.

I shall now be the *only man* at this Post who belongs in the other Army. I shall be retained here as long as possible & nothing but a positive order from the Department Head Quarters will get me away. There is a supposition here, founded on a recent act of Congress, that all extra duty pay will be stopped for the future. I & another clerk here will be exceptions. General Burnside is now in command of the Department of the Ohio & General Rosecrans command that of the Cumberland.

A sad accident occurred in the street yesterday. The Lieut. Col. of the 23rd Mich. Regt. was thrown from his horse & killed on the spot.[19] The shock of his fall burst a large artery & he bled to death in less than two minutes. The funeral procession of all the troops here accompanies his remains to the Depot for transmission to Michigan. He was attempting to rid an unruly horse & the saddle girth broke.

I suppose you received the countersign all right. With regards to my expected commission, I have never heard a word & probably never shall.[20] I will however write to the Governor of Illinois on the subject & get a decisive answer if possible. If I get it, my occupation will be such as to keep me entirely out of the field of active service. The private soldier will be far more exposed than I shall.

Many soldiers here who were not considered sufficiently convalescent from sickness for field service have enlisted in the Gunboat service. Their duty will be on the Mississippi which is intended to be kept clear by a fleet of gunboats & transports on the water & by bands of scouts on the land adjoining—the boats being the floating camp of this "Marine Brigade."[21] The men by this means prolong their stay in the Government service; but the prospect of a change & of a relief from fatiguing marches induced them to enlist in considerable numbers.

I understand that the "Hon. Member" Capt. Mayall[22] is about to resign his office here & take his place as Senator from his own. He is a very singular old codger & is the subject of many anecdotes & droll remarks. I mimic him sometimes & tell little conversations to the great amusement of our mess, which is chiefly composed of young medical students acting as hospital stewards &c.

I hear nothing of the 129th Ill. except thro' the papers which occasionally give accounts of their exploits in driving off small guerilla parties. I received the *Sentinel* & the neck-tie which answers very well. It is just a little too wide. I had a new linen collar given, one which I am now wearing.

The weather has lately been fine & bracing & rather warm in the middle of the day. Today is bright & beautiful. Yesterday two ladies brought the general a bouquet of flowers which stands in glass on his desk in the room adjoining ours.

The "shoulder straps" get all the attention & all the honors here but at home I suppose the private soldier is thought more of. The ladies think more of dandy officers than of the men in the ranks who do the most of the work. The dark damsels sometimes take compassion on them which I suppose makes some amends. But uniforms of both grades are so very common as not to attract much attention. I am almost sick of seeing them myself.

Since Brigadier Gen. Smith married a Miss Durham—the upper ten% of the aristocracy declare that they can't think of less than a *Major General* as a husband! Pride & vanity! Where will all these evanescent honors be in a short time? When the officer will sink into his former insignificance & the private soldier outrank him in civil life.

I will compose some more rhymes for the dear children—I think of them & you every day. You must take all the exercise you possibly can & get a wagon made. It is quite *necessary.*

With best love to you & the children,

WmHBradbury

I should like the photograph of the twins very much. I suppose they seem far dearer to me because I have never seen them. My affections tho' chiefly to Janey & Willie & Freddy to the youngest always feeling the dearest.

Our paymaster has not done anything for us yet. I thought he was going to pay us to the 1st March. The "Hon. Member" has no money with which to pay our extra duty with, so that I am dead broke & clean strapped.

My health is very good. We live first rate. What is good for sick men is certainly good for us. But you need not mention that I board with the Post surgeons & his clerks & attendants and they know where the things are.

A new Regt. came in on the cars from Louisville this afternoon. The boys are a rough, undisciplined lot.

Head Quarters US Forces
Bowling Green, Ky.
April 12, 1863
My dearest wife,

I received your expected letter this afternoon & was very glad when I got it. I was much pleased with Jane's sums in the long & short division. I think she does very well. I shall be very glad to hear from her again. She spells her words correctly. She will soon make a good writer.[23]

I am glad the children all got their birds. They must take care of them. I will send them some flowers next time I write.

The peach trees are in full bloom & all the shrubs & forest trees are fresh & green. The wind has been very cold; and we have not had many warm days yet.

I send the children some more verses which I think they will like. I think of you & them every day & my heart yearns warmly to you my dear wife & to those little ones at home. I long to see you again, but I don't like to ask for leave of absence anymore; tho' the Adjutant Genl. seems always willing to oblige me in everything.

My cold was quite gone & I felt very well indeed till just lately. I have been suffering from chills & colics, but nothing worth speaking about.

My map has been completed some time & has been much admired. The General was quite pleased with it. He took it with him to Louisville this week, & shared it with the Generals there. It will be engraved or "lithographed" at Cincinnati & if I get any copies for myself I will send you one. It shows all the streets in the town & the roads, fences, timber, hills, fortifications, river, bridges, Railroad, &c. I put my name on it "W.H. Bradbury Del." I had no proper drawing tools & I had to do it between spells. I, of course, know that it is defective, but others think it "first rate."

I am afraid we shall not get our Regimental pay—the Paymaster now here, has not funds enough to go round, & the "detached men" will stand a good chance of being left out.

There will be some more funds here by & by & then my turn will come, as I have taken steps to secure it. I am now nearly the only man belonging to the Army of the Cumberland who is not already gone or under orders to go to his regiment.

The Hon. Member Captain Mayall, has no money yet, tho' he

expects some this week. I feel sorry for your sake that I don't get any money to send you.

I can tell you some funny stories about the Hon. Member when I get home. He is a very simple minded man & the officers quiz him sometimes.

We have still a fire in our office tho' the sun is quite warm the wind has been very chilly.

I have not heard about the Kansas land from L.N. Walkley. I presume he thinks it too much money. I would take less now that Greenbacks are coming down.

You will be aware that our troops are blazing away at Charleston now. There seems to be nothing going on here, tho' the forces are under arms every morning from 3 o'clock to broad daylight. Two trains were captured near Nashville a few days ago & we are constantly on the alert.

There is a concert at the Episcopal church next Tuesday evening. There will be a great rush of shoulder straps & crinoline.

I took a long walk—there are two steamers at the landing.

The yellow soil will soon be covered with herbage. I am going to try my poetic machine on the hills of Kentucky. I send kisses to the babies & the other children & my best & warmest love to you.

Your affect. & devoted husband,
WHB

Bowling Green, Ky
May 24, 1863
My dearest wife,

I arrived here at 2 o'clock yesterday afternoon & was cordially received by all. Capt. Kise had written twice—last time enclosing $10 which I presume you have got.

The Hon. Member was very glad to see me & wished to get me into his office. He had seen Capt. Kise about it. He would pay me *extra* out of his own pocket. He wanted a man of "studious mind," (he said) like himself.[24]

They had a grand ball here on the 1st May given by Gen. Judah & staff. The rooms were decorated & there was a grand time. The Polish Sergeant had just gone back to his regiment which was under marching orders, so that I was in the nick of time; tho' Capt.

Kise says he did not expect me so soon as he had written that I need not be in a hurry. It will be impossible [for me] to get an appointment by the President confirmed before next session of Congress which takes place in the Fall.

I think Capt. Kise will pay me something out of his own pocket as he would not spare me for the Hon. Member. The trees are full of leaf & wave coolly in front of the open windows & their fragrance penetrates the rooms.

Our scouts report no organized force of the enemy in the neighborhood so that there is at present no fear of an invasion.

You must get a copy of the *Chicago Tribune* for next Friday or Saturday containing a letter from a "private soldier" respecting an extortion of 25c on the Railroad ticket to Louisville. I sent it to the *Tribune* today. You must write & say how you got home &c.[25]

I have no time to add any more before mail time—kiss the little twins & the other children for me—I send my best love to all.

Yours most affectionately,
WmHBradbury

Chicago Tribune, May 30, 1863 [publication date]
"Imposition Upon Soldiers"
Bowling Green, Ky., May 23, 1863

In Louisville I met with two soldiers of the 102nd Illinois volunteers, one, the Sergeant Major of that regiment, who had traveled from Chicago by the same route, and in the same train as myself. They told me that upon paying their fare, they demanded the omnibus ticket or the return of the extra quarter. The "gentlemanly clerk" or conductor, flew up, and insisted that the railroad ticket would include the omnibus ride. The martial representatives of the "Succor State" told him that they "couldn't see it in that light;" and the "gentlemanly officer" finally disgorged the extorted quarters. I should like to know whether my twenty-five cents was really credited to the Louisville Omnibus company, or spent in cigars. I have reason to suspect that many odd five and ten cent greenbacks are extorted by ticket clerks and conductors on soldiers' commutation fares. Small as are the amounts, the soldier has far more need of them, than these haughty, pampered officials. —Private Soldier

Head Quarters
Bowling Green, Ky
May 31st, 1863
My dearest wife,

I did not receive a letter from you today as I expected, but I will not on that account defer writing to you. I suppose you received my letter written last Sunday. Captain Kise says my extra duty pay will be paid by himself "right along." I told him I should go to my regiment, but he did not want to lose me.

I received my Regimental pay for 2 months that is to the 30th April, yesterday, & I now enclose you $20 which I hope you will receive safe. If you have no use for $50 of the money now on hand you had better get Kenyon to send it to Van Dusen by express. I had a letter from Frederic acknowledging receipt of the deed. He will advertize the land. I suppose you got the $10 sent by Capt. Kise. I shall not charge Capt. Kise with the time I spent at home. He will get his pay from the Paymaster now here.

The Greenbacks are flying round Bowling Green now. Capt. Kise found an officer beastly drunk, & cut his shoulder straps off. I have seen several drunken soldiers taken to the Guard House quite drunk.

I straightened up the books at the city hall prison & saw a man sentenced to be hung. He went to Louisville yesterday. He was a Rebel spy. Major Owsley of the Rebel Army is also in prison here.[26] His pretty little wife is trying her best to alleviate his sentence. So is the wife & mother of the other man.

We have a prison full of rebel citizens who must travel South by & by. A Negro got 75 lashes yesterday for shouting at the Captain of the Guard.

There are great changes about to be made here by which I shall endeavor to profit. In the first place General Judah will take a Division into the field & consequently there will be a new commander of the Post. He wants me to *steal* along with him. Capt. Kise will go,[27] but I shall not go unless I can better my position. The Post will probably become about third rate & some old Colonel will command here. The "Hon. Member" with whom I have just been conversing will leave if he can.

In the next place (20,000) twenty thousand men are to be raised in Kentucky to garrison the state. I think of trying for a recruiting commission in one of the new regiments. The troops here now are nearly all Kentucky. Capt. Kise says there are not two good clerks to be found in three Regiments of them. I shall be governed by circumstances.

During the absence of Capt. Kise & the General, Capt. Day & myself have been running the institution. The General returned today. I have heard nothing from Kansas expecting the money I sent there for taxes. I have heard nothing from L.N. Walkley—I shall sue him sure as fate.

A nice little red-haired clerk now rooms with me. He has been writing love letters & flirting with the girls opposite. He is a funny boy. It is tedious work to keep him in the office. Thompson has left the office. His Reg't & another have moved away. Captain Montgomery & Col. Chapin of the 23rd Michigan are gone.

The weather is warm, but quite pleasant. My desk is at an open window partially shaded by a large locust tree so that the sun never enters.

The Guard forms every morning under the trees in the square. Their deep green foliage makes a delightful view from my window & the sweet music of the band mingles with the fragrance of the dewy leaves of the ailanthus and catalpa—trees which we had on the farm.

The summer is now upon us. Vegetation is full of life. The earth is covered with its beautiful color & the wooded hills glow in their emerald dress.

The moon is, while I am writing, darkened by an approaching thunderstorm. It lights incessantly & the distant rumble sounds awfully among the hills beyond the river.

General Manson is in the field with a Brigade. General (somebody else) has a Brigade, but *our* General has a Division which consists of several brigades. A Brigade is 3 or 4 regiments.

Vicksburg is not yet taken. There will be a tremendous struggle there yet. Rosecrans is on the move or preparing to move. We are preparing here.

We will have first rate board—good bread & butter, pies & cake & sometimes stewed cherries &c rice, hominy, currants, milk, coffee &c beside beef & ham & sometimes fowl.

Oh dear, how I wish you could board with us. But I will send you enough money to keep a good table & I do hope you will use & enjoy it. That will be the only pleasure I shall take in sending—to think that you are getting fat on it. I think a great deal of those blessed babies. They feel now almost as dear as the other children.[28] Kiss their sweet faces for me.

I have been much engaged since I came here. The red haired boy is often out & I have been very busy for the last few days. I wrote to the Union League last week. I don't want to be writing all the time. But I shall always write to *you*.

Tell Fred that here they have fishing rods as long as our house & lines a great deal longer & they catch big fish—as big as his arm. I send Jane a part of a peacocks feather out of our fly brush which is made of this beautiful material.

This is Sunday & tho' churches are just over I don't wish to raise your hopes & disappoint you but Captain Kise promised me my extra pay. If I get [it], I hope you will have a girl & not weary yourself to death with your work. I shall expect a letter tomorrow to hear how you got home &c.

I send my warmest & best love to you & the children. My health is very good.

I remain,
Your affectionate husband,
WmHBradbury

5

"More Compliments than Coppers"

June 4, 1863–August 9, 1863

To his distress, Bradbury had to leave the relative comforts of Bowling Green for what he considered "the front"—Glasgow, Kentucky. Glasgow may have been in the region where Confederate General John Hunt Morgan planned his raids, but it was hardly the front. As many Union officers chased after Morgan, Bradbury was left, lonely in camp at Glasgow.

A dozen miles from the nearest railroad depot, Bradbury likely felt that he had burrowed into isolated, if not uncertain, country. A smaller town, Glasgow afforded fewer opportunities for grapevine gossip among old friends. Yet this post was not one of hardship. He missed his children and was entertained by a couple of mischievous boys who probably reminded him of his oldest sons Freddy and Willie.

Boarding with a local schoolteacher, his duties changed, and he joined the Commissary Department. While he might not have liked where he was or what he was doing, there were implicit advantages in being positioned in the Commissary Department, a duty that would offer another type of currency. Bradbury surely succumbed to the nearly irresistible temptation and pilfered from the Commissary. Every dollar that he did not spend on his own board was sent to Mary to take care of the children.

While he continued to fret about the payments on their Kansas lands and the proximity of John Hunt Morgan to his outpost in Glasgow, some two thousand residents of Lawrence, Kansas, were about to experience the fury of another guerilla leader, William Clarke Quantrill.

Lawrence, Kansas, not far from Bradbury's land claim in adjacent Shawnee County, was occupied by a significant settlement of "free-staters"—immigrants from the northeast who held antislavery views and had moved as intact communities of the Emigrant Aid Society. Quantrill's raiders burned and looted much of the town, savagely killing nearly two hundred non-combatant citizens who were caught unaware in the early hours of an August morning in 1863.[1] The sack of Lawrence, an unauthorized guerilla assault, was considered the worst civilian massacre of the Civil War. By the time Bradbury learned of the Kansas massacre, he would be out of Glasgow, on his way to Tennessee.

Head Quarters US Forces
Glasgow
June 4, 1863
My dearest wife,

I duly received your letter. In the meantime I had written you a long one to which, of course, I have had no answer yet. I arrived at this place yesterday afternoon with General Judah & his staff & escort much against my will as well my interests; for Col. Hawkins who succeeds Judah at Bowling Green offered me strong inducements to stay with him at B.G. in the shape of extra pay & the promise of a commission in his own Regiment with a view to being placed on his staff.

This was all spoiled by Genl. Judah, who insisted that I should go with him. If I don't like this place I shall write to my Colonel of the 129th & get sent back. I always get more compliments than coppers.[2]

I rode on horseback most of the way. The day was cool & very pleasant.

Jane will find the place 30 miles *east* of Bowling Green & 10 miles from the nearest station on the Louisville & Nashville RR.

I have had a diarrhea for several days and am still quite unwell.

We are just organizing a new & large command. Genl. Judah takes command of the Post here & of all the forces between this & the Cumberland River. He will, when this organization is complete, command the 3rd Division of the 23rd Army Corps. This corps is commanded by Genl. Hartsuff.[3] We have just sent off two regiments at 8 o'clock this evening. They will march rapidly all night.

Col. Hawkins offered me a Quarter Mastership in his Regiment, but I declined. I shall probably make my point after a while.[4] I saw Gen. Manson & Capt. Little here & shook hands with them. Old "Rugged" was very cordial.

I wish you would forward my paper which you received from Springfield.

If R.P. Morgan would take my papers to Springfield & apply to the Governor for a commission in the 107th Illinois Regt.[5] or any other Illinois Regt. in the 23rd Army Corps, Department of the Ohio, I think it might be productive & good. In the meantime I shall try Col. Hawkins again as he *must* have an experienced man with him at Bowling Green & Kentucky Regiments do not furnish the right kind of timber.

This is a poor little place & not near so convenient as Bowling Green. I have worked hard for a sick man since I arrived. The more I do the better chance it gives the officers to gallant around & enjoy themselves. I feel very spiteful sometimes.[6] I will not say anymore now. It is quite late & I feel unwell.

Kiss the children especially the twins & accept my best love.

Your affect. husband,
WmHBradbury

Head Quarters, Judah's Division
23rd Army Corps
Glasgow, Ky
June 13th, 1863
My dearest wife,

I received your letter of the 7th June yesterday afternoon. Capt. Kise brought it from Bowling Green along with a letter from L.N. Walkley in answer to my last, in which he states that the money to pay off the mortgage was on the way to Kansas. I have just written him to say that it was all satisfactory. Did I not send the taxes for that land by express? I have heard nothing from it yet.

The news today is that the train from Louisville had been put back. The Rebels captured the freight trains & took several hundred horses. The passenger train had reached as far as Munfordville so that it may arrive tonight or tomorrow & bring a letter from you in answer to my last. I do not see why my letters do not reach you sooner.

I do not know how to advise you about the house. You must get Mrs. Young to help you in some way & look out for a house. I don't approve of John building a house for you. I don't suppose he has money enough to build you a decent one. Besides it would take too much time. Your money would not be near enough.

I should prefer that you should go to the house on the bluff if Mrs. Miller would rent it. $375 is very cheap if we had the money.

I don't intend & never did intend to give Mr. Kenyon anything over $10 an acre except on that acre of timber land. I thought he might get $15 for it and the $5 could pay for his trouble.

I will take $2000 for the whole *half section* & the timber land, subject to the Mortgage & Keyt's contract. That is to say I want to have $2000 clear. I should require $1000 down & the balance next year. I don't wish to sell the south quarter subject to the *whole* mortgage because in that case I should only get $400 & have to wait on Keyt to the end of his contract. If anybody wants to buy, let them make me a proposition.

My diarrhea is all over now & I begin to feel better. I live on "hard tack[7] & sow belly" like the rest of the soldiers. I can stand it very well.

We have sent out several scouting parties lately & have given the Rebels *fits.* One party killed about 40—brought in 36 prisoners & 2 small guns or cannon—60 horses, several wagons, burnt a whole train of wagons, destroyed their camp, &c. I copied the order sending them out & saw the prisoners & guns come in. This work [was] by the 5th Indiana Cavalry.[8] They did not get a single scratch.

We are now in the front & Genl. Judah has command of the troops between this & the Cumberland River. Bands of guerillas are all around us. Our cavalry are constantly on the go.[9] Gen. Manson is in command here during Gen. Judah's temporary absence at Columbia.

The gardens here are all aglow with flowers—roses especially. There is a great profusion of them. Everything looks beautiful except the old buildings here.

We have had no very hot weather yet. In fact a few nights ago I could scarcely keep my feet warm. I like the country very well. We are going into tents as soon as the General & his staff get back. We shall soon be in *active* service & move forward when our organization is complete. My work will be less laborious & more responsible. I have orders to answer telegrams tonight—receiving the instructions from General Manson.

I am glad you have a cow that milks easy, but $24 seems a great price. How is the garden? Had you not better hire somebody to work in it a day or two?

Lots of bugs are flying round the candle. They are different from the bugs North.

We had a grand review of the 1st Brigade yesterday. I climbed a tree & saw the whole. The 24 Pounders fired the salute to Major General Hartsuff.

I am anxiously waiting to hear from you. Kiss the dear little twins & the other darlings for papa & accept my kindest & best love.

Yours affectly,
WmHBradbury

Head Quarters, Judah's Division
Glasgow, Ky
June 22, 1863
My dearest wife,

I have only time before the mail to write you a short letter & I do this chiefly because we may move before I shall have the opportunity to write again.

With regard to the house I think your best plan is to write to Mrs. James Miller & offer her $5 a month & 3 months rent in advance for the house on the bluff. I understand it is all clean & ready to go into. If you & Mrs. Hetzel could go over together for company, you could see Mrs. Miller & Mr. & Mrs. Waters. I think by this course you might get it.

I did not receive your letter till last Saturday, 9 days after it was written. The Rebels are giving us much trouble just now. We send out scouting parties nearly every day. Information just received of Morgan's advance into Kentucky renders it necessary that we move perhaps tomorrow, perhaps today. We were telegraphing till 12 o'clock last night. The order will fly around today.

Capt. Kise will most certainly pay my extra duty money & he has arranged things so that I go into the Commissary department today where I shall get more than I do now. I won't say how much till I get the money in my pocket.

I am expecting a letter from you today in answer to my last. I will write you again perhaps tomorrow.

In the meantime give my love to the children & those dear little twins & accept my best & kindest love yourself.

Your affectionate husband,

WmHBradbury

I have not heard a word from the taxes on the Kansas land? Have you?

Office of Commissary Dept.
Glasgow, Ky
June 27, 1863
My dearest wife,

I received your letter dated the 20th (but bearing the Dwight Postmark of the 22nd) yesterday—making the time 4 days.

With regard to the money sent to Kansas—I feel almost sure that I sent it by express, but I have no receipt for it. I will write to Judge Safford about it.[10]

I am now fairly in the Commissary business under Lieut. Davis. The Division moved forward several days ago—as I told you in my last short letter—leaving the Quarter Master's & Commissary's Department behind. The business is quite new to me & Lieut. Davis does not understand it very well; but I think I can get along with it.

It has rained almost incessantly for the last 4 or 5 days & everything looks dull and cheerless. The roads are bad & very dirty & the streams are almost impassable.

We have hundreds of tons of stores bacon, sugar, &c covered with nothing but tarpaulins & sheets. We sent a train of 30 wagons off this morning. I am afraid they will have a hard time crossing the streams. The provisions are for Genl. Manson's Brigade which is now near the Tennessee line.

The 129th Illinois is now at Gallatin, Tenn. Capt. Day on Genl. Judah's staff saw them a few days ago. The Colonel asked about me, Capt. Day said. I could not be spared unless I could get a 2nd Lieut's Commission in that Regiment. Our Division numbers about 12000 men; but many of them are left behind here.

I have been quite unwell with a severe diarrhea and feel very weak today. Our mess is broken up & I am boarding at a private house. They charge $2.50 a week. I shall pay in sugar and coffee which I can draw from the Commissary Stores.[11]

I earned $2 from Capt. Day by making out his Inspection Report. I am on good terms with all the Staff officers & they are disposed to help me to any good thing. I should feel comfortable but for this miserable diarrhea. The weather is dull and warm and damp. I sleep in the office at night & awake very early in the morning for sufficient reasons.

Capt. Kise has no money till the paymaster comes round again which will be in a few weeks probably. I shall then send you at least $35.

I am sure it is very kind of Mrs. Eldredge to have a sewing bee for you. If you can spare it, you should pay them $5 on the old account. I hope you will get your sewing all done & the garden in good order.

You will tell Kenyon to see that Keyt sells his corn so that Van D's claim can be paid. I will send him $5 next pay day.

I imagine Mrs. Miller would let the house to a good tenant especially if the rent were paid in advance. I should make a strong effort in that direction if you cannot be allowed to stay where you are. You should go over with Mrs. Hetzel as I proposed in my last letter. I wish I were with you to attend to your wants.

I suppose the pleasure of seeing & playing with the babies compensates for the trouble of attending to their many wants. Poor Jane has a hard time with them. You must not be cross with her. I will write to her in answer to her letter when I feel better. I hope the dear children will have a good time on the 4th July which will soon be here. Did Freddy cry when his tooth was pulled out? How is little Willie? I suppose he is boisterous & funny as ever.

I wish you could send me a couple of good white shirts and a light pair of pants, not very light in color. You will make them up for a small parcel & address them "Lieut. O. S. Davis A. C. S. Judah's Division, Glasgow, Ky." Get some soldier on furlough—Mr. Riggs if he is not gone back—to leave it in charge of some officer at *Cave City*. We have communication there every day. It is only 13 miles from this place.

Lieut. Davis is quite sick & his clerk—myself—is not fit for much.

I send my kindest regards to all inquiring friends & my best to yourself & the children. Kiss them all for me.

I am,
Your affectionate husband,
WmHBradbury

This is Saturday night. The Staff Officers are singing & having a good [time]. The Quarter Master's clerk is an excellent singer. We are all together.

Office of Division Commissary
Glasgow, Ky
July 5, 1863
My dearest wife,

I received your letter of the 28th June on the 3rd of July—5 days. I am what is called the "abstract clerk" in the commissary department & am now very busy making out my monthly returns which is a difficult & tedious job.[12] I shall be less exposed in my present capacity than in my former one; in fact I am really doing the duties of a "citizen clerk" at $75 per month. Quarter Masters & Commissaries are allowed clerks from $100 to $50 per month. We have arranged a sort of "hocus pocus" by which Uncle Sam is deluded but not defrauded. I shall receive at least as much as my extra duty pay—perhaps more. I understand my work very well considering my want of experience & have no fear but that my returns will be all right.

The regiments have been scurrying round the country this hot, rainy weather after Morgan. Bad roads and swollen streams have impeded their progress. They are now back at Glasgow preparing for another excursion in another direction.

General Manson who commands a Brigade of this Division positively refused to send out his men early this morning as they were quite exhausted by previous marches. Some words ensued between the two Generals. I am afraid there will not be any good feeling between them. "Old Rugged" does not believe in so much red tape.

The men have had a very hard time lately. We have had heavy rain & thunder for the last week & today & yesterday have been very oppressive. There have been no refreshing breezes for 8 or 9 days.

I am sorry Anna Lower cannot stay with you. I was in hopes you could get somebody. I like the dress patterns very well & the candy. I hope you did enjoy yourselves on the 4th July. There was nary enjoyment here nor demonstration of any kind.

I am sorry that I cannot help you by any advice about moving. I have said all I can think of. But by way of cheering you up I will say this—that on the 15th of this month I shall have earned (from the 15th of last month) $63. The arrangement is that somebody else signs the receipt for the amount while I do the work & get the money. I don't see any doubt whatever but that I shall get it. $50 is for my extra services & the other $13 is my regular pay. Capt. Kise, Capt. Little, & others urged the matter & Genl. Judah assented to it after considerable hesitation. I took a favorable opportunity to put them all together & the result was favorable. I did not mean to tell you this until I had actually got the money but as the arrangement is all secure, I think there can be doubt but that I shall get it. If Davis continues as Commissary, I shall be retained & if he does not I have other irons in the fire which will get me a place equally lucrative. You need not mention this to anybody as it is really an evasion of the Regulations. I consider it quite as good as a second Lieutenant's position with less responsibility.

Since writing the former part of this a wholesome cool breeze has sprung up which is quite refreshing. I think it will be cooler tonight. The 1st (Manson's) Brigade left for Munfordville this afternoon.

There was no mail yesterday owing to some stoppage on the Railroad. Morgan's men to the amount of about 4000 are in central Kentucky having been driven this way from the Cumberland River. It is generally supposed that he can hardly escape this time. He will be hemmed in.

I still board at the house of a Yankee schoolmaster $2½ a week payable mostly in rations.

This morning (Monday) is somewhat cooler. I slept very well & had a good wash all over in the adjoining room. We have breakfast about 7. The mail closes at ½ past 7. It is carried by an old fashioned English-looking coach drawn by four horses. There was no news yesterday.

I wish you would pay Kenyon the $5 & get him to look after Keyt & see that Van Dusen is paid.

The Quarter Master's two clerks are sick. Lieut. Davis is improving. I am very well myself. I have got over the diarrhea &c. I drink plenty of buttermilk. The schoolmaster keeps cows. I should like above all things to see the twins again. They must be quite interesting.

I should like two nice new shirts. They look clean & feel cooler this sultry weather. Homer Kenyon will hand them to the commissary at Cave City—Captain Johnson's—who will send them here. Clothing is very dear here. I will send the money to pay for them.

I send my best love & kisses to all of you.

Your affect. Husband,
WmHBradbury

Office of Division Commissary
Glasgow, Ky
July 13, 1863
My dearest wife,

I received your letter of the 5th July on the 11th. My health is now very good again. There is no hurry about the shirts. If the parcel was left in the station house at Cave City it would be sufficient. I can get along without any pants from you as the Quarter Master has *given* me a new pair. I can really do without the shirts if necessary.

With regard to the house I should make a strong effort to get the one on the bluff. I cannot advise you further. The weather will probably change so that you can move about.

You have heard of the incursion of Morgan & his men into Indiana. Genl. Judah & his staff with nearly one whole division pursued him thro' Kentucky & I understand that Genl. Manson & his brigade are after him in Indiana.

It was a great chase & great pains are being taken to catch him. He is supposed to have from 5000 to 7000 men now, tho' he crossed the Cumberland with only about 4000 men. It will be a grand thing if we succeed in capturing him.

There was tremendous excitement here a week ago by a report that our pickets had been driven in and that the Rebels were upon us. This was after the Division had left. The Commander of the Post ordered everything carried to the Fort. The store keepers closed their doors and windows in a twinkling. A Jew from Bowling Green exclaimed, "My Gott shall I lose all mine goots!"

I was at my boarding house & hurried over to the office to take care of my papers. When I arrived the consternation was over. It had been ascertained that it was nothing but a squad of 25 Rebel prisoners from East Tennessee whom the Pickets mistook for Rebel soldiers. It is supposed by some that as all the troops or at least a large proportion are chasing after Morgan, an attack may be made here.

The weather has been very close & damp. It is now raining again. We have had no refreshing breezes. I am glad the children had a good time on the *fourth*. There was nothing doing here.

I am glad you paid Kenyon the $5. Get him to attend to Keyt & see that Van Dusen is paid.

The babies must be very interesting. I should very much like to see them & you & all.

There are rumors of peace propositions in the papers. I don't know what they may result in the fall of Vicksburg & the defeat of the Rebels in Pennsylvania may lead to something.

I get first rate board at Mr. Morse's house. We have meat—beef or mutton or ham & pastry or pudding after—all very good. It will cost me nearly a dollar a week besides my rations. I can get sugar & beef whenever I want any & have the run of the stores. I sleep in the office. Lieut Davis is gone to Louisville.

I must now close this time as the mail leaves in an hour. It is Monday morning.

I send my best love & kisses to you all.

Your affectionate husband,

WmHBradbury

Glasgow, Ky
July 20, 1863
My dearest wife,

It is now nearly two weeks since I heard from you. I have been expecting a letter from day to day. I begin to feel somewhat alarmed lest some disagreeable cause may have prevented your writing. I have deferred writing hoping to hear from you previously.

I have been quite sick for the last 10 days. I have had diarrhea & chills & fever & have been taking medicine. I am still very feeble & wretched.

Genl. Judah & all the officers are still absent on the Morgan-hunting expedition & the news now is that he is as good as captured. It has been quite a long chase.

There are indications of an advance into Tennessee. I hope we shall not go just yet. I don't feel able to stand the fatigue of a ride.

The weather has been quite cool & pleasant but it is now becoming sultry again. It is possible that your letters may have followed the Division in its careening thro' Indiana & Ohio.

I feel lost here without news from home. I never longed to be with you so much as I have for the last few days. I have not much to do and have no disposition to do anything. I trust I shall feel better "in the course of human events" as one of the boys remarked.

Basil Duke, one of the leaders of Morgan's gang, has just been captured.[13] Incursions thro' Kentucky are nearly over. Scottsville was attacked the other day & the stores robbed &c.—one soldier was shot while going to his hospital. The Union men ran; and the Rebels committed great destruction.

I hear nothing from the 129th Illinois. I suppose they are still at Gallatin. There has been a sale of Negroes today[14] and speeches by rival political candidates.

You have heard of the Fall of Fort Hudson & Vicksburg & the great number of prisoners we have taken.

These great achievements seem to indicate a speedy close of the war. I certainly never felt so heartily tired of it as I do now.

The trees are beautiful & green & the flowers are still in bloom. It is a very fine looking country.

We had a thunderstorm last night which has left the air cooler this morning. I slept very well. The office is my bedroom and I have a wood cot in one corner. The Quarter Master's Room is adjoining. The Telegraph Room & the office of the Commander of the Post are on the same floor. The building fronts the public square where the Court House stands on a grassy lawn shared by locust trees. Among these trees are pitched the tents of the Division Staff & that of Genl. Judah, but they are occupied only by orderlies & servants. I think the staff will be back soon as Morgan & his band must be used up by this time.

There is any quantity of blackberries here. The hedges & fields are full of them. There is one kind called the Dewberry which creeps along the ground. The soldiers go out with their cans every day. We have plenty of them to eat. The children would have a good time picking them. The Kentuckians don't seem to think much of them.

I hope by this time you have made some arrangement about a house. It seems very hard that you should be driven out of Dwight; but the man is of course entitled to his house. Your lot is indeed a hard one. I hope the children are all well & the twins growing.

With my kindest & best love to you my dearest wife & to the dear children.

I remain,
Your affectionate husband,
WmHBradbury

Glasgow
July 23rd, 1863
My dearest wife,

I was very glad to receive your short letter of the 18th Inst. It arrived yesterday. I thought it best to write again immediately as my health improved considerably since I wrote last. I am still afflicted with headache & some neuralgia & feel quite weak & languid, but I am gaining every day. I think I shall be quite recovered in a week.

I hope you have the whole of Clarkson's house? It is not any too large. How did you arrange about the garden?

I often think of my dear sweet wife & her strivings & troubles. Oh! That I could relieve you of some of the burden. I send you ten thousand sympathetic kisses & blessings.

The division has not yet returned, but some of the officers are expected this week. I shall be very glad when they do return as it is very lonely. The long hot days pass monotonously one after another. Even the daily paper fails to raise an excitement.

Morgan's band is now for the most part captured. This will render our presence here unnecessary and I think we shall soon advance into Tennessee. It is consoling to reflect that the Summer is half over & that the days, tho' hot, will be shorter.

I shall send over to Cave City for the parcel. I am glad to hear that Jane is a good girl. She is generally a good girl. I will write to her next week. I suppose Willie & Freddy are big rough boys. I should very much like to see you all. My heart warms towards you my dearest sweetest wife. I would give a good deal for one embrace.

The paymaster will probably be here next month when I hope to be able to send you at least $50—I will write again when I hear from you. I suppose I may expect another letter in two or three days more.

I send my best love to you & the children & remain,
Your affect. husband,
WmHBradury

Office of Division Commissary of Subsistence
Glasgow, Ky
August 3rd (Monday) 1863
My dearest wife,

I sent you yesterday by Express from Cave City $60 which I hope you will receive safely. There is no express office here. Capt. Kise owes me $15 which he will pay when I can meet with him. He has been relieved by Genl. Judah & will be, in future, with Genl. Manson, who with his brigade is at Lebanon—about 10 miles from here.

We have only a few troops here now. I don't know what the next move will be. Morgan & his band are captured and we have nothing to fear from incursions. There will be probably another organization of the Division. Capt. Kise was taken prisoner, Lieut. Price (of the staff) was severely wounded.

I shall get my regimental pay as soon as the Paymaster comes round when I can send you (with Kise's money) about $40 more. I know you will use it to the best advantage & it gives me great pleasure to send it you.

General Judah is sick. He is troubled with piles & rupture & he has been running after Morgan's five or six hundred miles. He is also much hurt by an article reflecting upon his conduct, which appeared in a newspaper.

There is to be a grand pic-nic tomorrow, I am debarred from going by a boil on my leg which makes me limp about like a wounded soldier. My general health was never better in my life. I have a comfortable place to board, but I sleep in the office at night on a hard bed made of boards & blankets.

We have plenty of music & singing. I have as good a time as an officer without so much responsibility. However, Lieut. Davis is going home on leave of absence soon & he wishes me to take charge of the whole institution during his absence of 20 days. The Quarter Master and his clerk occupy the next room & I've had jolly times. These clerks & Lt. Davis get up the Pic-nic. It will be an extensive affair. I may go on horse-back, for I can have a horse whenever I wish. I have the confidence of Lt. Davis & the respect of all my superior officers.

Stevens wrote me that he could not find anybody to receive the shirts at Cave City & he took them forward to Gallatin like a fool. He should have left them with *anybody* at Cave City & they would have been forwarded to Glasgow. I wish that Stevens & I shall get them "in the course of human events."

I have not heard from you for more than 10 days, I believe, except a little note. I am anxiously waiting & expecting a letter from you everyday. I am busy now making out the July "RETURNS" which are written out on large sheets of paper & must be *quite* correct. It takes a smart man to cheat the Government; but it is done extensively, and the accounts are fixed accordingly. This is done both in the Quarter-Master & Commissary Department.

The Rebels took Capt. Kise's horse, sabre, money & pistols & came very near taking his *Boots* but the officers permitted him to retain them. There were several funny incidents connected with this memorable expedition which I have not space or time to relate.

Lieut. Davis is a droll & very good-natured man. He has a deep bass voice & talks very deliberately & makes us laugh with his dry remarks.

I frequently sleep at the Commissary Depot where the stores such as bacon, rice, coffee, hard bread, flour &c. I send you the heading of a spoiled "RETURN" from which you will see what articles we issue. The soldiers are entitled to nearly all these. They cannot draw peas *and* beans nor rice *and* hominy. They can have Peas & Rice or Beans & Hominy & mixed vegetables, which are *all sorts* of vegetables *pressed dry* & packed in cakes in airtight tin packages.[15] They are good in soup & swell out amazingly. A ration of flour is 22 ounces or a loaf (when the bakery is in operation) of 20 ounces.

The store house or Commissary Building is a large wooden tobacco warehouse like a barn & it is cooler & more airy at night than my office. We give 15 lbs. of sugar to 100 rations. Can Jane tell how much that would be for one ration, or one man?[16] 15 multiplied by 16 to get into ounces then divide by 100—two ounces & nearly one half—that is 2 2/5 ounces of sugar every day to every man.

I will write Jane this week. I send my best love to you my dear wife & to the dear little children, especially the twins.

I am,
Your affectionate husband,
WmHBradbury

Glasgow, Ky
August 9, 1863
My dear little daughter,

Mother says you are a good girl. I am very glad to hear it. You were nearly always a good girl. I love you when I think you are kind to your mother. If you become a good example to our little brothers and they are good and kind too, it will be like—"birds in their little nest agree"-ing.

I hope you like the new house. Do you go round by the Railroad crossing to school? Mother will buy you what books you require. But I will tell you what my father used to tell me—never work and play together. When you study, study as hard as you can; and when it is play time, play as hard as you can. When you work for Mother, work away till it is finished; and then you can read or do anything else.

There are roses here which bloom every month so that we have lots of flowers all the time. I board at a very nice place where there [is] a little boy called Benny and one called Frank. Frank cannot talk yet. Yesterday he got hold of some ink and poured it all over his clothes. He did not know he had been doing anything wrong.

We shall leave this pretty place soon, and go perhaps to Lebanon which you will find on the map about 60 miles Northeast of this place. I am very busy now making out accounts on large sheets of paper. I wish I had you with me to read while I write.

The bell is ringing for breakfast & I must put this in the post office before I go to breakfast. The mail closes at 7½ o'clock.

I remain,
your affectionate father,
WmHBradbury

My dear Jane,
I send you this piece which you perhaps have not seen before.

A little girl was looking at a picture of ships, when she remarked, "See what flock of ships!" We corrected her by saying that a flock of ships was called a *fleet,* and a fleet of sheep was called a *flock,* and here we may add for the benefit of those who would master the intricacies of our language where nouns of multitude are used, that a flock of girls is called a *bevy* and a bevy of wolves is called a *pack;* and a pack of thieves is called a *gang;* and a gang of angels is called a *Host,* and a host of porpoises is called a *shoal,* and a shoal of buffaloes is called a *herd,* and a herd of children is called a *troop,* and a troop of partridges is called a *covey,* and a covey of beauties is called a *galaxy,* and a galaxy of rubbish is called a *heap,* and a heap of oxen is called a *drove,* and a drove of black-guards is called a *mob,* and a mob of whales is called a *school,* and a school of worshippers is called a *congregation,* and a congregation of engineers is called a *Corps,* and a corps of robbers is called a *band,* and a band of locusts is called a *swarm,* and a swarm of people is called a *crowd,* and a crowd of gentle folks is called "*the elite,*" and the elite of the city's thieves & rascals are called the *Roughs,* and a miscellaneous crowd of city folks are called "*the community*" or "the *Public.*"[17]

6

"Bully for Us!"

August 14, 1863–October 13, 1863

The movements of troops and supplies over the Cumberland Mountains was a daunting logistical task, and it was the first time that Bradbury moved into a truly dangerous environment away from headquarters behind the lines. His destination, Knoxville, would become the site of an unforgettable campaign and siege.[1] Bradbury's account of moving troops and supplies across hostile geography, in range of shot by Confederate sharpshooters, provided excellent imagery for the newspapers:

> The entire wagon train consisting of 240 wagons and the three batteries, were taken over roads so precipitous that it required from fifty to one hundred men to each wagon besides the horses to make the ascent. For want of forage, a great number of horses perished, and the necessity was forced upon him [Brigadier General Julius White] to destroy the greater portion of the supplies to enable him to get his batteries safely over.[2]

Major General Ambrose E. Burnside sent a message to Major General Halleck on September 3 that troops under the Department of the Ohio had successfully crossed the Cumberland Mountains and occupied Knoxville and other key positions in the region. A column of General Carter's cavalry division under Colonel Foster had taken Knoxville without much difficulty. A column of cavalry under Colonel Byrd had taken Kingston; another column under General Shackelford fought its way into Loudon, finding that the Confederate army had burned the bridge before they retreated.[3]

Known for its divided loyalties,[4] eastern Tennessee—especially Knoxville—suffered in harsher ways than had Nashville, under occupation a year earlier. From a civilian's perspective, the enemy in Nashville was easy to identify: they were men in blue uniforms. However, Knoxville had a strong history of Union support along with active Confederate participation.[5] The mixed allegiances in that geographical pocket amplified to a frenzy among residents, as Confederate General James Longstreet[6] moved in, then out of Knoxville, much to the dismay of his supporters. General Bragg needed General Longstreet to help reinforce his troops behind the Chickamauga to the southwest.

In the face of so much movement and heightened anxieties, local residents couldn't help but speculate. Who was winning? Who was in control? What goods should they hide from the sight of both armies?

General Burnside was criticized for remaining in eastern Tennessee while the Army of the Cumberland was getting battered in the Southwest. Bunkered on hills surrounding the city with a fort under construction, Burnside methodically created an impenetrable Union block in eastern Tennessee.

With General Orlando B. Willcox[7] positioned in the Cumberland Gap to the Northeast, Burnside was ready for whatever would develop—a Confederate retreat out of Virginia or an open channel for reinforcing the Union army.

Bradbury's movements during this period cannot be precisely tracked, but from his assignments and descriptions of vistas and homes, he likely spent a considerable amount of time in the Mabry home, on Summit Hill. Working under Captain Samuel H. Lunt of the Quartermaster Corps, he would have found the Mabry home a most pleasant place to settle.[8]

Captain Lunt, Bradbury's commanding officer, became active in Knoxville's social circles with locally known women such as Mrs. Kain and Miss Ellen Renshaw House.[9] Captain Lunt not only socialized with them, but he shared military information and traded goods for rations under the table. Bradbury also wrote about similar experiences with "Mrs. Cain" and others, indicating that he was also known among local residents, along with Lunt.

In Knoxville, perhaps more than anyplace else that Private Bradbury had been, women were in positions of influence. Miss House's diary mentions unnamed Union "gentlemen" frequenting her home, where various officers stayed.[10] Similarly, Mrs. Kain was not a minor player in the Confederate's activities in East Tennessee. Her husband, Confederate Captain W.C. Kain, commanded the artillery there.[11] Captain Kain participated in John Hunt Morgan's violent raids in 1862 through Kentucky and Tennessee, resulting in the destruction of segments of the Louisville & Nashville Railroad.[12]

Knoxville had been a city of some wealth before the war. More than a dozen households had a net worth of fifty thousand dollars or more in 1860.[13] While there was less slave ownership in this region than in Georgia or South Carolina and while many residents actively supported the Union, Tennessee had nonetheless seceded from the Union.

Bradbury wrote for the newspapers about Parson William Brownlow. Brownlow was a prominent figure in Knoxville's past; he was well known for his fire-and-damnation speeches against secession.[14] There were many reasons for East Tennessee to oppose secession: religion, economic structure, immigration patterns, the high number of female heads of households—and a public figure like Parson Brownlow, whose capacity to stir up the angels was legendary, had a significant impact.

As mid-November of 1863 approached, civilians noticed the increasing commotion of cavalry and infantry racing up and down Knoxville's Main Street.[15] Bradbury either did not write home during this time or his letters did not make it through the lines—another possibility is that for some reason the letters were not saved. However, based on future writings that were retrospective in style, he was in Knoxville during this time and was stunned by the scenes and sounds of horror.[16]

What Bradbury witnessed was truly worthy of many memorable writings. Perhaps the subjects were too graphic and disturbing for letters home. Burnside's engineers were constructing the fort using the veterans from regiments that had served as widely as in the northeast at Gettysburg and in the southwest at Vicksburg. Just before its completion, Union Brigadier General William Pitt Sanders[17] of Kentucky was shot in front of the battery of Lt. Samuel N. Benjamin[18] by Longstreet's sharpshooters from the tower of Bleak House.[19] General Burnside stayed with Sanders for hours until he died.[20] Crushed by the loss of Sanders, General Burnside named this formidable fort after him.

Fort Sanders was approximately 125 yards by 90 yards with 13-foot-high walls and a twelve-foot-wide ditch in front of it that was in places eight feet deep.[21] The garrison there was also supported by Captain Buckley's Battery D, the First Rhode Island Artillery, part of the 79th New York Infantry and part of the 2nd Michigan Infantry.

Private homes, churches, and shops were converted to hospitals almost instantly as the siege of Knoxville commenced. Scarcely a fence, a tree, or a sack of flour was spared. Even Captain Lunt's wagoners took shelter under Miss House's woodshed.[22]

By late November, the fates of Generals Longstreet and Burnside at Knoxville were largely decided. One company each from the 2nd Michigan and the 29th Pennsylvania advanced toward the deadly ditches in front of Fort Sanders and secured the surrender of the Confederate soldiers who had for days been trying to assault the fort. Artillery Lt. Benjamin had obtained a supply of short-fused shells that were lit as grenades, when the Confederate army led by Brigadier Generals Wolford, Humphreys, and Bryan attempted their assault over the fort's walls at 3:30 a.m. on the misty, icy November morning.[23] The carnage was appalling: men in grey were heaped in the ditches surrounding the fort after their failed attempts to scale the earthen walls.[24]

General Bragg sent General Longstreet a message to "depend upon his own resources."[25] During the first days of December, the siege ended, and Longstreet moved out of Knoxville to make his way to Virginia. With the presence of the Union army behind him, he was prevented from rejoining Bragg's forces to the South.

Yet Confederate sympathizers like Miss House, living in emotional denial, still held out futile hope: "So many poor fellows want things that can't be had for love or money, so many begging for something to eat. They are on less than quarter rations. Oh! If Longstreet would only come."[26] Longstreet would not fulfill the hopes of Miss House and Confederate sympathizers who prayed for his return, re-inforced and re-energized. Miss House and Mrs. Kain, along with large numbers of women and children, were forced to leave their homes and go further South.[27]

Bradbury had described the unusual beauty of Knoxville for newspaper readers before the siege. When the battle was over, though, his pen was still. The Confederate sympathizers were on the way out, the dust had settled, and his view of Knoxville would become appropriately mournful in the weeks ahead. Knoxville's moments of high drama were over. Parson Brownlow returned to the pulpit and his newspaper. For Bradbury, the timing could not have been better; he headed home for the holiday season on an extended furlough.

Lebanon Junction
Aug. 14, 1863
My dearest wife,

I am now on my way from Glasgow to Lebanon where I shall

arrive today noon. I shall still be with Lt. Davis in the same capacity. We are in the 2nd Division under Genl. Manson. I have just learned that we are likely to march in two days, where to I don't know, probably into Tennessee.

I have not heard a word for some time. I wrote to Jane 3 or 4 days ago—I sent you $60 dollars by express. I presume you received it. I have just received my shirts. I got them from Cave City yesterday. They were left there by someone coming down on the train.

My boil is getting better. I am in great haste.[28]

With best love,
Your affectionate husband,
WmHBradbury

Lebanon, Kentucky
August 16, 1863
My dearest wife,

I am writing this before breakfast at the hotel called the "Campbell House" in a bedroom in which are two beds. Last night was the first really cool night we have had & good sleeping was the consequence. My leg is still troublesome & I have to poultice it. I use bread & milk everyday. There is proud flesh[29] in it. If I could keep my trousers from chaffing it I think it would heal without poultice.

Col. Moore, who fought so heroically at Jebbs Bend on Green River & drove back a greatly superior force of Morgan's Band, has just been in the room and announces "marching orders." We shall move sometime today in the direction of Columbia which is south east of this place. We shall probably go thence into east Tennessee.

I have both of my shirts. They are very nice & feel quite comfortable, this hot weather.

Gen. Manson is sick. Col. Moore commands the 2nd Division until Manson's recovery. This Division (which is ours) consists of two Brigades. Col. Chapin commands the 2nd Brigade. I understand Capt. Kise will be here this morning. He had a quarrel or some misunderstanding with Gen. Judah & left him. He will be with Gen. Manson as before.

I have an easy pleasant position which I shall keep as long as the war continues, unless my captain should make a fuss about my absence & induce Gen. Rosecrans to order me back by special order. My papers are all in good shape, and my "Monthly Returns" are put in a little ahead of those of any other Commissary of Subsistence.

Capt. Lunt—a regular Quarter Master appointed by the President—offered me a permanent position as one of his clerks, & would pay at least as much as Lt. Davis, but he would not take me from Davis as long as he required my service—consequently I feel quite sure of a good position in some capacity or other.

There is no restraint on the liquor saloons here. The quantity of whiskey consumed (by officers chiefly) is enormous. The soldiers are encamped out of town about 5 miles distant where there is water. The number of shoulder straps staying at this & the other Hotel is very large. Colonels, Lt. Colonels, Majors, Capts, & Lieutenants swarm around, and the bar often is thronged from morning to night. Their officers ought to be with their commands & not loafing about town.

We are taking along an extra quantity of spades, shovels, picks, &c from which I apprehended that we shall undertake some siege operations or perhaps fortify ourselves.

L.H. Williams, formerly ticket agent on the Railroad running thro' Dwight, is the other clerk with Lt. Davis. He is a smart business man & well educated, but inclined to get tight occasionally. He is well known to R.P. Morgan, Mr. Roadnight and all that class of Railroad men.[30] Mr. Morgan will remember him.

I have not heard a word from you since I wrote last. I told the Post Master at Glasgow to forward my mail to Lebanon. I expect a letter today *sure.*

I shall ride in a wagon or ambulance & my baggage will be carried—I must now conclude as there are papers to be made out.

I have heard from Topeka. The tax receipt has been sent to you *allright.* Tell Kenyon to attend to Keyt & see Van Dusen paid.

With best love to you & the children. I am your affect. husband.

WmHBradbury

Jamestown, Tennessee
Hd. Qtrs. 2nd Division, 23rd Army Corps
Aug. 27, 1863

My dearest wife,

After a long & tedious march over rocky & precipitous mountains where scarcely any body lives, we rest for a day or two at this poverty stricken village waiting for the arrival of more troops for this expedition. When we are all gathered together we shall move upon Knoxville at some point on the railroad leading to Chattanooga.

The roads over which we have come were sometimes so terrible steep & rocky that the cannon & wagons had to be dragged up by 60 men on a rope. It is surprising how we have progressed without breaking everything to pieces.

I have an unexpected opportunity to send this to Columbia, Ky. It may take a few days to reach you by way of Lebanon from which place (which is on the railroad) I wrote to you before we started on the march.

Gen. White is now our General of which Lieut. Davis is Commissary & I am his clerk.I was issuing rations of provisions last night till after 12 o'clock. I have issued to 7 or 8000 troops. Things are badly arranged & I am afraid we shall suffer for want of supplies. Gen. Burnside, I understand, will command the whole of the troops when collected here. We have about 70 head of beef cattle which we drive along & the boys are now eating fresh beef on the top of a lofty mountain. It was quite cold yesterday & last night.

The houses are very poor & the inhabitants poorer. One village called Albany in Ky. was nearly deserted & the houses very much dilapidated—the work of the Rebels.[31]

I must hurry as the commissaries leave *very soon.* I don't know when I can send word to you again. It must be a long time. First unless we are successful in taking Knoxville & the railroad. . .

My health is pretty good. I ride in the wagon belonging Hd. Qtrs. drawn by 4 horses. Gen. Manson & Capt. Kise are both at home—Manson sick—they may never come to this Division any more. Capt. Kise owes me $18. I never got any acknowledgment for the $60 I sent by express.

I send my best & warmest love to you & the dear children.

I have no small envelopes.

Your afft. husband,

WmHBradbury

Loudon, Tenn
September 14, 1863
My dearest wife,

I understand that a mail leaves this place some time this afternoon which will be the first for a long time. The mail will now be more regular.

I received your letter containing news of the death of Mrs. Charles B.[32] I shall write to him as soon as possible. Perhaps you will send me his letter.

I received yours containing note from Judge Safford also a few lines from Ann on the subject of the farm. Frederic is a good honest fellow but it is out of the question that he can pay anything handsome down & I would not sell it on any other terms. He would probably make a good tenant. Has he the *means* to work the land?

I suppose you have heard of our successes. Knoxville has been ours for some time. Chattanooga has surrendered & the railroad is in our possession. There is also a rumor and in fact it is positively said & generally believed that a dispatch has been rec'd by Gen. White that Bragg's whole army has surrendered to Grant & Rosecrans. If such is the case the war in the West is at an end.[33] Bully for us!

We are encamped on the Tennessee River, and are busily engaged in seizing & confiscating wheat, barley, lumber, grinding flour, building a pontoon bridge & putting ourselves into good shape generally. We are short of provisions & have to get as much as possible from the country. Rebel property is not spared.

I issue only half rations of sugar & coffee. Soap & candles are played out. We have plenty of salt which was confiscated. It was sent by the rebel authorities & intended to be distributed to the inhabitants in small quantities.

I have not received my regimental pay as the Paymaster has not been here, but I have $50 of extra pay for the month of August which I will send you the first opportunity. My regimental will be $52 more up to the 31st Aug.

Gen. Manson and Capt. Kise have not yet arrived. The Capt. owes me $18. These amounts with my extra pay for September will make $170. I can steal enough from the Commissary department to pay my expenses.

My tent is pitched on the bank of the river near the piers of the once magnificent bridge. The Rebels fired it as our advance attacked them and the State of Tennessee is deprived of one of her most important means of communication. We completed the Telegraph along the piers yesterday & now have Railroad & lightning connection with Knoxville. Until the pontoon bridge shall be completed, we have ferry boats running constantly day and night. The river is half a mile wide nearly.

I think the children would be delighted if they could see the long canoes shooting across the River & the ferry boats loaded with horses and men & rowed by Negroes, slowly swimming over.

I issue provisions to the whole division & have charge of the papers and do nearly all the business. Lieut. Davis is busy on the other side of the river with the grist mill & the bakery.

My health has not been very good lately. I am too much confined, and I don't get my meals regularly & the food is not of the right kind. Butter, eggs, milk, good bread & good cooking are not to be obtained. The weather is dry & warm & the roads & the ground everywhere is very dusty.

The inhabitants are poor and dirty. A young man stays with me as a sort of servant & assistant & we trade with a woman commissary stores such as sugar, coffee &c for board—the soldiers have stolen nearly all her dishes & knives &c & the table at which we sit is by no means inviting. I hope to do better when we get across the river. This town, like the rest, is deserted. There is nothing to be bought but a few things left over in the sutler's wagons. We are prowling thro' the country to keep up our stock, & the corn fields & barns suffer tremendously.

The scenery is very beautiful on the banks of the Tennessee. I wish I had time & means to take a sketch of it.

I understand there are only two bridges destroyed between this place and Nashville. I think in a week or two the mail will be able to go thro' to Louisville. At present I believe it is carried from Knoxville into Kentucky.

We had an awful march over the Cumberland mountains. I wrote to you from Albany or Jamestown. I received a letter from you on the march. It was sent to the 3rd Division of which these troops formerly made a part & was handed to me by Capt. Day.

I feel very desirous of seeing you & the children. I think of you every day tho' I can scarcely imagine what the twins look like. One great satisfaction is that I am earning sufficient for your support & that the dear little ones do not run about hungry & half-clad like the squalid tribes of young ones in this region. I wish I had Freddy & Willie here. We could have a good time in the river and walk about on the hills where we could see a long way.

I should like to hear what has been done with Keyt & whether Van Dusen has been paid & if Caldwell has redeemed his land by paying the mortgage.

If the news is true about the surrender of Bragg we may be home this Winter.

I send my best & warmest love to you & the children.

Your afft husband

WmHBradbury

I will write to Jane next time.

Loudon, Tenn.
October 10th 1863
My dearest wife,

I write this while waiting for the train which will take me to Knoxville this afternoon.

Your letter sent to me at Glasgow, Ky did not reach my hands till day before yesterday when it was handed to me at Knoxville by a man just arrived from Glasgow. Capt. Kise told me he had another letter for me, but it was inconvenient to get it at that time.

I am glad you did so well with the garden. My health is now pretty good. I hope you & the children will keep well. I wrote to you from Lebanon & from this place, so without noticing your letter now before me of the 26th July except to say that you had better stay where you are through this winter. I will tell you my present position & prospects & the news generally.

Lieut. Davis has been relieved & is likely to go home on account of his health for 30 days. I have received my extra pay—$100—for August & Sept. which I shall endeavor to send by him to Louisville or Cincinnati where he will express it to you. I shall get something additional for making out the September papers—perhaps $15 or $20. I did not receive any regimental pay yet nor my money from Capt. Kise who by the way is sick at Knoxville.

We have been deprived of all news from "America" as we call it for nearly two months tho' we have heard of a "*big mail*" coming over the mountains any time for the last 20 days. It has not reached us yet, but we do really expect it today. If it does not arrive our Post master will go himself thro' Cumberland Gap & see "what's the matter."

While up at Knoxville the other day I made an engagement with Capt. Bailhache,[34] Chief Asst. Quarter Master of the 23rd Army Corps. He will give me $70 per month in addition to my regimental payoff $13 per month. This is a "big thing"—$25 per month more than I had with Lieut. Davis—making my total pay $88 per month & board & clothes. My board, however, will cost me something as there will be great inconvenience in cooking my own rations & when working at the desk I cannot digest coarse food such as soldiers generally get when far from any railroad. I don't know how long this will last but I shall endeavor to satisfy Capt. Bailhache & he will probably keep me with him as long as he stays in the service.

He is from Springfield, Illinois, and one of the editors of the *Illinois State Journal.* His office as A.Q.M. (Assistant Quarter Master) is permanent, & he is not liable to be removed like one merely *acting* in that capacity.

We have been at this small town about 35 days. It is beautifully situated on the banks of the Tennessee River. Our pontoon bridge has been in use sometime & troops pass back & forwards constantly. It is of great service.

The Rebels give us considerable trouble sometimes. They have been so near that we could hear the cannons roar. I packed up my desk & papers & was ready to leave for the other side of the river at a moments notice.

Many of the inhabitants—in fact all the women & children left town, but it was nothing but a scare. We were prepared for an attack & had men in the fortifications & in the field all night. This was the case last night also.

General Manson is at Knoxville & and in temporary command of the 23rd Army Corps. I shook hands with him when I was in Knoxville.

I will write you again from Knoxville after I receive that letter from Capt. Kise.

I am your affect. husband
WmHBradbury
I send especial kind regards to Mr. & Mrs. Lower, Mr. & Mrs. Hetzel, Mr. & Mrs. Eldredge, Mr. & Mrs. Young &c.

Knoxville, Tenn. [a continuation of the letter above]
Oct. 10, 1863
Dearest wife,

I have just arrived here & obtained your letter enclosing one from Charles which I will answer. Lieut. Davis will start for home tomorrow & I shall send the $100 by him. You ought to get it about the 20th of this month. You actually need not feel any anxiety about actions at present. I shall endeavor to conduct myself so as to ensure good pay as long as the war lasts & even after it is concluded. I have friends who appreciate my abilities & will very likely employ me. I have had an offer from a Lawyer in Ohio.

A train starts over the mountains tomorrow and this letter will go with it. I shall write you again in time to send off by next mail to Kentucky. The letters go by way of Cincinnati. The *Big Mail* has arrived. The post master was sorting the letters as I left Loudon, but I could not afford to lose the train. I shall get any letters that may have come by it tomorrow. The post master will bring them up here for me.

I am glad you got the $60 all safe. You must buy some apples & let the children eat them at meal times along with bread & butter. It is better so than eating them between meals. Good bye to you & the twins & the bigger children—till I write again in a few days.

Knoxville, Tennessee
October 13, 1863
My dearest wife,

The long letter I wrote you a few days ago from Loudon has not probably left this place & you will get this & that & one to Jane all at once.

I have no doubt but I have received all your letters including the one before me which is the last & is dated Sept. 11th. I received one dated August sent to Hd. Qtrs. Gen Judah and two addressed in care of Lieut. Davis. They reached me nearly all at once. I will answer more particularly the present one—it being the latest.

The letter I wrote from Loudon will contain considerable in answer to your previous ones &c. I am conscious that I have not made remarks on the contents of your letters at least on some of them; but the subjects were rather trifling & I preferred to fill up my letter with something else that I thought you would like to hear perhaps better.[35] I wrote a long letter to Charles & sent our sympathizing regards & the children's to their motherless cousins.

I send you by Lieut. Davis who will leave tomorrow for Michigan, $90 not $100 as I wrote you first. I shall receive $75 from Capt. Bailhache at the end of this month. The pay master has not been here yet & I have obtained nothing from him or from Capt. Kise who handed me one of the letters from you. Gen. Manson is in temporary command of the Corps.

I wrote a long letter to Kenyon in answer to his just received, offering to sell the 1/4 for $2000 on the terms mentioned which Mr. K will read to you. The land does not pay interest & taxes. I think you will like the terms as it will relieve us entirely from the mortgage.

You did not send me the list of prices from the *Sentinel.* Butter here is 50¢ a pound & scarce, coffee a dollar a pound & everything else is very high. Only think—that this large army has to be supported out of the country[36] & supplies drawn in wagons 150 miles over the worst hills & rockiest mountains you ever saw.

Provisions may well be high. I pay $6 a week for my board. My rations will reduce it to $3 or $4 a week. They will take them on the board account. We get no milk in our coffee & live chiefly on pork, bacon, and sausages with greasy heavy hot biscuits. I can't go the biscuits. I wish I had some of your bread.

I think you sold Nellie for a good price—$16 or was it $10? $10 was enough anyhow.[37] I suppose you are glad the children go to school again. I should like to know if Freddy learns anything from his new teacher. What has become of Mr. Pearre?[38]

You seem to have done very well by buying the garden. I suppose you take much pleasure in gathering things out of the garden especially the Fruit. We have a bag of good apples in the office and I eat all I want—at least three a day. I use them as an antidote to the everlasting pork. I did not get but a few peaches in the season. I got them out of an orchard on the line of march to Loudon. Fruit is generally scarce where soldiers are.

I shall send you some more money at the end of the month when I hope the mails will be more regular & reliable. I hope you will clothe the children well & warmly. The little dears must be taken care of and be provided with the necessary books. If you can get a girl to help you I wish you would do so. I feel sure of a good position as long as the war lasts unless Capt. Walkley makes a fuss & wants me back.[39]

I have been obliged to buy some underclothing—$5 worth. The Govt. had none & I was needy. It will be impossible to save my whole pay. My position exposes me to expenses which I should not be liable to in the ranks. Many of the teamsters & soldiers are suffering for want of clothing. If our supplies should be cut off we should be in an awful fix. You did not send me a piece of your dress.[40] Two of the clerks wear boots which cost $18 a pair! Clothing is very dear.

I should very much like to see those dear little twins. I saw a very pretty baby yesterday belonging to an English woman. It came to me quite willingly. They have a little dog which did not approve of the change & commenced biting my shoes most vigorously.

You must be very poor in flesh with the two babes suckling. I hope you will take good care of yourself and live well this winter.

I sleep in the office on the carpet. Somebody stole my blanket & I traded my overcoat for another. Still I ought to have *two* blankets. I find I am getting delicate & susceptible to cold.

It is now raining, which will make it tedious for the wagon trains. Capt. Lunt brought in a train of 500 wagons a few days ago. Capt. Day is expected with another. We had 54 wounded come in from Greenville where a fight had been going on.

I will now conclude with my best & kindest love to you & the children.[41]

Your affect. husband,
WmHBradbury

7

"After the Loaves and the Fishes"

February 5, 1864–April 1, 1864

With a Christmas-New Year's furlough behind him, Bradbury had to return to the war in early 1864. He was worried as he returned because General Thomas had restricted furloughs after the battles of Chickamauga and Chattanooga. Had Bradbury not have been so well-liked and needed in his official capacity, he might not have obtained this much-needed leave, and he would have missed knowing his twins, Elwood and Edwin, as infants. His lengthy six-week furlough gave him the time to negotiate timber and corn sales while encouraging Jane and the other children on deportment and their studies.[1]

With Mary's hands full with the five children, Bradbury returned to the field from the home front. Through the kindness of Bradbury's comrades traveling to and from home, his wife was able to continue receiving extra income as opportunities materialized. Concern for his family's welfare and comfort was never far from Bradbury's mind. No doubt Frederic Bradbury's three letters in this chapter were also a comfort to Jane and Mary during William's time in Eastern Tennessee.

He also wrote the children that they should help their mother. He asked them to remind her to fulfill tasks in which he believed she was falling behind, such as getting their smallpox vaccinations.[2] Yet much of his correspondence with the children contained recommendations for improving their spelling, geography, diet, and conduct. Bradbury's description to the children of his living quarters, his "shebang," was intended to bridge the distance that separated him from his children.

As he had followed the officers to Knoxville and onward to Lookout Valley near Chattanooga for the start of the Atlanta campaign,

Bradbury continued to search for opportunities to earn extra income. He began writing as a newspaper correspondent for the *Chicago Tribune.* On February 5, 1864, from Loudon, Tennessee, he wrote a fourteen-hundred-word article, "The Situation at Knoxville and Vicinity." Stationed at Loudon, a smaller community southwest of Knoxville, Bradbury was able to provide a depiction of the conditions under commanding officer, General Sheridan:

> Coal mines, saw mills, grist mills, &c are here in full operation under the Government and preparations are being made for the reception of gunboats and transport vessels with a view to the accumulation of a great amount of stores. A substantial bridge across the river will be ready at the end of this month . . . which will be a great improvement on the present ferry. The vast expansive energies of the military power are seen everywhere and there is no profession, trade or occupation which is not called into request by this gigantic undertaking. . . . Loudon is quite an important post.

As Bradbury continued, reinforced by the newspaper's acceptance of his articles for pay, he seemed to pander to the political winds of power. For instance, he described Captain Lunt, as A.Q.M. his commanding officer, as "one of the most efficient officers in the whole regiment and a most generous and wholesome gentleman."[3] These remarks, however, belied his true feelings about the man he worked for in Knoxville, which he would express in a letter from Atlanta to Capt. Bailhache (included in this chapter).

Fiery-tempered Knoxville native Miss House shared many of Bradbury's feelings about Captain Lunt, but for different reasons. She wrote in her diary that "He [Lunt] is quite handsome . . . but the vainest creature I have ever seen."[4] Ingratiating, and eager for companionship, Captain Lunt's image, whether crafted by comrade or foe, was not very flattering.

Beyond descriptive details of the region, Bradbury's newspaper correspondence ventured into imparting rumors, if not outright gossip, which catered to the reader's desire to know an insider's perspective. An example are these remarks disparaging another officer: "Gen. Foster, who is not yet relieved, is distrusted by many of his inferior officers, and there seems to be an impression that he is not adequate to the emergency. . . . General Foster is sending rebel women and children out of Knoxville. They leave Loudon by the boats and will enter the enemy's lines in Georgia."[5]

Ellen Renshaw House would soon join those exiled from home by the Union Army, on the grounds that this nineteen-year-old woman was "a very violent rebel, one who would sell her soul and body for the benefit of the Confederates."[6]

When Bradbury described the anticipated Confederate defeat near Knoxville, he wrote about the prospect of "losing face" in war. His conclusions of impending events in the war were as follows:

> East Tennessee will undoubtedly be the scene of conflict this summer, and the Army of the Ohio will have the most important part to perform. If we continue to hold this portion of East Tennessee and drive the rebels out of the remainder of it, their campaign will have been a failure, while the lapse of another half year will have materially increased their embarrassments, as regards finances, supplies, and everything which goes to make an army effective.[7]

Yet after the battle of Knoxville in November 1863, the plight of noncombatants from both sides was very bleak. Residue of the lamentable conflicts in Eastern Tennessee was not embarrassment but incarceration, disease, starvation, and madness.

The more Bradbury wrote for the newspapers, the more frustrated he became. Why wasn't the *Tribune* paying for his articles in a timely manner? Many of his letters to Mary would focus on accountings of articles submitted, his desire to see them in print, and whether Mary was paid for them. Assuming that he wrote to the newspapers as frequently as he did to Mary, the task of reconciling this matter must have been a complex one.

But as he continued writing, Bradbury summed up his view of Knoxville for the *Tribune* just before orders came through for him to return to his regiment, which was proceeding to northern Georgia. Knoxville had greatly changed. From Bradbury's description (including a rare invocation of a biblical passage), Knoxville can be remembered as the city he saw in early 1864:

> Knoxville was a beautiful and attractive place before the war; but now the shade trees and shrubbery, the majestic cedars and the stately oaks—once the ornament of this picturesque city have disappeared forever. The smooth sides of these sunny hills are gored with long red gashes; and their lofty slopes are no longer graced

with the ever-green plumes. . . . Their beauty is marred; their glory is gone! The elegant mansions in the suburbs are now only noted by black and crumbling walls. The tasteful gardens and yard fences with flower beds and bushes—brace the joy and pride of many a household—are now, alas, utterly destroyed. When shall there again be "beauty for ashes and the oil of joy for mourning?"[8]

Chicago Tribune, February 18, 1864 [publication date]
"From Tennessee, (From our special correspondent)"
Loudon, Tenn. Feb. 5, 1864

Chattanooga has the appearance of a vast brickyard surrounded by low hills of reddish color, intersected by disjointed pieces of streets, including the inevitable "Main Street," studded with chubby churches, long sheds, spacious depots and warehouses and straggling buildings of all kinds. It is an uninviting and bare-looking place, being unrelieved by a single tree. The whole is nearly enclosed by cetaceous looking mountains, with their bold bluffy heads towards the river and their ridgy backs mingling away in the distance. In this vicinity was fought the most decisive battles of the war; and "Lookout Mountain" and "Mission[ary] Ridge" will be as prominent in the pages of history as in the landscape of this romantic region. . . . Neither private freight, nor passenger, soldier, or civilian, is allowed to go up the river without a special permit from Major-General Thomas who commands here. . . .

On board our flat-bottomed stern-wheelers I noticed several barrels marked "Hospital Stores from the Sanitary Commission, 66 Madison Street, Chicago." This reminds me of the Sanitary Commission at Chattanooga where in addition to the ordinary arrangements, a reading room and a writing desk are free to all soldiers, and a prayer meeting takes place at one o'clock every day. What shall tell the amount of good done by this institution? Where is the parallel to it in the ancient or modern times?

Gen. Foster who is not yet relieved, is distrusted by many of his inferior officers, and there seems to be an impression that he is not adequate to the emergency. Our forces and those of the enemy are on the south side of the Holston [River]—the rebels occupying Strawberry Plains. The transportation of the 23rd army corps has been sent over the mountains that the animals, fifteen hundred in number, may be foraged in Kentucky. Brig. Gen. Manson, and a portion of his personal staff, have just left on leave of absence. Brig. Gen. Judah again has command of the 2nd division, 23 A.C. (Late under Brig. Gen White, now sick in Chicago.)

Knoxville
February 6, 1864
My dearest wife,

I arrived here last night all right and safe. I succeeded in getting a good new overcoat in Loudon from Capt. Little with whom I staid all night. I shall have to pay $11.50, which is the present Government price.

I sent a letter off to the *Chicago Tribune* from Loudon but you need say nothing about it. I felt uneasy and uncomfortable till I got on board at Chattanooga. The officer came round for the "orders." I gave him mine in fear and trembling. He read it over several times & handed it back—*all right.*

I then felt gay as a lark. I saw Genl. Manson & Capt. Kise at Loudon. The Genl. said "Did you get a discharge or did Capt. Lunt give you leave of absence"? I said—"leave of absence"—tho' not strictly according to Military Rule—"It was *perfectly right—Perfectly right*" said the General. Bully for him!!

I left some of my things in Capt. Little's camp chest which will arrive in a day or two. I am boarding at present where I formerly did with the English woman. Mrs. Cain & family & other secesh women & children have been sent South.[9]

I have a less troublesome position in the office than before. Capt. Lunt's duties are changed—better for him. He has a good active chief-clerk and the office feels pleasanter to me than before.

I have seen Lieut. Davis. He wants me to make out his September papers and I dread the job. Suppose you had six weeks washing & ironing & mending to do besides your regular every day work. He says that when he first saw the account in the paper of his death—he knew "it was a d—d lie."

We only get two meals a day—half past 7 & 3 o'clock. I think it will suit me very well. If it would be no inconvenience to Capt. Lunt, I should prefer to be at Loudon with Capt. Little where my board would be less and my pay perhaps greater. I should also have more air and exercise which I feel to be a necessity.

The fortifications have been materially improved & strengthened tho' it is said by some that Longstreet could take the place any time. Foster is not much thought of as a General.

I have a little potted beef left yet. The preserved milk is in Capt. Little's camp chest.

I shall write another letter to the *Chicago Tribune* tomorrow. It may appear in about Tuesday's or the 16th inst. I received two letters from you & one from Kenyon which of course contained old news.

I think you had better buy the house, but I would *first* sell the timber land for $200. I don't think you will get more. You can offer Kenyon $5 on condition that he makes sale of the timber land for at least $200 & also sells the corn. I can send you at least $100 at the end of this month.

I feel anxious to hear from you in reference to the stove grate and the hay and other things besides the children. I can fancy I see Chodger [nickname for Elwood] and Eddie & Willie and Freddy & Janey and Mother fussing & scolding. If I was back I should cuddle you all up most tremendously. I am sure I "never forget the dear ones that cluster round my home."

All the boys at the office were glad to see "Brad" again. Several of the old clerks have left. I have a nice desk covered with green baize & containing drawers and four little cupboards all to myself.[10] This will perhaps go over the mountains instead of going by Chattanooga on Monday by boat.

I now send my best love to you my dear wife and to my dear Jane & my dear Freddy & my dear Willie and my dear little Chodger and Eddie. I shall not write again until I hear from you. Then I shall send a letter to Jane.

I am your faithful & affectionate husband,

WmHBradbury

I write with the gold pen.[11]

Chicago Tribune, February 29, 1864 [publication date]
"From Knoxville (From our special correspondent)"
Knoxville, Tenn., Feby, 16, 1864

The army of the Ohio, isolated without adequate supplies for the last six months is now receiving rations and clothing quite liberally. The cars run regularly from Chattanooga to Loudon and from that point another train runs to this place. . . . It is the intention of the military authorities to run seven daily trains from Chattanooga to Loudon, in order to accumulate a large quantity of supplies in this menaced and mountainous country. . . .

Siege guns of long range have arrived from Richmond. It is evidently the intention of the enemy to complete the bridge at Strawberry Plains, move their heavy guns down by rail towards Knoxville, and attempt another siege. It is reported that they can shell the city at a distance of four miles. . . . Gen. Grant has just telegraphed that he will send Gen. Schofield all the troops he wants. Gentlemen who wear red shoulder straps are on the alert. W.H.B.[12]

Knoxville, Tenn
February 17/64
My dear daughter Jane

I received your letter which you sent me last December. I mean the one in which you made the letters of the alphabet. I thought they were very well done for a little girl who had not been learning to write very long. I also saw Freddy's & Willie's and the babies' letters which were very good—especially the babies'.

Now I want you to try and earn the 5 cents a week by behaving prettily & keeping yourself neat and tidy about the hair and face and dress and shoes and everywhere as a young lady should do. Everybody likes to see neat and graceful little girls. You know what I mean. When I come home next Fall I shall be so pleased to find my daughter Jane not only a good girl and a good scholar (which she is now) but a nice, neat, and graceful girl and then there is no telling what Father will think of her and do for her.

Now I will tell you what you must do besides. You must do just what you know is right and what your mother and teacher tell you, and never mind what any of your school-mates or anybody else says.

When I write to you next time I will send you some letter as a copy, though I suppose you have regular copy-books.

I am sorry dear little Freddy and Willie and Chodger are sick. You must kiss them all for me & tell Mother that you should all be vaccinated for the smallpox. Don't lose any time.

Your affectionate Father

Knoxville, Tenn
Feby 17, 1864
my birthday
My dearest wife,

I received your short letter today enclosing one from Frederick and one from Mr. Safford of Topeka. I sent you $85 by Mr. Butterworth which you will probably receive before you get this. I enclose you a letter which you will please forward to Frederick & enclose to him by express $200 & $400 if you sell the timber land.

I am glad you have bought the house. If you can let it I would not move into it until April. And if you do move into it before that time, I would use the barn for the corn & pay Mrs. L rent for it. I should stay until grass comes if possible.

I am sorry to hear of the children's sickness. I wish I was with you to share the care & trouble & sympathize with you & them. My health is better than it was when I arrived here. I think I can save $75 a month *clear* by turning in my rations & using contrivances & economy.

The preserved milk was all spoilt. I sold the butter at $1 per lb. I shall charge $3.50 for the green tea & I bought some excellent black tea at the commissary's which I shall charge my Landlady $2.50 per lb. for. The hop-cake was all right.

I am trying to make a little money by buying vouchers and checks. My February pay will soon be due and I shall use some of it for this purpose; unless you require any when you know I shall take great pleasure in sending it to you. John Hetzel said he could let us have the $100 to help buy the house & you [should] ask him for it. The interest will not amount to much. Never mind it. This $100 with the $85 I sent you & what you can spare will make $200 which you can send to Frederick. I shall always have enough to send you so that you will have plenty of money till next Fall when Aaron Harford's payment is due.

You will see my letters in the *Chicago Tribune* (if they print them) above the signature WHB.

You must take a dollar—which I will send you next time I write & divide it into 10 equal parts and give Jane 5 cents a week, and Freddy 3 cents a week and Willie 2 cents a week if they are good children & deport themselves well. As Jane has the most, she must keep herself neat and tidy & have her hair well combed back &

behave like a lady. You can tell whether she earns her five cents or not. This is Father's dollar and it will last 10 weeks. The children must have little bags or cases to put their money into. Freddy can have postage stamps which Jane can send to Father and Mother will pay her money for. Five postage stamps will make 15 cents.

Willie can have little two cent checks which Mother will give money for—5 of them will be worth 10 cents. I enclose 10 checks. Now Mother, I want you to do this. It is not too much for the children & will teach them to save their money. This will be instead of the money you give them weekly. If little Chodger and Eddie behave themselves, they must have a kiss all around & a nice piece of cookie or something good every Sunday.

The Rebels are reported as getting nearer & threatening us from several points.

I send you my dearest wife & children my best & sweetest love.

I am your ever faithful & affectionate

WmHBradbury

Don't fail to send me as soon as possible three or four ounces of good strong unground ginger. Send it by mail. Want it for ginger beer.[13] Knoxville Tennessee, Feby 17, 1864. Put sufficient stamps on it.

I sent you by Mr. Butterworth, who left this place this morning for Cincinnati & Chicago, eighty-five dollars. This includes my wages for January. I put $10 to the $75 & have enough left to carry me thro' till the end of this month when I shall receive another $15. I wish you to buy the house, as in case you sell the timber land, you will have enough to do that and pay Frederick too—his $400.

The money will come from Chicago to John Hetzel who will hand it to you. I have written so much lately—three letters to you & one to the *Chicago Tribune* tonight—(not three to you *tonight*), that I have nothing more to say only that you are the dearest & sweetest & best of women & I send my love to you & the children.

Yours ever faithful & affect.

WmHBradbury

The rest of my things have come from Loudon. The butter & a little of the potted beef left is still very good.

Chicago Tribune, March 3, 1864 [publication date]
"From Knoxville [From our special correspondent]"
Knoxville, Tenn., Feby., 24, 1864

The spring campaign is now commenced in reality. The enemy has retreated from his late menacing position, and is hurrying towards North Carolina by way of Bull's Gap. . . . It is probable that the sudden departure of the rebels is caused by the news of the destruction of several bridges in their rear, by means of which communication with their base of supplies becomes endangered. They have been apprehensive of such a disaster for some time and the news is therefore likely to be correct. We can now act in direct concert with our troops at Cumberland Gap and keep our men straight and strong. . . .

A spy of the name of Hincky is under sentence to be hung next Friday—an unlucky day for him. He deserted from the rebels and took the oath of allegiance, and has since been acting the vile part of a perjured traitor and a spy. . . . Thirteen hundred deserters are on their way to this place. They confirm the reports and state that they are heartily sick of the war. . . .

We receive the Louisville papers on the fourth day from that of publication and Nashville papers a day later. The Knoxville *Whig* ventilates rebel atrocities and its vindictiveness every Saturday. This feeling is excusable to some extent, but will not heal an old wound or make new friends. Brownlow is a more generous and charitable man in private life. If his sheet were less savage, he would be more popular. He abstains from any remarks on the Emancipation or Negro enlistment questions, which now occupy the Nashville and Louisville papers.

[No location written, but Knoxville]
Feb. 28, 1864
My dearest wife,

My health is getting to be first rate. I expect a letter from you tomorrow when I shall write again. I rec'd a short letter from you day before yesterday. Don't write me again till you hear from me, for it is not certain whether I stay here.

I enclose $60. Capt. Bailhache will send it to you from Chicago.

The Tribune Co. will pay me $5 a letter. They want me to continue. I shall get $25 from them this month. This with $75 will make *$100.* Bully for me. I can save it *all.* My regimental pay & rations will pay my board &c.

With best love to you & the children.

I am your affectionate & ever loving husband,

WmHBradbury *in haste*

Capt. Bailhache will send you $20 or $25 from the Tribune office.

[letter fragment, February 29, 1864]

. . . But I wish to know why the deportment was not sent me. If Freddy gets lots of postage stamps for his good behavior, Jane can sell them to me & I will send her 30 cents for 10 stamps.

The darkey had taken my shirt which I left here and I made him pay me $2.50 for it. My board has cost me very little this month & I am now going to a place where the woman charges on $1.50 per week in addition to the rations. I am therefore sure of saving $15 per month at least & as much more as I can get from the Tribune office.

Now I will tell you a small secret which you must not divulge. Gilchrist has applied for me to return to my regiment and Gen. Grant has ordered Gen. Schofield to send me back. I imagine that Gilchrist who is at present commanding the company thought I was desirous of coming back from what I wrote to Walkley from Dwight. The commander of the post has been instructed to find me & send me back. I don't suppose the commander of the post will try to find me *very bad,* & then the whole thing will be dropped. However, if I should go to the regiment . . .

I am now in a position where I can earn something for you & I mean to do it honorably. I should be glad to get $200 for timber land and pay up Frederic.

I had only two meals a day ever since I arrived until now. The folks did not cook only two—at half past seven & two o'clock. I begin on the 3 meals plan tomorrow morning—March 1st. I think it will suit me better.

I am quite satisfied that you did well by buying the house, but I would not tell anybody what you gave for it. If we ever come to sell it, the price *paid* might interfere with the price *asked.* I would not insure unless the Doctor is a careless fellow. The rent ought to be $5.50. If he is a good tenant, $5 will do very well. I did not expect the boilers would last forever. They have now been in use upwards of 7 years.

I am sorry the hay turns out badly. I would put in the barn sufficient for the winter & sell the [rest].

My health is now first rate. A dose of salts did me good.

It is now raining like sixty & the water drops just where my bed is—Plague on it.

Davis neglected to bring up his papers for me to work on several nights, till finally he said if they were not on hand next time I called, I need not make them out. He failed to bring them & I am absolved. I have plenty of writing without them.

With my best & sweetest love to you & the children.

I am your afft husbd,

WmHBradbury

Knoxville
March 5th 1864
Dear Jane and Frederick,

I have not had a letter from Mother for a week and it seems a very long time. I thought I would write to you today and to Mother tomorrow. Next Monday I am going to Chattanooga (can Freddy spell that word?).

I shall see Mr. Gilchrist and Mr. Judd and Mr. Smith and all those that came from Dwight.

I send you some of the new money. There is one ten cent paper for each of you and one for Willie. The babies would tear theirs if I sent one. You must be good children & I will write to you again. Mother must send me the deportment because I want to know how good and dutiful my dear little children are while Father is away. You must keep your money in a safe place.

I send you a nice piece out of a newspaper.

Can't Mother cut some of the *Tribune* with W.H.B. under them & send them to me?

Your affectionate father

Camp in Lookout Valley
Near Chattanooga, Tenn.
March 11, 1864
My dearest wife,

I arrived at Chattanooga on the 8th & on the next day ascertained that the 129th Regiment had been ordered to the Front but had not arrived but that they were expected every hour.[14] On the following day I proceeded down the Railroad to Lookout Valley & after waiting by the side of the track about 3 hours sure enough the whole brigade came along & stacked ammo in the woods directly opposite.[15] I then reported to the Regiment & was made very welcome by everybody from the Colonel down. They all look first rate. I write this in Capt. Walkley's tent with Chilcott's gold pen.

My letters will be sent after me to Chattanooga. I waited two days in Knoxville in hopes of getting some letters but was obliged to start without any. I wrote to you on the Sunday previous—that is—last Sunday—and to Jane on Saturday & I wrote my last letter from Knoxville to the *Chicago Tribune* last Monday—the day I started.

They are all very glad to see me & treat me like a visitor. Capt. W & the Colonel excused themselves for sending for me. They were obliged to do it, but did not hardly expect to see me. The Colonel wished that the rest of the absentees come up as promptly as I had done. I shall probably get detailed from Corps Head Quarters & work my way up to as good a position as the one I left.

We are camped in a very pleasant place near the Railroad but shall move a short distance tomorrow. Lookout Mountain is directly in front of us & the railroad winds all around its base. After we have staid here a week or two we may be ordered forward into Georgia & if there is any fighting to be done, I think we shall have a chance to do it.

The men are all polishing up their guns to be ready for inspection tomorrow. They have plenty of rations & clothing & are in good condition throughout. I carried my knapsack & blanket in soldier fashion for the first time in more than 12 months. I walked about 8 miles down the road.

I have never seen any of my letters in print. Can't you cut them out & send them to me. You can find out from John Hetzel in what papers they are—I don't remember any of the dates in February but in March they would be printed in the papers of about the 8th or 9th & the 12th or 13th. Including the first letter descriptive of the siege [Knoxville], I shall have earned altogether $45 or $50 by this correspondence.

I am sorry the ginger & hops did not arrive during my stay in Knoxville. I wanted to sell them to the man with whom I was boarding—to improve his small beer & keep up the supply of hopcake. I shall direct one of my acquaintances in the office to sell them to him & send me the money in a letter. The gold pens I sent to Frederick for will be sent after me & the music which I wrote for to Case.

With my best & sweetest love to you & the dear children.

I am your ever faithful & affect. husband,

WmHBradbury

New York
March 17th, 1864[16]
My dear Jane,

I am very much pleased with the letter I received from you a short time since. It is very well done for a girl of your age, which, if my memory serves me right is now not far from nine years and half. Have I guessed or rather remembered right?

It is now nearly six years since I saw you last, and that was when you lived near Morris by the old windmill (though why I should call it old, I don't know, for it can't be more than nine years since it was commenced). The subject of that old windmill has a funny side to it, although it proved such a bad speculation and I think your mother will agree with me that during its erection it was productive of a good deal of merriment.

Now you live at Dwight, a place about which I know nothing except I have heard and read. I suppose you recollect the visit of the Prince of Wales for the purpose of shooting the prairie chickens. That day, doubtless, constitutes an era in the history of Dwight.

I should like very much to see you and Freddy & Willie, and the twins one of whom was just beginning to walk when your mother wrote to me last. I am pleased to hear that you are getting on so well with your studies. But, above all, I am pleased to hear that you are a good girl and that you help your mother all you can in her numerous and trying duties.

I see I shall have to use another half sheet of paper, for there is not room enough on the first for all I have to write to you.

I suppose you have pleasant companions to take the place of Mr. Case's children who, your mother tells me are now in Chicago. Choose good companions who love and obey their parents and apply themselves to their studies and respect and obey their teachers.

Will you please to send me a copy of that letter in verse or rhyme as you call it which you received from your father last year? Your father, when a very young man, was fond of rhyming, and I recollect well, one of his poems was printed and circulated amongst the good people of Ashton-under-Lyne, in England.[17] Ashton-under-Lyne, as your mother can tell you, is very near to the place where your Uncle James lives.

Perhaps "when this cruel war is over," as the song says, I shall be able to pay you a visit. You are so very far away (about a thousand miles) that it takes a good deal of time and of money to make the journey. Till then I shall be very much pleased to hear from you often.

And now with love to you and Freddy and Willie and the twins and Mother and Father,

I remain,
Your affectionate Uncle
F. [Frederic] Bradbury

No. 106 Pearl St., New York[18]
March 17th, 1864
Dear Sister-in-law,

I duly received your letter of the 1st Inst, and day before yesterday I received D. McWilliams' draft for one hundred dollars on Messrs. Stone, Starr & Co. of this city. I cashed it yesterday. There was nothing but the draft to indicate whom it was from, but from the post mark on the envelope, I judged it was from you, and I hereby acknowledge the receipt.

It seems the man with the $85 has not yet turned up, for which I am sorry for your sake as well as my own. I trust he has not been "gobbled" by guerillas and that he will yet turn up with the "greenbacks."

I am glad to hear William's health is better. I quite agree with him about the Kansas land & hope he may be able to get along without selling it. I will send a statement of account soon.

I omitted to acknowledge the receipt of my niece Jane's little note. It would not be right to leave it unnoticed and so I have tried, on the other leaf, to talk a little to her.

In conclusion, with love to you all,
I remain,
Yours affectionately,
F. Bradbury

Head Quarters, 1st Brig. 1st. Div. 23 A.C.
Wauhatchie, Tenn.
March 19, 1864
My dearest wife,

The whole Brigade is gone off to Review and I have time to write once more to those who are nearest and dearest on earth to me. I have not yet received any letter from you of a later date than Feby 19th tho' I have sent several times to Chattanooga for the mail which I expected to be sent to me from Knoxville. I am in hopes of receiving something by next mail.

My position here is that of clerk to the asst. adjutant general of this Brigade which is at present commanded by a Colonel (Col. Harrison) & Lieut. Culver of our regiment is acting adjutant in place of Adjutant Mitchell who is absent on leave & has been injured by a Railroad accident in Indiana. I was ordered to report at Genl. Hooker's Hd. Qrtrs.—11th Army Corps, but Colonel Harrison made a particular request that I should stay here a few days at least.

There is no extra pay attached to any clerkship short of Department Hd. Quarters at Chattanooga or some post where much business is done. I shall not stay here any longer than I am obliged. I have been accustomed to control my own movements to a great extent and I shall keep a sharp eye to all the opportunities for advancement.

I have about $30 in cash & $65 pay due besides the clothing

allowance which at the end of this month will amount to $17.50 making a total of more than *$100 that I can save.* My expenses here will not exceed $2 a month. The officers treat me very kindly & respectfully & wish me to stay, but I am after the loaves and the fishes & so are they all. I am ambitious to be something more than a clerk at $13 a month. While others have the honor & credit & big pay, I won't do it neither.

The change has been very beneficial to my health. The air and exercise & better diet than at Knoxville has made me feel much better bodily, tho' I have suffered much from the cold at nights. The weather has been quite raw for the last five days. The men & all of us have built cots & we have a fire in our office but it smokes most intolerably & I have been crucified between the cold and fire. We are encamped in Lookout Valley with Lookout Mountain on the East behind which the sun looks out about 7 o'clock every morning.

We have in our brigade 3 Illinois regiments, one from Ohio & one from Indiana.[19] There is a Grand Review of the whole corps (pronounced core) going on today by General Howard or General Hooker and the troops are all neat and clean and on their best behavior.

Captain Walkley says that if he had been, at the time, in command of the company, he would not have sent for me; but Gilchrist thought it was his duty to comply with orders. It is all right. It will do me good to be in the field a short time.

I have not written anything to the *Tribune* since the 6th March. It is nearly train time & I must close. We are stationed on the Railroad near the Depot & are building a bakery, more houses &c.

[letter torn]
New York, March 23rd, 1864[20]
Dear Sister-in-law,

My letter acknowledging receipt of D. McWilliams' draft on N. York for One hundred dollars . . . Do not distress yourself at all for the balance as I should be very sorry if you pinched yourself and the children.

William, it appears, has been ordered to his company, and this I suppose means active service for him. I hope he may be detailed to act as clerk and that he may return at the expiration of his term of service, "Sound in wind and limb," as the horse jockeys say. . . .

I am yours with affection,

F. Bradbury

Chicago Tribune, March 31, 1864 [publication date]
"From Tennessee"
Wauhatchie, Tenn., March 24, 1864

Did any mortal ever know or hear of such severe weather at this season and in this latitude? It has been for several days very raw and cold, but we certainly did not expect to see such a phenomenon after the equinox in the "sunny South."

The headquarters of the brigade and also of the 1st division are at Wauhatchie Station, in Lookout Valley, which has just been made into a Post, and will be a depot for supplies and store for the whole command. . . . Spacious buildings for quartermasters and commissary stores, and a large bakery capable of supplying several thousand men with daily rations of soft bread (in contradistinction to hard-tack) have been completed and will be in operation tomorrow. . . .

We are now in the front and subject to be ordered into active campaigning at any moment. . . . An esprit du corps has already sprung up and the soldiers show a zeal and emulation which shines forth in bright buttons, blacked shoes, well brushed clothes, and general neatness of person, accoutrements and quarters . . . the munificent sum of $1,000 has been subscribed for the purchase of a complete set of instruments for the band. . . . We hope to have the best brigade band in the corps. We think we have already the best brigade. The insignia of this corps is the crescent which appears respondent on a "field of blue" on the soldier's coat or cap. Other corps have other insignia but the crescent of the 11th indicates, almost derivatively, the increasing and expansive power which we claim to have. . . .

The railroad trains crawl around the base of the huge mountain like caterpillars. Lookout Creek, like a green ribbon, loosely ties the dark ravines and the track of the iron horse to the glorious Tennessee [River], which waves its wide bands around the peninsular city, and meets the waters of the bloody Chickamauga at a distant and lonely bend of its majestic course. On the right, the blue hills of the Cumberland recede in the far distance, and on the left mountains behind mountains extend bold outlines to the nearer gaze, and lift their dark ridges like a wall against the blue sky. Surely such a land was never made for slaves. —W.H.B.

Head Quarters 1st Brigade, 1st Div. 11 A.C.
Wauhatchie, Tenn.
Sunday, March 27, 1864
My dearest wife,

I received yesterday from Lieutenant Gilchrist your letter of the 18th inst. enclosing one from Charles and photograph of his late wife. I am glad that you received both packages of money safely & the $25 from the Tribune office, which still owes me at least $10 more, for I wrote two letters since the first of March, which I presume have been printed.

I would not send Frederick any unless you can easily spare it. There is no *absolute certainty* of me being able to send you more than $10 or $11 per month after I have forwarded you what is now due to me which, when I get it, will amount to four months wages (to the end of February) or $52. I shall then send you $70.

I have never seen *one* of my letters in *print* yet except the "siege." I don't know whether they use them *all* or not and I wish to ascertain if they are still acceptable, and if I can count on $5 each for them when my means of obtaining news is so very small here. $5 per week would help considerably.

As I stated before in my last letter, there is no extra pay allowed except at Department or Post Head Quarters. I shall therefore endeavor to get into one of those offices. Lieut. Culver is willing to let me go if I can better my condition.

I received the hops a few days ago. They had arrived at Knoxville & were forwarded to my present address. I have no use for them here. I wrote a friend in Capt. Smith's office instructing him where to dispose of them & the ginger (when it should arrive) but presume he did not get the letter in time. I hope the ginger has not been sent.

Did Hetzel owe us $50 besides the $100?

I am afraid the corn won't amount to much. If we could rent the timber land for pasturing purposes for about a dollar an acre, it would be better than getting nothing for it. I am glad that you have let the house. You should get the rent in advance every month. I have always felt satisfied with the purchase of the land office[21] and I think the rent could be advanced to $5½ or $6 a month without any impropriety.

I can imagine what a hard time you must have had with the children & am sorry that you strained yourself by carrying them about. You *must* take care & avoid all such dangerous things in the future.

I did not *seriously mean* that there was any secret about my coming back to the regiment tho' it was not generally known in the office that I had been sent for and if the Commander of the Post had not heard where I was, I might still have been with Capt. Smith. My leaving had nothing to do with Capt. Lunt's reports tho' he, like many other Quarter Masters, is behind with his accounts. I don't see where Mr. Young obtained his information.

I suppose I could qualify myself for a commission in a Negro Regiment & get detailed on some staff, but the war will not last much longer and I may get into a good position where I can save as much money. After I have made up my Returns & Reports for 1st of next month I shall look around & strive for a better place.

I sent a long letter to the *Tribune* dated March 24th from Lookout Valley which will let you know how we are situated here, provided they print it. It will probably appear about the 31st. Please send me the paper if it is not too much trouble. I shall write today to Capt. Bailhache & and find out what he can do for me.

I shall also write to Charles & get him to pay James.[22] I believe he honestly owes me at least that amount, but we *jumped* at the settlement without making out a regular account.[23] I suppose Mr. W.H. Sutcliffe pays for his [Charles's] children's tuition and no doubt the old folks help as they have no other family ties in England.

I am glad to hear that the children are good in their deportment. You must give them the dollar in the proportions I designated. As soon as I receive a letter from Jane & Freddy I will write to them again.

My two pairs of boots are very serviceable this muddy weather. I wish you would send me a little black & white thread also some more postage stamps as I only received *four* in the letter from

Gilchrist, & none in any other letter lately—Now for your mistakes *on a separate paper.*[24]

My health is very good. The mountain air is pleasant & bracing. The mud is now drying up there is a prospect of fine weather.

I send my best love to you & the dear children. You must take care of one another. I wrote to you three or four days ago. I expect to hear from you again next Thursday. I will write again on receipt of a letter from you.

Your affectionate husband,
WmHBradbury

Head-Quarters Department of the Cumberland
Office of Judge Advocate
March 27, 1864[25]
Dear Captain [Bailhache],

The application which you were kind enough to make on my behalf has hung for a long time. I delayed the matter myself in the first place, afterwards a delay arose in consequence of the movement of troops and the absence of officers. Now I have got a favorable endorsement from my Captain, but the Colonel *disapproves.* He says it would afford a bad precedent of which others might avail themselves and thus fritter away his regiment. I shall make another effort when Col. Harrison—the Brigade commander comes back. He is a *quasi* friend of mine and may further my views. If the Colonel of my regiment would endorse favorably, I think it would be all safe. If I should fail altogether I should be glad of a position with you when my term of service expires—Sept. 8, 1865 (?)

I will now give you the news in the Q.M. &c Depts. Capt. Farnum, whom I saw in Chattanooga, relieved Captain Dunbar A.Q.M. in charge of transportation at that place. Capt. D's clerk refused to do business after office hours at the solicitation of a number of Gen. Sherman's staff who had come from the front for some special purpose. Members of staff expostulated and insisted. Clerk deprecated and refused. High words insued and the vials of wrath were poured out, until at length [a] member of the staff jumped over the wooden railing and "went for" the clerk. Capt. Dunbar came in at this *juncture* & had good evidence that his *sub* was getting the worst of it. After considerable altercation, peace prevailed; but the joke on Capt. D. was, that he was relieved, and sent to the *Front* and Captain Farnum AQM reigns in his stead.

Lieut. Lyon of the 23rd Mich. is AQM & has charge of the tools, workshops &c of the 23rd Corps. He is now here, tho' the command is "over the hills and far away." He has the same old staff with him with the addition of Congdon (Capt. Lunt's "boy") and our mutual friend, the "immaculate Williams" (now home on leave) as his clerks. His papers &c have been burnt or destroyed twice, which may help to account for his being at present "all up and square."

Capt. Lunt was relieved as Disbursing officer in June last, to give him an opportunity to make up his papers, which, as everybody knows, were most unconscionably behind. It may be presumed that he has rendered in his papers and accounts by this time, as he has already reported by letter to Col. Boyd, the angelic Quartermaster of the 23rd Corps for assignment. He is probably now on duty with some part of that command in the field. Lieut. Lyon says it will kill him if he gets *only a Brigade.* Col. Boyd is reported to be a very capable and active officer. Under his hands, the Q.M. Dept. of the 23rd Corps has attained great efficiency (*sub rosa*—not before it was needed).

Capt. Winslow A.Q.M. has still a Division. He is in trouble and "confusion worse confounded," and seems to be an object of pity and derision to Lyon & that ilk. The letters "A.Q.M." will have a terrible cabalistic meaning to him as long as he lives. He is in the field with his command.

Lieut. O.S. Davis is now fairly out of the service. He was discussed for exceeding most outrageously his leave of absence and reinstated as Q.M. of his own Regt. Gen. Judah promised him a place on his staff, but he failed to "come to him" in some important respect and lost his position. It seems that another officer had in the mean time obtained the Commission as R.Q.M. during Davis' meanderings. At all events "Old Honest" is now a citizen & at home in the State of Michigan. It is stated that *Honest* and Williams together made upwards of Four Thousand dollars out of the A.C.Q. Dept. Of course Williams got the lion's share. I learn all this news from Lyon, &c.

Capt. Huntingdon has resigned and Capt. Lunt has Bailey, one of his clerks, with him.

I saw Capt. Hertig during this campaign. He looked as usual.

Genl. Manson commands the Div. Of East Tenn: Hd. Qrts. Knoxville.

Capt. Kise recently resigned his commission and is now Lt. Col. of the 120th Ind. Vol. Infty. I saw him in Atlanta a short time since. He is not in good health.

Gen. Judah is at Nashville awaiting orders. He was relieved and sent to the rear after the battle of Resaca.

News has just reached us that the construction train which left Atlanta this morning was captured & burnt about 10 mile south near the Chattahoochie River. The Rebs are very spiteful just now. Sherman is chasing them into Alabama.

I give the Illinois public the benefit of my observations occasionally through the CT [*Chicago Tribune*].

In conclusion, Hurrah for "Old Abe."

With best regards to yourself & Hart, I am,

Yours very truly,

WmHBradbury

8

"I Don't Like This Field Work"

April 1, 1864–July 27, 1864

Back with the 129th Illinois Infantry, Bradbury rejoined many of his old comrades, now near the front of the upcoming campaign. The reunions were a source of companionship and enjoyment to him. He had especially missed Lt. Culver, and he now joined "old Cul" in his mess nearly every night.

The tension of the campaign building in northern Georgia was spreading throughout the ranks. An unusually wet and muddy Spring seemed to bog them down—with extra time on his hands, Bradbury wrote frequently. Writing to his family was not financially lucrative, however; newspaper correspondence was.

By the late spring of 1864, Bradbury was serving as a clerk under Colonel Benjamin Harrison, who had learned of his phonographic skills. Bradbury wrote about Colonel Harrison for the *Tribune*, describing him to readers back home:

> A man of far more than average intelligence and shrewdness while his energy and military capacity are manifested by the good condition of his brigade, and the estimation in which he is held by his superior officers . . . He is supported by an active and zealous staff and it is a remarkable and unusual feature as in his headquarters there is no whisky-guzzling with its attendant boisterous comment and drunken profanity. The Colonel is a moral and religious man . . . there are other Generals and officers in the corps to whom the above remarks are by no means applicable. Military reforms to be effective, must begin in high quarters. The force of such examples

> produces wonderful results among subordinates, and the influence for good is felt on every hand.[1]

It's impossible to know Bradbury's motives; he was either pandering to his new commanding officer and friend or he was honestly in awe of him.

Writing to the newspapers as a paid correspondent was not a sanctioned activity, especially for a soldier working directly for a general. While Bradbury was not the only correspondent to the *Chicago Tribune,* when inappropriate military information was leaked to the paper, he felt as though all eyes were on him. The tension mounted between seizing the opportunity to earn extra money to support his family and respecting the propriety of his position by keeping quiet. As an attorney, Bradbury surely knew that he would not have had much of a defense were he to be found in violation of Article 57 of the "Articles of War."[2]

Correspondents were under military law and subject to court-martial if they were found guilty of aiding or abetting the enemy, either directly or indirectly. Offenders could be sentenced to death by a court-martial hearing. General Sherman became irate when the *Indianapolis Journal* published a report regarding his movements in Atlanta, asking authorities to find "that fool" who provided the information.[3] While there is no reason to believe that Sherman knew about this clerk's prolific newspaper writing, the general's outburst must have given Bradbury some pause. With prime information coming out of army headquarters where he worked directly for General Daniel Butterfield, the frequency of Bradbury's letters was increasing, and others knew that he was writing for the newspapers. Over time, the information grew more descriptive and potentially useful to the enemy. Bradbury was walking on the proverbial razor's edge.

Fieldwork experience for Bradbury was different than it was for most soldiers during the Atlanta Campaign. The constant movement and unpleasant conditions discomforted those in headquarters as well. In many ways, field commanders fared worse than regular soldiers, who by this time were well equipped. The general officers, still transacting a considerable volume of clerical work with the help of soldiers like Bradbury, went without basic mess equipment such as tin plates when they reached Snake Creek Gap.[4]

While Bradbury mentioned dodging bullets while taking down notes for General Butterfield, it is unlikely that he returned fire himself. His comrades from the 129th Illinois Infantry, though, were in the thick of battle. From early May through the end of July, the regiment was continuously under deafening fire, often restricted to muddy trenches for extended periods. Regimental comrade Laforest Dunham wrote in a letter that forty-seven men of the regiment were killed or seriously wounded during this stretch, which included some hand-to-hand warfare.[5] Lt. Joseph C. Culver's letters to his wife turned quite solemn, with each closing paragraph written almost like a church prayer.[6] The letters of Colonel Benjamin Harrison of the 70th Indiana Infantry to his wife reflected pride and the belief that victory would follow, even if incrementally, as they inched forward to Atlanta.[7]

Private Bradbury's exposure to high-risk situations in the Atlanta campaign is uncertain; he did not write home about it very much, but he may have wanted to spare them from worrying. Instead, he wrote about his boredom when General Butterfield went home sick and there was little to do. Writing to Mary served another function: it helped clear his conscience about his unauthorized writing for newspapers.

Bradbury did not feel well in the field. Living conditions in an active campaign were far more primitive than those he had experienced. Making a meal of hard tack, coffee, and berries was a far cry from his fare just weeks earlier. Unlike his comrades, his constitution had little time to adjust to this significant change in his diet.

For most Union soldiers, though, dietary inadequacies were secondary to staying alive. The places from which Bradbury wrote—Ringgold, Dallas, Ackworth, and Marietta—would be remembered by old soldiers for a lifetime, but only if they were very lucky.

On the homefront, Bradbury asked his wife to obtain the help of a servant girl because her lack of letters suggested to him that her many domestic and business assignments were exhausting her. Yet it's unlikely that Mary grew up with the familiarity of hired domestic service—as William probably did. She may also have been uncomfortable with the prospect of squeezing another body into a house already brimming with people. William probably viewed a domestic servant as a way for Mary's time to be freer so that she could serve his business activities. But in the U.S. at this time, having a servant did not mean that Mary thought her life would necessarily become one of rest and leisure.[8]

We cannot know why Mary's efforts, perhaps halfhearted, in securing domestic help to appease her husband never lasted long. By the mid-19th century, nearly 25 percent of Chicago households employed live-in servants.[9] Yet during the same period, young women began to be attracted to factory work, which generally provided shorter hours and often higher pay.

Many periodicals and books like the *Englishwoman's Domestic Magazine*[10] aimed to educate women about the "scientific approach" to efficient household management. While we do not know if William subscribed to the magazine, he was certainly a subscriber to the same worldview. When William complained about Mary's inability to hire and keep domestic help, he showed himself to be out of touch with the reality that a prairie wife would have to compete with manufacturers for a labor pool that had changed considerably since their emigration from England. With the changing times and relations between domestic servants and employers, Mary's level of enthusiasm was understandably questionable. Further, there were many published reports that domestic assignments were growing more volatile and short term in nature.[11] Hired household help? Maybe not.

Head Quarters 1st Brigade 1st Division
April 1st, 1864
My dearest wife,

I received your letter of March 26th yesterday, only 5 days. I received the hops which were sent to me from Knoxville. Today I got a letter from you of March 2nd—one from the *Tribune* office saying they would pay me well from plans [maps] &c—one from Captain Bailhache enclosing express rect & one from a friend in Knoxville enclosing express rect for $60 which with the $25 from Chicago made $85 which with the $85 from Butterworth makes $170. I did not receive any other letter from you addressed to me at Knoxville except the one of March 2 which also contained a letter from Jane.

I have not received the ginger nor do I need it now. My friend in Knoxville will forward anything that comes to my address. I presume you forwarded my letter to Frederick along with the $200. I have not received the gold pens yet.

I wrote Charles a very long letter in answer to the one from him. He takes quite a different view of the Rebellion from ours.[12] I asked him to pay James £10 for me. I shall repay him sometime.

I shall be glad when you get the photographs of the twins taken. You must of course send me one of the cartes.[13] I hope you can get them well taken in Dwight, but Chicago would be the best place. Could you not make time to go up with them? It would not cost more than $6 & you could save at least $1 in difference in charges.[14]

If Aaron Harford does not pay for the timber land in two or three weeks, don't let him have it unless he pays interest at 10 per cent from the time he promised to pay—which will be 40 cents per week. You can then send $200 more to Frederick which will make $400 altogether & pay off his whole claim. If Harford hangs back a great deal, I would not say anything more to him. It is cheap enough at the price when farm produce is rising almost every day and a gold dollar is worth $1.70.

I was very glad to hear that the children were doing their best to earn the dollar. I should be glad to know that Jane is improving in her writing. Her spelling and composition is good but I don't think her writing is anything extra. I will write to her next time I write to you. Which uncle was her letter addressed to? I told Uncle Charles all about the children, beginning with the twins and going clear up to Jane.

You did tolerably well to get $7 clear for the hay. I hope you will not lose any rent of the land office. If I get into a good position, perhaps we can put an addition on one side of it & live in it ourselves. It will cost at least $100. I am afraid the house you live in at present is not very wholesome on account of the lowness of the rooms.[15]

The Chicago Tribune Co. still owes me about $10 according to my calculations. I shall write them a letter every 10 days or so.

I am in hopes of getting into some better position in the course of this month. I have been asked for by several staff officers and I am making friends among men who have influence in High Quarters.

I burnt your last letter by mistake and don't remember exactly all you wrote about. I wish you would send me a little more thread, black & white. I received the postage stamps. I don't hear anything about any pay-master; but I think we shall be paid about the middle or last of this month unless we move way towards the extreme front.

The Rebels are active just now & we send out mounted patrol & scouts every day. I wrote a short letter to the *Tribune* yesterday. I sleep on the floor of the tent using for a bed a lot of leaves in a sack which makes a great dust when I shake it up. I take my meals with the orderlies who carry dispatches to the different regiments. The Company (B) & the Regiment are only a short distance across the Railroad.

Lieut. Culver is just going to bed. He wants you to kiss the babies for him. He is a very kind hearted man & allows himself to be imposed on sometimes. I send my best love to you & all the children. It is now 11 o'clock. I shall expect another letter from you in a week or less.

Your affect. husband,
WmHBradbury

Wauhatchie Tenn
April 6, 1864
My dear daughter,

I told Mother that I would write to you next time I wrote to her. I received your letter written in pencil. It was spelled very well, but I did not think the writing was very good. You must practice writing with ink and try and become as good a writer as you are at geography and spelling.

We are in a valley about 7 miles from Chattanooga (is not that a funny name?). You can tell where that place is by looking at the maps. Georgia, Tennessee and Alabama meet together somewhere. Sometime I would like to know how far Chattanooga is south of Chicago and what is its latitude.

Now you know you are generally a good girl, and if you become a tidy and graceful girl and a good scholar, how proud Father and Mother will be!

You must tell Freddy that I and another man have just put up a tent made of cloth with poles to keep it straight and we have each made a little bedstead and we have nice evergreens placed all around on the inside. It looks very pretty. There is room for two children in my bed. Would you and Freddy like to come, or Freddy and Willie or Janey and Willie or the two little twins. I should be very glad to have you with me, but we must wait till next Fall and then have a good time.

There is scarcely any grass yet and the trees have no leaves; but the day has been quite warm and we shall soon have fine, warm weather.

I shall think of you every time I go to my bed in the new tent or

"Shebang." We call them all "Shebangs." The office in which we work is built of logs and is made very comfortable. We put it up in one day and a half. We have no windows but a large hole in the roof and a large cloth is stretched over it, which lets the light through.

Your affectionate father

My love to you and all the chuckies

Head Quarters 1st Brigade 1st Division
Wauhatchie, Tenn
Apl 6/64
My dearest wife,

I had some hopes of receiving a letter today from you, but the trains have been behind and very irregular.

We are still at this place tho' there is some talk of our proceeding by way of Knoxville towards Richmond. This army corps (which is the 11th) and the 12th will probably both be joined together and known as the 1st Army Corps and we shall then be *1st* Brigade, *1st* Division, *1st* A.C.

There is nothing definite known but there are some indications of it. I don't hear of any change likely to benefit my condition at present except that Col. Harrison said he had told the Quarter master to put me on his rolls for extra-duty pay. I have written to Capt. Bailhache on the subject; they will do what they can for me.

I have no news to send to the *Chicago Tribune* and that source of profit is cut off. Perhaps I can make a few dollars by writing something. I hope you have, by this time, received the $200 from A. Harford and sent it to Frederick.

My position here is pleasant tho' somewhat confining. Lieut. Culver is very kind & allows himself to be imposed upon by the other officers. We sing together and play chess evenings. He is *great* on an old Methodist tune. We sing Sunday school tunes with the Colonel sometimes. We have plenty of fun and *"Cul"*—as they call him is as *great a boy* as anybody. Some of the officers quote Shakespeare and get up gay scenes. We get the Nashville papers containing the latest news.

I shall make a few drawings or maps & forward them to the *Tribune*. They write me that they will be glad to receive them & pay me well. The scenery is very beautiful and romantic.

If you hear of any express package being made up at McWilliams, perhaps you will send me something.

The rumor about the changes is now confirmed. This brigade will have a new commander and several members of the staff will be sent back to their regiments. It will probably make no difference to me.

I send Jane a drawing of a few of our tents which we call "Head Quarters" 1st Brigade. She can copy it if she thinks she can do it and has time. I will send her some more bye and bye.

This is the first real warm Spring day. I think the season is quite as backward as with you unless you have an unusually backward Spring.

I have just received your letter of April 2nd—today is the 8th—I also recd my letter to the *Tribune.* I think with you that it is a pretty good one. They are talking about it in the office while I am writing.

I have not recd the ginger—I wrote to Case not to send it. Case paid me for the butter.

If Wilson puts 4 horses in the stable I should charge him at least $1.75.

I imagine produce will gradually get higher in price therefore you should lay in at least two barrels of flour and other necessary articles of food & clothing. I don't wish you to stress yourself at all. I think I can [earn] nearly enough to pay current expenses. I can surely write 3 letters a month or 2 letters and a map which will be about $15 a month in addition to say $10 saved out of my Regiment pay = $25. This with the cows and the rent *free* will help a good deal. In the mean time I shall look out for something better. If I let Hetzel have the money—$75—I would make it payable *on demand* if he only gives 6 per cent. If A. Harford does come forward with the money, you can make up $100 for Fredk with a part of that amount & what I shall send you when I get my pay. As I said before, I can send you $70.

I am glad Eddie can walk about. It will be less trouble for you. I would not feed him too much greasy food—You don't say anything about Elwood.

I would not sell milk for less than 6¢ per quart if you can get it. It is no higher in proportion than other things.

Send me a few *more* stamps next time. I lost the last lot or someone stole them.

I send my best love to you & the children. I hope to hear from Jane & Freddy.

Your affect. husband,
WmHBradbury

Chicago Tribune, April 15, 1864 [publication date]
"From Lookout Valley [From our special correspondent]"
Lookout Valley, Tenn., April 9, 1864

We are constantly hearing of large bodies of troops passing through Shelbyville, Tullahoma and other places on this route. Their destination must be northern Alabama for only a few pass through this valley, and those travel on the railroad. Trenton, Bridgeport and Whiteside are very important places and are menaced by the enemy to such a degree that our scouts are kept constantly on the alert. . . .

A recent general order from the War Department has created quite a furor among the men of this command. It is to the effect that a non-commissioned or private, on the recommendation of his immediate commander, can obtain a furlough of 80 days, at the end of which time he reports at the Philadelphia Military School, where, if found eligible, he is instructed in military science and practice, with a view to being commissioned as an officer in a Negro regiment. The combined attractions of the furloughs and commission will induce quite a number to make applications. The example is set by officers who are allowed to resign in order to accept positions of a higher grade in the "U.S. Colored Troops." Lieutenants become Captains and Majors; Captains become Colonels and Majors, and Colonels become Brigadier-Generals in the Corps D'Afrique. The Engineer Department and the Marine and the Telegraphic and Topographical Corps also afford opportunities to improve a position by transfer out of a regiment. . . .

The fact that we are gradually but surely making a considerable army of colored troops is overlooked by many of us at home. They in connection with their white officers, will be the future army of this country; and in the meantime will play a very important part in the present war. Regiments of sable soldiers are forming every day and boards of examination sit regularly at Nashville, Chattanooga and other places to pass judgment on applicants for commissions in them. . . . Here we have an answer in part to the question of "What shall we do with the Negro?" Make soldiers of some and laborers of others. Let them have the protection, civil and religious, accorded to American citizens. . . . —B.H.W.[16]

Head Quarters 1st Brig.
Wauhatchie, Tenn.
April 14, 1864
My dearest wife,

I have just recd your letter of the 7th April. I thought I would write you a short one now and another in a day or two. There is a grand review today and I shall have no time to write a long one. I will write to Mr. Jones—give my kindest regards to both of them. I did not receive the *Tribune.*

I am charged with writing the letter to that paper giving an account of this Brigade. I don't admit it & I don't care a straw what they think. Neither do I care any thing about the scandal and I don't see why you should. There is no respectable person that knows you, will believe it.[17]

As for the Jew and his customers, their good or bad opinion cannot injure us a particle. Don't let it trouble you at all. If you get the rich man's property—all right. It is too bad to have the *name* without the *game.*

The weather will soon be warm enough that the twins can go out and Willie can then take care of them. I should be glad if you could get a girl to help you. I don't wish Jane to be forced too much in her schooling. She should play and take all the exercise she can. I sent her a letter last time I wrote to you.

You should get Wilson's rent in advance if possible. When the weather becomes warm I would move into the land office provided you can have the rest of the barn until grass comes & longer if necessary.

We have planted trees all around our Head Quarters in a most beautiful style. They won't grow and they have scarce any roots and some are sharply driven into the ground.

You must read my letter in the *Tribune* of about the 15th or 16th. Don't tell anybody that I write. I might possibly get into trouble—It is dated Lookout Valley & signed WHB [BHW]. It is very long; cut it out & send it—I enclose a little picture for Willie.

The review now being held is thought by many to be preparatory to an advance. I have got a new pair of pants and a new pair of drawers & two new pairs of socks. The socks soon wear out at the heels. I have not heard from Capt. Lunt or Capt. W.H. Bailhache. I should like to see the piece in the *Tribune* affecting Capt. Lunt.

I received letters from Westcott. He is tired teaching school & wants to be a citizen clerk in the army with some Quartermaster. I am endeavoring to get a paper for him. I have written to him & expect an answer in a few days.

I am making a sketch of the scenery & encampment here which I shall send to *Harper's Weekly* if I ever get it finished. I have neither pencils nor paper suitable. I should be glad if you could send two dark shading pencils one *dark* and the other *darker* that is "B" & "BB." They could be sent at different times in a letter. John Hetzel knows what kind I need & can buy them in Chicago—one pencil should be rather hard.

With regard to your teeth, if you think you can spare the money I should be very glad if you would get them. You know what the prospects are.

I think I can get enough to support you & the children and I have hopes of getting into some better position bye and bye—perhaps I may be adjutant in some Negro Regiment. I have been requested to prepare myself for that position. These changes are of constant occurrence.

I have not heard a word from Frederic.

My health is pretty good. I find that the more exercise I take the better I feel; but I am somewhat confined & the recent wet weather has rendered exercise impossible. I am obliged to be in the official day-to-day [business] because Lieut. Culver is at the Review.[18] I must be in when he is out.

The *Chicago Tribune* owes me (as I consider) about $25 which I have directed them to send you. I don't think we shall be paid before next month in which case we shall receive up to the 30th April making six months pay coming to me or $78. I have twenty-three dollars besides.

I will write you again in three or four days. I send my respects to Mr. & Mrs. Young, Mr. & Mrs. Hetzel & all inquiring friends. I send my love to you & the children and I hope to hear soon from Jane.

Your affectionate husband,
WmHBradbury
Seal your letters *well* with something. The envelopes won't stick.

Wauhatchie, Tenn.
April 17, 1864
My dearest wife,

I wrote you a few days ago a rather short letter in answer to your last.

Our brigade has now changed commanders & I am at present out of a place. I have just applied to Department Head Qtrs for a clerkship with the Judge Advocate. I shall probably get it. At all events I shall get some desirable place soon.

Col. Harrison goes back to his Regt. & Gen. Ward takes the Brigade.[19] We had a very comfortable place here—our quarters being beautiful with shrubbery & fixed up in very handsome style. I can get a place almost anywhere, but I want to have a choice in the matter myself. I have heard nothing from Capt. Lunt.

I can get a commission as adjutant in a Negro Regiment but I feel undecided about binding myself for a period of service longer than my remaining term. I am practising short hand with a view to taking down proceedings of courts martial which will be my duty with the Judge Advocate if I get the place.

This is Sunday & they are just preparing for preaching.[20] The mail starts in a few minutes. I will write again when I hear from you which will be in two or three days more. I have really nothing to communicate at present. I will write again and let you know of any change that may take place. Hoskins will probably be Major and Culver will be Captain of both.

I send my best & sweetest love to you & the children every one. Kiss them all for me & the twins twice. I hope to hear from Jane.

They are singing just outside and I am writing inside a very comfortable "shebang" with a large fire.

Your affectionate & devoted husband,
WmHBradbury

Head Qtr, 1st Brigade 3rd Division 20th A.C.
April 27, 1864
My dearest wife,

I only received yours of the 20th inst. enclosing extract from the *Tribune.* I see the *Tribune* regularly. I don't think I shall write much more. I have no news to communicate and if I had, everybody would charge me with it whether it was of an important nature or not.[21]

I think Frances would look well in the dress you describe but the colors would not show much in a photograph.[22]

I hope you will have grass soon and thus have no trouble with the cows. Yesterday was very fine & warm in fact the first really warm day we have had. I was at the Head Quarters of Maj. Gen. Butterfield[23] & walked back to camp in the evening a distance of nearly three miles.

Genl. Butterfield sent for several shorthand writers to take down his reports at length & copy them out afterwards. I was the only one who could do what he wanted. I made out two long documents for him yesterday and I go down again this morning to await any further instructions. The other shorthand writer could not "begin" as the saying is.

I am still on duty with the Brigade Inspector and have just worked late and early getting up *four* copies of his monthly reports.

I had a fit of indigestion last week & was relieved from duty for two days. After violent purgings & pukings I got better and am now pretty well again. This trifling sickness & hard work must be my excuse for not writing more promptly.

There is considerable talk of a move into Georgia in a short time. Preparations are being made. No tents will be carried & all the rations necessary will be placed in as few wagons as possible so as to make a rapid march. There is every indication that something will be done *soon.*

Can't you hire someone to dig the garden? There is no need for you to do it. You can make the beds & weed them.

I should like some of the eggs you speak about & also some milk & butter, but these are luxuries that we never see and scarcely think of.

I received a letter from you dated last February which has just reached me from Knoxville. It speaks of Frederick having anticipated his salary on the strength of my promise to let him have

$400. I suppose you have only sent him $200. I should have been glad if you could have spared him another $100.

I send you a sketch of a portion of Lookout Valley. You can forward it with the letter to *Frank Leslie's* or *Harper's Weekly* unless you would rather keep it yourself. I persevered under all difficulties.

I have not received the ginger. I will write again to Jane & send her some capital letters. It is strange that A. Harford does not take the timber land but it is only just like them. They talk big & it amounts to nothing.

In conclusion I send my best love to you & all the children.

Your affectionate husband,

WmHBradbury

I am just going to walk down to Genl. Butterfield's. It is warm & pleasant & the trees are about half leaved out. Don't forget to send me *20* postage stamps. You don't send enough.

Head Quarters, 3rd Division 20th A.C.
May 1st, 1864
My dearest wife,

I received yesterday two letters one from Jane and from Freddy. I think they were both written very well. I will write to them today or tomorrow.

I am now engaged in writing the Military History of Maj. Gen. Butterfield and reports of operations in Virginia &c. The Genl. dictates and I take notes in shorthand. I then copy out the notes at length and revise and correct and arrange until the manuscript gets into proper shape. The Genl. sent for 7 or 8 shorthand writers. I was the only man to suit him.

The confinement and coarse rations have had a bad effect on my health. The weather has been very sultry and disagreeable with heavy thunder showers. So much coffee does not agree with me, and the food does not relish without it. I shall be better when I get more exercise and the weather becomes cooler.

We are making preparations to march and shall in a few days more be on our way into Georgia. I shall probably remain with Genl. Butterfield in which case I shall have my baggage carried.

The papers on which I am engaged are very long and tedious. Just before coming to the General I had completed four copies of a long Inspection Report. The paymaster is expected every day. I don't know whether he will be here before we move or not. I have now six months pay due amounting to $78. Perhaps I shall only get four months pay or up to the end of February.

I am at present in a comfortable hut built of split timber. I sleep on a wide shelf fixed at one end like a bunk in a ship. This is also my "office" with documents and messages from the General. I am in fact his private secretary & see papers & documents of great importance.[24]

I shall give the General a hint about extra pay bye and bye. In the meantime I have several wires working in other directions. Capt. Bailhache says he can't do anything at present tho' he would like my services very much.

The $25 you received pays me up to the 10th April for my services as correspondent to the *Tribune.* They still owe me for three communications.

My present quarters are about 2½ miles from the Regiment nearer Chattanooga and opposite the point of Lookout Mountain. If you conclude to send the sketch [to the newspaper] I sent you, you can at the same time forward the enclosed letter.

We have received orders to be ready to move at 4 o'clock tomorrow morning. I don't hardly think we shall start then.

I have not written to Mr. Jones yet. I have heard nothing from Frederick. I suppose you have heard nothing from A. Harford.

Could not you get a boy to attend to the cows for his board? I mean in part payment, some boy who is going to school & lives at a distance.

Our mess consists of a lot of New York boys from the Army of the Potomac. They are gay and festive youths—well-educated and full of fun. We have also some Englishmen in the crowd—one who talks just like that man that used to be with Banyons on Roadnight's farm.[25] We play cards in my "Shebang" at night.

I expect a letter from you today. Next time you write send a common sized needle. I have only the darning needle left. I have plenty of thread.

The clerks are packing up papers preparatory to leaving tomorrow morning.

I send my best love to you & the children and remain,
Your affectionate husband,
WmHBradbury

Head Quarters 3rd Division 20th A.C
In the field Nr. Ringgold, Georgia
May 6, 1864
My dearest wife,

I have just been to the creek & washed myself and two shirts and two pairs of socks. I therefore feel better.

We are encamped in the high rolling timbered land of northern Georgia. We started unexpectedly this morning and arrived at this place, which is called Leet's Tanyard about noon today. Major Gen. Thomas was at our headquarters today also Brig. Gen. Kilpatrick & Brig. Gen. Whipple.[26] They held a consultation and partook of something out of a bottle. The result of their conference was an arrangement that the troops should make a move forward tomorrow morning without baggage, wagons, non-combatants or other impediments. They will be provisioned with 5 days rations. It is supposed to be a concerted double flank movement on Dalton or something preparatory to it.

I am writing to my wife as I would write to a newspaper. I presume matters of a domestic character should now come in. I received a letter from Jane & Freddy with which I was very much pleased. I also received some time ago Jane's composition about babies which I think I did not acknowledge at the time. I think it is very good. I keep it and read it sometimes. I have not heard from you for some time; but there is now a mail at Division Hd. Qtrs. which will be distributed tonight when I shall get welcome news from home—sweet home!

Our mail will now come thro' Chattanooga & Ringgold and reach us quite regularly. This will also be the case in sending out mail matter. I have written several short letters to the *Tribune* which they will call—"special dispatches." I sent a plan or map of the country with the names and positions of Corps & Genls commanding.

It is probable there may be a fight tomorrow a few miles to the front of us. I sent this short letter & map to the *Tribune* yesterday. I should like to know if they print it in any reasonable time. It should appear about the 12th inst. It is dated Gordon's Mill. I worked very hard on the plan & have now material for a very long letter, but I feel afraid that being now secretary to Genl. Butterfield, I may be accused of writing improperly. But when I think of $5 a letter, I feel to risk it. I keep a diary for Genl. Butterfield & a separate one myself.[27]

My health is very good again. The exercise and change is far better than steady work in an office. Just previous to our departure from Lookout Valley, I staid up till 2 o'clock in the morning writing letters for the General. He dictated seven letters. I took them down in short hand & wrote them out afterwards while he & every body else were asleep. But I have my baggage carried & ride in an ambulance which is of course pleasanter than marching in the ranks.

We heard cannon at a distance today and if the rebels don't retreat tomorrow we shall drive them. I will finish this after I have had my hard tack bacon & the inevitable coffee. The supper consisted of some beans as well, only they were slightly burnt. I suppose I shall get a letter thro' Brigade Head Qrs tonight but I dare not wait till tomorrow as the mail goes at such uncertain hours.

You will now have no trouble feeding the cow as you must have grass by this time. The season is no forwarder here than I have known it in Illinois. The country is very fine & the weather glorious.

I will write again when I get your letter. I send my best love to you and the children every one. I shall be glad to hear from Jane & Freddy again.

I am your affectionate husband,

WmHBradbury

The band is playing beautifully & the shades of evening are closing o'er us and my clothes are not dry. Well, I must take them in anyhow. Goodnight.

Head Qrs 3rd Div, 20th Corps
Nr. Dallas Ga
May 30th, 1864
My dear wife,

I have received no letter from you since I wrote last from near Cassville but, as the mail leaves tomorrow I thought I would write again.

You will see by my letter to the *Tribune* what we are doing &

where we are. We had a tremendous attack by the rebels last night along our whole line and the artillery & musketry were used incessantly. We were in the rear fast asleep, but we soon awoke & hastily packed up our things & prepared to leave. It sounded worse than the storming of Fort Sanders at Knoxville.

We are in the timber just behind the troops who are in the breastworks & it is quite common for a bullet or a piece of a shell to come amongst us. Yesterday a bullet passed between me & Genl. Butterfield as I was within a few feet of him—the day before a large price of a shell came down near where I was writing for the General. I dodged a little & went on with my work.

We have made no impression on the enemy at this point yet. The musketry has been rather quiet; but is now waking up. We may have another attack tonight.

I had a severe cholic and diarrhea this morning from eating fresh beef. I hope to be better tomorrow.

We are about 30 miles from Atlanta. Our regt tho'—it has done as well as any has; not lost but a few. The Dwight Co. only [had] a few slightly wounded. They have been very fortunate.

I have very little to do. My knapsack is always carried & I frequently ride in the ambulance. Our rations were stolen the other night & at present we are living on what we can catch. A man called Dan generally looks out for me in such cases.[28] You know I am a poor provider for myself.

When we have taken Atlanta (if we do take it) the campaign for the summer will be over. I don't like this field work.

I boiled my shirts & washed them yesterday. The color came out. I have lost my toothbrush; I wish I had another.

We expect a mail tomorrow. I hope to hear from you & will write again by the return mail. Please send me some more postage stamps & a few envelopes.

The guns are continually popping away averaging nearly one in a second about 3/4 of a mile from where I am writing.

The mail will close in a few minutes & I must close too.

I hope you have got your new teeth and that they are well adapted & suit you.

I send my respects to Mr. & Mrs. Hetzel, Mr. & Mrs. Young & all inquiring friends.

I send my love to you & the dear children. Kiss them all for me.

I saw Capt. Kise a few days ago. He is now Major of the 120th

Indiana Regt & on the staff of Genl. Hovey who relieved Gen. Judah. I also saw Montgomery & several others of the 23rd Corps. They look war-worn & weary—some of them.

The weather continues quite hot.

Your affectionate & faithful husband,

WmHBradbury

I hope you will keep your girl—

Nr. Ackworth, Georgia
June 12th, 1864
My dear wife,

We have been staying here several days waiting for our supply train. It has rained every day since the 3rd of 4th of this month and between the showers the sun has been very hot. It is raining very fast while I write. Everything we have is wet and damp; but we manage to make fires & cook our coffee & bacon or beef. We have just had some very good beef soup for dinner today. We steep crackers in it and it tastes first rate.

The roads are now so very bad that we shall be compelled to march slowly if at all. Our position is well fortified with a breastwork of logs and earth.

I wrote to you three or four days ago in answer to yours of the 29th May. I expect the mail just arrived has a letter for me from you.

I have stopped writing for the *Tribune* as they did not print my latter productions and it is difficult in my position to find out what is really going on. If they pay me according to what I have written, they owe me $50 at least.

I hope to get another & a better place than this when we reach Atlanta. The mail has just been distributed and I did *not* get any letter from you. I got a tri-weekly *Chicago Tribune* of the 1st June (Daily of the 31st May) which contained a short letter from me. This is the only one I have seen with the exception of *two short ones* since the 1st May. Perhaps I may write again if I have anything worth sending.

I have written at least 12 letters since we left Lookout Valley. They owe me for April and May which cannot be less than $50.

It is raining, raining, raining all the time. My blanket and everything I *have* is wet & damp. I shall have a damp bed tonight. I am perfectly disgusted with the weather. We shall soon be covered with mud.

There has been some little fighting this afternoon. We shall probably stay here some little time. The roads are awful.

June 13th—It is still raining and everything looks wretched tho' there is skirmishing going on in front.

Head Quarters 3rd Div. 20th Corps
In front of Marietta, Ga.
July 7, 1864
My dear wife,

I received yesterday your letter of the 28th June. I wrote you on the 29th in answer to your enclosing one from the *Tribune* office. Before you get this you will have seen my three letters of the 24th, 26th & 29th June which (*if they print them*) will appear between the 1st & 10th July. These with another letter of mine, which appeared on the 22nd June ought to entitle me to $25 more which they will send you. I shall probably write to them again if I can obtain any news worth sending. The officers are perfectly willing to give me all the assistance they can.

Genl. Butterfield is home on sick leave. He would have taken me with him if he could. It is supposed by many that Genl. B will never come back here.

I have applied to Major Thruston[29] of the Department of the Cumberland and Judge Advocate on Courts Martial for a clerkship with him. I was very strongly commended by Col. Benj. Harrison & Captain Speed & Captain Thomson. I have received no answer yet. He is perhaps in Chattanooga. If I get this place, I shall be sure of $12 a month extra and very likely a great deal more. If I don't get it, I shall get a place at the Corps where I shall have far more opportunities of knowing what is going on so that I can make my letters of more interest to the *Tribune.* Other correspondents have horses & are on familiar terms with the generals & officers from whom they get everything they want. They receive salaries of $100 to $200 per month. My chance is poor compared with theirs.

We are now encamped in a grove 10 or 12 miles from Atlanta which can be seen from some of the adjacent hills. It is a very large

Professor Mary A. Grant, University of Kansas, granddaughter of William H. and Mary Bradbury, circa 1920. Courtesy of the Spencer Research Library, University of Kansas.

Mary Brown Bradbury with her daughter Jane, circa 1856. Courtesy of the Spencer Research Library, University of Kansas.

Jane with a doll or baby brother. Courtesy of the Spencer Research Library, University of Kansas.

Private William H. Bradbury with one of his children, probably Charles, circa 1865. Courtesy of the Spencer Research Library, University of Kansas.

William H. Bradbury, circa 1880. From *History of Dwight, Illinois.*

Charles T. Bradbury. Courtesy o the Spencer Research Library University of Kansas.

Charles Bradbury's home, Riversvale Hall, Ashton-under-Lyne, England, circa 1890. Courtesy of the Spencer Research Library, University of Kansas.

Captain William H. Bailhache. Courtesy of the Richard K. Tibbals Collection, the U.S. Army Military Institute.

General Julius White. Courtesy of the U.S. Army Military History Institute.

General Benjamin Harrison, formerly colonel of the 70th Indiana Infantry. Courtesy of the U.S. Army Military Institute.

Captain and AQM Samuel H. Lunt. Courtesy of the U.S. Army Military History Institute.

Captain Gates P. Thruston. Courtesy of the U.S. Army Military History Institute.

Brigadier General Henry Case, 129th Illinois Cavalry. Courtesy of Picture History.

Major General Daniel Butterfield. Courtesy of the U.S. Army Military History Institute.

Lieutenant Joseph F. Culver, 129th Illinois Infantry. Courtesy of his grandson, John C. Culver.

Colonel Marshall W. Chapin, 23rd Michgan Infantry, formerly Co. I, 4th Michigan Infantry. Courtesy of the Dave Ramsey Collection, the U.S. Army Military History Institute.

Parson William G. Brownlow. L.C. Hand, photographer. Courtesy of the McClung Collection, East Tennessee Historical Center.

U.S. Internal Revenue Stamp for Duponco's Golden Periodical Pills, a patent medicine. Grant-Bradbury Collection, Spencer Research Library, University of Kansas.

Illustration of Champ Ferguson and his guard from *Harper's Weekly*, September 23, 1865. Courtesy of Prints Old and Rare.

Colonel William Jackson Palmer, PA 15th Cavalry, formerly Captain, PA Independent Cavalry. Courtesy of the Jackson C. Thode Collection, the U.S. Army Military History Institute.

place. We are still on this side of the river. The country is nearly all covered with timber & tho we have some shade, the breezes are nearly shut out by the woods. It is hot now every day. We get our mail from Marietta—8 miles north of us.

There are no military movements going on at present. The whole army appears to be resting. Detachments are cutting roads to enable the various commands to get out on the main roads when we move again.

I wish you would keep the girl until you hear from me again. The weather must be very tiresome for you. If you get the other $25, you can surely afford to keep the girl awhile longer. I have about $150 coming to me this summer which was due 1st of this month.

I should think you had work enough without sewing for anybody.[30] I would not do it. If you have milk enough for the family, I would not buy another cow at present, but you know the circumstances better than I. There would be no harm in waiting a few weeks.

My health is just middling. I feel weak & languid. Hard tack & bacon & hot coffee is not the food this climate requires. I gather blackberries & huckleberries, and English bilberries or whinberries. I have nothing at all to do just now. I send my respect to all inquiring friends & Wm Bartholic.[31]

I send my best love to you & the children.

Your afft husb.

WmHBradbury

Headquarters Second [crossed out] Third Division, Eleventh [crossed out] 20th Army Corps Ordnance Office
Near Atlanta, Georgia
July 11th 1864
My dear daughter,

It is very hot this afternoon and as I had not much to do I thought I would write to you. We are now near the banks of the Chattahoochee River and about ten miles from Atlanta. We have been here several days—almost a week. I and several other soldiers sleep under a large tent which is open at each end. The country is all covered with trees which are very pleasant as a shade from heat of the sun. I go out picking blackberries sometimes. These are getting ripe every day and are very good to eat, especially with sugar; but we don't get sugar for that purpose. I had some very nice string beans for dinner today. I saw in the woods a few days ago a very singular plant which shrinks up its leaves when you touch them—as much as to say—"don't touch me!" It is called the "sensitive plant."[32] I suppose you have read of it in your books. I also got a sprig of acacia which has a beautiful flower like golden hair tipped with red, and very pretty green leaves.

You can tell Freddy and Willie that I saw a big spider two inches long. If it bites anybody it is dangerous. We see lizards every day. They are about six inches long and live about old logs where they feed upon insects. They don't harm anybody. I have not seen a snake yet. I saw some lizard's eggs the other day. These eggs make young lizards.

We have flies and ants and mosquitoes, but as we live outdoors in the woods, we see more of these things than if we lived in the house.

The ground is yellow & the roads also. The woods are green and the sky is blue; and these three colors are all we see.

I wish you and Freddy and Willie and the twins were here for a few days to gather blackberries and huckleberries. There are plenty of them.

I get the Chicago papers two or three times a week. On the 4th July there was a letter from me, date of June 26th. There should be one of the 24th & one for the 29th.

There are lots of men and horses and big guns which make an awful noise; and the men shout and run with fixed bayonets and the bullets fly all around sometimes. Everything is very quiet now and the rebels are across the river.

I should like to receive a letter from you, in which you must tell me what books you are reading and how you get on with your writing. I should like to know what Freddy and Willie are studying and to see Freddy's writing.

You must tell Mother that I soon expect to have some good news to tell her. I received her letter of the 28th June & answered it on the day after I got it.

Gen. Butterfield is gone home, and I have scarcely anything to do. Tell Mother to send me a common needle & both kinds of thread. Send my love to Mother and you and Freddy & Willie and the twins and kisses for every one of you.

We get a mail every day.

Your affectionate father,

WmHBradbury

Near Atlanta, Ga
July 19th 1864
My dear wife,

I received your letter of the 5th July enclosing postage stamps for which I am obliged. I also received a few days previous tooth brush & envelopes which will be very useful.

I received two letters from the editors of the *Tribune* acknowledging that they had credited some of my letters to the wrong man. The mistake will be rectified & you will receive (or have received before this) $20 up to July 3rd. Several of my letters were delayed & arrived too late to be of any service. They wish me to continue my correspondence. I shall do so. I sent about a column this morning—speaking of crossing the river, marching by moonlight, &c It should appear about the time you get this.

I hope you & the Barstows had a good time at John's. I am afraid that Timothy seed[33] on the farm will not amount to much this year owing to the drought.

I think I would not buy another cow. Keep the girl. You must consider the price of hay. I wish you to make yourself comfortable and easy and not work hard. I can surely let you have $35 a month and Uncle Sam owes me nearly nine month's pay which with my other due will make upwards of $160 due 1st August every cent of which I expect to get. I shall send you $150.

I have heard nothing yet from my application for a better position. I have influential friends and strong recommendations, but clerks are not much needed in an active campaign. Wait till we take Atlanta. There will be no more hard fighting at present.

I hope your eyes are better and general health also. I am very well myself. The weather has been cooler. Yesterday was quite pleasant.

I wrote to Frederic on the 29th. I have heard nothing from him. Nor have I heard from Charles.

I have been studying phonography lately. I have borrowed a book for advanced students. I intend to practice it when the war is over. My abilities in certain directions are pretty well known and I feel that I can get employment anywhere in my line of business when the war is over. Capt. Bailhache would give me $100 per month.

I feel pretty sure that this Fall will enable us to see when the war is going to end. The executions [command activities] of Grant &

Sherman & the presidential elections will tell something definite & enable us to form a correct opinion.

I am sorry Willie's face is breaking out. You must make the children wash themselves often & take plenty of exercise & not give them too much animal food.

I wrote to Jane a few days ago. I would send her a specimen of the sensitive plant if it would not spoil. It is now in flower. There is plenty where I am writing under a tree also a few whinberries or bilberries.

I should very much like to see you & the children especially the twins. I hope Eddie is better. He was too forward at first. I should like to know how Jane and Freddy are progressing at school. I suppose Jane will write pretty soon. Is Willie in the First Reader? How is "little" Doc? And George Flagler?[34]

You must of course draw on Hetzel's. You can't live on nothing these times. Now don't be *stingy*.

We get a mail from the North every day—one goes out every day. This will go tomorrow morning.

We are within a few miles of Atlanta and moving down upon it from the North. Our corps staid in camp all day yesterday.

I have a small quinzy[35] or obstruction in my throat which is very unpleasant. The weather is fine & not very hot. We are encamped in a very nice place. We have not received any marching orders yet this morning (the 20th July).

I send my best love to you & all the children & respects to Mrs. Barstowe.

I hope to receive a letter from you every mail.
Your affectionate husband
WmHBradbury

Head Quarters Department of the Cumberland
Chattanooga
July 27th, 1864
My dear wife,

I wrote to you next day after I received your letter of the 5th July. I have sent within the last seven days *four* letters to the *Chicago Tribune*—one map and one long list of wounded. They now owe me for five letters—$25 at least.

You will perceive from the heading of this that I am at Chattanooga.

I obtained the position I have been seeking so long and am now with the Judge Advocate on Gen. Thomas' staff. I get 40 cents a day or $12 a month extra and 40 cents a day in place of rations which will enable me to get wholesome & comfortable board. I have a good place to sleep in the office. I think I shall be as comfortable as I was at Bowling Green and out of reach of those pesky guns.[36]

My last letter to the *Tribune* was dated Vining's Station on the Chattahoochie River July 26. The previous ones were 19th, 21st & 23rd. I shall still write occasionally to the *Tribune* perhaps three or four times a month.

I enclose your letters which I received from Chicago in answer to my letter to them. You ought to have received $20 from them about the 7th or 8th of this month. I have not heard a word from you since yours of the 5th July which I got about the 16th or 17th. I have diverted the Post Master of our Division to forward my letters to my present address at Chattanooga. If you can send me any *Chicago Tribune* containing my letters I should be glad.

The express runs to this place and there will be no difficulty in sending me a package containing preserved milk &c. I should be glad if you would send me a quart or upwards. It should be securely packed. John Hetzel can tell you how.

I shall probably stay here a month when I shall again go to the front. I wish you would send me about $5. I have not got a cent until I receive my regimental pay in a short time now.

There will be no difficulty in getting a furlough this fall. I shall apply for one in October or November. This letter will reach you on 3rd July. It will leave here tomorrow afternoon. Please notice what day you get it.

I don't think I would buy another cow. You have plenty of work and hay and feed will be very scarce. If you could keep the girl and preserve a quantity of milk for winters' use I think you would do well.

I will write again to Jane and Freddy when I hear from them. It will take only about 4 or 5 days for letters to go between us.

I received the tooth brush & everything else you sent. I think if I had staid much longer at the front I should have had the scurvy or some skin disease.

I hope the children are better. I send my best love to them & you.

I will write again when I hear from you.

Your afft. husbd.

WmHBradbury

9

"Let It Go to Thunder!"

August 12, 1864–September 20, 1864

Annoyed with Mary and itchy with poison ivy, William wrote some angry letters home in the late summer of 1864. Mary could not or would not keep up with his requests that she mail him the newspaper clippings of his articles. He also was unable to enforce his business affairs. As Bradbury had time on his hands and was more comfortably situated in Atlanta, he seemed to have plenty of time to assess everyone's performance—his tenants', his lawyers', his brother-in-law's, and, of course, Mary's.

The high command issued an order that may have been initiated by Private Bradbury in response to another frustration—his own colicky stomach: "By order of General Butterfield, of this date, company cooks are to be detailed, and fresh meat is to be boiled instead of fried or broiled."[1]

However, frustration could not begin to describe the plight of the citizens of Atlanta who had been ordered to leave their homes. Private Bradbury, a scholar of protocol, knew that Union General William T. Sherman and Confederate General John Bell Hood[2] were having a secondary battle on the very subject. General Hood complained to General Sherman:

> You order into exile the whole population of a city; drive men, women, and children from their homes at the point of the bayonet under the plea that it is . . . an act of "kindness to these families of Atlanta." I characterize what you call a kindness as being real cruelty.[3]

General Hood's dispatch to General Sherman would only be flung back at him later that day with the following response:

> War is cruelty, and you cannot refine it; and those who brought war into our country deserve all the curses and maledictions a people can pour out. . . . You might as well appeal against the thunderstorm as against these terrible hardships of war.[4]

General Sherman intended not only to occupy and subjugate Atlanta; he intended to see to it that the many vestiges of its civilization were scattered to the wind.

Private Bradbury would see and mention the long trail of wagons and people leaving the city on foot. Of immediate concern to Bradbury was not any twinge of conscience over the diaspora of the people of Atlanta, a tragedy that would preoccupy generations of Georgians; he was more bothered with a bug trapped in his ear.

Office of Judge Advocate
Hd Qrs Dept Cumberland
Chattanooga
Aug. 12, 1864
My dearest wife,

I received your short note of the 2nd inst the other day. The coat, shirt & socks came safely to hand yesterday—so did the can of milk which we tried last evening. It was all right. Did you buy it or make it yourself? I was disappointed in not getting a letter. I have heard nothing from home for a very long time except that short note of the 2nd. No letter has yet reached me from my former address at the third division tho' I have written twice to the Post master with the army.

I am glad that you are all well. I hope to hear more particularly by next mail. I received the book and pencils from Fredk. I shall write him this week. I also received the $5 from you. I thank you for all the things you sent me. The coat fits very well. I like the color and style. It looks like one John Hetzel once had. I want a needle and thread of both colors. I wrote for them before. They may be now on the way.

It is really provoking that I have such difficulty in finding out whether the Tribune Co. prints my letters or not. I always either leave the signature blank at the end or sign with a star (*). It matters little—I shall not be likely to write any more at present. "Guy" is another correspondent.

I have just heard from Capt. Bailhache. He says he sent you $25 on the 8th July. I have received no notice of it from you. The Tribune Co. still owe me for four letters if they have printed them, and a long list of wounded from north-western regiments in the 20th Corps. I also sent them a map showing Atlanta & vicinity & the battle ground of the 20th July. I send another map to Capt. Bailhache today. If the *Tribune* won't give $5 for it Capt. B will keep it. It shows the Rebel Fortifications at Atlanta & our troops on the outside, giving the numbers of the Corps.

There is no Chicago newspaper to be got here. One of my letters contained the new rebel general's address to his troops. You never did send me one of my letters and I suppose you never *will*. You need not look any more. Let it go to thunder.[5]

Where did you get the Phonographic wafer?[6] The motto is—"Speak every man truth of his neighbor." I must teach Jane Phonography when the war is over. As soon as I receive her letter I shall answer it and send her some capital letters which I promised her. I hope she will improve and make as good a writer as she is a speller. I should like to hear about Freddy and Willie. I think of them very often. I hope they are good boys.

I have a very pleasant place here and my health is getting to be very good. I shall take some exercise when the weather becomes cooler. The last evening was the hottest we have had lately. It rains heavily nearly every day.

The prospects of a speedy close of the war I don't think very good. Both Grant and Sherman soon to have their hands full. Every thing seems at a stand still as far as important results are concerned. I rather think we shall have to stay out our time. A great many Regiments [will] be mustered out this Summer and Fall.

The presidential campaign will show which way the winds blows as regards peace. I sleep soundly every night almost on the bare boards raised from the floor so as to make a bunk. The windows are always open night and day. The Chief Clerk and the Postmaster of the Anderson Cavalry sleep on the floor in the same room. Our boarding house is a short distance from the office. A little darky comes and tells when the meals are ready. We have coffee in a morning—generally nothing but water at dinner and supper. We get plenty of apples.

The Chief Clerk is a watchmaker. He practices his trade in his leisure hours & makes lots of money—from $5 to $20 a day sometimes. He is a very amusing fellow and can imitate the various caterwauling of cats. He is a very intelligent German. His time is out on the 20th September when I expect to take charge of the whole office myself.

I write again when I hear from you.

I send my best love to you & the children.

Your affectionate husband,

WmHBradbury

You must send me a few envelopes. They cost 10 cents for *four* here.

Office of Judge Advocate
Chattanooga, Tenn
Aug 25, 1864
My dear wife,

I have just received your letter of the 18th inst. I have never been able to hear anything of the *two* or *three* that miscarried. I have written to the Post master at Nashville on the subject as letters *from* the Army to Chattanooga frequently go through to Nashville, *first* where they are distributed & sent back here.

I wrote you acknowledging the receipt of the thing. I also wrote you and Jane a few days ago. The affairs on the Farm are turning out just as I thought they would. *We must have nothing to do* with Petzer.[7] Aaron Harford is the man we deal with. I will write him a letter & forward it to you next time I write. I have not received Kenyon's letter which he was going to send me.

I feel disposed to take the $350 & call it about 84 bushels of grass seed or *one bushel and a peck to the acre!* rather than have an expensive and doubtful lawsuit. If I were at home it would be quite different. I must confess I have little faith in Kenyon's *making* Harford do this, that, and the other. He did not do anything with Keyt beyond collecting the amount of the mortgage—$4 a bushel seems a big price but remember it is only equal to about $1.60 per bushel *in gold.*

I think Aaron [Harford] ought to deliver as much seed to the acre as the same quality of land produces this year in the neighborhood. I would be quite content with *three bushels* to the acre or 240 bushels altogether. It is not our fault that the land is weedy. It has been in Timothy [seed} *two years.* It ought to produce something now.

How would it be to let your brother do the business if he would or could spare the time. I should prefer to have the matter arbitrated in Morris and let John[8] state the case on our side and Baron could state the case on his side and thus avoid a lawsuit. Suppose you send John this letter. If John could arrange this arbitration I think it would be the best way. He could pick one arbitrator and Baron another. Both could pick a third and a majority of the three could decide. We should have had some seed last year but did not get any.

The arbitrators would require to be paid. I think you had better let Aaron have the timber land as it is not likely that anybody else will buy it, tho' I hate to let it go at the price equal to about $75 in gold or $4 an acre!

I will wait to hear from you again before I say anything more about the grass seed.

There is no satisfaction attending any of our arrangements about business matters. How is it! Is it our fault? Or is it the dishonesty of others? We cannot make any bargain *stick.* I shall be out of the service when the next payment is due and will give it my *best attention* at that time.

Unless Petzer has made considerable improvements on the place he might find it to his interest to throw up the agreement with Harford, and we might perhaps have the place on our hands again. Until I hear again from you and Aaron Harford, I shall not decide.

I enclose receipt which you *must not alter or add anything to.*[9] You can give it to Aaron or Petzer when you get the money or the seed. If you get the money, find out how much seed that will amount to at the market price & insert the number of bushels.

The giving of this receipt will not invalidate our claim for since than the amount stated, unless you insert "full." Suppose you get Mr. Hetzel to drive you over to Morris and meet John there and state the case and leave the agreement with him and let him do the best he can. I have more confidence in him than in Kenyon. I will pay him well for his time. He can consult a lawyer in Morris. I will leave the matter to you and him. In the mean time take what seed or money is offered on account of this year's payments.

I am making another sketch which I shall send to you as soon as complete.

It is reported that we shall make a grand attack on Atlanta today. Something will be done very soon. I hope to receive another letter from you in a few days upon which I will write again.

I send my love to you & the children also to brother John & Ann & their children.

I am your affect husband

WmHBradbury

Always consider *money* paid as so much *seed* at the market price.

Office of Judge Advocate Dept
Chattanooga August 31, 1864
My dear wife,

I received your letter of the 25th Aug yesterday (enclosing Photographic cartes of brother Charles and his family). I also received two letters of old dates which have been so long on the road. In one there were the needle and thread which I had been expecting and for which I thank you. There is still one letter missing which contains the one from Charles.

One of your letters spoke of John being very busy & all, a muddle as usual. In this case he will have no time to attend to our business on the farm and I should dislike to trouble him with it. Perhaps you had better see Mr. Strong and let him do the best he can without bringing on a lawsuit. The receipt for the Timothy seed which I sent you will be all that will be required to be signed on my part unless it should be arbitrated when I should have to sign an agreement of reference. I am afraid Kenyon would make a great *blow* and accomplish nothing.

Is the $350 that Petzer proposes to pay, the product of the whole 160 acres or only of the 80 acres? We are getting nothing but just a *rent* for the place instead of a payment on account of the purchase money. I have received no letter from Kenyon. You must exercise your own judgment somewhat and get the best payment you can. I think three bushels to the acre a very low yield; but *two* bushels is better than *one.*

You can send me another can of condensed milk as soon as convenient also some green tea—about three or four ounces. I have been & still am sick with headache and diarrhea and chills. I had to get up five or six times last night. I also suffer from colic.

I received Jane's composition. I think the *composition* is pretty good; but the writing is not very nice. She always makes capital "W" instead of a small "w." I will correct it next time. With regard to the select school, it depends upon the teacher. I thought Jane was doing very well at the public school. If you think it will be to her advantage to go to a select school, let her go. Who is the Teacher?

You must excuse me writing a long letter this time. I am scarcely able to hold up my head.

I presume by this time you have received another payment from the Tribune office. I understand that my letters appeared tho' I did not see them myself. I wrote to Capt. Bailhache & the Tribune Co. on the subject.

It runs in my mind that we have received altogether from the Tribune Co about $150 and the amount now due will make $175.

I have had some trouble with my descriptive roll. Captain Walkley refused to furnish one and I had to [present] the old one. I made a statement of the whole fact in this case and an order was issued from Department Head Quarters directing him to furnish it. It is here now and I expect to get my pay in the fore part of this month.

You can read to Mr. James Strong such parts of my letters as have reference to the farm, from which he will be able to gather what my ideas & views are.

I send my best love to you and the children and
Remain your ever faithful
& affectionate husband,
WmHBradbury

Do you remember the contents of Charles' letter?

[The following was crossed out, but was still legible.]

He did not do anything with Keyt beyond collecting the amount of the mortgage. I think Aaron ought to pay or deliver as much seed per acre as land of the same quality generally.

The 1st of September 1864
[continuation of a letter to Jane; the earlier part is missing]

You must be a good girl and do as Mother and the teacher tell you. I think a workbox would be a very nice thing to have so that you can take care of your little things. This reminds me that I want a needle and thread myself.

How much will a little box cost?

I am glad you wrote to Uncle Frederic. I suppose you told him all about your studies.

I received Freddy's and Willie's letters. I did not think they could write so well. I am glad Freddy is making so much progress. I should like to see him when the chickens come out of the shell.

I suppose you don't have much trouble now with the babies. They can both walk I think and Willie takes care of them a good deal.

I have now written you a long letter. You must write to me again. Could you write to me twice every month; do you think, or once?

I remain,
Your affectionate father,
WmHBradbury

Chattanooga, Tenn.
Sept. 10, 1864
My dearest wife,

I have just received your letter of August 27th also the envelopes for which I thank you.

The only letters now missing are yours of the 9th enclosing one from Charles and one from Kenyon. I have seen nothing of either of them. Yours of today contained a photograph of what I suppose to be Charles' oldest daughter and her aunt—Mrs. W.H. Sutcliffe. They are all very well executed. I have now the cartes of Charles, his wife and family. I send them back to you. You should buy a photographic album of the right size and place them in for safe keeping. They will be safer with you than me.

A great change will be made in our arrangement owing to the capture of Atlanta. Nearly all the staff departments heretofore quartered here have been ordered to proceed to that city. It was supposed that we should remain; but we received "*marching orders*" this evening. We shall have our stay until the arrival of Major Thruston who will be here tomorrow.[10] It is understood that the army will take a months rest and then commence the Fall campaign.

I wrote you two letters giving you my views on the farm. I can only add; get the $350 from Petzer or Harford and as much more as you can and employ Strong or Kenyon but avoid a lawsuit. I did not think it worthwhile to write to Aaron. I sent you a receipt for the Timothy seed in my last letter. I should be willing to give Kenyon 5 per cent over all he could collect above the $350 which you said Petzer was willing to pay. I will write about the Kansas taxes and attend the payment as soon as I hear what they are & get the money.

I have found the drawing or sketch of the view from our window. It is almost an exact copy of the scene and is considered by good judges to be well exacted. I shall send it to you perhaps next mail. You must get it framed and hang it some where. I took a great deal if pains with it and worked patiently for a long time upon it.

You say nothing about any payment from the *Tribune* the month of July. I sent them *four* letters since last settlement (July 8th) and two short ones in August making five full letters for what (if they printed them) they owe me at least $25.

If you have received this money, I wish you would send me $5 for I have not obtained any regimental pay or extra duty pay either. The Government owes me 10 months pay and upwards of $200 altogether.

My health is good with the exception of an intolerable itching caused by little watery tumors on the hand & various parts of the body. I have taken sulfur and cream of tartar as prescribed without much benefit.[11]

I shall be very glad when I can send you $20 by express. I wish you to enjoy yourself & take comfort with what I can send you. It will be pleasant to me to hear that you are comfortable. I am now in the last year of my term and have every prospect of a good, pleasant time until next summer.

I suppose the only advantage attending the select school to which Jane now goes is the improved society—that is to say—it is more *select*. It will be better for her on that account, but the training may not be quite so good.

With the great depreciation of paper money every thing is and will be high in price. You should lay in a supply of coals sufficient to serve until January or February next. If the Fall should be wet, coal will be very high. Do you get the rent regularly for the house?

I am sorry Charles' letter miscarried. I should have liked to answer it. The road is again in running order and I hope our letters will be no more delayed. A big mail came in today. It is not yet all sorted. I hope to receive another letter from you tomorrow. I cannot find the photograph of Charles' wife.

I have heard nothing else from Frederic, tho' I wrote to him about two weeks ago. I will write to you in the future once every five days unless something extraordinary happens. I will find something to say. We have not received a newspaper from the North in nearly 10 days! None came in today.

There are great events ahead. In a few days more I may be in Atlanta. The old address will answer once more.

Well my best love to you and the children.

I am your affectionate husband,

WmHBradbury

I shall try hard for a furlough this Fall—

Atlanta, Georgia
September 16th 1864
My dear daughter,

I am now in this city which you can easily find on the map of Georgia. It is 128 miles by Railroad from Chattanooga in a South-easterly direction.

It is a very pretty place with plenty of nice white houses surrounded by evergreen trees and flowering bushes. The gardens are filled with flowers and vegetables.

There are scarcely any stores open now. The streets are very dry and dusty and have a bright yellow color. The fine houses are nearly all painted white and enclosed in railings or fences. The sky is bright and blue.

The rebel people and boys and girls are being moved out of town and wagon-loads of them and their furniture pass thro' the streets every day.

Do you write a copy every day? Who is your new teacher?

Your affect. father

WmHBradbury

Head Quarters Dept Cumberland
Office of Judge Advocate
Atlanta, Ga
Sept 16th 1864
My dear wife,

I received on the 14th your letter of the 4th Sept. I wrote to Kenyon yesterday stating that, if you have not made other arrangements, I should be willing to give him 10 per cent on all he could collect above $350—he to pay *all* expenses. I wrote to Kansas to know what this year's taxes were. I also wrote to the Chicago Tribune [Co.] requesting them to send you what was due since July 8th.

I have not yet received Kenyon's letter on the subject of the farm; nor have I received yours enclosing Charles.'

We arrived here early last Tuesday morning and are now settled in a pleasant office (formerly a private house) on Peach Tree Street close to Genl. Thomas Quarters.[12] I board with the old mess of the 3rd Division, 20th Corps. It is upwards of a mile from the office but the walk is beneficial as the weather is fine and dry. I was ever compelled to do this as I have not a cent of money to pay for my board elsewhere, or buy provisions from the commissary.

Talking about commissaries, I saw yesterday Mr. Webber formerly of Morris.[13] He is now a captain and C.S. or "commissary of subsistence." He will be assigned to some division or brigade in this dept.

I have not received any pay whatever; tho' we expect it every week. The commutations of rations or 40 cents a day is consumed in buying provisions. The 40 cents extra duty pay we have not yet received—even for July—consequently I am hard up. The paymasters are here and the army is in course of being paid; but owing to a delay in my descriptive list, I shall not get my regimental pay for at least two weeks.

My health is somewhat better than it was. The roof of my mouth is sore and I fancy I have some indications of scurvy.[14] The itching continues and last night some insect entered my ear. It is still in and I shall apply to the Medical Director. I understand sweet oil will have a good effect—it is very disagreeable. I was awakened the other night by it.

We get potatoes & onions where I board. I intend to get some pickles if possible. I can buy from the Commissary on my own order but alas, I have, at present, no money.

Major Thruston the Judge Advocate is gone to Louisville to his home. There are three of us in the office which makes the work light. Two hundred and fifty-six clerks are employed in the various offices of this Department of the Cumberland which is the largest, most important and best regulated in Sherman's whole army.

The 1st Brigade (in which is the 129th Ill.) will be here today from the river—about 6 miles in the rear. The rest of Thomas' Army of the Cumberland is camped in the neighborhood of the city. The 23rd Corps is to the left at Decatur. The Army of the Tenn. is away in front nearly 30 miles from this place. We shall most probably stay here thro the winter, tho the army will make another advance this Fall.

Considering the depreciated currency I don't think $7 a ton for coal and $6 a ton for hay very high. When you receive some money from me & the farm you will feel more at ease and perhaps feel disposed to hire a girl. You have too much work with two cows. In a few weeks more you might safely send me a little butter in a preserved milk can thro' the post office.

The weather is fine and sunny and the travel thro' the streets raises clouds of fine sandy dust. The nights are cool & musketoes abundant.

I sleep on the office floor and am serenaded by three of the musical insects every night. I shall write to Jane & Freddy and enclose in yours this afternoon.

Citizens are being removed out of town by the military authorities that they may be supported by the rebel government & not by us. Some go North where they will be obliged to earn all they get. We don't intend to feed anybody but our own army.

I send my best love to you & the children.

Your affect husband,

WmHBradbury

Atlanta, Ga
Sept 20th, 1864
My dear wife,

Your last letter of the 4th Sept. I received on the 14th. I wrote to you on the 15th enclosing a short letter to each of the children. I forwarded the photographs & drawing some time since from Chattanooga.

I am now pretty well situated in this city, tho' I have not yet drawn any pay. I still board with the Division Head Quarters which is distant from the office upwards of a mile. The walking is very fatiguing when the weather is hot. My health is improving tho' the itching continues and I have been troubled with a sore mouth and tongue and some symptoms of scurvy. I use castille soap to wash.

I am expecting the concentrated milk & the tea for which I wrote from Chattanooga. Hard tack & bacon and coffee is not exactly conducive to convalescence. I expect to get entirely well as soon as the weather becomes cool.

The 129th regiment is now quartered near town. Capt. Walkley is on the brigade staff as Inspector which relieves him from duty as captain of the company. Gilchrist is with the Division Pioneers and Chilcott has consequently command of the company.

Rebel citizens are being moved out of the city in great numbers with their household goods and furniture. Some go North by railroad to Chattanooga & Nashville—others to a place where the rebel authorities receive them—about 12 miles South of town. The people don't like it at all, and a very interesting correspondence has taken place on the subject between Genl. Sherman and Gen. Hood.

Prisoners are now being exchanged. 650 went by a day or two since for that purpose. They had come from Nashville. A place called "Rough and Ready" is where the lines meet and at this point Union & Rebel officers effect the removal of citizens and exchange of prisoners. An armistice of 10 days was arranged to facilitate these objects. It expires tomorrow night at 12 o'clock.

I have just made out my muster and pay rolls and have been promised my regimental pay next Thursday afternoon. I will send you a remittance the first opportunity afterwards.

There are plenty of flowers in the gardens and the shrubbery still looks very fresh and green, tho' the forest trees begin to show the touch of Autumn. I send Jane a small rose which I plucked this morning at Division Head Quarters.

I have heard nothing from Frederic tho' I wrote to him last. I have never yet received Charles' letter nor that sent by Kenyon some time ago respecting the farm. I did however receive one from him on another subject dated on Aug 19th and addressed to me at *Nashville* (!) Perhaps the lost letter was there addressed also.

Yesterday we had for dinner an excellent stew made out of what do you think? Can the children guess? Our Dutchman called it—

"*goat beef.*" It was the flesh of that animal & tasted like mutton. It was very good.

Next time I write I will send each of the children a letter. I have Jane's composition yet. I expect a letter from you tomorrow when I shall perhaps know which of the boys wears the "*pretty*" on his cap. You should make them a blue star of the enclosed pattern which may be worn on the cap or fastened on the left breast. It signifies 20th Corps (pronounced *core*), 3rd Division (red denotes 1st & white 2nd Division). The material can be silk or any other fabric & it can be trimmed lightly. They are sometimes made stiff and firm. You can make it a little smaller than the pattern.

When Jane writes she must tell me the name of her teacher and give some account of her school. I suppose Freddy is still in the *second* reader or *third* which is it? It is time he began to make figures and add up sums. What does Willie read in? First reader, I suppose.

We have had rainy weather lately and it threatens rain again this afternoon. The roads will become quite muddy—red clay and fine sand mixed with water.

A few furloughs have been granted but it is now stopped for the present. This is also the case with officers leaves of absence.

Another forward movement or an attack by the enemy or *something* of the kind is on that account expected. If I get furlough, it will not be before December.

I shall write you again on the 25th. I wish you would *send* me the address of Mr. Jones. Is it *Spring Grove* or what? I will write to him.

Please send a blue star a little smaller than this and a few pins.

I send my best love to you & the children.

Your affectionate husband,

WmHBradbury

Please send me three or four buttons for my shirts. The *red color* has all washed out.

10

"All I Live For"

September 22, 1864–November 24, 1864

With Private Bradbury's health languishing in Atlanta, he wrote more letters during the fall of 1864 to his children than to his wife. He may have felt that his survival was at stake because the letters contain more thoughtful remarks than usual. Explaining the practice of foraging from civilians was not necessary, but he tried to explain the concept to the children in the simple terms of "good" Union soldiers and "bad" Confederate soldiers.

Before too long, the men of General Sherman's army would commence the historic march to the sea and the 129th Illinois Infantry would be part of it. Captain Walkley, persistent in his efforts to retrieve Bradbury to Company B, was now a thorn permanently removed from his side. Walkley was assigned duty as Inspector General of the 1st Brigade of the 3rd division of the 20th Army Corps. Lt. Culver would leave for home on furlough, making the old regiment a mere shadow of its former self.

From the relative comfort of the piazza of an Atlanta home that officers had confiscated for their use, Bradbury worked intensely to secure a position with Captain Bailhache. The home's owners were likely refugees of Atlanta now on their way to an uncertain future.

Perhaps Bradbury experienced great stress while in Atlanta. He had never been so far away from his family. Deafening noise during the siege of Atlanta, his firsthand experiences near the front of battle, and no doubt fear itself may have created what might today be called post-traumatic stress. He also saw newly released survivors of Andersonville Prison, a prisoner-of-war camp for Union soldiers. Their pitiful conditions horrified comrades—and the rest of the country.[1]

While friends were leaving for unknown destinies and some of those fallen in the weeks before were now forming the rows of internees of a national cemetery, Bradbury seemed incongruously delighted by Atlanta's gardens. With a nearly surreal attention to detail, Bradbury wrote of the botanical specimens in this garden, evoking an image of a soldier-clerk cocooned in a brick house, with roses in bloom, a cow and a sheep at the rear of the landscape, while the city itself began to live again—but under Union occupation. In his earlier life, the image, without the war, might have been a vista from his old home in England.

Contending with continuing downpours and mud, a persistent skin rash, and all-around unhappiness with the state of business affairs back in Illinois, Bradbury did have some good news to cling to—the prospect of a furlough in December continued to look quite promising. And he cheerfully received news that he would join General Thomas's headquarters in Nashville, which would bring him miles closer to home. This encouraging news seemed to inspire the few bright moments in his letters home.

Rare as letters from Mary to William were, her Thanksgiving day letter was doubtlessly treasured. Using simple language, Mary provided a peek into the family's life, the children's academic progress, and how remorseful she felt about the poor outcome of business affairs left in her hands. While the survival of a dozen or so of her war-era writings would have constituted a treasure, the two that did survive—an earlier letter to Ann and the 1864 Thanksgiving letter to William—help us understand Mary's life of hard work, worry, and pure devotion.

While the *Tribune*'s need for his correspondence had waned, now that he was leaving General Sherman and Georgia, it did publish one of Bradbury's poems. He quoted from the Bible in "The Soldier's Grave."[2] Perhaps he was inspired by the number of his old comrades from the 129th Illinois Infantry who were killed during the Atlanta Campaign.[3] While it was on the surface just another of his many poems, this one had great staying power. "The Soldier's Grave" would appear again and again in publications and recitals throughout the rest of Bradbury's life.

"The Soldier's Grave"
Where Lookout Mountain lifts his head
To gaze on lonely Tennessee,
And Chickamauga's silver thread
Gleams midst the rugged scenery—
Where Dallas' woods grow green and brown

Beyond "Burnt Hickory's" fatal plain,
And Kenesaw's twin summits frown
O'er landscapes marred by battle-strain—
Where Oostenaula's streams arise
And Chatahoochie's waters lave
Bright banks where Georgia's beauty lies,
The red mound marks the Soldier's Grave.
Not there alone but far and wide,
From fair Virginia to the West,
Our heroes life-blood swelled the tide
Poured at the Nation's grand behest.
To them this monument is reared,
An emblem of their scattered graves;
Here let their memory be revered,
Here let us mourn our fallen braves!
These lovely blooms and emerald wreaths,
Bedewed with tears and fraught with sighs,
Are tributes which the heart bequeaths,
A sweet and sacred sacrifice.
The south wind's fragrance-laden breath
Bears odors from the Land of Flowers,
Where sleep our heroes calm beneath
Bright summer suns and vernal showers.
These floral offerings catch the scent,
And richer grows the rare perfume,
In fancy's thought, together blent,
They smell like flowers of heavenly bloom.
God heals the wounds of war-worn lands,
The battle-blights and scars of strife
Are gently covered by His hands
'Till scarred Earth glows with wanted life.
So doth He also heal our hearts
With hopes of Heaven beyond the tomb;
The "oil of joy" for grief imparts,
"Garments of praise" for robes of gloom.
"Beauty for ashes" shall be given,
And fairer flowers and brighter wreaths
Shall deck the patriot's brow in Heaven,
Where Peace the sword for ever sheaths.

Atlanta, Ga
September 22nd, 1864
My dear wife,

I received your letter of the 16th yesterday—only 5 days! Your letter written the Monday previous never reached me and I wrote again to the *Chicago Tribune.* I am glad you got the $20 tho' I expected $30.

My health is very much improved and I begin to feel as if I did not care for anything except of course you & the children.

Wilson is obliged to go out of the house on a months notice. We have nothing to do with what he *understood* unless there was a positive agreement that he should stay a year. I think you should make him get out & occupy it yourself; and if the butcher will stable your cows, you will do pretty well. One cow is quite enough.

I feel very sorry that you have so much hard work and dirty work and I am puzzling my brains to make some improvement. You might just as well have kept the girl thro' the hot weather & let Jane go to school. I expect to send you $200 by express on the 3rd of next month after which I shall send you at the rate of $25 a month being my whole earnings except $3 a month. I shall do this in the hope that you make yourself comfortable & don't work so hard.

I don't know what makes you low spirited unless your mind is too sensitive. That little miserable house of Lower's has something to do with it and sleeping with the window closed makes it worse. We never think of such a thing.

I feel at present hopeful and confident; tho my mind is more sensitive & my health & constitution are not so strong as yours. I have made a serious resolution to fight the battle of life bravely & not to give in at all. People are in general subject to the "blues" or low spirits in proportion to the fineness of their mental constitutions—the low condition of their health, the state of the atmosphere and other surrounding conditions, which depress the vital energies & act upon the brain by supplying it feebly & insufficiently with *good* blood. A walk or exercise in pure bracing air will nearly always cure it. A French physician said that remedy would "almost cure a guilty conscience."

The more vigorous vitality a person has, the less he is liable to these fits of depression. We should all cultivate cheerfulness, and take plenty of oxygen and a *full generous* edict when we work hard. I hope you will attend to the latter injunction.

Capt. Bailhache has at my request made an application to get me out of the service that I may be with him. I shall get it well endorsed and approved by several officers here & forward it. I have not much hopes of its success; but I thought it my duty to try to *secure* a good place so that I need not lose any time at the expiration of my term of service. I mean if possible to *make* money and *save* money, and I shall continue restless until I accomplish something.

These endeavors are prompted entirely by a determination to provide liberally for you & the children and I have a right to expect that you will *make use* of the small means I have already furnished. I want to see you well-housed, well-fed and well-clad. This is all I live for.

Our cook was drunk yesterday and today. I have had nothing but hard tack & coffee for breakfast & bread, molasses & coffee for dinner. Supper—I should get till next morning as it is raining most dreadfully and I have a mile to walk. A piece of hard tack is all I shall have. Now if I had that package of tea, I could make a little at the office (for several officers have their quarters & mess in the same house) & enjoy a warm supper. I am afraid a generous diet of juicy beef and rich puddings would scarcely agree with me at present.

Last evening I ate some cracker & pork fat, which tasted very well—but kept me awake about two hours in the night with a sickness & strong inclination to vomit. My stomach finally consented to *let it go that time* & I fell asleep. My bowels are very strict & have not allowed any thing to pass for several days. The guards in the city are not so strict as that. I have not drank a pint of liquor in two months. I have no taste for it, but I would like some Sasids ale.[4]

It is dark, rainy, gusty, evening. The trees close by our window bend & sway under their load of green leaves and the wind sounds with a pleasant melancholy rush like the breath of autumn, but it does not affect my spirits for in about an hour I shall receive from Major Stillman, the paymaster, \$182—45—Regimental pay & clothing allowance I don't now require the \$5 I wrote for, tho' I suppose it is on the road.

I shall write to you again in a few days when I will not forget to send each of the children a letter. I shall make Jane & Freddy each a drawing of our office & send Willie some little picture. I suppose they are all good.

This will leave Atlanta at 11 o'clock morning of Sept 23rd, 1864

[Letter fragment, probably September 23, 1864]

. . . I wrote to you on the 15th and 20th Sept. and should not have written again until the 25th, but I thought I had better answer your letter as it arrived in so short time.

There is a good deal of monotony here as regards our office. We have little to do and the other two clerks are preparing to go home and talk of a big *drunk.* No "drunk" for me. I get up off the floor about ½ past 6 or 7 in the morning & walk up to breakfast, write or read or trifle till noon when I take another walk to the 3rd Div. HdQrts—that is—if the weather permits. In the afternoon I attend to my duties & go to supper about six. It is dark when I get back.

Bedtime soon arrives and I seek my humble couch round which not angels exactly, but musquitoes hover & "keep watch o'er my lonely pillar" (*knapsack* I mean). I wake in the night & tumble about for two hours. In the morning another day has passed. My term of service is one day less—so, alas! is my life.

I forgot the itching and scratching. A curry comb and horse brush would save my fingernails. A red, bleeding sore is preferable to this abominable irritation. I wash with castile soap but—I could *t-t-t-t-e-a-r the skin off.* It is however a common complaint and I must shed *some* blood for my country.

The socks you sent me are about used up. I shall get a complete supply of clothing this week—blouse, pants, drawers, and socks. My present pants have been in use six months and are shabby. I have had clothing from home or I should not have $42 to receive on that account. I also bought some in Knoxville—shirts I mean & books. I have not received the milk yet. I like it spread on bread. Do you sell the milk & buy butter?

A large body of cavalry went forward to the front yesterday. It looks as if some other move was to be made. We heard today of Sheridan's victory in western Virginia. Many officers in high rank are going home on leaves of absence but this probably is not the case in the other corps. I am watching for the paymaster clerk before I can finish this long letter. I am writing on a round table with two candles burning & alone in the room (except mosquitoes & bugs).

We received today 300 more of our men who had been imprisoned in the South. They have been exchanged & ought to be sent home to recruit their wasted frames.

I have just got the money—$182.45—Bully for me! I bought yesterday a knife, fork, and plate & cup for $1.25.

I send my best love to you and the children. I have eaten my cracker & must now go to bed. Good night!

Your affect. & faithful husband,
WmHBradbury

Head-Quarters Department of the Cumberland
Atlanta, Ga
September 25th 1864
My dear son and daughter Freddy and Jane,

I wrote to both of you and also to Willie on the 20th of this month. I wrote to Mother at the same time. I also wrote to Mother on the 23rd. I have not heard anything from home since her letter of the 16th which I received on the 21st.

This is a very pretty city. There is a large depot and engine house in the center, here three railroads come together and the cars start at the same place in three different directions. There are plenty of large stores, but they are all either closed or used for government purposes.

The private houses are very handsome and are surrounded by gardens filled with beautiful trees, evergreens and flowering bushes and shrubs. I send a little rose for Jane.

Our office is in a very nice house in the midst of a garden. I am in the front room where the window sash opens down to the floor and we can walk out of the window on the piazza. I must send you each a little picture of it. We have a cow in the backyard but I don't get any of the milk. I use the concentrated milk which Mother sent me. I received it yesterday. It is very good. We had some boiled beef for dinner today and some good bread made in loaves as Mother makes it.

We don't have any table cloth and use tin plates which are sometimes rusty. How would Freddy like to eat from a rusty plate?

My fork has one leg broken off and my tin cup is a little rusty. But we don't mind these things at all. I have bought a regular white plate for my own use. I spread the preserved milk on my bread instead of butter.

The rebels have torn up the track near Marietta and there may be some delay in the mails. A great number of soldiers were swarming around the railroad stations today, ready to go out in the direction of the cars. I saw the cars full of soldiers and the tops of the cars were covered with them. They were going to protect the road between this place and Chattanooga. Between three and four thousand soldiers went out today. (Capt. Kise is Lieut. Colonel. I saw him yesterday.)

We have had a great deal of rain lately and it was very cold last night. I should like very much to receive a letter from both of you. Jane can write very well if she tries and it is time for Freddy to write a little. I send kisses for all of you. Can Freddy read this letter?

Your affectionate father
WmHBradbury

Atlanta
September 26, 1864
Dear little Willie,

You must tell Mother that I think of her every day and that I shall write to her again next Wednesday. It seems to me as if you were a big boy. Can you read this kind of writing [cursive handwriting]? If you can't, Freddy can.

We have two little dogs and a cat in our house.

I saw yesterday a man who used to play wicket near our house at Dwight. His name is "Campbell." We used to call him "Kentucky." He is now a Quartermaster. Jane will read you what I wrote to her and Freddy.

Are you in the first reader? Do you take care of the babes? You must teach Eddie and Elwood their letters. Be sure and be a good boy and help Mother and I will come home this winter if I can.

Goodbye, little chap.

How heavy are you? Kiss Mother and the twins for me.

Your Affectionate
Father

Head Quarters Dept. Cumberland
Office of Judge Advocate
Sept 28/64
My dear wife,

I wrote you on the 15th, 20th, and 23rd of this month and to Jane, Fred, Willie on the 25th—I also wrote to the children on the 15th or 20th I forget which. I have heard nothing from you since the 21st when I received yours of the 16th.

I have not much to say at present as my last letter was very long and contained almost everything. Major Thruston, the Judge Advocate, who has charge of this office, has come back. He says I am his chief reliance and he will get me a furlough when he goes home himself sometime this Winter. Another officer is coming here which will lighten the work and leave him more at liberty. The other two clerks will not leave till the latter end of October. I should consequently not be able to send you the money as soon as I expected, but if you should require it some I will send it all the way by express. The cost of [sending] $200 to Chicago will be $2.75.

My itching still continues. I have had to take Epsom Salts by advice of a surgeon. If the medicine reduces me much more I shall be very thin indeed for I am rather slender to begin with.[5] My health is otherwise tolerably good.

The Quartermaster who pays for extra duty services has not at present any funds. I have owing to me from this source $28 at the end of this month. If I don't get this, I shall not be able to send you as much as I intended. I can however send you $150 at *anytime.* Please state in your next if I shall send it to you. There is also $20 owing to me by a Captain in the Regiment.

Homer Kenyon has been reduced to the ranks in order that he might be detailed as clerk to Capt. Walkley who, as well as Lieut. Gilchrist, is on detached service having the company in charge of Chilcott. The company is now very small.

I find that everybody is looking after the easiest place and the most pay. I have heard nothing from Chicago in answer to my letter to the *Tribune* of the 13th.

Capt. Bailhache's application has been favorably endorsed by Capt. Walkley & is now before Col. Case. I wish you *not to say anything at all about it.* I don't hope much from it, tho' I feel it my duty to try and better my condition by every means for the sake of you & the children.

There is a rumor of an advance of the 20th Corps in about two weeks. Troops are continually on the move in some direction by railroad. The rebels don't seem to be doing much. The rebel citizens, chiefly women and children, have nearly gone & the vacant houses are occupied by soldiers & officers to a great extent. It is a terrible hardship on poor families who are thus driven from their home, many of them without the means of subsistence.

You will see the correspondence between Sherman & the Mayor of Atlanta in the papers. The army will undoubtedly advance this Fall or Winter, for our office will remain here.

As the rebel territory becomes smaller & smaller, their space for the growth of the means of subsistence becomes less and less, while the influx of refugees into the already crowded territory increases consumption of their stores and embarrasses all proceedings. If this course is pursued after the Capture of Richmond, the rebels will have to fight their way out or starve. Another year will certainly see the end of the struggle.

We have heard of Sheridan's great victories in western Virginia. We get the Chattanooga paper generally the day after its publication. Any exciting news is written on the bulletin board for the information of the public. We have of course plenty of rumors which cannot be traced to any reliable source. These are called "*grape-vines*" telegrams, in contra-distinction to the regular reports transmitted on the genuine wires. One of these is that Grant has entered Richmond with 30,000 men. Another is that President Lincoln is in correspondence with Jeff Davis on the subject of peace.

I learned from Capt. Kise, who is now Lieut. Col. of the 120th Regt. Indiana Vols., that Genl. Manson is at Knoxville in command of the District of East Tennessee. Genl. Judah is back somewhere in Kentucky.

I expect a letter from you tomorrow. But there is a rumor that the road is cut between Chattanooga & Nashville.

I send my best love to you & the children &
remain,
Your ever faithful & affectionate husband.
WmHBradbury

Headquarters Department of the Cumberland
Atlanta Georgia
Oct. 21st 1864
My dear son Frederick,

I thought you could read this better than the other kind of writing.[6]

There is nothing here that you would like; I cannot get another wreath at present. When I come home in December, which will soon be here, I will bring you all something pretty. So you must be good children. Jane will make you a star if you ask her nicely.

The rebels tore up the railroad track several times so that we could not get anything to eat from Chattanooga. Now was not that mean? But I'll tell you what we did. We sent out a great number of men and horses and eight hundred wagons and went to the farms and took lots of corn, and oats, and sweet potatoes, and sheep, and geese and chickens and little pigs and other things good to eat. That was very hard on the poor farmers, but they should not have let their General tear up our railroad. We must have something to eat. We have good dinners now every day.

The rebels shot a man that I knew and killed him and they took away several of our men and horses and mules. They burn out cars and did much mischief. We have sent out a lot of men after them.

I live in a little brick house with a garden before it. Roses and flowers are still in blooms, but the weather is getting cold. I sleep in the back room where I have a little bedstead made by myself and a fire.

Good bye, until I come home in six weeks when I will tell you plenty of nice tales.

Your affectionate father

I should like to hear from you and Jane. Can't you write a short letter some Saturday?

Atlanta, Ga
October 22nd 1864
My dear daughter,

I have written you two letters and have received no reply. A mail is expected today which I hope will contain one from Mother and one from you.

I told Mother to let you have the drawing I sent as your birthday present. There is nothing here worth sending except little pictures and I thought you would like a picture that I had drawn myself as well as any other.

When I come home in December, I will bring you something pretty. Would you like a book or what?

I have made a nice star out of the blue silk which Mother sent me. I return what is left and the thread. You can make Freddy and Willie one a-piece to be given to them if they are good boys.

I send two little paper stars which you can cover with blue silk for the twins. The stars on the card can be given to the other boys.

The weather is very cold this morning and the leaves are falling and the flowers fading. We shall soon have Winter. Still, the sky is bright and clear and everything looks beautiful.

I forgot to tell Freddy and Willie that we had a sheep tied to a tree in our yard. It eats grass we feed it corn. When it gets fat, we shall have some mutton.

You were eleven years old on the 6th of this month. I should have written you a letter, but the Rebels had torn up the railroad track. In a few more years, you will be a young woman. You must remember that "Youth is the time for improvement," and learn housework and to read well and other useful acquirements, because in a few more years you will not have the opportunity to go to school. I and Mother would like to see our daughter grow up into a neat and industrious young lady, well behaved and well trained. You are generally a good girl, and Father and Mother will love you so much if you become a well educated and well-bred young lady. Girls that behave prettily always look prettily.

I have just heard that a mail came in last night, but there were only a few letters. I am afraid I shall not get any.

I send my best love for you and Mother & your brothers and kisses for all of you.

Your affectionate father

William H. Bradbury

I have just received Mother's letter for the 13th October (enclosed Charles'), the long one she speaks of not arrived yet. I will write tomorrow.

Head-Quarters Department of the Cumberland
Atlanta
Saturday, Oct. 22, 1864
Dear little Willie,

Can you read Freddy's letter? I suppose you can very nearly. Can you read this, little chap?

We had for dinner yesterday roast goose, roast beef and sweet potatoes and onions. We don't have any table-cloth and no chairs. We sit on a board. Most of the soldiers shout "Hurrah for Lincoln and Union."

I suppose you are getting into a big boy and helping Mother and learning fast at school. Mother must tell me when she writes again if you can read this. Tell her to send me some postage stamps.

It is now bed-time and quite cold.

Good night! Be a good boy until I come in December.

Your Father

Atlanta, Ga
October 25th 1864
My dearest wife,

I received on the 23rd your letter of the 13th October containing one from Charles which I answered yesterday.

I wrote to all the children, except the twins of course, on the same day. The only letter now behind is the one which you wrote between, the 30th Sept. & the 13th Oct.

While I am disposed to regard your instructions about eating rare beef, using sulphur (which I do) &c I am glad to say that the necessity for it has nearly passed away. We get plenty of fresh vegetables—onions & potatoes, also fresh beef, and the eruptions are passing away.

Our foraging party, which went out with a large expedition having 40 wagons, brought at two different times from the country—12 bushels of yams and sweet potatoes and three sheep, about 200 pounds of fresh pork, a calf, a quantity of chickens, and several very tough geese.

I can get onions and molasses at the commissary. All these things go into our mess which consists of 13 men. We have a good cook & live very well.

Your other tea has not arrived. I hope you received the $150 which I sent by Gilchrist. I got the $5 & $1.

I hope you have received something satisfactory from Aaron Harford. But we will say nothing more about it until I reach home, which, if things go right, will be in the beginning of December.

I am very glad Charles has paid your brother John £10. We can now easily get out of debt in that quarter.

I wish you would write to James and I will write to him also or shall we defer it until I reach home.

In a few days more I shall have entire control of the office as the other clerks are already relieved & will soon be on their way home. We have a fire every day in the office and sometimes one at night in the adjoining room which we use as a sleeping apartment.

I have heard nothing from Kansas about the taxes. I wrote to Judge Safford some time ago on the subject.

The weather is very fine and the scenery looks beautiful and bright. We have had some cold nights, but no frost yet.

The rebels captured & burnt a railroad train of ours some time ago. Just lately they took nearly all the mules of the 1st (our Brigade) which was at the Chattahoochee River. The mules were out grazing, in charge of a few men who were also captured. That's of course a good joke on the first Brigade. The soldiers will for the present be obliged to haul the wagons themselves.

There is a strong rumor that our headquarters will go back to Chattanooga in which case this office will go too. An entire change of campaign seems about to take place. I think Northern Alabama instead of Georgia will be the scene of our future operations this Winter.

The first Brigade, in which is the 129th Illinois, has not yet been paid, tho' they are expecting it every day. There is now nearly 10 months due them. I have not yet received any extra duty pay whatever.

I am glad you enjoy the cool weather. I hope you & the children take all the air they can and get plenty of good nourishing food & warm clothing. You certainly have the means.

I don't know what more to say. I count the days which separate me from you & home. I also count the months which I shall have to serve when I get back to the army after my furlough. It will only be seven or eight & then! We will enjoy a better time than we ever had before.

I will get a clerkship with Capt. Bailhache if the war continues, or something else if it does not. I imagine there will [be] a demand for my services after the close of the war. At all events I am quite hopeful on the subject.

The rumor is now that we shall go back to Huntsville, Alabama & spend the Winter there. It will be considerable nearer home than Atlanta.

Sherman's Army, or a good portion of it, is now west of Rome. Gen. Beauregard ("Bo regard") is reported to be in command of the Rebels. We are not likely to penetrate south of Atlanta this Winter.

Please send me a few more postage stamps—five or six—I borrowed some from the Major.

Having no more to say at present, I will conclude by saying that my health is improving & that I send my best love to you & the dear little children. I mean to buy them something in Chicago as I come thro.'

I send Charles a very long letter such as he will be glad to get.

I am your affectionate & devoted husband

WmHBradbury

Head Quarters Department of the Cumberland
Chattanooga
Nov. 2nd 1864
My dearest wife,

We have just arrived at this place & have now got the office and furniture all straight. All the Staff Departments are here and will probably remain here thro' the winter.[7]

My health is very good with the exception of a cold caught while removing from Atlanta. I spent two nights in the cars & got but very little sleep.

We have again the same office from which I drew the sketch of Chattanooga &c. I board at the same place, that is, with the colored family with which I boarded previous to going to Atlanta. I am *all right* as regards board. I have a cot whereon to sleep & an overcoat & plenty of blankets so that I shall be quite comfortable thro' the winter.

I wrote you the 27th or 28th or some day near the end of Oct. None of your letters are behind. I received the one enclosing Charles' & a long one written on the 7th Oct.

It is difficult to get beef rarely cooked. I have used the sulphur & lard.

The itch (as some Doctors call it) has returned, but not as bad as before. Owing chiefly, I believe to the *full diet* (which agreed with me very well), I am strong & vigorous compared with my condition several weeks ago. We lived high on the captured property—fresh pork, chickens, geese, sweet potatoes & onions & plenty of them.

The 20th Corps, to which our Regt belongs, is in daily expectation of marching orders. They are still in the neighborhood of Atlanta. The rebels are all in Alabama & an entire change in the campaign is taking place. It is possible that we (that is Genl. Thomas' Head Quarters) may remove nearer Nashville for the better protection of the Tennessee River.

I am now the chief and only clerk in the office—the other two having left two or three days ago. If nothing happens contrary to our expectations Major Thruston will recommend that I have a furlough about the beginning of December. In that case the furlough is pretty sure.

The Tribune Co. now owe me for 4 letters (if they print them all). I shall write them again bye & bye & send in my bill—$20, which will come in useful for you. If I had not written them to *wake them up*, you would not have got the extra $10. I am anxious to know whether you got the $150 I sent Gilchrist on the 10th or 11th October.

You will excuse this short letter. I wish to catch the mail which leaves soon after 12 o'clock. I will write more fully when I hear from you. Your last letter was dated the 13th October.

I send my best love to you & the children.

Your affectionate husband,

WmHBradbury

I have plenty of envelopes but no stamps. I can buy stamps here I think.

Chattanooga, Tenn.
Nov. 6th, 1864
My dearest wife,

I have just received your letter of Nov 1st, which is the only one come to hand since the one dated 13th October.

I wrote to you about the 28th October from Atlanta and two days ago from Chattanooga. You have doubtless got them both by this time.

As you say nothing about the payment on the farm, I conclude that you have received nothing more from Petzer or Harford than the 24 bushels of seed or the warehouse receipt. You should sell it as soon as possible, the *price* always goes down, I believe (in the Fall and Winter).

If you have given no receipt, *don't give any.* It is not half a decent rent for the place. I sent you a farm or receipt signed by me. You never spoke of it. I don't know whether you got it or not. I shall not consider such a miserable payment as $80 a payment at all. If it is worthwhile to turn Petzer off the place or sue Harford for breach of contract, I shall do so. I will find out when I get home in December.

I thought Kenyon had signed to collect the money. You never mention him now. Never mind, I will attend to it when I get home. Harford cannot get a deed till the whole 1400 bushels are paid and if he does not pay a fair proportion every year I will not give him a deed at all. *Don't fret about it at all.*

I don't know of anything which will prevent my having a furlough about the 1st Dec. We shall have another clerk in a few days. At present I am the only one. We have another officer here who has first entered upon his duties. I fully expect to be able to leave here in about four weeks.

The itching has nearly all subsided. My general health is pretty good and I am getting strong and fat.

I am very glad to hear that you have all got such vigorous appetite. I will take good care that you have something to satisfy them. I have a strong opinion that gold will rise still more and that prices will become accordingly higher. You will take note of this & lay in a moderate supply [of coal].

I have received no extra duty pay yet but expect it certainly this month for August, Sept, & October—about $40. Also two months regimental pay $32; making $72. The Tribune Co. owes me for four *letters.* I have just written to them on the subject. I don't know whether they print them all or not. I am afraid they have not. I sent them seven verses of poetry yesterday I thought would appear on the 12th or 13th—it is signed WHB & called "The Soldiers Grave."

With what money we have on hand & what I earn from

different sources we shall have more than sufficient to last until next year at this time without depending on the farms at all.

I got the *dollar, five* dollars, *tea,* & postage, stamps. A can of preserved milk would be very acceptable. They sell at $1 here. You spoke of sending me some butter.

The weather is rainy & cold & the streets and roads very muddy. Gen. Thomas is expected here from Nashville. He will organize the new recruits now coming in and make extensive preparations for next year's campaign which will be as severe as any. The rebels will put their slaves into the army next year and make every resistance they can.

While writing a telegram has just been received from Genl. Thomas ordering our office to Nashville! Only think—150 miles nearer home! I call that good news. I can hear from you in three or four days.

Expecting to hear from you in one or two days in answer to my previous letters. I send my best love to you & the children. I will write again when I hear again from you.

Your affectionate husbd,
WmHBradbury

Head Quarters Department of the Cumberland
Chattanooga
Nov 12th, 1864
My dear wife,

It is now nearly a week since I received your short letter of Nov 1st. I wrote you five or six days ago in reply to it. This will make the 4th letter to which you have not replied. One from Atlanta about the 28th Oct. & three from this place. I fully expect a letter tomorrow noon.

I get the *Chicago Tribune* three times a week—only three days from date of publication. The paper of Nov. 9th reached me today. If you had written on the 7th or 8th I ought to have got it.

I have nothing new to communicate. There is no immediate prospect of our going to Nashville. Major Thruston is still here and so is Genl. Thomas and some officers of his staff. They are making preparations for an attack by the rebels against some portion of western Tenn. on the Cumberland or Tennessee Rivers.[8]

I have very little to do just now in the office tho' I have been very busy. I don't imagine there will be any difficulty about getting my furlough in the 1st week of December. I shall make a strong effort for it. It will be two years next April since I had one as I told Major Thruston.

I am looking forward joyfully & counting the days which intervene between now & the 1st Dec. I picture you & the children in my minds eye every day. Jane & Freddy are uppermost in my thoughts. Willie a little behind, and the twins I think of them too, but not so much as the others. I certainly expected to hear from them before this. I suppose they have not time, or something. I mean Jane & Fred—I will write to them again myself in a day or two. I wonder if Willie will know me when I come home this time. I shall be so glad to see you all.

I wrote a long letter to Charles a few days ago on the subject of the American War & have since sent him several newspapers. I wrote the letter so that it could be published in an English newspaper if deemed advisable.

I see about half of one of my letters appeared in the *Tribune* of the 6th Nov. There was no signature to it. It was more than a column long, but they printed only about half for some reason or other.

The rainy weather is all over & it is now dry & windy & bracing. This change took place before the full of the moon. What do you think of that?

My health is very good; but I feel quite lonesome. I am alone in the office. I still board at the colored house. There are plenty of troops here & every vacant spot is taken up with camps. Atlanta will soon be abandoned.

With best love to you all,
I remain,
Your ever faithful & affect. Husbd,
WmHBradbury

Chattanooga
Nov 19th, 1864
My dear wife,

I yesterday received your letters of the 5th & 9th of this month. I cannot imagine why they should be so long on the road when my

Chicago newspaper never exceeds four days from date. I also received Jane's & Freddy's letters. I also received the postage stamps—two lots.

I don't think Jane improves much in the writing tho' the spelling is very well. I am glad to hear she is only 10 years old; there will be so much more time for improvement at school. Freddy makes *all sorts* of letters, which make me laugh very much. I will write to them next week. I am very sorry to hear that Freddy is sick. Poor little chap! Father thinks of him very often.

I am glad you did not trouble Gilchrist or Chilcott with butter (That blot was made in killing a mosquito). I thought you would send it in a milk can by mail.

I feel hopeful of a furlough during the 1st week of Dec, but like you, I dare not trust too much in it. I have worked very hard lately, having been the only clerk. Another clerk will be here tomorrow. As soon as he becomes somewhat conversant with the work I don't know of any reason why I shall not get the furlough, unless Genl. Thomas should refuse on the ground that every man should be at his post. I will come home if possible.

I am sorry to hear of John Hetzel's sickness. Give my respects to him and his wife. I suppose they are getting quite rich. Tell Mrs. H not to give the twins, that is Eddie, any sweetmeats between meals.

My itch has all gone away. I get rarely cooked beef when I can. In the present muddy condition of the streets it is very disagreeable to get anything. It is now raining like sixty and the roads are cut-up by wagons & are complete mortar beds. The cavalry men haul saw dust for bedding for their horses to save cleaning. Each horse is tied to a post with a white patch of saw dust round it. The weather will prevent any active movements. We have had a great deal of rain lately. This & the work of the office has prevented me going out. I have been closely confined & have no appetite. Have dreams &c

I have sent several papers to Charles lately. I will send some to James. It is time you had a little more money from the *Tribune.* They publish a letter of mine occasionally.

Good gracious how it rains! It is as dark as pitch, and all this soft water running to waste!

Right in front of our office, where the old fence and the back house stood, is a camp of cavalry. The fence, buildings & little trees are gone long since. You can tell where I mean by the drawing. Just beyond the camp & on this side of the fort they hang their clothes to dry. The scenery therefore is quite interesting. The house that had an old tent cloth drawn over the roof is now repaired with shingles instead. The willows on the flat are fast shedding their leaves tho' they are still green & yellow. The flat is now covered with water.

What a good thing that I am not with the 20th Army Corps & the 129th Ill. on their way to Savannah. We shall not hear of them for a long time—not perhaps until they reach the seacoast.

It is after "Taps" and I can't think of any more to say. This will leave tomorrow at ½ past one p.m. on the 20th & should reach you on the 24th or 25th at the latest. See if it does. I expect another letter from you in answer to two or three which you must have got now.

You say you can use a barrel of flour in (L) weeks. What figure do you call *L?* I can't make it out. Willie can do better than that. I am glad you have sent to Kansas.

Oh Lord how it rains! Good night! The mail leaves at nine in the morning, that is—leaves the office.

I must sweep a place on the floor & spread my blankets and think of home & you & the children. I send my best love. Gracious how it rains! Won't there be some wet beds tonight & blankets & soldiers?

Your affect husbd,
WmHBradbury

Head Quarters Department of the Cumberland,
Chattanooga
Nov. 24, 1864
My dear wife,

I received yours of the 16th inst today. I also recd a letter from Topeka which I enclose. I also recd a letter from Chicago Tribune Co.

I received your letter and I have now recd all your letters. I don't think any have missed entirely.

I am very sorry to hear that the children have been so sick. I hope they will all be better when I arrive at home. Everything looks very favorable for my furlough. The Major has promised to approve the application. I shall make it out in a day or two. The other clerk is becoming acquainted with the business, and there is not much work on hand, and will not be until we open our new books on the 1st January when it will be necessary for me to be back. You had better not write to me anymore until you hear from me again.

The letter from Topeka speaks of the taxes being from $15 to $18. I hope you sent sufficient to allow him a dollar or two for his trouble.

We will answer James' letter when I reach home. I am surprised to find that he considers the £10 in full of all I owe him. I don't think it is. I shall pay him some more as soon as I can.

It is Thanksgiving day today. We have had some milk punch made of whiskey hot water and concentrated milk. It is very good. I must make you some when I get home.

The editors of the *Tribune* wish me to discontinue the correspondence. They do not get my letters in time to be of much service and have made arrangements with some correspondent at Nashville. That is all right. I am aware that my letters are not worth much now. They have paid me nearly if not quite $200 which is "better than a bob in the eye with a burnt stick." I shall make arrangements thro' Charles with some English newspaper and pay the earnings to James.

Gilchrist did not reach the front in time to join the regiment. He is now here, I understand, with the detachments of the 20th Corps. Col. [Benjamin] Harrison (one of my friends) is also here.[9] He commands all the troops composing these attachments. I intend to go and see them both tomorrow. Culver will be left behind in the same fix. I suppose he has left Pontiac. Chilcott I imagine will also be behind. This will leave Company "B"—Dwight Company—without an officer, unless they send Walkley back or detail another officer.

I wish you would send up that drawing, that I sent you, to Chicago so that I can get a frame as I come thro' & give it to Jane. Send it to "A.B. Case, Root & Cady's, Chicago."[10] Roll it nicely so as not to injure it, or send it in a little box by Eldredge or Mack or John Hetzel or somebody.

With best love to you & the children,
I am your ever faithful & afft husbd,
WmHBradbury

Dwight, Livingston Co.
November 24, 1864[11]
My dearest William,

I received your letter dated 12th and one dated [left blank], 2 more others from Chattanooga that last from Atlanta was dated 25th. I replied to all but the last but I had written the day before and I have not had much time to spare. I enclosed a few stamps in the last to Atlanta also in the first to Chattanooga.

I wrote the day before I received your last enclosing a letter from my brother James and told you about the twenty dollars from the Tribune Company.

I am afraid you have not received mine dated the 8 or I should have an answer by this time.

Last Thanksgiving day I received sixty dollars. I felt that I would have given a good deal to have had a few lines from you today. Well I am glad the children are better. Willie has been out for the first time today. He has a lot to eat, the best dinner for a fortnight. I killed a chicken and made pot pie. They were all out on the ice in the morning. Mary Eldredge is spending the afternoon with them, both Eddie and Ellie can say Papa Bradbury. Eddie says gone to Chattnooga. He is very fretful yet; I cannot leave him five minutes without him crying. He is now siting on my lap while I write. He looks very slim and puny compared to Ellie. I won't say much about them because I expect you will be home before long.

I suppose Mr. Kenyon has written to you about the farm and sent it by Chillcot. I thought it was best not to mention it because there was nothing decided. Oh how I often wish you were at home.

When it is fine we get along very well but as soon as the weather is cold I find it very hard work in the morning with the babies. They will not be quiet while I make the fire. They cry and it makes me feel disheartened. We have a delightful day today, if the clerck of the weather is as fickle with you as with us the five days would not last long. I supose you remember that I [am] considerable weather wise. If you noticed the 5 and 6th days of the new moon were not any of them alike consequently the weather would be unsettled the whole of the month. The full of the moon has little to do with it.

Jane's school was out on 20th. She got the prise. She now goes to the publick school. They have been good children lately. When you come home I would not bring them play things unless it is a rubber ball for Willie. Jane says she would like a box of paints if you buy them any thing let it be some thing usefull. I do hope to have a letter tomorrow.

Eddie is crying and I must say good bye by sending our best love.

I am as ever your faithful wife,
Mary Bradbury

11

"Everybody has the Blues Sometimes"

December 28, 1864–February 8, 1865

Private Bradbury's holiday furlough of 1864 was likely far more enjoyable than the miserable trip back to headquarters in Chattanooga, Tennessee. At least the woman with whom he boarded welcomed him with the observation that Mary must have found his visit home "refreshing." It was probably very difficult to leave his family again and return to what must have felt like a perpetual war.

The facts of the war changed for Bradbury. The troops he was no longer with engaged in skirmishes, burnings, and battles as they moved through Georgia to Savannah and up the Carolinas, while he sat in headquarters in Chattanooga. As Bradbury tried to reconnect with Captain Lunt and others in the Quartermaster Corps, members of his own regiment were facing extreme hardship. Men had died, something that wouldn't change in their encounters with Confederate soldiers ahead.

As Bradbury expanded his writing to readers in England, he wrote about subjects that were not prominent in his letters home to Mary. Parson Brownlow, the morale in Knoxville, and his assessment of the impact of the African-American soldiers on the war effort were roundly discussed in his dispatches.

Quite touching among the letter collection was a short note written by Private Cornelius Smith,[1] a member of the 22nd Wisconsin Infantry, to young Jane Bradbury (included in this chapter). In spite of her father's advice that she had done enough and that it was time to reduce her charitable works for soldiers, another soldier surely touched Jane with these words of appreciation and affection. She kept the letter her entire life.

Rumors of peace swirled as Bradbury wrote prolifically for profit, but there was a lingering and unsettling issue that underlay his return to duty—the possibility that the "refreshing furlough" would prove to be a reproductive one as well. While he dismissed the probability that his wife might be pregnant, he encouraged her to take steps to ensure that she would not remain pregnant for very long.

Rare as it is in any letter collection, let alone that of a Civil War soldier who was devoted to his family, Bradbury's inability to welcome the prospect of an addition to the household is surprising. For Mary, now forty-two years old and with five children to deal with, the possibility of another pregnancy, William's reaction, and his admonition that she do what was necessary to stop its progress all surely combined to make a disconcerting time. After waiting so long for the furlough and the happy holiday reunion, the Bradburys were now greeting the uncertainty of the New Year of 1865 with heavier hearts.

Nashville
Dec. 28th 1864
My dear wife,

I arrived here last night & have reported at the office of the post commander. The trains run quite irregularly to Chattanooga & it is uncertain whether I get off tomorrow. In the meantime I have been staying at the soldiers' home which is full to overflowing & the accommodations are wretched & I slept a few hours last night on a dirty floor where were crowded 30 or 40 more closely packed like logs. I am trying to find a better place tonight.

It would have been quite as well if I had staid at home two or three days longer. The railroad had been cut near Elizabethtown about 50 miles south of Louisville by the destruction of a bridge. We had to walk thro' the mud a short distance & cross a deep river on a precarious bridge of fallen trees & rails. The train on this side of the river was insufficient & I had to stand on the platform for about 100 miles of the journey. We had thirty "bounty jumpers" on board & a man whose legs had been cut off. He trudged along on his stumps & was occasionally carried by another man.

Major Thruston is at Chattanooga but none of Gen. Thomas'

staff are now at Nashville. There is a break in the road to Chattanooga about 10 miles from this city. It will be necessary to walk five miles thro' the mud & carry my baggage. I shall be very glad to get out of this place. Gen. Thomas is driving towards the Tennessee River & the rebel army is stated to be in a very bad condition.

I will write you again from Chattanooga. I send my best love to you, my dear wife & the children.

I called for a few minutes at Mr. Scovel's—Mrs. Young's brother-in-law—& I write this letter in his office.

The weather is fine & bracing & the mud is drying up—I have never had my clothes off since I left home. I slept on a sofa at Banyon's. Case did not get my letter. Our engine broke down between Washington & Joliet & it was nearly eleven o'clock on Saturday night when I got to Banyon's. I could not find Case's house in the dark. You see my journey has been unpleasant & full of mishaps. I shall feel better when I get to Chattanooga.

Your ever faithful & affectionate husband,

WmHBradbury

A great number of officers and soldiers are on the way North to New York to join Sherman's army at Savannah.[2]

Head Quarters Department of the Cumberland
Chattanooga, Tenn
Jany 2nd, 1865
My dear wife,

I arrived here this morning about 8 o'clock having had a very pleasant time on the way from Nashville which I left at 3 o'clock yesterday afternoon in a private car. I was delayed in Nashville two days by a break in the road and two days more by Capt. Stone who wished me to go down with him.

I found everything all right & everybody glad to see me back. The office looks the same as before. My two phonographic pupils were waiting for me, having advanced but little. I shall give them a lesson tomorrow night.

I arrived here with only four dollars having been obliged to spend some money in Nashville. I shall get $12.40 for my December rations & very probably extra duty pay for the same month which will compensate in some degree. I also wrote you from the same place twice, enclosing one for Kenyon. The road is all right & now & I expect to hear from you in a few days.

I wrote to Capt. Bailhache from Nashville. I shall commence my letter to the *Manchester Guardian* tomorrow. They were glad of them, but will have to get someone to read theirs to them. The father of one is a preacher & can read pretty well. Aunt Reilly[3] was glad that I had a chance to see my wife. She was sure the visit proved "refreshing" to you!

The milk became a little sour before I used it. The butter and preserves kept very well. I have some of each yet.

I think of you my dearest & sweetest & best, every hour of the day & can almost tell what you are doing and what the children are doing. I think of dear Jane with those troublesome twins & Freddy with the hay and coals & you milking & cleaning the barn (what a job for my wife!) Oh dear!

I owe John Hetzel for 54 lbs. of corn which we had. John was with us. I did not tell Hetzel about it. I paid Newells the 30 cents you owed.

I enclose Culver's note for $10. Please put it in a safe place. I may lose it. I shall not be likely to see him again until my time is out.[4] I wish you my dearest & the children a happy New year tho' it is the 2nd of the month.

The weather here is so mild that I stripped & washed down the porch this morning (the 3rd). It is now raining and the street & roads will soon be very muddy. I found my blankets and other things all right & safe.

The 23rd corps is now with Gen'l Thomas & likely to remain with him. If it should be permanently attached to his army. I may perhaps get with Capt. Lunt or some other Quartermaster of that corps.

I shall do my very best to make all the money I can for the sake of you and the dear children. I felt very low spirited while waiting in Nashville. I feel much better now.

I shall be very glad to hear how you are making out in that little house this cold weather. I wish you had as much room as we have here.

When I write again I will write more at length. I will write to Safford at Topeka to send the $6 to you at Dwight. I presume you will have a letter from Charles or Frederic before long. Don't forget to write to James or Lucy.[5] Compose it all in your mind some night and then it won't take long to transfer it to paper. I rec'd yours of the 27th Nov.

With best love to you & the children,
I am your ever affectionate,
WmHBradbury

Head Quarters Department of the Cumberland
Chattanooga
Jany 7th, 1865
My dear wife,

I have just received your letter of the 2nd Jany. I wrote you a few days ago. I am now situated here as comfortably as usual, but I suffer from cold at night.

I miss my dear wife and the warm bed at home. I shall get some more covering by some means. I am glad the weather has been moderate for your sakes.

Major Thruston thinks we shall go to Nashville before long.

Please give my sympathizing regards to Mr & Mrs. Young. I will forward Chilcott's letter direct to Mrs. C and eat the cakes. What shall I do with Mrs. Gilchrist's letter? Send it to Savannah I suppose. I found out that I had left the map. I will get you to send it bye and bye to Charles or Frederic.

I don't think anything can be the matter with you. You had better take some pills (Dr. Hagerty has Dr. Duponco's pills) which will bring the required event with safety at so early a stage there can be no danger.[6]

I have just received a letter from Capt. Culver enclosing the $10 he owed me. Please send him the note which I forwarded you last time I wrote.

I wrote a long letter to the *Manchester Guardian* & sent it to Charles.[7] If acceptable, it will be worth perhaps two guineas or about $25 our money. If Charles sends you the March paper you can forward the letter to me. It is signed *B*. I shall write every week or ten days.

I find life here rather monotonous & tiresome and count the days as they pass by. This of course is childish. I shall brighten up and make the most of every day "in books or works or beautiful play."

The weather has been very wet & muddy, but it is now fine and drying up. The nights are very cold. I hope it will continue fine. I have obtained a tent which, spread on the floor, is a great improvement for sleeping purposes. Notwithstanding this, my feet were cold last night. I have also a bad cold in my head which affects my eyes & nose very much.

I think we shall soon receive our pay—the rolls are in course of being made out. I got my commutations of rations for the time on furlough—$12.40. My phonographic pupils are doing well.

I don't wish Jane to study too much. She is too young. I would rather she indulged in play. She will never be a graceful girl if she pours so much over her books. Let her read this.[8]

I suppose Freddy gets the hay out for the cows. He must be careful not to fall down between the boards. I hope Willie is better and that he goes to school as much as possible. I think you ought to buy Freddy a hatchet to chop up those long kindlings. I hope to hear from you again in 4 or 5 days.

I have written to Kansas to send you the six dollars.With my best & dearest love to you & the children.

I am,
Your affectionate husband,
WmHBradbury
How do Freddy's boots suit him?

Manchester Guardian [published February 7, 1865]
THE NEGRO TROOPS IN THE FEDERAL SERVICE
A letter, dated Chattanooga, 9th January, and received in this neighbourhood, says: —

The number of coloured troops now in the service of the United States is estimated by good judges at from 150,000 to 200,000. Of these there are eight or ten cavalry regiments. A good proportion serve with the heavy artillery batteries, which are retained exclusively for the defence of the various forts and posts scattered over our constantly increasing territory. The greatest bulk of these sable warriors, however, are infantry, and are usually employed for garrison duty and as guards in the blockhouses and stockades built for the protection of the bridges, culverts, and trestle work on the long lines of railroad by which we derive sustenance and stores for the large armies at the "front."

The United States coloured troops, or "U.S.C.T." as they are designated in military documents, fought well at the defences before Nashville; but as a general rule they are kept in the rear as much as possible. Those regiments which are deficient in drill, or have not the required soldierly qualities, are used as a corps of labourers, from which are made heavy details for work on the fortifications, handling stores, chopping and hewing timber, and any other "fatigue duty" that may be required . . . but the fact of his having for generations been cowed and kept under by the dominant race, give him a habitual if not instinctive, dread of the white man as an opposing force. When this dread shall have been overcome, I see no reason why coloured troops cannot be made as effective as white troops. A very intelligent and observant Polish gentleman told me that the Negroes of Kentucky were superior to, in mental qualifications, and quite as high in the scale of civilisation as, the Russian serfs and most of the European peasantry. This is certainly true . . . the future standing armies of this continent will undoubtedly be largely composed of coloured troops. In this neighbourhood, as in most others, coloured men, not in the army, are employed under the numerous quarter-masters and commissaries in the heavy work required in their departments, such as unloading railroad cars and steamboats, handling stores, &c. They receive $25 paper currency per month and rations. . . .

The females, in such places as Chattanooga, pick up a good living by washing and cooking for officers and soldiers. They and their families live in huts and cabins on the outskirts of the towns, and are liable to removal as military necessity or the caprice of the Provost Martial may dictate. Many women accompany the army as cooks, &c., traveling during a march, and sleeping in tents and under wagons, with their temporary husbands. Though they often have weddings according to their custom, I am afraid there are a good many bigamists and polygamists amongst them.

The "United States Coloured Troops" take fewer liberties in camp than white soldiers. Fewer cases of court-martial occur amongst them, partly because summary punishment is often inflicted on the spot. Their quarters, arms and accoutrements are kept in good order, and they generally yield an unquestioning obedience to all commands uttered by their superiors. There is, of course, none of that intimacy between coloured soldiers and their officers that exists . . . between the white troops and their officers.

The pay of the coloured private soldier is $13 a month, that of the white private $16 a month; clothing to the amount of $42 a year included in both cases. The coloured non-commissioned officers keep themselves neat and clean and some even wear paper collars . . .

In conclusion, I may safely say that there is quite as much difference in every respect—physical, moral, and mental—between any one Negro and another, as there is between any white man and another. By "Negro," I mean a person of African descent. I have seen them of all shades, with blue, grey, and brown eyes; with complexions slightly ruddy, and hair perfectly straight. These are proud of their near approach to the white race; and a woman with straight hair wears not the usual turban. Their mental characteristics are equally diverse and noticeable.

Chattanooga
Jany 17th 1865
My dear wife,

I received two days ago your letter of the 9th Inst. I wrote to you three or four days ago a short letter. I will certainly excuse a short letter from you when you have been washing, for I know what work and annoyance falls to your lot. I am very glad to hear that the weather has been so fine on account of your work out-doors. In another month the time for severe cold will have passed, and the days will be longer.

I think of you every day, and my remembrance of you calls forth nothing but associations of goodness and purity and truth. I feel as if I never could estimate you too highly. I wish my furlough was still to come. I count the months and days that intervene (How foolish and how vain!) between the present and that happy time when we shall meet again.[9]

I have had the blues all day today. I slept cold last night and have felt out of sorts today. The provisions we get are rather coarse and the duties of the office are very monotonous. I cannot take any interest in them. I made out some payrolls for the clerks who were recently here and they must be made anew. Botheration!

It is time for me to write another letter to the English paper and I hate to begin.[10] You must excuse me mentioning these little annoyances, but I have no one to tell them to. I hope I shall feel better tomorrow.

There is a rumor that the office will be moved to Nashville in a short time, but there is nothing certain. The Major [Thruston] may accompany Gen. Thomas on his campaign. I think sometimes I should like to go back to the Regiment and be with some Commissary where I could obtain as much pay as I do here.

The officers belonging to the 20th Corps, who are still here, will not be sent to rejoin their commands with Sherman. I don't know what that means. I suppose that Sherman will be near Richmond before long, and it may be possible and it looks very likely, that we shall have control of the Railroad thro' Knoxville into Virginia and send troops by that means, to Richmond or anywhere else.

Peace rumors are now very strong. It may be that the rebels, in order to prevent further destruction and bloodshed, will come to terms. It is quite certain that they are getting into a very tight place; and also that peace messengers are at work. I don't however think it will shorten my time.

I am glad you settled with Kenyon.

I notice what you say about the letter to the paper. I must not make my letters tame or one-sided. They should be candid & not shrink from the truth.[11]

[The] Cases were glad of the butter and thanked you for it. I did not know where Barstows lived. Besides the weather was very unfit to travel about in. I did think of them and should have been glad to have visited them. They must excuse me this time. [missing section]

Manchester Guardian [published February 21, 1865]
The Federal Campaign in the South-Western United States
The following letter has been received in this neighbourhood from Chattanooga, Tennessee, January 21, 1865.

The number of troops sent voluntarily into the field by any one state in proportion to its population is considered as an evidence of the amount of loyalty or allegiance of that state to the general Government. The rebels claim to have as many troops from Kentucky in their army as have in ours. This was probably the case two years ago; but now the proportion is changed in our favour, owing to the fact that recruiting for their armies has been stopped by our occupation of the state, while we have been constantly gaining some little accessions, though whenever the rebels do obtain temporary possession of a small territory, they conscript all they can "catch and carry away," both in this state and in the state of Tennessee, where bloodhounds have actually been used by them to track fugitives in the mountains. The number of white volunteers from Kentucky is estimated at about 40,000. Governor Bramlette claims 70,000 altogether, including Negroes and conscripts. The aid and countenance frequently given to raiding parties and guerilla bands, and the opposition shown by this old and Conservative state to the measures of the present Administration in reference to Negro enlistments, "arbitrary arrests," as the are called, &c have induced the sneering remark that "half her population are half loyal." The Civil Governor and the Military Commander of the district have been at loggerheads for some time. The Governor, who represents all that class who voted for McClellan, enjoins implicit obedience to actual laws; but claims the right to discuss and agitate any intended measures. The Military Commander finds it difficult to draw the line between those who thus agitate and raise obstacles and avowed enemies. The conduct of Brigadier General Paine, who ordered the summary execution of guerillas and bushwhackers without even a form of trial, and held reign of terror over Western Kentucky, has not tended to conciliate the people. Though great numbers have taken the oath of allegiance in Kentucky, it is questionable whether there is much more loyalty in that state now than at the commencement of the rebellion.

The state of Tennessee had furnished about 30,000 volunteers to the Union army, and one third of its population—chiefly the mountaineers of East Tennessee—is considered loyal to the old Government. This loyal element is fast becoming abolitionised. There is every indication that the laws of the new state government, now in course of formation, will be such as the most ultra free-soiler could desire. Tennessee has virtually joined Maryland and Missouri, and no possible successes of the Confederate arms can root out the leaven that is fast "leavening the whole lump."

The Union party in Tennessee are decided in their loyalty. They are not "half loyal." Parson Brownlow, once a virulent advocate of slavery has rightly read the signs of the times, and is the nominee for Governor of the state in the Convention just held. He has ever been unflinching and outspoken in the Union cause. His past martyrdom accounts for his present vindictiveness.

The Western States lack but very little of filling up their quotas. Illinois in December last, had furnished 197,000, Indiana 165,000, and Michigan 80,000. Some of the Eastern states had recourse to recruiting among the Negroes emancipated by our advancing armies; and regular "state agents" were sent out for that purpose. The states of Kentucky and Tennessee, and others in our actual possession, were, however reserved; and recruiting agents caught "poaching on these preserves" were liable to punishment. An officer of a coloured regiment was court-martialed, and very heavily fined, with imprisonment in default of payment, for sending Negroes from Tennessee as recruits to fill up quotes in Massachusetts. He was compelled to disgorge the bounties he had pocketed, amounting to nearly $3,000. Only Georgia, Alabama, and Mississippi are legitimate recruiting grounds for coloured men in this region. For military purposes "the Negro is just as good as the white man"; and, instead of being sold as formerly, he now sells himself for the highest bounty he can get. The brokers, of course, make a good margin on such transactions.

In the future, all Negroes in Tennessee are to be retained in that state for the purposes for farm labour. This is at the request of the War Department. Many of the poor people in the mountain districts of Kentucky and Tennessee are extremely ignorant. Some can neither read nor write. School houses are very scarce. Spinning wheels and hand looms of the coarsest and clumsiest structure are to be seen in their log huts. . . .

Their fare is very coarse. "Lincoln coffee" is a traditional luxury, and eagerly sought. Though these poor people are generally loyal, their ignorance frequently made them the subjects of the grossest impositions by the Northern soldiers. Counterfeit Confederate money, manufactured by the ram, and sold as an article of commerce, and worthless trash of broken banks and spurious paper money of every description, has been foisted upon them in exchange for their farm products. . . . "Courts of claims" are established for the settlement of the millions of irregular accounts, and the offices are daily besieged by the miserable victims of war presenting scraps of dirty paper, and patiently waiting for an investigation of their claims. . . .

On another occasion a Dutchman came running into camp in a state of great excitement. "Vare," said he, "is dat quartermaster? He come to mine house; he take mine hay he shteal mine corn; he speak mit mine frow; he kiss mine daughter; and he never leave no voucher!" The people of Kentucky, and especially those of East Tennessee, are vindictive, and unforgiving of the wrongs inflicted upon them by the partisans of the usurping Government during the time they were under its ban, as traitors to the new dynasty. The spirit of old Brownlow animates these hardy mountaineers. Re-occupation of the country by the Union army has afforded them much revenge already; but the uttermost bitterness still prevails. How obnoxious individuals now in the rebel army can hope to return and live in peace with their exasperated neighbours, is difficult to conceive. Even the women express their feelings in such words as "devilish; hell; infernal," &c.

I heard Parson Brownlow say in his speech at Knoxville, on his return from exile, in the fall of 1863: "But as for you," alluding to his persecutors, the rebels, "we have no shake of the hand for you; we mean to confiscate your houses, your lands, your Negroes, and your infernal necks at the end of a rope!" About the same time a storekeeper in Knoxville, who claimed protection as a British subject, remonstrated against being deprived of trade privileges, as he had not taken sides in the struggle. Brownlow, who was treasury agent and controlled trade regulations, published the remonstrance and his own reply in his paper. He accused the "British subject" not only of having taken up arms himself in the rebel cause, but of having encouraged others to do so. He concluded by saying that an officer would wait upon him at a certain hour next morning for the key of his store and shut up his concern. If Brownlow should be elected Governor of the state, he promises to "keep down this infernal guerilla warfare and bush-whacking."

I saw a "British subject" in Indianapolis, the capital of Indiana, who came off much better than our Knoxville storekeeper. Strange to say, he was a young Irishman, but Protestant. He was at a boarding-house, and one of the inmates, an American, jeered and twitted him, and asked him why he did not fight for his adopted country. He urged, in reply that he was a British subject, and spoke strongly in favour of that Government. The abuse immediately increased. The Irishman resented it, and invited his adversary to "come out on the sidewalk" and gave the American a good drubbing. Persons claiming British protection are not in very good repute here, but this man's nationality was respected for some time afterwards.

While I was waiting, a short time ago, in the clerk's office at

General Miller's head-quarters at Nashville, an elderly gentleman, dressed in a plain black suit, entered the room. He seemed well acquainted with the clerks, took a seat by the fire, and opened a conversation on the subject of General Thomas's recent victory before the city. "I got five more this time," said he; "and that makes 117." Turned round and looked at him inquiringly. "One hundred and seventeen what?" said I. "One hundred and seventeen rebels," replied the old gentleman in black. "Ah, don't you know me!" he continued. "I am the old Tennessee sharpshooter and while out in front of the city during the last fight I fetched down five more rebels. I don't count those I shoot in partnership, because I can't tell whose shot it was. I only count those I am sure of myself." I noticed the absence of his uniform. "Oh!" said he, "this is my citizen's dress. I am a surgeon by profession, and not on military duty at present. I only lack 27 of my number now." "What is your present number?" said I, becoming more interested. "One hundred and forty-four," said the sharpshooter; "I'll make it up yet." "A curious number," I replied; "How did you fix upon it?" "Well," said he, chuckling, "it's just a gross; and I've been grossly injured and grossly insulted by these villainous scoundrels, and I'm now taking my revenge. I thought I'd make it a gross." He then went on to state that for his strenuous adherence to the old Government, and some severe language against the new, he had been deprived of a great amount of property—only his house and lot in the suburbs being spared to him, as this was made over to his wife. His name is William Dawson Dorris.[12]

He invited me to his house, and narrated to me his long and interesting life. He was, and still is, extensively employed as a guide and scout, and has a carte blanche from General Thomas to go where he pleases within the lines. He is 62 years of age, but quite vigorous and active.

**B

Head Quarters Department of the Cumberland
Chattanooga
Jany 22nd 1865
My dear wife,

I have just received your letter of the 16th. I am very sorry to hear of your headache & general bad state of health. Indigestion is enough to make anybody low spirited and that's what's the matter with me.

I do hope that the expected change will take place and that you will be yourself again.[13] I am inclined to think that nothing serious will result. You ought to understand such matters. I do not say this reprovingly.[14]

Some pain killers would remove the face ache perhaps. I think some good patent medicine would do you good. You can get Mrs. Hetzel to get it for you. I suggest these things for your considerations. You know best.

I am glad to hear that the children are well. I think about them every day. I can call up in my imagination the faces of all of them. I will write soon to Jane & Freddy & Willie.

I have not received a cent of pay yet. I have more than $100 due. I can send you $10 at the end of this month and perhaps $5 more in a week after. I can send it by post office on Chicago & Case can forward it to you. It would be safe by mail I think. Judge Safford ought to send you the $6. Keep the big notes if you can.

It is just as well & better that you did not get the flour, as gold is going down fast & provisions will follow suit. I was wrong & you right about this matter.

Our great successes and peace rumors have had a good effect. I am glad you bought some more coal. I presume you have enough for the Winter.

We had a grand entertainment last Thursday evening in honor of Gen. Thomas' victories. I say we—but I mean officers, citizens &c for of course there were no private soldiers invited. There was music & dancing &c. The supper was very elegantly got up by a Chicago Lady. I wrote her a very nice letter of thanks from the committee this afternoon.[15]

I earnestly hope that nothing will result from my being at home. If it should, it will be all yours & not mine.[16]

I suppose you have written to James by this time. You did not send me Fred's letter.

With best love to you & the children.

I am your affectionate husband,

WmHBradbury

Send me some envelopes

Head Quarters Department of the Cumberland
Chattanooga
Jany 26th 1865
My dear wife,

I received yesterday your letter of the 20th making five days. I did not get Frederick's letter. I have answered all the others. In one you said there was not much in Freddy's & I suppose that was the reason you did not send it.

You need not make any apologies for sending such a doleful letter. I was of course sorry; but it relieved your mind and you had no one else to tell your troubles. I am glad that you are resigned to your fate tho' I am still hopeful that nothing serious will result.[17]

I did not get any of the good things left at the ball. I did not go there. It was a magnificent affair.

With regard to the clothing I am sure it must be much cheaper in England. You know what John gave for his clothing which James sent him. I do not mean bed clothes entirely but other clothing as well. If some emigrant could convey the box of things to Frederic he would forward it to us and we should save the duty which is now very high; they will not search emigrants closely. There is plenty of time to send the list, but you might consider what things will be most useful. If we need the things, we should try and buy them as cheaply as possible. I thought we were in want of bed clothes more than anything else.

It is not likely anybody will come to visit you when you do not go anywhere yourself.[18] Mrs. Hetzel I suppose & Mrs. L. goes with the quality & finds it more agreeable.[19] Some quiet motherly woman would suit you for company better than anybody else.

I should like you to go to the tableaux[20] if you could conveniently. The ladies who get up such things deserve some praise. I am afraid you will begin to mope. I must stir you up a little.[21]

I practice short hand every day & expect to be able to write very fast when I get out of the service—only about 30 weeks! My pupils have paid me $5. I expect the other $5 shortly. I think of advertizing in the papers.

I will write to Jane perhaps tomorrow & send her 50 cents. I do not know what little thing to make or send her. I looked around today & could see nothing worth sending.

The soldiers get plenty of paper and envelopes & housewifes[22] and cheap books and everything necessary for them at the Sanitary

& Christian Commissions. I think if she was to knit me a night cap, it would be the best thing she could do.[23]

We are having a very cold time here just now. This morning we had ice on the floor of the room less than three feet from the fire. I find it difficult to keep warm in bed. I humble when I think how cold it must be for my wife and children on the bleak prairies of Illinois.

It is time for me to write another letter to English newspaper, but it is inconvenient writing where my desk is, so far from the fire. I wish I knew whether my letters were acceptable or not. I suppose it will be the same as before. Shall never see half of them. It is time we heard again from Charles.

We have not much to do in the office but sit around the fire and burn on one side & freeze on the other.

My bad cold has passed away. It has been a common complaint. We have had a very fine spell of weather, but it is now soft & rainy.

Part of Thomas' army has gone to Virginia. Every thing is dull here but if the rebels do not come to terms this Winter, the Spring campaign will open very lively.

Jan. 27 [letter continues]

I wrote a long and good letter to the English paper yesterday. I shall write another in about 10 days. The whole will be from $40 to $60 but "we must not count our chickens before they are hatched."

I am very glad to hear that Fred has the most head marks & that his boots please him. Let him tell how many days it is to my birthday from today and how many weeks to the 8th Sept.[24]

My dear wife, I wish I were with you to nurse you and comfort your head. I am glad to hear that the children do as you tell them. I will remember them for it.

I am trying to get Banyon a place in the commissary here. He had nothing to do in Chicago. It will be worth $70 a month to him, if I get it for him.

I send my kind regards to Mr. & Mrs. Hetzel & all enquiring friends & my best love to you and the children.

I am, your affectionate & sympathizing husband,

WmHBradbury

Is John's address Morris or something else—I think it is Morris.

Head Quarters Department of the Cumberland
Chattanooga
Jany 28th 1865
My dear daughter,

I received Mother's letter today. It was dated Monday afternoon which would be the 23rd. I wrote her on the 26th and promised to write to you the following day, but it was so very cold last night that I did not. I suppose you will not scold about it.

The soldiers have plenty of paper and envelopes and pens. They can get all they want at the Sanitary and Christian Commissions.

I send you and Freddy one dollar. You must have 50 cents for yourself to spend for some useful purpose and Freddy must have the other fifty cents and as much more as will buy a hatchet.

Mother will give him what is required to make up the price & I will send some more money to Mother in a short time.

You may send some little things to the soldiers, but I would not send any paper or envelopes. I'll tell you what I will do. I will hand to the Christian Commission here, those envelopes that Mother said she would send, and which I shall receive tomorrow. We have plenty of envelopes in the office and I don't need them. We have just got a supply.

The weather at night has been very cold for some time. It is a little milder during the day, but still we feel quite uncomfortable. We burn a great deal of wood in the stove and try to keep warm. I think how cold it must be for my poor little chuckies, but if you sleep all together and put plenty of clothes on, you will be warm.

I will write to Mother in a few days, so you look out for another letter in Hetzel's window[25] in two or three days after you get this. I never got the letter Mother send me enclosing one from Frederic—I mean Uncle Frederic.

If you could knit me a night-cap and send it by mail, I should like it very much. One that would fit Mother would fit me. If you cannot knit one, you can make me a housewife, for the one I have got is nearly worn out. You must do as Mother thinks will be best. If you make something for me—that will be working for the soldiers—won't it?

There is a great talk of peace. It would be very nice if we could all come home in two or three months. I should be so glad if peace would result.

You must tell Mother that I have not received any money yet, but I will send her a little next week. I think I shall get some.

Freddy must mind and not cut himself with the hatchet. I was very glad to hear that he had got so many high marks.

I think it would be best to go into the Land office with Spring, about the middle of April or 1st of April. How would you like it?

I don't think it will be so cold tomorrow.

I think if Willie was to go without meat and not eat much, perhaps his foot would get better. What does Willie think about that?[26]

You must all be very kind to Mother. Kiss Mother and the babies for me. I send my love to you all.

I am my dear daughter,

Your affectionate father

Head Quarters Department of the Cumberland
Chattanooga
Jany 31st 1865
My dear wife,

I wrote to Jane a day or two ago acknowledging the receipt of your letter written about the 22nd.

I am glad to hear that your general health is better and that you are determined to take things easy. If there is to be an addition, we can surely make room for it, and you will be well provided for during the time.

Instead of letting it be a source of trouble to me, I immediately set to work on my English letter which had been on my conscience for several days & which I dislike to commence and finished a pretty good one to my satisfaction and sent it off yesterday. It makes the fourth letter this month and it will be something for the little stranger.[27]

I have not received any pay yet, but I think I shall be able to send you a few dollars perhaps this week. My fellow clerk owes me about $12 lent money. I heard that there were some paymasters on the way from Nashville and we must wait patiently.

I don't mean to be low spirited or have the blues. Nobody with a healthy mind & body should be. When I feel that way inclined, I pitch in and practice phonography with all my might & main. I find I am improving fast. If I get paid one guinea each for my letters, I shall have earned about $50 this month besides my regimental pay. I only wish to be assured that you are comfortable at home.

"Never say die!" I find that every body has the blues sometimes even the richest and the highest. Your poetry is very good but you don't spell adieu ("adu" is wrong.)

You had better move into the land office in April when the barn can be dispensed with. The cows will come up if fed awhile. Our severe cold spell is just over. I hope the same with you. It has been quite warm today & it threatens rain. I have a good bed now. I should be glad if you could send me a few pounds of butter and anything else that is tasty & will keep about 10 days by express. Pack in a little box weighing about 10 pounds altogether, some sausage meat or something of that kind. In fact anything that is good to eat & will pack close. I will send you the money for it all out of the profits on the butter which is worth a dollar a pound here. Get something of this kind ready, but don't send it till I write again.

I presented the envelopes as Jane's present to the Christian Commission "for the use of the soldiers"—this was written on the cover.[28] The agent was very much pleased with them as they were just out of envelopes. He says he will write her a letter of thanks. Her name & address were on the paper.

I send my love to you & the children.

Your affectionate husband

WmHBradbury

Having written you a few days ago I have not much more to say. I am glad the twins are less trouble. I can fancy how cold it must be with you now, and how unpleasant doing the chores. Freddy will be dancing round the stove when he comes in & Willie standing first on one leg & then the other with his hands in pocket & his top lip lifted up. Jane will wrinkle her brows & look blue & Mother [will] say her feet & legs are as cold as a stone &c. I am very glad you have plenty of coal. This will be the last severe spell of cold this winter most likely.

I suppose you have plenty of peace rumors. There will be no more fighting here I think. We are all in Winter quarters.

With my best love to you all,

I am your affect. husband

WmHBradbury

U.S. Christian Commission Rooms
Chattanooga
January 31st 1865
My Dear Little Girl,

Your envelopes came to hand in the right time. We had none to give the dear soldiers who called at our office when your father brought your present to us. In a moment after they were given, they were being given out and before night they were all distributed.

On behalf of the soldiers who received each one I thank you. May the blessing of the Lord rest upon you through all the years of your life is my prayer.

Those envelopes will enclose many a soldier's blessing to his loved ones far away.

Good bye

[Added by WHB] This is written by a soldier. His name is Cornelius Smith. His dear home is at Geneva, Halworth, Co., Wisconsin. He, too, has a daughter whose name is Jane.[29]

Head-quarters Department of the Cumberland
Chattanooga
Feby 8th 1865
My dear wife,

I received yesterday your letter of the 30th Jany and Jane's composition. I think the composition was very good & well written with scarcely any mistakes in spelling. I suppose by this time she received the letter from the agent of the Sanitary Commission. He told me he had written to her.

The Major is gone to Nashville, and we are awaiting orders to follow. We shall probably leave this week. When we get established, I will write you again.

My health is pretty good with the exception of colds brought on by the changeableness of the weather. Our severe cold spell is over; but it is still quite raw & snowy. The mountains are white over. It thaws a little during the day. In a week or two more the sun will have more power and the days will be more pleasant.

I have just taken another load off my conscience by writing a long letter to the English newspaper. I feel disposed to wait a while now and see how they take. This makes five—altogether about seven columns of newspaper reading. I was in hopes of getting another letter from Charles.

I am glad your health and appetites are so much better. I want you all to live well and enjoy yourselves as much as possible. It always adds to my pleasure to know that you are well provided for.

I have not received Frederic's letter yet. I presume it is lost. There was no vacancy for Mr. Banyon. Poor fellow! I am sorry for him. I wrote to him a short time ago. I have sent Gilchrist's package or letter thru' the mail. He will have to pay the postage.

I sent you $5 last time I wrote. I have now signed the Rolls for above $100 which ought to have been paid long since. We have good reason to expect some in three or four days (This is the old story). You need not send me any butter or anything else until I send you some money. The other clerks owe me $13.

Major Thruston has promised to endeavor to get me a place when I can earn more money than I am getting now. It will probably be as reporter on some military commission where my short-hand will come into use.

I am in good spirits and quite confident of making a living while in the service and something more when out of it. It would be strange indeed if I could not. Do you think I had better wait and hear the result of my letter to England or keep writing still?

You must eat all the beef you want and everything else; you will feel so much better for it & it will be better for the _______ [left blank].[30]

I wish you would send me a little black thread.

The peace rumors don't seem to amount to anything. The general opinion is that this year will terminate the war. Having nothing more to say I conclude with my best love to you all.

I am your afft. husband,

WmHBradbury

I return this composition.[31]

12

"The Federals in the Southwest"

February 10, 1865–May 1, 1865

Bradbury appreciated the benefits of being back in a city like Nashville as he began to settle into his position with Major Thruston. He counted on his earnings from newspaper reporting, encouraged by letters from brother Charles in England (two are included in this chapter), and from other freelance work that a city like Nashville provided. Bradbury felt it was quite a "grand thing to be a soldier" and that it would not be such a bad thing for him financially if the war continued a little longer.

Bradbury's exhaustive analysis of detached servicemen, or "bummers," provided British readers with a classification scheme that could be likened to civil service. He wrote to entertain, satirize, and sometimes to inform. It seems that Bradbury could describe the nature of "bummers" with remarkable authority. When his older brother Charles wrote to him quoting *Hamlet,* it was probably a comfort for William to learn that his Civil War correspondence to the *Manchester Guardian* was acceptable. However, the letter exemplified how the brothers' views on the war and reconstruction were fundamentally different. If Bradbury replied with words of protest to his brother, they did not survive in the U.S. collections.

Bradbury was succeeding with the newspapers; both the *Chicago Tribune* and the *Manchester Guardian* were paying for extensive reports covering the close of the war and the president's assassination. He might have been considered a mercenary correspondent, yet for most of the close of the war, the professional correspondents were focused on the final military negotiations in North Carolina and Virginia. Bradbury, by contrast, had to rely upon reports that were by then somewhat dated, but he enlivened them with speculation and hyperbole, all of which translated to cash.

Finally, Bradbury had a voice, a venue, a chance to speak his mind. He took the opportunity of being a published correspondent to vent his feelings of the peer pressure weighing on a volunteer soldier, which "all tend to keep him in the well-grooved track of what the world has ever called 'glory.'"[1] And as Bradbury wrote disparagingly of the elite young Philadelphia men who sought to "crush the rebellion seated at a desk in some elegant secesh mansion,"[2] he could, ironically, have been describing himself. When he wrote about ethnic generalizations, he was likely catering to British readers—German-immigrant soldiers would probably not have been amused to read in print that their best contributions to the war effort were described as bakers.[3]

Writers, though, were beginning to bring new insights to readers about current events, leaders, and the ludicrous side of war. Some writers for the British magazine *Punch,* like the American Charles Farrar Browne under the pen name Artemus Ward, were finding new ways of integrating humor in their journalistic pieces. Bradbury was no Ward, but his creative writing for the British may have been an attempt to incorporate a bit of Ward's style. Small world that it was, their paths would cross in the months ahead.

With Mary having settled any lingering issues about a sixth child, her husband's advice as family medical authority was interesting. If, as William suggested, she had consumed three glasses a day of Hostetter's Bitters, which was composed of 45 percent alcohol, she would have likely been inebriated for much of the time.[4]

Headquarters Department of the Cumberland
Nashville
Feb. 12th 1865
My dear wife,

I received your letter of the 7th Feby yesterday on my arrival from Chattanooga. We are now "fixed" here pretty comfortably. I really don't see that you ought to help the soldiers at all, except one soldier in whom you have a direct interest. They are very well provided for—far better than some of them deserve. In Chattanooga there is the Sanitary Commission, the Christian Commission, and the Ohio and Indiana agencies who attend to the wants of soldiers from those states. Those who have a surplus of money can of course spend it in this fashionable way. It is a good thing for storekeepers who sell the articles.

I *am* glad Mrs. Hetzel has a pet of her own.[5] There will be no danger of Eddie being spoiled with fruit and candies at unreasonable times.

You can send the box as soon as you like. You need not send any pork or sausage. Perhaps some butter & potted beef will be best.

Not having been paid & having but some money I have only a few dollars left—not enough to live upon during this month. We have been put off so long as regards pay that I don't count upon it anymore. If they can't pay us at Nashville, they can't pay us anywhere. There was $140 due me on the 1st of this month.

I don't remember whether I ever told you that I had paid Newell's (while I was at home) 30 cents, I think, for the repair of the can, & that I had not paid Hetzels anything for the corn I got for John's horses when he was over. It was thirty-eight pounds & would be worth about 40 cents.

Not having made any eating arrangements yet and most of us being out of money, we board at the "soldiers home" where the provisions are plain & substantial but, of course, not nice.

I caught a most terrible cold while coming up from Chattanooga. It was a common box-car without fire & the night was very cold.

I saw Mrs. Young's sister in the street today. She appeared to be going to church. I did not speak to her, being behind. She looked rather seedy. She wears ringlets—a woman of near fifty. They live a short distance from our office which is in a fine healthy place near the Capitol.

I have a new desk—large and convenient with plenty of drawers & pigeon holes. Right in front of the chair there is a paper label which reads "O! Be joyful!" I don't know what for particularly. You must excuse this short letter for my head aches.

With best love to you & the children.

I am your affect. husband

WmHBradbury

Please write by mail the same day as you send the box.

Head-Quarters Department of the Cumberland
Judge Advocate's Office
Nashville
Feby 19th, 1865
My dear wife,

I received yesterday your letter of the 14th.

I sent you $20 two days ago which I hope you will receive safe. I will send you some more as soon as you acknowledge rect. of it.

We are very comfortably situated here and the weather today is like May warm & clean & very pleasant. The season is about a month earlier than with you. I would have the house plastered and white-washed & eaves & troughs put up. It will pay to have all these things done.

Buy whatever you need that will conduce to your comfort. I will find a way & earn some money yet. I almost think I shall wait till I hear from Charles before I write again tho' I have matter for another letter or two.

I should like Jane to be dressed pretty well. It will keep up her self esteem.[6] I am glad she got the letter from Chattanooga. Is it not time the twins had pants?

I wrote to John a few days ago enclosing photographs of Generals Sherman and Thomas. I suppose you never heard how they got home that snowy day. I wrote Grant for information about the lawsuit.

You have probably sent the express package. Butter here is 60 cents a pound & other things in proportion.

I am glad the people of Dwight are troubled about the draft. They have made enough by the war & can afford to pay pretty well. It will be the last draft for I regard it as certain that the war will terminate this year.

We may have a foreign war in regard to Mexico but there will be sufficient soldiers without calling for another draft.

If you wish the alley open, you should apply to the Commissioners or Trustees or else refuse permission to nail or join onto your fence.

I have been boarding at the old soldiers home and buying meals occasionally. We start to board at the house of a colored family on similar terms to our arrangement in Chattanooga. I think I can make myself very comfortable. The weather has been mild and I sleep very well at nights.

Gen. Thomas spoke of my being a good clerk to Maj. Thruston. The Major stands very high on the staff and can do something for me, but he dislikes to do anything irregular or wrong. He is in this respect the reverse of Captain Lunt. I shall write to the Regt. today.

With best love & the children.

I am your afft. Husband,

WmHBradbury

Nashville

Feby 22/65

My dear wife,

As the mail closes this evening I have only time to say that I recd. yesterday yours on the subject of the express package. There is of course an express office here. I shall expect a letter by mail saying when you send it. I wrote another letter to the English paper today.

There has been a grand salute of guns in honor of the fall of Charleston. We are very busy at the office.

Your afft. Husband,

WmHBradbury

Manchester Guardian

March 16, 1865 [publication date]

"The Federals in the South-West"

(From an Occasional Correspondent)

Nashville, Tennessee, 23rd February

As the evacuation of Richmond, which has long been rumoured, is now likely to take place very soon, and as the Confederates will most probably retreat in the direction of the mountains beyond Lynchburg—which are spurs on the Alleghenies, and are grouped about the interwedging corners of Virginia, Tennessee and North Carolina—and attempt to hold the East Tennessee and Virginia Railroad, extending from Lynchburg into the former state, it may not be amiss to give some idea of the country in a geographical and military point of view.

Knoxville may be said to be the head of navigation of the Tennessee River, though the city is really on the Holston, which, with the Clinch River, forms the Tennessee proper at Kingston.

According to some the river assumes its own name at the junction of the French Broad; much higher up. These rivers are navigable from Chattanooga to Knoxville only by small steamers of light draught. Last winter, owing to the low stage of water, stores were unshipped at Loudon, where the river is bridged, and sent by railroad thence to Knoxville, a distance of thirty miles. The river, however, is a valuable accession, as a means of transportation or carriage, to the East Tennessee and Georgia Railroad, which connects Chattanooga with Knoxville by a line 110 miles long. . . .

The East Tennessee and Virginia Railroad, of which the Federals have control, and which they have repaired as far as Bristol on the Virginia line, connects Knoxville with Lynchburg by a road 344 miles long. The distance from Knoxville to Bristol is 130 miles, and from Bristol to Lynchburg 204 miles. From Lynchburg to Petersburg, near Richmond, is 122 miles. East Tennessee, driven like a wedge between Virginia and North Carolina, has been truly styled the "Switzerland of America."

The rugged and precipitous Cumberland Mountains afford only a precarious wagon line of communication between the railroad terminus in Central Kentucky and Knoxville, the capital of East Tennessee. This route, though only about 150 miles in length, is almost impracticable in winter, and very tedious and uncertain at all times, both on account of swollen streams and wretched roads and of the prevalence of guerilla bands in the mountains. For this reason the campaign for the occupation of East Tennessee was deferred until more reliable communications were on the point of being established by way of Louisville, Nashville, and Chattanooga. President Lincoln urged the construction of a railroad connecting Central Kentucky and East Tennessee three years ago. Chattanooga is the grand depot of supplies for East Tennessee. It was used also as a field base for the Georgia campaign. Since that time additional buildings have been erected; and the storehouses now in use would, if placed end to end, stretch nearly three miles. These buildings are kept full; and from them, Knoxville and points further east could be supplied by river and rail.

The importance of Chattanooga may be inferred from the fact that there are twenty quarter-masters stationed there, who employ above 2,000 citizen artisans and labourers. Knoxville is extremely well-fortified. It is situated close on the Holston, amidst a group of hills and abrupt swells of land, which afford excellent sites for the numerous forts, redoubts, and earthworks which extend for some distance around it. The adjoining forests have disappeared before the axes of the Yankee soldiers and the once beautiful hills are now bare.

The Virginia Railroad crosses the Holston at Strawberry Plains, about 15 miles above Knoxville. There is a wagon bridge at this city, built by the military authorities last year. The whole line of communication, from the shores of the Ohio into East Tennessee is so circuitously long, resembling three sides of a square, as to render Knoxville no more available as a point d'appui for a large movement than Atlanta could have been. The difficulty of procuring supplies increases in a geometrical ratio to the increasing distance. . . .

This is one of the most elevated habitable regions on the continent. The ordinary roads are necessarily crooked and rough; and the railroad makes all sorts of sudden curves to dodge the mountains. The railroad which connects, via Chattanooga and Nashville, this romantic country with the rest of the United States takes a course in many respects nearly parallel to that of the Tennessee. This singular river may be compared to a whip, the stock resting on the Ohio, at Paducah, reaches across the states of Kentucky and Tennessee. The thong, attached at right angles, as it were, at Eastport, in the north-east corner of Mississippi, flies with a curve through the northern end of Alabama, grazes the frontiers of Georgia, strikes the elevated valleys of East Tennessee, and splitting into a thousand strings, smites the recesses of the Alleghenies, in Virginia, and lashes right and left the Bald mountains of North Carolina and the blue hills of the Cumberland.

The climate of this mountainous district, so near the sources of great rivers, is more salubrious and cooler than on the banks of the lower Ohio. The increase of altitude more than compensates for the difference in latitude. I have seen 15 inches of snow near Chattanooga on the 23rd of March, in latitude 35.

General Thomas has gone to Eastport to start off some of the cavalry and mounted infantry which have been collecting at that place, and form the land expedition against Montgomery and Selina. Mobile, after following the fate of Charleston and Savannah, will pave the way for the speedy capture of the inland cities, while the land expedition or "raid" will destroy the railroads, depots &c.

. . . If Lee should attempt to enter the Gulf States through East

Tennessee, Thomas will have a lively time of it. The passenger train from Louisville was attacked by guerillas, last night, near Bowling Green, Kentucky.

Head-Quarters Department of the Cumberland,
Nashville
February 27th 1865
My dear wife,

I have this afternoon received yours of the 23rd. I also received an old letter from you dated the 3rd Feby. I think that is the one which should have contained Frederic's letter but it did not.

When you send the box let me know by mail about it so that I may be on the lookout. I am much pleased with Jane's composition, also with the little notes from the teachers about Willie & Freddy.

I think articles of dress will be cheaper after a while as gold comes down. At least it ought to be. The ladies here dress very finely. To see some of them you would suppose there was no war going on. Splendid houses—fine carriages & horses & everything grand & gay. I suppose they are only the fortunate ones who have escaped the many disasters. This is a gay & fast city for citizens & officers &c; but a soldier cannot get a glass of lager-beer!

It is grand thing to be a soldier! I have a pleasant time enough in one sense; but there are lots of others who do no more work nor so much who live on the top shelf. They read the newspapers & attend to business for five or six hours during the day & pass the rest of their time in riding, social festivities &c—fair thing to be a staff officer!

I spend my leisure time in practicing shorthand. I wish I had Jane to read to me.

I am glad Hetzels are doing so well; but I don't envy them a bit. I have often thought that Mr. H would like a partner in whom he had confidence & who would relieve him of some of the care and anxiety of the business.

I am really sorry for Mrs. Case. You ought to write to her. I wrote to Case the other day. I also wrote a note to Charles. It is quite time we heard from him.

I wrote to the *Chicago Tribune* a short letter this evening speaking of the movement of the 4th Corps towards Knoxville. If they print it, it will appear in the paper the same day you get this—perhaps the day before.

If you had eave-troughs put up, you could catch the rains water in the tubs without cistern. I think you should have it done.

I tried so many things for my itching that I don't know what cured me. Sulphur and magnesia or carbonate of soda, salt and water—Epsom salts—Castile soaps and sulphur and lard on the outside—frequent washings in cold water.

I have received extra duty pay up to the end of Jany. & have plenty of money. I send you a $10 bill. I have nearly $30 more which I will send $10 at a time. Two of the bills are compound interest bearing bills which you must keep if possible. The one I send you does not bear interest.

I have six months regimental pay due now. We shall probably receive 4 months very soon.

I have now a very nice cot made on purpose by the Quartermaster. I have also just got a place to board where a colored woman cooks our rations on the same terms as at Chattanooga. It is more economical than pleasant.

The Major does not wish to spare me, I imagine, nor does he like to do anything out of the way of propriety. I have urged the matter several times, but he does not think it would be allowed. He says, "$10 a day would be a very nice thing." I think so too. I could get this sum if I were out of the service as reporter for the Military Court now sitting here—$200 to $300 a month! Only think of it! If this war would only last about a year after my time was out what a fine thing it would be.[7]

I send my best love to you & the children every one of them. The weather is mild & warm & threatening rain.

I am,
Your afft. Husband,
WmHBradbury
I sent $10 last time.

Dukinfield [England]
[Undated segment of a letter from Private Bradbury's brother, Charles T. Bradbury]

I hope to receive them [letters] regularly. Bear in mind that any early and reliable information about facts & the state of feeling of the northern people as regards either the continuance or giving up of the war would be of direct & great money value to me. It just occurs to me that if you could send a readable letter or two about the doings of Sherman's army that they might be of value to some of the newspapers who would pay for them & be glad of a regular correspondent.

Mr. & Mrs. Tomlins are in good health & desire to be remembered to you. Along with the carte of the children I send my own from which you will see if I have changed much since you saw me & the children will be able to see what their uncle looks like. I also send a carte with Kate[8] & her aunt, Mrs. Sutcliffe. Mrs. S. joins me in love to yourself, wife & children.

I am your brother,
Yours affectionately
C. T. Bradbury

Head-Quarters Department of the Cumberland
Judge Advocate's Office
Nashville
March 2nd 1865
My dear wife,

I received this afternoon your short letter enclosing one from Charles. I now answer briefly to let you know that I am very much gratified with Charles' letter. If the Manchester paper prints all of my productions, there will be one hundred and fifty dollars due to me for the letters I have already written. As you did not read Charles' letter very attentively, I suppose you did not notice all that he said. I shall continue the correspondence, but I should like Charles and you to be more prompt in forwarding the letters containing extracts from the paper. Two guineas and a half or $25 of this money for each letter is a very nice thing.

I will send you another $10 as soon as the railroad is free from danger. We had a guerilla attack yesterday near Bowling Green.

Major Thruston promises to give me information about any movements that he may know of. He will do his best to improve my position in a pecuniary point of view.

With love to you all,

I am your afft. Husband
WmHBradbury

Have you not received the newspaper containing my letter dated Chattanooga, Jany. 6th—it was printed in full. The one you sent me was cut down considerably. They only printed about a third of it. I will write more fully when I hear again from you—in haste,

Yours, WmHB

Manchester Guardian
March 27, 1865 [publication date]
"The Federals in the South-West"
(From an occasional correspondent)
Nashville, Tennessee [written March 3, 1865]

In my last letter I spoke of the organization and concentration of cavalry in General Thomas's extensive territorial department. The rendezvous of this important arm of the Federal service in the South is at Eastport, on the Tennessee river. There are now at this point 15,000 cavalry and mounted infantry, equipped and ready for the expedition against Selma, Montgomery, and Mobile. The difference between mounted infantry and cavalry is that the former use their horses merely as a means of locomotion, and always fight on foot. . . . They will co-operate with the forces of Generals Granger, Canby, and A.J. Smith, in the capture of the cities and destruction of the railroads in Alabama and Mississippi. This programme, however, might be changed by the sudden appearance of Lee's army in East Tennessee.

The tremendous and continued rains now falling have already swollen the two great and, to the North, vitally important rivers, the Cumberland and Tennessee, to such an extent that steamboats, of considerable capacity, can run up with supplies almost as far as is needed . . . on the Cumberland, the highest point to which it is necessary to convey military stores, is Nashville, and at this place there is a perfect flood, and the rain is still falling in torrents.

. . .General Thomas is now busily engaged in inspecting the fortifications at Cumberland Gap, Knoxville, Loudon, Kingston, and Chattanooga, with a view to having them put into the best possible condition for defence. At the same time the fourth corps, the only large infantry force left here, consisting of three divisions, under General D.S. Stanley, is on the move towards Knoxville; and new regiments are constantly arriving from north of the Ohio to take the place of those veteran troops. . . .

Six thousand new levies, mostly raw recruits, were lately quartered at the barracks here at one time, awaiting means of conveyance to "Dixie." A Michigan cavalry regiment, which had been home for the purpose of recruiting, passed through the other day to Knoxville. A large Illinois regiment, the 154th, numbering eleven hundred men, volunteers, and conscripts, landed here on the Cumberland a few days ago, and immediately took the train for Chattanooga or Bridgeport. There are also then thousand new troops in camps of instruction north of the Ohio, destined for Thomas's army in Tennessee and Alabama.

. . . The streams in that romantic neighbourhood are very torturous, and have a few more crooks in them than the railroads, which deviate so very suddenly that a train of more than ordinary length frequently assumes the form of a letter S. The railroad from Chattanooga to Dalton in Georgia, crosses the Chickamauga Creek no less than thirteen times in less than twenty miles.

Guerillas still abound in Western Kentucky. Trains from Louisville to this place have been attacked three times within the last week. On the last occasion two of them were burned. . . . The loyal citizens of Kentucky are constantly clamouring for "protection," and the state has not sufficient loyalty to take the lead and make an effective movement for her own safety. The desertions of her soldiers are more numerous than those of any other state.

There is now a bill before Congress which provides for the muster out of the army of men who enlisted in old regiments, the term of service of these regiments having expired or being about to expire. These men enlisted with the understanding that they should be mustered out with the regiments in which they agreed to serve. If the bill passes—and it will depend on the result of the draft—the three-year term of this class will be shortened by six or eight months, and it will take place now, at a time when their services are urgently needed. They are all glad to hear of this bill; and I know of none patriotic enough to refuse the benefit of it, unless they have a prospect of a commission or hold the reversion of a good, easy place, commonly called "a soft thing." The soldiers are all envious and jealous of the citizens, who run no risk and are making all the money. The fact is, that though the war is successful, and consequently popular, and the newspapers keep up the interest and the tine of public opinion, yet real patriotism and enthusiasm, such as prompted the first levies, are, to use another slang term, "played out." The authorities seem chary of attempting to enforce the present draft. Notwithstanding all this, the soldier, and especially the volunteer, cannot consistently deprecate his own calling and occupation. Must he cry "stinking fish?" And the volunteer is a representative man. The power of public opinion—the honour of his state, his country, his own honour—the approval of his relatives and friends—the value of his paper money—all tend to keep him in the well-grooved track of what the world has ever called "glory."[9]

Nashville, March 4, 1865.

The Cumberland is very high and still rising. The flood has cut off our communication with Chattanooga. I apprehend very extensive damage. . . . Army movements by land are out of the question at present in this part of the theatre of war.

B.

Manchester Guardian
April 3, 1865 [publication date]
"The Federals in the South-West"
(From an occasional correspondent)
Nashville, 10th March

For the purpose of aiding the people of Tennessee in their efforts to restore the laws of the state, General Thomas has just issued an order turning over—that is, transferring, the court houses and jails in certain counties in which civil courts have been organized to the sheriffs of those counties. . . .

The amendment to the constitution of Tennessee, abolishing slavery, has been ratified, and the new state Government has been organized.

We may judge from the present condition of Kentucky, how far this restoration of civil law will benefit Tennessee. So long as standing armies are required to enforce the decrees of the civil authorities, so long will the power controlling those armies dictate the state policy. Hence, the trouble in Kentucky.

An army like this composed of all trades, occupations, and professions, is competent to furnish men of the necessary skill and ability for any purpose whatever: from a judge advocate of a court-martial to a railroad conductor; from a sign-writer to a stonemason;

from a topographical draughtsmith to a tailor. Artists, photographers, engravers and clerks, engineers, bricklayers and carpenters, boilermakers, blacksmiths and bridge builders, teamsters, tentmakers, and typesetters, all find their appropriate spheres in the diversified work required to be done.

There is in this army a large organization of artisans, known as the 1st Regiment Michigan Engineers and Mechanics. . . . There are also two regiments of regular troops of the same class. Officers and men needed for any special or extra duty are detailed by the general commanding. Men detailed as clerks, messengers, typographers, &c by the department commander, and for duty at his head-quarters, are paid 40 cents per day, in addition to their regimental pay. This latter class of "detached men," from the permanence of their duties, scarcely merit the appellation of soldiers. They are non-combatants to all intents and purposes; and some of them never had a musket in their hands. The rank and file sneeringly call them "head-quarters bummers."

The word "bummer" implies a combination of shirk and loafer, and is also frequently applied to petty staff officers, who land about head-quarters on light duty or frivolous pretences. A squad of clerks, orderlies, and teamsters is always attached to the head-quarters of every military organization, from a regiment to a large army. The most intelligent and impertinent of this class are the clerks, who do the official copying and other drudgery of the staff departments, and must be good penmen and pretty well educated. At regimental head-quarters a clerk is sometimes unnecessary. With a brigade there are perhaps two; with a division, seven or eight; with a corps, 15 or 20 and at head-quarters' department of the Cumberland, the last roll contained 165 "extra-duty" men.

Many of these young gentlemen are "gay and festive youths," smart, witty, and handsome. They "put on style" in proportion to the size and importance of the command with which they serve. The despised uniform of a private soldier is thrown aside as much as possible, and a nondescript dress is adopted, which sometimes calls forth from commanding officers the questions, "Who are you? Are you a citizen, a soldier, or an officer?" Paper collars, tasteful neckties, well-blackened boots, and a profusion of bright buttons, give them a distinguished and neat appearance.

Most of the clerks at General Thomas's head-quarters are taken from the 15th Pennsylvania Cavalry—very much to the mortification of the colonel of that regiment. This command was enlisted from the elite of the young men of the city of Philadelphia and its neighbourhood, and comprises gentlemen of intellect, refinement, and wealth. Many of them are better satisfied to perform clerical duties, to which they have been trained, and "crush the rebellion" seated at a desk in some elegant secesh mansion, than to scour over the mountains of Tennessee at the behest of Colonel Palmer, the prince of scouts.

The Colonel occasionally makes a desperate effort to get back some of his men. His last haul was very successful—much to the chagrin of the smooth-faced handsome young gentlemen, who expected to spend a comfortable winter in Chattanooga, as orderlies and clerks. They did not take to "seek the bubble reputation at the cannon's mouth," and consider "the pen mightier than the sword."

In the Topographical Engineers' department are sixteen "extra-duty" men, who compile and elaborate those minute and beautiful maps illustrative of every foot of country over which our armies have passed. When a complete map is made, copies of it are lithographed on linen in the field, and during a march, and distributed to all the generals and brigade commanders. Photography on sensitized paper is also used; and tracings on a large scale are thus multiplied. The drawing paper, colours, instruments, and apparatus of various kinds are very extensive in this department, and the maps, views, designs, photographs, &c are numerous and valuable. Long before Sherman left Atlanta, I saw skillful draughtsmen (all private soldiers) busy at work with fine pens and delicate pencil-brushes delineating the cities of Macon and Columbus, with their approaches, fortifications, &c and gradually introducing the intervention of topography, as fast as deserters, refugees or scouts furnished the information. The prismatic compass is used on a march when strict accuracy is not required. The topographical engineer of the 20th corps made an exquisitely beautiful set of maps for General Hooker, illustrative of his part in the Georgia campaign as far as Atlanta. It will be very useful to him in making his official reports. Among German and English soldiers are found the best draughtsmen.

Germans also furnish the best bakers, but a Yankee must superintend the ovens. On one occasion, a major general commanding a large division of the 20th corps required the services of a short-hand writer to assist him in compiling some long reports.

He accordingly wrote to Nashville to a phonographic teacher there for a list of pupils from his division, who had been studying the art during their stay in that city last winter, and had three of four of them ordered to report to him for trial. The last one alone was found to be capable; and wrote out a full report of the journey to Washington of the chief of staff of Major General Hooker, then commanding the army of the Potomac, showing why reinforcements were withheld at a time when "Fighting Joe" fully expected to take Richmond. General Halleck advised the President on that memorable occasion that if those troops left Washington comparatively unprotected, the rebel population and sympathizers would rise up and burn the Government stores and public buildings. Only 4,000 men were realized to reinforce the army of the Potomac, and Hooker was relieved at his own request.

Some soldiers earn plenty of money while on "detached service." I knew a fine intelligent German, who, while on clerical duty at the Department Head-quarters, made, in his leisure hours upward of $200 per month, by repairing watches of officers and men; and this continued for several months. He had a little drawer in which he kept his tools and materials. He was an excellent watchmaker, from the shores of the Lake of Geneva.

There was also a member of the 15th Pennsylvania Cavalry, who conducted a bakery on his own account, and made a fortune by selling pies and cakes, &c in Chattanooga and Atlanta. He had been a steward in a large hotel in Philadelphia, and was successively purveyor for General Rosecrans and General Thomas, by whom, or by whose staff, he was materially assisted and protected in his exclusive privileges.

Tailors and shoemakers can make money; and so can gamblers. The time is past when ten thousand dollars in gold lay on the "chuc-a-luck" board in the army of the Potomac; but greenbacks are gambled for in every way, and to a great extent.

There is another class called "hospital bummers," who, from being patients, have become convalescent, and are returned, generally at their own request, to lighten the labours of the surgeons and nurses, and do the menial drudgery incident to hospitals and barracks. These men hang around such cities as Nashville or Louisville, and some finally get on duty in an obscure capacity, with third rate staff officers, as cooks, orderlies, or anything to avoid being sent to their commands. Bye-and-bye regimental commanders become clamorous for their men, and a rigid sweeping order hunts up and ferrets out these "hospital bummers" and drives them to their respective companies at the "front," or wherever they may be. Their occupation is gone. They can now no longer bleed Uncle Sam gratuitously; nor insult the generosity of the charitable people at the North by consuming the good things of the Sanitary and Christian Commissions. They can no longer pretend to be unfit for field duty, and at the same time earn a dollar a night as supernumeraries or scene shifters at a theatre. There are plenty of shirks in the army who would rather do any low menial work, in which nothing could have hired them to do at home, than stand up in the ranks and march and face the enemy like men.

. . .There are three gunboats now here, and the sailors, in their nautical uniform of dark blue and flat circular cap, present a novel feature on the streets. . . .The steamboats stand on a level with the houses; and streets for half a mile in length are submerged to the depth of two or three feet.

Manchester Guardian
April 7, 1865 [publication date]
"The Federals in the South-West"
(From an occasional correspondent)
Nashville, Tennessee, 14th March

I have the following information from excellent authority and it may be regarded as perfectly reliable.

The fourth army corps, which is the only large organized body of infantry in General Thomas's extensive territorial department, is now on the move to Knoxville. It consists of about 18,000 men. This movement was delayed by the heavy rains. A cavalry force of 6,000 men, under Major General Stoneman, has already started from Knoxville for Virginia. The infantry, under Major General Stanley, will follow the cavalry as fast as practicable; and the combined force will spend the spring and summer in the occupation of the rich country stretching between the Saltworks and Lynchburg. No opposition is anticipated on this side of the Saltworks, which are some distance across the Virginia line. If General Lee should approach with a large force, the Union army will retreat and destroy the railroad to prevent his advance.

The cavalry force, which has been waiting at Eastport for the subsidence of the great flood in the rivers, will positively start in three or four days. The number of this expedition is 10,000. Its destination is ultimately Mobile, and its object destruction of railroads, &c. The remaining force will be held as a protection against guerillas, and for other emergencies.

The freshet has enabled us to accumulate great quantities of supplies, and gunboats have arrived over the mussel shoals into the Upper Tennessee, which, with the Holston, is now quite navigable to Knoxville. This city will constitute a sort of field base of supplies, though Chattanooga is the grand depot. The new troops which have been lately passing through Nashville will take the place of the veterans now proceeding into Virginia.

Subsistence is said to be plentiful after penetrating the mountain range and east of the mountains in the vicinity of west of Lynchburg, where the expedition will attempt a junction with Sheridan. General Thomas and his adjutant general have already gone to Knoxville to superintend this large and important movement.

Head-Quarters Department of the Cumberland
Nashville
March 19th 1865
My dear wife,

I have not heard anything from you since your letter of the 6th March. A train was captured between this place & Louisville sometime last week. It is possible that a letter from you may have been destroyed at that time.

I wrote to you in answer to that letter about a week ago. The days are now getting long and warm. The streets are dry and dusty and we shall soon have Summer. By the time this reaches you there will be little more than five months to serve. The war will not have ended by that time and there will be plenty of profitable employment for such as me.

I have written 9 letters for the English paper and have only seen about half of one of them. I mean the extract which you sent me. I shall not write again until I hear from Charles; tho' his letter was very encouraging—offering 2½ guineas per letter. Still my subsequent letters may not have been so well appreciated.

The fall in the price of gold will of course reduce the amount we shall get for the English letters. I wrote Charles about three weeks ago to send what might be due when it amounted to £10. He will send it payable to you, but it will not be here for some time. At the present price of gold, 2½ guineas would be about 20 dollars. I wrote a good letter on the 22nd January which we should certainly hear from by this time. I also wrote one about the 1st February. The last two or three letters contained accounts of the movements of Thomas' Army.

I have written two or three short letters to the *Chicago Tribune*—only one of which I have seen in print. I thought if I could make a few dollars, it would help pay my expenses here for I have been obliged to buy several meals lately.

I have not received any regimental pay yet. The rolls are made out for six months which will be $9. I wish I could be at home to help you thro' the summer months. I can imagine what a wearisome time you must have. But never mind—cheer up—I will provide for you handsomely when I do get home. My health is pretty good. Hoping to hear from you tomorrow & with love to the children.

I am,
Your afft, husband,
WmHBradbury

Head-Quarters Department of the Cumberland
Nashville
March 23rd 1865
My dear wife,

I received yesterday your letter of the 15th March. As you had not written for so long a time, I had become somewhat uneasy. It is strange you have heard nothing more from Charles. I have not written to Frederic yet.

I should take no notice whatever of what Hetzel said in reference to your being close and tight. It was rather a natural remark, and such as we have often passed upon them; but we perhaps did not have any one to repeat it to the parties interested. They have done considerable for the soldiers & good fortune. I know that everything is very high, but we cannot help it. We must neither complain nor be curious, but endeavor to profit by experience & do better next time. I am sure Hetzels have been good friends to us and we ought to throw into their hands what little trade we have, provided we can do as well there as elsewhere.

I think it is about time to stop making things for the soldiers. Let the Govt increase their wages. I know several men here who are able-bodied & have plenty of money who stay behind & board for nothing at hospitals & soldiers' home & get clothing & good things from the Sanitary Commission when the Govt furnishes clothing & they are quite able to buy everything they need. But they spend their money going to theaters &c & then sponge on those benevolent institutions for what they need. I would not give a cent more. Quite enough has been done. I don't think that a family that has one member in the army should be called upon at all. "Charity begins at home." If I had not seen these sanitary stores misapplied, I should not feel so severe on the subject.

The weather here is now quite warm with a tendency to occasional rains. We have two extra clerks so that I have three under me now, and of course I have not so much work. I think the Rebel General will soon report to Jeff Davis that he cannot fight much longer with his present troops and then the war will terminate. We are sending troops into East Tennessee & western Virginia which will finally proceed towards Lynchburg & cut off the Rebel supplies in that direction. I don't see how the war can last longer than this year.

I see by the papers that the guerillas continue to molest the R. Road or I would send you another $10 for I have just received extra duty pay for February. We expect our regimental pay in a few days.

I wrote a letter to Charles yesterday, but I shall not write any more for the paper at present. The *Tribune* does not print my letters. I suppose the news is contraband for none of the other papers have a word about it.

Major Thruston had an offer of a Colonelcy of a one year regiment, but declined the honor. He seems to intend to stay here. We are fixing up the yard & office permanently.[10]

The shirts I have (except the red flannel) are nearly worn out. I shall draw some from the Govt pretty soon. I shall also require a few other articles of clothing which will amount to about $10 leaving me about $10 to draw on clothing account. There is also $75 bounty coming to me next September.

The news from all sources is very encouraging so much so as to render the speedy conclusion of active hostilities certain. But it is the opinion of officers here that it will still be necessary to maintain a considerable force. I shall look out for a good place where I shall be near home, unless something better should present itself.

Having nothing more to say at present, I send my love to you all.

I remain,

Your affectionate husband,

WmHBradbury

Head-Quarters Department of the Cumberland

Nashville

March 27th 1865

My dear wife,

I received yesterday your letter of the 21st enclosing extracts from the Manchester paper which I was very glad to receive. I thought the letters read very well. We have now evidence that they have printed four of them—making at the present price of gold—$75. The remaining 5 letters will make about $75 more. If gold falls, the necessaries of life fall too, so that it makes little difference. As soon as I hear from Charles I shall write to the paper again. I have nothing important to communicate at present, but I don't see why I cannot write at least 10 more letters before my time is out.

I have given up the idea of going to my regiment at present. It will be necessary however that I should arrive there 20 days before the time expires so as to be mustered out with the rest. If I should manage to get to Dwight about the end of July or beginning of Aug. there would be nothing unpleasant in leaving for there in four weeks. I think I could get full fare or transportation to Chicago & from Chicago on by New York to wherever Sherman's army or the 20th Corps might be.

I am glad that the weather is becoming fine so that the children can run about. The peach trees here are in full bloom & some of the early trees here are clothed in pale bright green. I took a walk yesterday 3 miles out of town & gathered some peach bloom & some of what is called the "burning bush." I enclose blossoms for Jane, also a blue flower. Peach trees grow by the road side.

I would either have the rooms in the land office papered or white-washed. The ceiling should of course be white-washed. If we have to leave it, it will sell for more. I believe in fixing up things and enjoying them as we go along. Can't you hire somebody to help you move?

Freddy is quite handy with a spade. If he was only strong enough, I think he would be quite a man and Willie, I suppose, is not so lazy as he was. I wish I could come home this Spring and help make the garden.

I don't suppose gold will go below $1.30 even if peace should be declared. I will bring two blankets home with me and overcoat &c.

I will write again in a few days—my health is very good.

With best love to you & the children.

I am,

Your afft. Husband,

WmHBradbury

The children must be good & play out of doors when it is fine, but they must help Mother when she wants them.

Nashville, Tenn.
March 31, 1865
My dear wife,

I have just received your letter of the 28th containing one from Chas. which was very gratifying. By the same mail I received one from the *Chicago Tribune* saying that my letter of the 17th appeared in their issue of the 22nd, but as usual, I have not seen and cannot get that paper. The Tribune Co. owes me for 3 letters which I know they have printed. They wish me to send them important news and promise to pay liberally.

You had better send me the draft for £10. It is not available without my signature. Hetzel would be glad of it. It is worth about $73. How would it be to send it to Frederic? It would save express charges if we send by mail.

I think of sending Hetzels a nice photographic view of a part of Lookout Mountain. There are several very beautiful pictures or views of the city.

You did right to get the eaves-troughs. Get anything you need, but save the gilt or compound interest money.

I really don't see why we need be penurious. I am certainly earning $50 per month clear at the very least.

I finished & posted a letter to the *Manch. Guardian*—a column & a half long containing extracts from letters written by Rebel ladies & important war news. You ought to get it about the 30th May.

I shall write occasionally to the *Chicago Tribune.*

I should be very glad if you could get someone to help you move and assist you occasionally in your heavy work. If Jane is unwell, she cannot be of much use—give my especial love to her and tell her I think of her every day.

At the present price of gold I have earned $150 from the Manch. paper and about $10 from the *Chicago Tribune.*

I shall write to Grant tomorrow to know what [he] is doing in the lawsuit. I have not heard a word about it.

I think if you were to get a bottle of genuine Hostetter's bitters & take it—a wine-glass full—three times a day, you would feel much better. Now do please get a bottle from Chicago. Hetzel will get it for you. I am sure it would do you good.

I shall be glad to receive the newspaper or extract when it arrives to your hands. I want to see the letter—I forgot what it was about.

We have not received our pay yet. I have seven months due.

We are now very busy in the office and getting behind with the work. I shall have to pitch in like sixty[11] tomorrow.

I send my best love to you all. Keep up courage—never say die. I feel "bully."

Your afft. Husbd
WmHBradbury

Dukinfield [England][12]
April 1st, 1865
Dear William,

I have duly received your letters, both private ones and those intended for the *Manchester Guardian.*

I wrote to you some time ago remitting £10 in bank draft on London. Any apparent remissness in writing has had a justifiable cause either waiting to see the editor[13] or because the mail did not leave for a few days. I saw the editor yesterday & since I was writing to you I wished to know if he had any remarks to make & he said "No" as you seemed to know what was required. . . .

I hope to have the pleasure of remitting £11 by next mail.

I always forward you the papers in which your letters appear & also any papers in which there are leaders on the American question. I hope you duly receive them as the reading of them may furnish you with a few hints.

I am much obliged for the map & when the interest of the American question centres on the district of country there represented I intend to give it to the editor as a present from you, till that time I shall keep it as its value would not be appreciated before.

We are all well at home. The children are getting on well in their studies & have good health for which I am very thankful. Mr. W.H. Sutcliffe has been ailing lately but is now rather better. Mr. & Mrs. Tomlins are pretty well. They take great interest in your letters, also Mr. Sunderland, your old teacher.

I am always glad to hear anything about you or your family. That letter in which you gave an account of your children gave great pleasure to Mr. & Mrs. S [Sutcliffe] & Mrs. Tomlins.

I notice the jubilant tone of your remarks occassioned by the successes of the North & acknowledge your retort about "wicked" hopeless & delusions as a palpable rhetorical bit but not as an argumentative one. "Let the galled jade wince my withers are unwavering."[14] To most people the great successes recently obtained by the North seem to promise them an early suppression of the rebellion.

To me the case of the North appears as wicked & hopeless as ever. I know faith in moral principles & such a wanton violation of them for mere lust of greatness & power will assuredly be avenged on the North & if they are cursed by granted prayers most fearful of all—failure would [come] to them [and would] be the greatest blessing. Can intelligent human beings believe that the atrocities perpetrated by the North [missing segment]. . . can possibly be the means of bringing them back on terms of brotherhood with the people subjected to them. Does not common sense & all history shew that it will make a wide gulf between the two peoples which can never be passed.

The good from the war will be the abolition of slavery but that cannot be credited to the North as it was never their object & is not now except as a means & not an end.

I must now conclude but I had a great deal more to say on the subject.

Mrs. W.H.S. joins me in love to you & your family.

I am,
Your affect. brother,
C.T. Bradbury

Manchester Guardian
April 22, 1865 [publication date]
"The Federals in the South-West"
(From an occasional correspondent)
Nashville, Tennessee, 31st March

A large body of infantry, consisting of two divisions of the fourth corps, and several unassigned regiments and detachments, are now, most probably, well advanced into South-western Virginia. The infantry were accompanied by numerous batteries of light artillery; and a cavalry force numbering 6,000 men, under Major General Stoneman, of raiding notoriety, preceded the rest of the expedition by about ten days. Among these were a large regiment of troops known as the "Merrill's Horse,"[15] and General Thomas's scouts or head-quarter escort—the Fifteenth Pennsylvania Cavalry. The brigade of which these well-mounted and effective troops form a part, is commanded by that intrepid and indefatigable prince of scouts Colonel W. J. Palmer, who knows all the mountain paths by intuition, and never hesitates to execute any mission, however hazardous. The elegant young Philadelphia gentlemen who compose to a great extent Colonel Palmer's regiment will be apt to remember the pleasant days they spent in the various department offices in Chattanooga and Nashville before they see the termination of the impending campaign.

The Nashville and Chattanooga Railroad, and the Tennessee and Alabama Railroad have been heavily taxed in transporting this army, and their baggage and supplies, to the temporary rendezvous at Bull's Gap, 70 miles above Knoxville,—a place in the mountains, where the railroad, being out of repair, ceases to be available. . . .

Knoxville is the immediate destination of all the loose and disposable troops—infantry, cavalry, and light artillery—that can be spared from the camps, garrisons and posts in the rear. Not counting the troops within the department of Kentucky which report to General Thomas, and are at his disposal, though under the immediate command of General Palmer, Thomas's whole forces comprised, a short time since, 110 regiments of infantry—of which 13 are coloured—93 regiments of cavalry, and about 90 batteries of artillery . . . but there is no doubt that an army of not less than 25,000 or 30,000 men, including all arms, is now surging up the Tennessee Valley, and crowding through the portals of the Alleghenies into the elevated and fertile regions of South-western Virginia, to form a link in that enormous and contracting chain which the concentrated armies of the Confederacy can neither resist nor rend asunder.

. . .The infantry force of the expedition into Virginia is under Major General D.S. Stanley, and the cavalry is commanded by Major General Stoneman. General Gillem also goes with it. The great cavalry raid into Alabama is conducted by Brevet Major General J.S. Wilson, who was sent from the army of the Potomac last fall to reorganize and command the mounted troops of this department.

I never hear any doubts whatever expressed of our speedy and complete military success. It is taken for granted. Being an inmate of the building in which is the office of the Provost Martial General, I see squads of deserters take the oath every day. The term of service of the volunteer troops of 1862 expires next summer. Their removal will leave a great gap in the ranks, unless the draft shall be more productive than it has been hitherto. . . . This has been done in many instances. The soldiers don't like it at all.

Nashville
April 2/65
My dear wife,

I enclose letter to *Chicago Tribune* which you will please forward with the map of Northern Alabama & Georgia which I left when I was at home last time. You can wrap it up in brown paper & send it by mail or by John Hetzel or somebody but don't lose any time about it. Don't tell anybody what is in it.

With best love to you all, I am in post haste.
Yours affectly,
WmHBradbury

Head Quarters Department of the Cumberland,
Nashville, April 9th, 1865
My dear wife,

I received a day or two ago a few words from you enclosing an extract from the *Manchester Guardian* containing one of my letters which I was very glad to see. This makes the fifth which they have printed. I have sent 10 altogether. I shall write some more bye and bye. I have heard nothing from the *Chicago Tribune* lately. I wrote to you enclosing my bill and requesting you to send them the map. I expect to hear from you and them tomorrow.

I am glad to say that our rations are now committed at 75 cents per day instead of 40 cents as before. This is money that we get in place of rations—amounting to $22.25 a month instead of $12—I can either save money or live better.

There is now built for the use of the clerks at Headqtrs a large and commodious house consisting of a large dining hall, wash-room with water—basins and taps & pipes—an enormous coal stove and every other convenience on the bottom floor. On the upper story there are nineteen good-sized bedrooms—each containing four single bunks & furnished with a table and stools. Each room has a key belonging to it which will unlock no door but its own. It is well arranged throughout. Downstairs in the large room are eleven large round tables with polished tops—suited for 11 messes of seven men to a mess. I sleep there but board near the office with a darky woman who cooks for us. I shall try to find a better place next month.

We are making arrangements to stay here thro' the summer. Gen. Thomas will not move his Headqrs. any more during the continuance of the war.

We had a gay time on hearing of the capture or rather evacuation of Richmond. The city was gay with flags and many officers and soldiers at Headqrs were drunk. But I was not. We were disappointed that the General Lee who was captured was not Gen. Robert Lee. The war cannot possibly last much longer. The Rebels have nothing to fight for their army is dwindling away. But we whose time expires next summer will not gain anything—we shall serve out our term which is now only five months.

I suppose you sent the map to the *Tribune* as I requested. If they don't answer my letter & pay me something, I shall write no more at all, at all to them.

If you would like to see my letters to the Manchester paper again, I will send them to you. I suppose you had scarcely time to read them. I don't like to write again to the *Guardian* during the present excitement of the fall of Richmond for that news in England will naturally exclude all minor topics of interest.

We have not yet received our regimental pay nearly 8 months due me. They are paying some troops now but have not got around to us yet.

I am ashamed to say that I have not written to Frederic yet but I must this week.

I send my best love to you & the children and remain,

Your ever faithful and affectionate husband,

WmHBradbury

Head-Quarters Department of the Cumberland
Nashville
April 14th 1865
My dear wife,

I received your letter of the 7th inst. enclosing a cheque on London for £10. I tried to sell it in Nashville today, but nobody wanted to buy any Foreign Exchange. I wrote to Frederic about the beginning of the month. As soon as I hear from him, I shall send him the cheque and he can dispose of it in New York. From all I can learn, gold will not get much lower at present.

I am glad to hear you have moved into our own house. I suppose by this time you have got everything straight. I can fancy you all tugging away at baskets and pails and Jane helping you lift the tables & heavy things and Willie trying to get out of the way & sticking his hands in his pockets and saying he had done enough & keeping his upper lip away and Freddy straining and calling on Mother to see how much he had done; and the little twins always in the way and taking hold of things that they should not touch and making themselves so dirty.

I am sorry to think you have so much drudgery to do, but I suppose you don't think so hard of it as I. I wish I were with you to help.

I was pleased with Jane's composition but she should keep the paper nice and clean; and make a copy of it first, and get it all right, and then copy it off on a nice piece of paper without mistake.

I think it is best that you should keep Willie at home. The other two are learning now as fast as they ever will, and should not be interrupted. Willie has not begun to learn much yet.

I don't feel as if anything more that I could write about would interest them now in England, but I suppose my conscience will soon become so uneasy that I shall try & say something. The war is so nearly over that I imagine nothing but the exciting news of the concluding scenes will be interesting.

I have heard nothing whatever from the *Tribune.* It makes me feel mad that they don't send me their paper. I never know whether they publish them or not. Send them the map.

Everybody feels free and easy about the prospects & staff officers will be discharged & difft. department reduced in force.

A war with Mexico or rather with France and Austria may result.

There will be a grand gala day tomorrow & a big drunk.

With best love to all,

I am your afft husband,

WmHBradbury

Manchester Guardian
May 12, 1865 [publication date]
"The Federals in the South-West"
(From an occasional correspondent)
Nashville, April 17

The anticipated pleasures of a day set apart for rejoicing by the municipal authorities of the city were at once marred and blighted by the shocking report of the assassination of President Lincoln and Secretary Seward. Wreaths of black and white crape [a type of decorative paper] soon mingled with the gay flags and bright banners that waved proudly under the green trees, and fluttered from a thousand housetops and pinnacles. Long pendants of funeral hue hung from lofty windows, swayed in festoons from high balconies, and intertwined sadly with the brilliant colours in front of the Government offices. The city was draped in mourning.

It was a sudden change from "beauty to ashes"—from "the oil of joy to mourning"—from "the garment of praise to the spirit of heaviness." In the midst of all this grief, the malignant animus of secession could not conceal its gratification. A man on Church street was so indiscreet as to think aloud in reference to the shocking event, and say he was "glad the d-d abolition son of a b-h was dead; he ought to have died long ago." Before the words had fairly left his lips a soldier shot him through the heart, and, plunging his bayonet into the falling body, pinned him to the ground. So far from his being arrested, a by-stander immediately offered to give him $100 towards a testimonial to the avenger of a national insult. In another part of the city, a man of Copperhead or Democratic proclivities expressed his satisfaction at the calamity, and said that "Lincoln was the cause of the war." He was instantly felled to the ground and, after a severe mauling, left for dead on the side walk. Strange to say, he was a Federal captain; but he was quickly deprived of all insignia and rank—his very buttons being cut off.

Several other similar cases occurred in the course of the day. Some fighting also took place, in which the "Copperheads" were badly handled, and many arrests were made by the military authorities. A reign of terror now prevails. Woe to the man who betrays any hostile feelings towards the Union cause under the present circumstances.

This city is the home of the now President of the United States, His home is only a stone's throw from the deck of your correspondent. Andrew Johnson never was a very popular man here, and the 4th of March inauguration scene did not shed any additional regard on his name. In his case it may be truly said, "the prophet hath no honour in his own country." A vulgar man, sprung from the lower classes, whatever may be his ability, is never reverenced by the aristocratic South. His low habits and previous political history have become the target of reproach even for his own party. His election to the office of vice President was not from any intrinsic merits of his, but from the strength of the ticket on which it was deemed advisable to place his name. If the rebels were unwilling to make peace with Lincoln as President, they will not be more disposed to treat with a man of Johnson's antecedents, one whom they now decide as a drunken apostate.

In addition to the actual transfer of state and county buildings and restoration of civil law in many parts of Tennessee, the loyal people of Northern Georgia and Northern Alabama have been invited by the military authorities to elect officers and re-organise their County and District Courts, with a view to the complete restoration of civil authority in such parts of those states as are occupied by Federal troops; and General Thomas makes it incumbent on the commandants of the various garrisons and posts to give adequate protection to such as may undertake this reconstruction. The disaffected citizens say they will not vote or take any part in the matter, and the Union party by no means crave their assistance. Time, however, tries all; and there malcontents may after a while find it to their advantage to follow in the footsteps of thousands of others once equally violent, and make the best of what they are powerless to prevent, by endeavoring to modify where they cannot change.

Previous to the assassination of President Lincoln the military grasp in this department had begun to relax, partly in expectation of the speedy termination of the war, induced by the recent great victories, and partly with a view to conciliate animosities and interests in this part of the South. Negro recruiting was entirely stopped, post establishments and armaments were about to be reduced, many prisoners, soldiers and civilians were set at liberty, trade permits were extensively granted to those who had been notorious rebels, much to the mortification of Union men who had been refused these privileges, and a spirit of indulgence and forgiveness was manifested in every direction. . . .

If the new government of Tennessee shows an ability to cope with the emergency in its own state, it is probable that a part of General Thomas's army, now there, will in due time be turned over to Governor Brownlow, and under a tried Federal general, be used as a protection to loyalists, and for the extermination of guerilla bands.

In Kentucky General Palmer has completely broken up many of these organizations and hung their leaders, not withstanding all their protests that they belonged to the Confederate army, and all their threats of retaliation. He now declares all existing parties and bands of this character to be "outlaws" and calls upon the inhabitants to rise up and destroy them wherever they may be found.

The people of Kentucky and Tennessee think no more of shooting a man than of killing a hog. In the Federal army the 9th Ohio Regiment boasts that none of their men ever took any prisoners. The conversation of some soldiers reveals the utmost barbarity and vindictiveness. Officers in high position also display the most savage traits of character, and nothing but death and destruction will satisfy their demands. The roving cut-throats and pitiless plunders in Tennessee will now receive no mercy whatever, for Forrest's cavalry has been utterly routed and mainly captured, and no independent warfare will for a moment be tolerated. Even citizens of rebellious propensities find it to their interest to assist in the destruction of these lawless bandits.

There is now no organized Confederate force east of the Mississippi, except that in the vicinity of Mobile and the remnants of the armies in Virginia and North Carolina. West of the Mississippi, Kirby Smith has about 30,000 men in Texas, near the Arkansas line. The intentions of this army are becoming a subject of much speculation; but their destination is generally supposed to be Mexico. . .

On the afternoon of the 15th, the day on which the news of Lincoln's murder arrived, a meeting was called of the Grand Council and subordinate lodges of the secret association called "The Union League" and held at four o'clock the same day. The next day (Sunday) the following warning was posted up at the street corners in the shape of a small handbill—

"Our country mourns."

"A great a good man, the Chief Magistrate of our beloved country, has been assassinated by a fiend of the hellish rebellion. Those who do not desire to be regarded as in sympathy with this most foul crime are hereby requested to show the contrary by nine o'clock Monday morning. Let our national emblem, appropriately draped in mourning, betoken the nation's grief, not only from the dwellings and business places of is friends, but from those of its enemies also. Treason is death, for we swear that persistent traitors shall be extirpated."

"Soldiers who are in earnest."

The citizens of all classes and opinions thought it best to pay attention to the threat, and this (Monday) morning badges of mourning in the shape of stripe of white and black cloth were displayed on every building in every street. None dared to ignore the warning. Where the scores of thousands of yards of decorating material came from I cannot imagine. It is a most sad and imposing sight. A self-constituted Vigilante Committee of soldiers went the rounds on Saturday night, to see that the Secessionists or rebel sympathizers indulged in no demonstration of joy. A number of those who published the threatening notice were arrested today, and sent to the military prison.

It is the intention of General Wilson to occupy Selma and Montgomery, and maneuver about in central Alabama, subsisting his large cavalry force on the country, and preventing the retreat of the Confederates from Mobile, which is now reported captured. Selma was found very little injured, and scarcely anything of military value has been removed. It will be properly fortified and held.

The Legislature of Tennessee have recently passed the most stringent criminal laws. Grand larceny is made a capital offence. In Kentucky, horse stealing is now punishable by death. It was necessary to pass these "blue laws" in view of the deplorable anarchy prevalent in those states. In Ohio, the Legislature have been considering the propriety of disfranchising such citizens as have run away to avoid the draft. The bill has by this time probably become a law, as a great majority were in favour of it a clause inflicting also six months' imprisonment on such delinquencies was appended to it.

The death sentence passed on deserters and soldier criminals is frequently commuted to imprisonment for several years at the Dry Tortugas, one of the islands off the coast of Florida, in the Gulf of Mexico, where the Government has forts and other defensive works. Even commissioned officers have been reduced to the ranks and confined there; and in flagrant cases the officer's name, crime, and sentence are published in the newspapers of the county where he resides. There is little doubt that on a declaration of peace all offenders, except in very aggravated cases, will be set at liberty.

The military prison here has never less than 500 inmates, about a third of whom are citizens. Some remain six or eight months without knowing what are the charges against them. We have now an excellent idea of a despotic government. Handsome, young ladies, who are generally the worst rebels, frequently are leniently dealt with, for provost martials are by no means exempt from susceptibility. In the office at these head-quarters a young lady took off her jockey hat, and handed it to the Captain for inspection. "Just look! Aint it pretty?" said the fair and saucy rebel. He looked and saw the "lone star" and the words "Texas Rangers." Major General Rousseau is considered so far too lenient in this connection. Union ladies who are neither young nor handsome are much mortified at these unfair distinctions. . . .

Head-Quarters of the Cumberland
Nashville
April 20th 1865
My dear wife,

I received your letter of the 13th on the 17th which is much sooner than usual.

I am glad the Tribune [Co.] paid you $35. They generally "shell out" when I get after them in earnest. I sent them a few lines for nothing on the 17th. They have not sent their paper. If I want, I suppose I shall have to send them the money for it.

I have [am] glad you have got the eaves troughs all fixed up. I suppose you have a tub or something to catch the water. You must make all arrangements and contrivances that will save you labor in the summer.

I wrote another letter on the 17th for the *Manchester Guardian*. I enclosed a 10¢ new paper money for cousin Kate & a 10¢ for cousin Harold & a 5¢ for that other little cousin—I don't remember her name.[16]

I have not heard yet from Frederic neither have I sold the cheque! I don't think gold will get much lower at present.

We are expecting a regimental pay positively next Saturday. There is $96 coming to me. How shall I send it to you? Perhaps I had better wait til I get it.

You must tell the children that I have just caught a pretty little bird which flew into our office tonight while it was raining outside. It has blue wings and a yellow beak. We, some of us, think it is a canary. I don't know what we shall do with it. We have no cage. We have put it in a dark room where it can sleep tonight.

The river is very high and large steamboats come up every day from the Ohio River. I counted 18 one day. The water is nearly two feet deep in some of the streets. The boats come thro' the railroad bridge which swings open as the bridges do in Chicago. When the bridge is shut the trains pass over.

All the buildings are decorated with white and black crape [sic] & muslin in mourning for the President. Several men have been killed here for expressing the satisfaction at his death. Yesterday a grand procession consisting of about 15,000 persons & 5 miles in length present thro' the streets & by our office. It was an imposing sight. In Cincinnati the funeral procession was 15 miles long.

Today has been very hot and now—tonight—a heavy thunder storm is raging. As soon as I have written this I must go down and post it at the office and then go to our Quarters in that large new building built expressly for our accommodation. We do not board there because we have no kettles, plates, knives and forks or cook. Where we board now we pay a dollar a week for our cooking & eat in a Negro kitchen. I can get along for the next four months.

I had a letter today from a man in our regiment—Frank Angle is killed, Charles Rawlings taken prisoner & Pat Skuge badly wounded. I suppose you have heard.[17]

I hope you are now comfortably fixed in the house and that the warm weather will relieve you of the care of the twins. You must live well and enjoy yourselves. I shall come home as soon as I can. You must get help to do the hard work, always.

Many of the officers at Headqrs are gone to a party tonight. They will have a jolly wet time getting home!

If Johns[t]on's army surrenders, the war is now nearly over.

I send my best love to you & the children,

You affectionate husband,

WmHBradbury

Nashville
April 24th 1865
My dear wife,

I received yours of the 19th in due course. I enclose you $20 compound interest note which you will put away with the rest of the same kind of money. I received pay last Saturday—$96. I will send you some more as soon as I decide how to send it. Many of the clerks have spent more than half their pay already. I am saving mine.

We don't have hailstorms here, but violent thunderstorms and rainstorms and yesterday & day before were very cold. It is now becoming warm again. I am afraid the heat this summer will be very obnoxious.

The city is built of brick and home and stores [are] on a limestone rock which will reflect the heat very much. Our office is large & airy & we have plenty of doors and windows. The building where I sleep will be very hot except in the morning.

I don't understand about Hetzel's house. Have they sold the store? I don't remember if you said anything about it before.

I don't think Lincoln's death will make much difference except that the rebels will be more hardly dealt with and the war prolonged somewhat.[18]

Jane's composition was pretty good and the writing was much better than her previous attempts tho' it is very strong and heavy for the penmanship of a young lady. I think she will make a good writer.

I have heard nothing from Frederic yet. I shall send him the cheque on London when I do hear.

The tide of war is now flowing towards Texas which is the only state not held, in some places by our troops. I shall write by this mail a letter to the *Tribune* which will appear about the 28th or 29th of this month. It will be probably on the second page and perhaps the only news from Nashville.

I wrote again to Grant to know what was doing in the law suit. He never answered my first letter. I also wrote to Banyon in answer to a letter from him wishing me to get him a place for Fred who is now just discharged. Banyon is in the coal business.

It is about time we had another newspaper from England. My conscience urges me to write again, but I am disposed to wait until I hear from Charles.

In conclusion I have to say that you must enjoy yourselves all you can with the money I keep sending and keep in the best possible state of health. Let the children play as much as they want to & get plenty of fresh air. With best love to all,

I am,
Your affectionate husband,
WmHBradbury

Manchester Guardian
May 20, 1865 [publication date]
"The Federals in the South-West"
(From an occasional correspondent)
Nashville, April 30, 1865

General Thomas, in pursuance of orders from the War Department, is now concentrating at this city what is called in military parlance his "movable column"—chiefly infantry—consisting of the fourth army corps, under Major General Stanley, and such detached commands as have been spared from the numerous garrisons and posts within this large department. The whole available force will not exceed 30,000 men, and this amount will be very considerably reduced by the expiration of the time of service of the non-veterans during the approaching summer months.

Nearly all the cavalry are with General Wilson in Alabama and Georgia. The contest in the East being now virtually at an end, the propinquity of Thomas's column to the only concrete force now remaining to the rebels, indicates a campaign by that General into Southern Arkansas and Texas, where Kirby Smith with an army of 30,000 men is waiting to cover the escape of a fugitive "President" who presides over nothing but deliberations for his own personal safety, and that of a few of his accompanying Cabinet adherents.

If the authority that controls this relic of the once powerful Confederate army does not speedily throw it into the scale of one of the Mexican belligerents, the head and tail, body and bones of the Southern Confederacy are gone for ever; for Texas will be invaded at half a dozen different points, and the army of Kirby Smith and his "distinguished" guest would be only a mouthful for the swarm of hungry veterans who would enjoy the chase like a pack of hounds on a keen scent, and willingly put in two months "over time" in a pursuit so congenial. . . .

In view of the possible necessity of the campaign alluded to, preparations are being made for the transfer of Thomas's movable column to the Arkansas river; and stores are accumulating at Little Rock, the State capital, with the intent to make that city the base of supplies and operations for the army of the Cumberland. . . .

There is a large Federal force already in Arkansas, carefully watching the movements of Kirby Smith, and ready to advance whenever the arrangements are completed. . . .

A recent order from the War Department enjoins the stoppage of all works on fortifications, except on a few specially reserved; and requires the reduction of all supernumerary organizations and armaments, the dismantlement of forts, and the immediate muster out of men thus rendered in excess. All bounties were stopped on the 24th inst. There is no recruiting in this department, except of Negro troops, who come forward willingly, without any other inducement than $16 a month, rations, and clothing. Their new mode of life may not be so pleasant as on "the old plantation" but it is more in accordance with their awakened ambition, and far preferable to a miserable existence during the winter months in abolitionised cities, and exposure to the kicks and cuffs of the poor vulgar whites, who regard them as a gang of Irish harvesters are regarded by the English farm labourers,—with the jealousy of competitors and the contempt of superiors. . . .

The coloured troops, now numbering 200,000, are considered part of the regular army, their term of enlistment being five years. The officers are all taken from the volunteer service, except second lieutenants, who are appointed by the Secretary of War on recommendation of officers in good military standing. . . .

The white troops of the regular army now number about 40,000. Of these there are 19 regiments of infantry, each containing three battalions, having a major and adjutant to each battalion, and averaging in number from 1,200 to 1,500 men to a regiment. . . . There are also in the regular army five large regiments of cavalry, and many well-filled batteries of artillery.

The present war has developed in many, among the vast numbers engaged in it, a taste for military display, a relish for the exciting scenes and incidents of active campaigning, and a craving desire for a wild, adventurous life and for those opportunities for plunder and ravage which are so attractive to the unscrupulous and vicious mercenaries who enter into the composition of all large armies. From this class the United States regular army will receive its greatest accessions to the exclusion of many worthy men, who would otherwise join from purer motives. . . .

In the machinery of the various staff departments—upon the proper working of which the success of the whole depends—the greatest improvement is manifest. At the beginning of the war, with true American enthusiasm and confidence, anybody thought he could fill any position in a regiment, and all rushed ahead with the organizations, calculating to find their proper places while the military train was moving. This overweening confidence brought its natural results. Colonels, quartermasters, commissaries, captains, and all accounting officers got into trouble. They could not straighten their papers; they were refused supplies on account of the informality of their requisitions; they received orders which they could not fill; and in process of time their pay was suspended for failure to render the required monthly returns to the bureaus at the War Department (corresponding to the House Guards at London);

and many found themselves obliged to resign commissions for which they were totally incompetent.

. . . the Southerners, impatient of restraint, ignorant, and unmethodical, had many bitter and violent contentions with their Northern colleagues, with whom they were thrown into business relationship. Regiments from these states never furnish any details for clerical duty; they are frequently unable to make out their own pay rolls, and confusion and delay have often resulted from defects in their army papers. A quartermaster, at an early period of the war, having been repeatedly solicited by the Quartermaster General at Washington for his returns for several months back, finally stuffed all his papers promiscuously into a nail keg, and forwarded them to Washington with a letter of transmittal saying that "all accounts were there; and if they could make anything of them they could do more than he could." Some officer at the War Department wrote back, threatening to have him brought under guard to Washington. He replied that he had never been there, and would like very much to visit the "City of magnificent distance" at the expense of the Government.

Even recently there has been published a list of 800 commissaries and quartermasters whose pay has been stopped for their delinquencies. Regular army officers, and others acquainted with the forms and mode of making out army papers, had no patience with the ignorance of the new levies, and refused to point out their numberless errors. All these forms and regulations, however, having, during an ordeal of three or four years, been "learned with difficulty," are now "remembered with ease"; and there are many large commands in which everything moves with precision of clockwork, whether the army is in camp or on a rapid march. . . .

The octavo volume, called the "Revised Army Regulations" is the grand textbook which determines everything within the scope of military affairs, and from which even private soldiers make glib quotations. It is, when well enforced, the great bear which licks Uncle Sam's amorphous cub into shape. In its terse paragraphs are contained directions for folding a letter and marshalling a division; for the hire of a transport ship, and the discharge of a teamster. Against its authority there is no appeal; even an act of Congress has been set aside as inoperative while the text of the "Regulations" remained unaltered. It has been found necessary to add to it an appendix to meet the requirements of the volunteer force, and conditions consequent on the unprecedented movements of such large bodies of troops. The Government furnishes every officer with a copy of it.

. . . If the present difficulties should be permanently settled on the basis of a restored Union, it would be unwise for any single foreign power to go to war with the United States. If Kirby Smith surrenders the struggle seems to be at an end, unless by some hocus-pocus Napoleon and Maximilian should unite in sympathy with "one Jefferson Davis," once more raise the "bonnie blue flag," and "cry havoc! And let slip the dogs of war."[19]

Head-Quarters Department of the Cumberland
Nashville
May 1st, 1865
My dear wife,

I received your letter of the 25th April yesterday and wrote you a short note the day before. I received the letter from Charles which enclosed the draft to you.

I finished & sent off my English letter last night. It makes the 13th letter—amounting altogether to 32½ guineas or £34.2.6 or about $240.

I send you a compound interest note for $20 a short time ago. I hope you received it. I have not heard from Frederic yet & still have the first draft for £10. I have not heard from Grant in regard to the trial.

I suppose you have seen the General Order announcing the reduction of the army to a peace footing. Some of us are sanguine enough to believe that we shall be mustered out & sent home next month.

Our time will be cut short to some extent, for the Government is anxious to reduce its tremendous expenses; and none will be kept in the service but men absolutely necessary.

I shall try and find out what Fred knows when I come home. I am glad to hear that Willie is improving.

I was much pleased with Jane's composition about the strawberry. I send her a yellow rose which grew in the garden closest to our office.

I received the figure of the Phenix—who sent it, Jane I suppose. I send her some scribbling with my pencil. I will send Freddy & Willie something next time.

I don't know how to advise you about the cows. I suppose they are not much trouble now that [missing word] is come.

The *Tribune* have printed three short letters of mine lately. I shall write them when I have anything of importance to send.

There is now only Kirby Smith to encounter in Texas and he will soon have to surrender or fight. The war will soon be over and this is the general opinion (very cold today here).

I am disappointed in not receiving the English newspapers more promptly. My letter of the 3rd March should have been here long since. It was included in the 11.

I will write you more at length next time when I hear from you.

With love to all.

Your affect. husband,

WmHBradbury

13

"Headquarters of the Cumberland"

May 13, 1865–July 1, 1865

As the close of the war brought thoughts of the future, Private Bradbury continued to write newspaper reports, now more characteristic of essays. His writing style became more verbose, and the earnest tone was no doubt intended to stir up British interest in U.S. issues, thereby insuring readers for his columns. Brother Frederic, who lived in New York, was a very infrequent correspondent to William, yet he wrote in support of his journalistic efforts.

Bradbury's remarks to the *Guardian* were often insightful. His article "What will be done with the Negro?" is the closest we have to knowing his attitude about the prospects for African Americans in the new world order, the postwar United States.

As Bradbury's duties changed under Major and Acting Judge Advocate Thruston, he became the chief court reporter of the trial against Champ Ferguson for the Military Commission of the District of Middle Tennessee. The charge against Ferguson was that he conducted warfare as a guerilla (or without lawful military authority) and in so doing acted in barbarous, inhumane ways including committing more than fifty murders.[1]

Itemized specifications on the charge against Ferguson were gruesome and numerous. He seemed to be proud of not "giving quarter" (or mercy) to captured Union soldiers. During his trial, Ferguson's defense was that he felt no Union soldier would take *him* alive as prisoner-of-war if captured, so he was simply operating under what he claimed were routine conditions of war when he killed those he captured.[2]

But during the war years, Champ Ferguson also terrorized civilians in their beds at night and hospitalized soldiers. Over and above Ferguson's identified victims, some would forever remain unnamed and unknown, including several African-American soldiers.[3]

Both sides of the war considered Ferguson a tremendous menace at times. His methods of execution, such as methodical dismemberment, were horrific, and might be compared to serial murderers in modern times. Yet his supporters argued that Ferguson was a man of steely courage who lived according to the custom of the times in the remote Cumberland Mountains.[4]

Court reporting seemed to suit Bradbury because so many of his skills intersected—phonography, detailed accounting, and law. Bradbury creatively embellished what were otherwise very routine court reports, as he indulged his fondness for allegorical references to Shakespearean characters. On the front of the court report of the "Charges & Specifications against Champ Ferguson," Bradbury wrote a verse from Act 2, Scene 2 of *Macbeth*, an apt commentary on the Ferguson case:

> Will all Neptune's Ocean wash this blood
> clean from my hand? No, this my hand will rather
> the mulitudinous seas incarnadine
> making the green one red.[5]

Head-Quarters of the Cumberland
Nashville
May 13th 1865
My dear wife,

I received this morning your letter of the 8th May. I duly received yours of the 4th enclosing one from Charles which I answered on the 7th May. I also received Jane's letter enclosed in your last.

I imagine the 129th Regt will be mustered out some time in the early part of June. Sherman's army will arrive near Washington about the 25th of this month and I cannot see the necessity of maintaining a large army when they have nothing to do for it.

Unless an active war should commence in Mexico, which is not at all likely, the 20th Corps will certainly be disbanded soon. But we must remember that it must be done gradually as railroad carriage could not be provided for so many all at once.

I have been waiting to hear from Frederic & have been keeping the draft for £10 to send to him. If I don't hear in another day or two, I will forward to you. Gold is going down every day. The draft is worth $5 less than when I got it.

Jane writes and composes very well, but she should have no scratchings out & blottings out. I will write to her soon. If the children are good, I will send them something next time I write.

I sent an English letter on the 7th. I shall have another ready tomorrow. I think I am keeping pace with my conscience pretty well. It is quite time there were some printed copies coming back from England.

I cannot think what it is that Jane is studying unless Phonography or music. I know it must be something good.

The weather is quite changeable. The other night we nearly had a frost. My feet were cold in bed and a few nights before it was warm enough to sleep without blanket almost.

I have $50 in compound interest notes & some other money besides. We expect regimental pay bye & bye. If I send you no more, I hope to bring home about $375 including the pay for the letters I am now writing. This is to the 1st July by which time I imagine we shall be citizens again.

With love to you all.
Your affect husband,
WmHBradbury

Manchester Guardian
June 5, 1865 [publication date]
"The Federals in the South-West"
(From an occasional correspondent)
Nashville, 15th May

The officers and soldiers of the surrendered and virtually disbanded rebel armies continue to arrive here in great numbers. They,

> "Come as the waves come, when navies are stranded,—
> Come as the leaves come, when summer is ended."[6]

They are very like leaves too—dead leaves—in colour. Like them also they be wearily on the ground, or flock in and out of the Provost Martial's office, until the breath of Federal kindness and authority sends them home rejoicing; and away they drift up and down the Cumberland, along the railroads, into Kentucky, Missouri, and distant parts of Tennessee; or down the streets of Nashville, disappear through open doors and fall into the arms of sobbing women and gleesome children. The homes of many are thriftless and desolate. No luxurious meal awaits these returning warriors. They have no brilliant achievements to relate; no successes to rejoice over; no trophies to display; no bounty money or pay to expend. Ignorant, enthusiastic, and brave, they staked their all on a delusion, and lost. Our soldiers do not twit them with their failures. I have not heard a word of exultation or a single sneer over a fallen foe. On the contrary, they mingle with them, and, like men of the same profession, compare notes and talk "military."

The prevailing colour of the ex-members of the so-called Confederate army is a dirty white as to their upper garments, and a warm brown as to their lower encasements. This last hue is the veritable and celebrated butternut, made from the infusion of the husk of the nut of a tree of the name, resembling a walnut. . . . You may be sure these men are glad to get home and see the end of a hopeless war. The officers come up cheerfully as their names are called. Colonel Smith, Major Jones, and Captain Robinson walk up the steps and receive their papers. "Now Colonel," says the Provost Martial, "cut off these insignia of rank. You too, Major. Cut your buttons off also." A couple of officers get out their penknives and reciprocate services. . . and off come the stripes of gold braid from the collar, and the C.S.A buttons from the double-breasted coat. "That's right," says the Federal officer, "Now I'd advise you to get some other clothes as soon as you can." Two rebel colonels and their staffs, who appeared in full uniform at the theatre a few nights ago, were arrested and taken out by the guard. One was the noted Colonel Chenoweth, who surrendered his command to a regiment of Negro troops some months ago. This same Colonel and his former comrades in arms now board at the City Hotel, and dine and sup regularly with Federal officers and promiscuous guests.

Coming out of the office I mingled with the joyful and patient crowd who were waiting for their papers; and being considered versed in the business in hand, I was asked many questions as to their destination, and the nature of the oath they would be required to take. There were many who had been paroled by Wilson and

Stoneman. They had been rightly informed that such paroles would not be respected and seemed anxious to know what oath would be used in substitution. One man, whose face and head were nearly lost in hair, said, "I don't care what they give me, so they give me no more fight." Another—a tall bright-eyed stripling, of about 19, said, "this is my home, and I've seen the old house this morning. I'd take a hundred oaths if they want me to." Another said he lived only five miles from the city and he was "ready to take a bushel of the strongest kind of oaths." I said to some of them: "Are you willing to become citizens of the United States?" One replied, "That's what we come for; if they'll let us." Another said emphatically, "That's my hand too." I asked if Jeff Davis were to come back with an army, would they join him? They said, "No; they intended to keep their path as long as they stayed in the country, and when they could not keep it any longer they would leave." One young man—very tall and slender, with a Roman nose and blue eyes, delicate as a woman's,—asked me, "Supposing Jeff Davis had surrendered himself and his army three months ago, did I not think he could have saved his own scalp?" I said I thought he could then; but not now. "That's just what I think," said the tall young man. After a lot had been sworn (for they are sworn in squads as couples are married in the Old Church at Manchester), one exclaimed, "Now, I'm a citizen of the United States, and I mean to continue so." No oath is required in case of men of Lee's and Johnson's armies. The parole list signed by the Confederate officers is sufficient. He gives his "honour."

On the boat going down to Clarksville there was an inebriated ex-rebel, who insisted that the Confederate army was not whipped—never had been whipped—and never could be whipped! "But," continued he, with the vehemence of a drunken man, "I'm a citizen of the United States now; just let anybody else say 'secesh' to me, and I'll be eternally rotted if I don't fix him." Out of a squad of 300 but four declined to take the oath of allegiance—preferring to be sent to one of the paroled prisoner camps, north of the Ohio. In another batch of 200 there were two who also preferred the restraint of Confederate prisoners of war to the liberty of United States citizens. All such are kept under guard, and sent north as speedily as possible. One man, meeting his parents in the street, abused them for being Yankees. All are Yankees who are not Southern men or rebels. Another man met his mother in front of the Provost Martial's office, and they entered one of the apartments. The soldier seemed dubious as to the parental reception he should get, and both held off for a while, until nature prevailed, and they rushed into each other's arms. Several ladies made their appearances on the sidewalk, with loaded baskets, and distributed pies and cakes among the hungry crowd. Had they been Yankees, how different would have been the treatment? No pies and cakes for Blue-coats, I ween [fancy].

It seems to be an easier matter for Northern soldiers and civilians than for Tennesseans to fraternize with the returning rebels. It is much to be feared that ignorance and passion and prejudice will revive old feuds engendered between neighbours at the initiation of the war. The dominant party will be apt to bear down a little too hard, and the numerical majority will kick at what they already stigmatise as an illegal and void assumption of power by an executive and legislature not popularly elected. Until the assuaging of time, or the modifying influence of a large Northern immigration shall have worked its usual results, nothing but a government almost despotic will be able to curb this turbulent element, for, though completely broken and destroyed as an organized unity, the virus of disaffection still remains, and it will continue to break out in little irritating sores all over the body politic of the Southern country. The disfranchisement and electoral disabilities of white rebels, and the social and political status of the Negro, will be fertile subjects for the bitterest animosities. Of this nobody who reads the proceedings of the Tennessee and Kentucky legislatures can entertain a doubt. Congress at Washington has no power to prescribe voting qualifications in states for either white men or Negroes. The mass of the coloured population, however loyal, whether soldiers or citizens, will never be allowed to vote at state elections, and by consequence, not at presidential elections.

In Louisville, Kentucky, there is already great apprehension of a scarcity of employment for the Negroes who flock in from the surrounding country, and are becoming so numerous as to be obnoxious. Schemes are being devised to send them off in some direction where they can shift for themselves. In this connection the Freedman's Bureau is of great avail. What is to be done with the lame, the blind, the old, the insane, is a matter for grave consideration by the state legislatures; and to this end civil jurisdiction should be encouraged, and left untrammeled by military dictation. If a great revolution does not yet supervene it will take many years to completely restore these disrupted states, reconcile startling differences, and lay down harmoniously the mosaic pavement of the old Union. . . .

If pacification shall be achieved in Tennessee, there need be no apprehensions of difficulties in any other state. A plot is now afoot to resist the decrees of the petty tribune's created by the late military Governor, to depose his officers by violence and to discredit their whole proceedings. There is also a plot brewing to assassinate Governor Brownlow; and the detectives are already on the track of a villainous ex-member of Wheeler's cavalry who was sworn to do the deed.

At the Baptist Church the other Sunday, the prayer for the Executive was very meager and vague, and prefaced by the words, "O Lord, we are commanded to pray for our rulers." It was quite evident that, had the military pressure been removed, prayer would have been loud and strong for Jeff Davis and his colleagues. The Methodist Episcopal Church, on the other hand, contains a large United States flag, draped, in mourning, and hung on the wall behind the pulpit. The inscription upon it, in large letters, reads "The Trinity M.E. Church at Cincinnati to the McKindree M.E. Church at Nashville—Greetings." I heard in this church, yesterday, a sermon by Colonel J.F. Jacques,[7] of the 73rd Illinois Volunteer Regiment, who became so notorious on account of his fruitless interview with Jefferson Davis, and the favourable impression made upon him by the insurant chief, as detailed in an account published by Jacques himself. He preached in his full uniform of a colonel of infantry. His language was vigorous, but not polished; and his discourse abounded with martial metaphors. . . . All seemed deeply impressed. But the effect was still further increased when he read a small paper which had just been handed to him. "This," said he, "has not much connection with my subject. It is the capture of Jeff Davis!" and the Colonel suddenly sat down overcome with emotion. A deep silence succeeded, which was soon broken by a clapping of hands all over the church. The sonorous voice of the regular pastor quavered as he gave out the lines:—

"All hail the power of Jesus name,
Let angels prostrate fall."[8]

The congregation joined in the hymn with great feeling, and the impressive services concluded. As we reached the street the newsboys were scudding along the sidewalk with little strips of printed paper, crying out at the top of their voices,—"Here's yer extry. 'Capture of Jeff Davis!'"

The capture of Jeff Davis destroys all apprehensions of danger from any possible combination between Kirby Smith's Trans-Mississippi forces and those of Maximilian. The brains of the Confederacy are now gone. The rebellion is now completely and permanently hors de combet [disabled]. The severed members may twist and wriggle and be obnoxious, but they can never re-unite, and never become formidable. Jefferson Davis will be hung by President Johnson just as surely as the fanatic, John Brown, who raised the standard of Negro insurrection in Virginia, was hung by Governor Wise; but the spirit of secession, or the soul of Jeff Davis, unlike that of the old Abolitionist, will not "go marching on." Secession is dead for the next century, at least.

Nashville
May 18, 1865
My dear wife,

I wrote to you not more than 5 or 6 days ago and you have probably got the letter by this time. I have just received yours of the 13th inst. I think I wrote you twice since I received the letter from Charles.

I have written two letters to the English paper this month and one to the *Chicago Tribune.* I am writing another tonight to the Tribune which will appear about the 22nd or 23rd. It will be signed "W" same as the last one you mentioned.

I received a letter from Reading of Morris saying the trial could not be reached at the Spring court and would not come on until the middle of Nov. by which time I shall be at home.

Sherman's army is now at Washington and I feel pretty sure that it and all belonging to it who are not veterans will be mustered out next month. I fully expect to be home by the fourth of July.

It is quite time I heard again from Charles. I have not heard a word from Fred. I wrote again a few days ago.

I send a $5 bill of Confederate money for Jane. A Rebel soldier gave it me. I also send two pieces of gold braid cut from a Rebel officer's coat collar—the larger piece for Freddy and the smaller for Willie.

The weather has been & still is very warm & showery. The shrubs and plants are all in full bloom and everything looks lovely. But the streets will soon be hot and dusty and very disagreeable.

I will write to Jane in a few days. I wonder very much what she is going to surprise me with. I intend to send you $20 bill next time I write.

We have had pie-plant long ago in the markets.[9] We also have salad of all kinds, strawberries & ice cream two weeks ago nearly.

Jeff Davis will pass thro' tonight perhaps.

With love to you all,

I am your affectionate husband,

WmHBradbury

Nashville
May 24th 1865
My dear daughter,

I have received your compositions and letter. I am glad that you are making so much improvement, but you must not study too much. When I come home, I shall have plenty of time to see what progress you have made. Your writing is very plain and neat, but it does not look like a young lady's hand. It should be smaller and not so heavy.

We have very fine weather now after the heavy rains. The gardens are all in bloom and the trees growing on each side of the street and almost meeting overhead make a cool, pleasant shade.

There are lots of Rebels coming in every day. Eighteen hundred arrived here at one time. There are lots of little boys, black and white, selling lemonade and ice cream and pies and cakes on the street. The little darkies drink soda water and eat ice cream. Everybody seems to have plenty of money. But when Winter comes, I don't know what will become of them all. The soldiers will be gone and the money too.

The river is very high and large boats come up from the Ohio. You know the Cumberland River runs into the Ohio and the Ohio runs into the Mississippi and so much water has gone down that river until it has burst its banks near New Orleans and has flooded the country for 40 miles in width causing great destruction of property. The late heavy rain-storms have washed away many of the bridges in Kentucky and Tennessee. There have been no mails for several days and it may be some time before you get this letter and a long time before I get another from Mother.

I see lots of school girls skipping along the shady sidewalks with their books and slates. Well-educated scholars are scarce here. There are no public schools at present, except those where black children go, which are supported by the government. There are select schools for the white children where the teachers are well paid by the parents of the scholars.

I am in hopes that I shall be home by the 4th July. I don't see why so many soldiers should be kept any longer and when Sherman's army comes home you may expect me about the same time.

I received this morning a letter from Uncle Frederic. Tell Mother I shall send him the draft today. I also received a letter from Capt. Bailhache. He has sent in his resignation and is going to Springfield, Ill.

There is a large mulberry tree growing close where my desk is. We have large catalpas and ash trees and maples and elms and sycamore and laurel trees and lilacs and trees-of-heaven and weeping willows and vines and pretty flowers which are made into bouquets or nosegays & sold at 25 cents each.

I send my love to you and Mother & Freddy and Willie and the twins.

Your affectionate father
WmHBradbury

Nashville
May 29, 1865
My dear wife,

I duly received your letter of the 23rd. The *Chicago Tribune* don't print any more of my letters. They get news by telegraph from Nashville & anything that comes by mail is not fresh enough for them. I could send news by this means, but if they did not print it, it would be my loss. I have written three or four short letters that did not appear. I shall write no more. They owe me about $20.

I received and answered a letter from Frederic. He has been at the same old place for seven years! The draft will reach him when gold is up again. I wrote a short letter to the *Manch. G* & one to Charles & sent them off today. The *Guardian* has of late printed only a portion of my letters.

The time of my arrival at home will depend upon circumstances. If I can be mustered out here, I may remain until the end of the month of June. If it is necessary that I should go to my regiment at Washington, I shall reach home with the rest! I shall find out about these matters. I suppose it will be at least a fortnight before the regiment reaches Dwight, perhaps more.

Major Thruston will, if possible, procure me a place with some quarter master or other officer—will bring in not less than $100 per month. Capt. Bailhache is coming back to Springfield, Illinois. He says he may be able to find me a job that will be congenial. I wrote to him at Springfield.

The weather here is extremely changeable, sometimes very hot & then quite cool. The catalpas & magnolias are in full bloom. We have plenty of beautiful shrubs and trees.

I wrote to Jane the other day. I will write again in a few days,

Your affect. husband,

William H Bradbury

Hdqrs Dept. Cumberland
Nashville
June 1/65
My dear wife,

I expected to have rec'd a letter from you today. But as I have good news to tell you, I thought I would not wait any longer.

As soon as the Major can get some clerks in the office to fill up the coming vacancies, I shall start for home, provided I can leave and get back before an important military trial takes place here. If the trial should come on soon, I shall probably stay here to attend to it, and not get home till latter end of July. I shall be appointed Recorder or Reporter (rather) of the Court and get about $8 per day for my services—making about $200 altogether. This will be "better than a bob in the eye with a burnt stick." You need not say anything about it at present.

I shall endeavor to find some clerks, but they are very scarce & I will try to get home in the early part of this month and stay with you about 20 days perhaps. The railroad fare will most probably be paid by the gov't as I come back. It certainly will as I go home. Some of the witnesses required at the trial are at Indianapolis and I may be sent to take their evidence. This place is about 150 miles from Chicago. I will say no more at present.

I hope to hear from you tomorrow when I will write again.

I got a letter from the *Chicago Tribune.* They wish me to discontinue writing as they are receiving telegraphic news every day.

With love to you all I remain,

Your afft. Husband,

WmHBradbury

I enclose a $20 compound interest note. What shall I bring the children?

Nashville
June 4, 1865
My dear wife,

I have received your letter of May 30th and the newspaper extracts. I also received yesterday the letter you sent me from Charles.

The trial that I spoke of is expected to come on very soon, and if I wish to be reporter of the court, I cannot, of course, go home. Maj. Thruston wishes to get thro' with the trial and go home himself about the 1st July. You need not expect me before that time. I know it is disappointing to you and the children as well as to me, but $150 will be a great bandage for such a wound. My intention was to go home and stay a short time and then come back to the trial; but it cannot be done now, as I should have no time to stay at home.

I should feel much better if you went to spend the $50 you say you would give if you were out of that fix. $50 would do a great deal of your work. I shall not be pleased if you don't get somebody to do your washing every week. What is the use of me earning money if we are not to have the benefit of it?

If the *Manchester Guardian* prints the rest of my letters, they will owe me another 20 guineas or $130. The *Chicago Tribune* owes me not less than $25. Without counting these sums, I hope to bring home about $350. I sent you $20 last time I wrote. I now send you $5 which must be used only to pay for washing and cleaning until I come home and I expect that you will use it all up and more too, for I have plenty more to send.

I think Freddy, who is a young and active boy, ought to fly around and help all he can. When folks are lazy they feel the heat just as much as when they are working and more too. I have to work hard every day and the weather here is very hot. When I get to Chicago I intend to buy something for good, industrious children that live at the land office in Dwight, Illinois. I know where that place is.

I heard from a member of the Regiment that Co. B and the rest of the Regiment would not get home until the end of the month as their papers were not made out right. If so, I may be at home as soon as they.

The *Chicago Tribune* of June 2nd contained one of my letters dated May 26 & 27.

With love to you all.
I am your afft. husband,
WmHBradbury

Head Quarters Military Division of Tennessee
Nashville
June 25th 1865
My dear wife,

I arrived here early this morning all safe and sound.[10] I stayed at Abraham Barstow's on Thursday night and had a pleasant time with him and the old lady. She looks very old but nice and trim, & with care might last some time yet. I just saw Case at Root & Cady's. I dined at Joseph Barstow's on Friday & started for Louisville at 6 the same evening.

They were all glad to see me at the office, particularly the Major. The trial has not yet come off but is expected to commence this week.

A telegram has been sent to Washington for authority from the Secretary of War to employ citizen clerks and it is quite likely to be given. My pay will not be less than $100 per month. When the trial comes on, I shall have about $8 per day as reporter as long as it lasts, which may be three weeks. Before the trial and after it, my pay will be at the rate before mentioned of at least $100 per month.

I got your letter which had been waiting for me. It was well written and well spelled. I also recd one from Banyon which had arrived in my absence & was written in April. I was disappointed at not receiving any word from Fred. I wrote him again today saying that I had sent him the draft for £10 the 25th May.

Now that I am here I begun to reflect that I might have done more for you and fixed up more at home. I feel sorry that I did not begin at first & continue till all the little chores were done. I will do penance in the shape of self-denial here for it.

General Thomas's territorial district is now much enlarged and is composed of five states—Kentucky, Tennessee, Alabama, Georgia, and Florida. Major Thruston will be retained on the staff and assist in organizing the new command which is called the "Military Division of the Tennessee." His services are almost indispensable to Genl Thomas, and he will be retained until everything is straightened out—perhaps two months. I think I shall be at liberty by that time and will come home before a certain event transpires.[11]

I shall see about my muster out tomorrow. I don't suppose I can get any pay further than the 10th June. There is (including the bounty) $160 coming to me up to that time. I shall send you at least $100 of it as soon as I get it. I think it will be best to send it by mail, a small quantity at once.

The weather is very sultry and oppressive. We have had a thunder storm this afternoon. I suppose it is about as hot here in June and September as it is in Dwight in July.

I shall write to Charles and Capt. Bailhache tomorrow.

As soon as you get the money I shall send you, I would get some carpenter to put up the rough addition at the back of the house. I would have the door at the North and the window at the East. Any common carpenter can do it in about two days I should think. The extra room & convenience will more than pay the cost which will be about $30 perhaps less. Mr. Hetzel could tell you. 200 feet for the floor—250 for the roof about 400 for the sides & nearly 400 for floor joists, rafters, studding, &c. This will make a thousand feet of lumber worth $20.00. The work, nails, glass, putty, hinges, handling &c will cost at least $10 more, or $30 altogether. The floor should be laid first, then the sides & then the roof.

I think of you and Jane and Freddy & Willie and the twins every day and I do hope that the children will all be good until I come home again. I have seen some red bladders blown full of wind which are so light as to almost float in the air and sometimes will rise to a great height.[12] They are bright red and shiny & very nice play things. I have not seen any Chicago or anywhere north of Louisville. I will bring one each for the twins if they are good and I shall remember Jane & Freddy & Willie also.

Mrs. Barstowe & Mrs. Joseph Barstowe as well as the rest of the folks desire to be remembered to you. Mrs. Jospeh B. was particularly pressing to have you call when you came up. I did not see Banyons—any of them.

I will write you again as soon as I get my pay. Be of good cheer and I will write twice a week. I do wish you had somebody to help you do the work.

With best love to you all.
I am, Your ever affect husband
WmHBradbury

Head-Quarters Department of the Cumberland,
Nashville
July 1st 1865
My dear wife,

You must excuse a long letter tonight for I have been working hard all day and shall have to work all day tomorrow—Sunday.

The trial comes on next Thursday—the 6th. There is nothing certain yet about the amount of my compensation, but it will not be less than $100 per month. The trial will last into August. I wrote you a few days ago but there has not yet been time for an answer. I wrote to Charles & Fred & Capt. Bailhache & 3 communications to the *Tribune.* I sent them today the Charges & Specifications against Champ Ferguson. I want to send them a long letter on another subject, but my regular duties take all my time.

Genl. Thomas now has an important command—six states, & Major Thruston is his legal adviser & secretary in many respects.

I shall get my regimental pay, about $180, next Monday. I was mustered out on the 26th June.

I have not yet written to Jane. You must give her my love and tell her I will write next week.

Blackberries are ripe. I wish all the children were here to gather them.

The veterans are very uneasy and want to go home—they say the war is over and they ought to be discharged. Some have more than a year to serve.

Lacey's wife has been here & she & Lacey[13] have had a "high old time." This took place while I was at home. He does not bear a good character here. They left the city together.

My health is pretty good but the weather is very hot especially in the evenings. I think it is hotter here than in Chattanooga.

The darkies here offer me $10 to take a report of their convention next August.[14] It will last three days.

If I was not so driven with work in the office I could write an interesting letter to the *Tribune* twice a week. I want to send them the charges against Col. Crane but I really cannot yet find time to copy them.

The Legislature now in session would have paid very handsomely for a good short-hand writer, nearly two hundred dollars a week—that's so. I will write again in a few days.

With love to all, I am as ever,

Your afft. Husbd,

WHB

14

"General Fisk and the Freedmen's Bureau"

July 5, 1865–August 30, 1865

During Nashville's steamy and hot summer of 1865, Bradbury was confined in stuffy court proceedings during the day and in unpleasant quarters at night, the "Hotel de Cumberland." Because of his restricted movement, his letters home provided a descriptive view of the beginnings of postwar reconstruction. Before society could move forward, though, the Bureau of Military Justice had to bring more than sixteen thousand records of courts-martial and military commissions to the attention of judge advocates and reviewing officers. Many expected the affairs of the Bureau of Military Justice to grind on for at least another solid year after the close of the war.[1]

Judge Advocate Major Thruston resolved to face the duration of the courts in Nashville with his right-hand man Private Bradbury, now a citizen-clerk, right by his side. For Bradbury, the end of the war was bittersweet; his comrades in the old regiment were going home to their families while he remained with this "Court on the Cumberland."

With Champ Ferguson's trial completed, the court-martial proceedings of Colonel and Quartermaster John C. Crane came before Bradbury for reporting. While he did not address this case in great detail with Mary, on the surface the circumstances were far less interesting than the murders committed by Champ Ferguson. Colonel Crane faced five main charges:

1. Accepting personal compensations for awarding U.S. military railroad supply contracts.

2. Fraudulent conduct by making large purchases without requisitions and approvals.
3. Neglect of duty by procuring unsuitable supplies at high prices.
4. Conduct contrary to good military discipline; namely, suggesting gifts and bribes of persons conducting business with his office.
5. Conduct unbecoming an officer and a gentleman.[2]

Bradbury complained about the time-consuming court appeals that affected his own life—his return home.

Crane's defense attorney appealed directly to President Andrew Johnson to intervene, arguing that the amount in question from all the charges in dispute, roughly $1,000, was insignificant when compared with the total cost of the goods that had been administered through Crane—$8,000,000. Capping his argument, Crane's counsel suggested, without subtlety, to President Johnson in a private memorandum, that the charges were trivial if Johnson would stop to consider another important reason for his presidential intervention and dismissal of the case:

> It is true that Col. Crane did receive money from parties engaged in purchasing supplies to [those] who were favourable to the election of Mr. Lincoln and yourself [President Johnson]. Not a cent of it was used by him, but it was all paid over to the National Executive Committee. . . .[3]

Unaware of the private memoranda darting back and forth, Bradbury's attention was on the incomplete tasks back home. With Mary's delivery date approaching fast, he felt that the family needed hired help and a larger kitchen. Regardless of his plans, fate was not cooperating.

While Bradbury awaited the conclusion of the Crane court-martial proceedings, he was also coming to grips with the uncertainty of his future career plans. His old friend Captain Bailhache had returned to work as managing editor of the *Illinois State Journal* in Springfield. Comrades from the 129th Illinois Infantry were returning to their businesses, churches, and farms throughout Livingston County and beyond. Yet Major Thruston was encouraging Bradbury to stay right where he was, with a respectable paycheck from his work as an army court recorder for the military cases in Nashville. Things left unsettled, unsettled Bradbury. Uncertainty seemed to buzz at him just like the mosquitoes during the hot, humid nights in the "Hotel de Cumberland."

Whatever the future held and wherever it was to be, at least Bradbury had his health. His former commanding officer from Knoxville, Captain Lunt, was far less fortunate. He survived the war yet lost his battle to fever near New Orleans that summer of 1865.[4] If Bradbury had accompanied Lunt, as he had first hoped months before, he might also have become another statistic in the close of the prolonged war.

For a brief time during the summer of 1865, Bradbury was involved in the establishment of a branch of the Bureau of Freedmen, Refugees, and Abandoned Lands. The Bureau, outlined by Edwin Stanton of the War Department, approved by an act of Congress,[5] and led by General Oliver O. Howard as commissioner, had two major objectives: to ensure that former slaves were truly emancipated, and to support and reinforce the stability of the Union by continued presence of troops in southern states. Commissioner Howard divided the former slave territory into fourteen districts and appointed assistant commissioners. General Clinton B. Fisk was appointed Assistant Commissioner for Tennessee, Kentucky, and Northern Alabama.

Assistant Commissioners were authorized to hire bureau agents to implement new practices and laws. Bradbury's new assignment as Fisk's assistant was to draw up contracts and various legal agreements between freedmen and their employers. In this role, he was entitled to earn fees for contract work.

In those early days, there was great optimism about the bureau's high goals. General Fisk was reported to have told his agents to strive for justice and peaceful relations in the fulfillment of their duties.[6] The Nashville newspaper indicated that they were pleased that General Fisk was in charge of their region.[7] Yet Fisk's territory was not without its problems. A superintendent of a refugee home in Nashville was attacked for fiscal mismanagement and bookkeeping irregularities. In Murfreesboro, a petition was signed to oust another of Fisk's agents for misconduct.[8] It seemed that the intricacies of the bureau's management was fraught with potential abuse and controversy from its earliest days.

A man of impeccable reputation, General Fisk would not stand idly by while such abuses soiled his efforts. By October 1865, he ordered that the refugee homes and freedmen's camps be disbanded.[9] If the bureau's early efforts had proceeded more smoothly and if President Andrew Johnson had supported its work, Bradbury might have stayed in Nashville, not with Major Thruston, who had been asking for him, but with General Fisk.

While the Bureau would attempt many strategies, its days were numbered under President Johnson, Tennessee's inheritor of the presidency. One of the bureau's successes, though, was the education enterprise under the guidance of General Fisk. As Bradbury wrote home about his observations of their elementary schools, leaders from both the North and South were interested in the performance of the schools. In spite of the bureau's brief history, the stomping grounds of General Fisk's early days of trial and error in the creation of the Freedmen's Bureau in Nashville gave rise to an enduring legacy—the founding of Fisk University.

Headqrs. Military Div. Of the Tennessee
Nashville
July 5th 1865
My dear daughter,

I am here again in Nashville working away on the office as if I had never been home. I think every day of my little girl and boys and wonder what they are doing at different times. I think I see Jane helping Mother with the dishes; Freddy getting in kindlings and chopping with his hatchet; Willie playing with the babies and Eddy standing up in his chair at the table with his eyes wide open and his mouth ready to say something big, and Ellie [Elwood] hiding behind Mother and biting her dress.

Oh dear! Don't I wish I was back with plenty of money and plenty of nice tales to tell you all. Well! Never mind. I'll be at home, if possible, in about 7 weeks and see what I can do for good children and Mother and all.

We had fourth of July here yesterday. I went out to see them in the morning and again in the evening and we had fireworks in a half a dozen different places. Rockets and Roman candles and wheels and crackers and rip-raps and paper lanterns & balloons. I saw two boys chasing each other and shooting fire balls along the street. Some of the balls were red and some green. It was not all over until 11 o'clock.

Now I must tell you about the school for colored children which I visited. They had 160 scholars and two teachers. I attended the examination and we had recitations & declarations & dialogues from little darkies who bobbed their heads & repeated their pieces very well. A colored girl played the piano & another sang very well. They repeated their geography lessons and spelled words of six syllables. One boy made a blunder in the word 'forceps' spelling it 'forseps.' Some were nearly white and some nearly black. The whitest were not always the smartest.[10]

They repeated the states of North & South America & their capitals—their voices going all together with a growling base and a treble squeak. They repeat everything twice—thus: "Brazil—Brazil" "Rio Janeiro—Rio Janeiro" "Patagonia—Patagonia." "Has no capital—Has no capital."

They are learning very fast and carry their books & slates to & from school like other children.

I remain,
Your affectionate father

Head-quarters Department of the Cumberland
Nashville
July 5, 1865
My dear wife:

I duly received your letter of the 28th June. I am glad to hear the children have been so good. I hope they had a good time yesterday at Pontiac. We had some fireworks and some music, but the weather was so very hot that we could scarcely enjoy it. It is very hot today also.

I am glad you sold the calf and that the cow came up. I think Rosey would stand without tying. I suppose Fred milks Bossy. How does your milk house answer?

The trial begins tomorrow and will continue 4 or five weeks. I shall not get less than five dollars a day and as much more as possible. I received $180 of the paymaster the other day which includes Bounty & anything up to the 25th when I was discharged. I have received about $20 more for extra duty pay & converted the money; [it] is all in compound interest notes of a late date. I enclose you a $50 note. I dare not risk the $$. Some means will be devised if possible to pay me for my services since I was discharged to the present time. I mean to be economical and save as much as I can for the dear ones that cluster round our home. I never forget them.

I still board at the same place—$6 a week now. I lodge at the "Hotel De Cumberland" as we call it. I did not go to sleep last night until 12 o'clock on account of the heat. Today is somewhat cooler. The river is very low and everything hot and dry.

I am glad to see that by the cotton reports Charles must have made some money if he purchased on the strength of his calculations about the time I wrote to him. I wrote him fully on the subject & sent him some papers. I must write him again in a short time. I have not received a word from that wretch of a Fred. I don't know whether he received the draft for £10 or not. I have sent word to him by a man going to New York.

I enclose you some pens. I hope you don't have it quite so hot as it is here.

With my best love to you all,
I am your affectionate husband,
WmHBradbury

Head-Quarters Department of the Cumberland
Nashville
July 7th 1865
My dear wife,

I wrote to you and Jane two or three days ago enclosing $50. I have not much to say now. We have terrible hot sweltering weather—thermometer at 98 or 100 in the shade frequently. There is a little breeze stirring this afternoon which makes it pleasanter. We have ice water to drink and cool off, but the sleeping at night is nearly played out in our hot rooms, which are shielded from the sun only by a thin pine roof. We hope for some cool breezes bye and bye.

I have heard nothing from Fred & I shall write to Charles again tonight. I sent word to Fred by a man who is going to New York.

I saw Gen. Sherman the other night. He came here from Louisville to see old Thomas. He calls him "old Tom." He was serenaded in the evening.

We have not done much in the heat, yet all the members of the court are not here. I don't think we shall begin fairly before Monday or Tuesday. We sit from 9 in the morning till one in the afternoon, after which I write up my notes on the record. I have made some enquiries today about cotton & shall send the information to Charles tomorrow.[11]

I am expecting to hear from you something about the 4th at

Pontiac. I suppose the children went except the little chaps who staid at home. I do hope that it is not as hot with you as it is here. The brick and stone reflect the heat during the day and retain it during the night. Nashville you know is built on the rocks. It is called "Rock City."

I enclose you three $10 compound interest notes. Don't you think I may risk the $100 note next time? When I have sent you that, I shall have only about $12. You will have to send me some more in about two or three weeks.

Can't you get somebody to build the kitchen. It will be very useful.

The Tribune Co. don't print my contributions—confound 'em! I'll fix 'em bye & bye.

I think I shall fetch up my blanket from the Hotel de Cumberland and sleep out of doors tonight on the porch at the office. It is so very hot in our room. My face streams with perspiration as I write, but after all, I have not near so much to contend with as you who have to strive and labor every day. I think of you, my dear very often and hope & try to make some alleviation.

By the way, how does the sign look? Did you get paid for it?

I now conclude with my best and dearest love to you all.

I am your affectionate husband,

WmHBradbury

Nashville
July 11th, 1865
My dear wife,

I duly received your & Jane's letter of the 6th this morning. By this time you will have received the $50 & the $30 I hope.

It is now just 9 o'clock and I have just finished my days work for which I shall certainly get between $5 and $10. It is the exchange price allowed and the Major will sign the papers at that rate and do his best to get them approved by the Adjutant General. If that is considered too much, there may be a little taken off. I had no difficulty in transcribing my notes, but I expect to have a hard day tomorrow.

The court sits from 9 to 1 o'clock and I take down the questions and answers of the witnesses and keep in proper shape all the papers. In the afternoon I write out in full my shorthand notes in book form which then becomes the record of the proceedings of the court. I will send you a printed copy of the charges which I prepared with great labor for the *Chicago Tribune,* but they never printed it. The Cincinnati paper got it for nothing.[12]

Gifford and Palmer Groceries and Provisions counts 38 letters which at 12½¢ per letter makes $4.75. I counted them wrongly as 39 letters which would have made $5 lacking a shilling. But it was E. Gifford and Palmer which makes just 39 letters of $4.87 ½. He agreed to give me a shilling a letter & I mean to have it. It was so near $5 that I thought he would not object to paying it. The price here for similar work is 50 cents per letter of the same size & style. How Baker got his $4.55 I can't imagine.

It is now near 10 o'clock. The night is cool and the band playing close by. It has been very hot.

I hope you have started the kitchen. Have you any money that is not compound interest money? If I save this whole $100 bill (May 15), I shall soon need some at the end of this week. I should have some; my pay for the present work will not be received till the trial is over next month.

I am glad the garden is finished and that the children have got in something to burn. I feel sure they will be good children & I shall soon come home again.

Blackberries are now over. We are having corn, green tomatoes, [and] new potatoes long ago.

The hot weather seems over for a little while. It is cloudy & cool now. My health is pretty good.

I wrote to Charles—not a word from Fred.

I send my best love to you all. Hoping to hear from you again soon,

I am your affectionate husband,

WmHBradbury

Nashville
July 15th 1865
My dear wife,

I received yesterday your letter of the 11th July. You do not say whether you received the $50 compound interest note. If you have no money at Hetzel's, you had better spend that first as it is dated only a short time ago. You should spend those first of the latest date. I don't suppose anybody would allow anything extra for those which had run less than a year.

I enclose [a] letter received yesterday from Fred.

I have worked eight days on Col. Crane's trial and have earned $80 or $90 since I got back. The court does not sit today. We shall have a big day on Monday.[13] I have every reason to expect $10 a day for my services and I think today will be counted in.

The labor of taking down the notes is not much but in the afternoon & evening I have to copy them all out. Thursday afternoon & night I wrote out 20 pages of foolscap[14] which took me until 10 o'clock. But I can stand it very well when I think about the $10. The trial will probably last 6 weeks or 40 days, not counting Sundays. This will give $400 for my services. Bully for me!

I hope you have lost no time in building the addition. A rough carpenter that will work fast at moderate wages would do. John Hetzel will understand. I would not put any more nails in than necessary as it may be taken down some time & the lumber used for something else.

The weather has not been very hot lately. Last night was quite cool and refreshing. The Summer is nearly half over. Blackberries are over here, but you can get some from Chicago. They will be in season very soon. Tell Hetzel to bring you down a small pailful or send a few by express. There is no need to send any from here; it is so far. Green apples are now in season here.

I think the trial will be over about the latter half of August tho' there are many witnesses to examine.

I think you should bespeak the services of Mr. Cutler & hurry up with the back kitchen. I fully expect to be at liberty by the 25th August.

Owing to the mustering out of service of another clerk, I have the bedroom at the "Hotel de Cumberland," as we call the government building, all to myself. I wish I had carpet for the floor. I have a wash stand & basin & a pail & wash tub. I only need a darkey to wait upon me & black my shoes & then I shall be all right.

I hope you will use and enjoy the fruits of my labors. I shall have to break my $100 notes next week. There is no interest on it yet. These interest notes don't sell any more until they are about a year old. A few months interest makes no difference. They are of course good to keep.

My health is good. I hope you & the children all keep well.

I send my love to you all and remain,

Your affectionate husband,

WmHBradbury

Nashville

July 22nd 1865

My dear wife,

I received yesterday your letter of the 18th. I intended to have written two or three days ago, but I have been working for several nights until after 12 o'clock writing up my short-hand notes. Today the work has been lighter and I have deferred the writing or copying until tomorrow.

The verbal testimony is drawing to a close and a few more days will complete my labors on this trial. There is however, another case to be tried by the same court on which I shall probably be engaged. It will not last more than a day or two.

I have also been asked by one of the editors of the *Cincinnati Gazette* to write two or three letters on the trial I am now reporting. I expect the present trial will close this next week and I shall then do what seems best to make the most money until towards the end of August. I think I can get perhaps $150 per month in some capacity.

I now pay $7 a week for board & unsatisfactory at that. The bread is always sour. I must change [even] if it costs more.

I am glad you got the $50. I send you $20.

The weather is very hot again and drinking & sweating is all the go. I suppose you too are having a streak of hot weather.

I am glad to hear the garden looks well & I am sure Jane is very good to take so much pains to keep it clean.

What is Freddy doing and Willie? I suppose Willie is a very good boy and minding the twins & making himself useful. I wish I could just drop in & see what you are doing—all of you. I shall be home next month in about 4 weeks from the time you get this.

I would send you some peaches, but you can get them in Chicago better & cheaper. It would cost to send my express as much as the peaches are worth in Chicago. I think you should secure Mary Kochlein as soon as possible or you may lose the chance.[15]

I saw today one of the Capt. Lunt's old clerks who told me the captain died in New Orleans of delirium tremors. Poor old Lunt.

I send my best love to you all & will write again in about 3 or 4 days if I can possibly find time.

Your affectionate husband,
WmHBradbury

Head-Quarters Military Division of the Tennessee
Nashville
July 27th 1865
My dear wife,

I received your last letter a few days ago & answered it next day enclosing $20 which I suppose you got. I shall perhaps receive another tomorrow.

The weather today has been very hot, so it was last night & will be again tonight.

The court-martial has adjourned while the depositions of distant witnesses are being taken. It will meet again at a very bad time, the 4th of September, tho' I don't think there will be anything requiring my services as there are only a few witnesses to be examined verbally.

Another case will be tried before our court on Saturday if the witnesses attend. I shall endeavor to get a job on one of the district courts if possible, but the result is doubtful. There is, however, plenty of other work at which I can get at least $100 a month. I think I had better make all the money I can until the latter part of August when I propose to come home.

It is extremely sultry tonight & we shall have a big storm before morning. I suppose you have the changes of weather just as we have.

I feel anxious to come home and see what you all are doing but I suppose $50 more would be better than to have me loafing round the house this hot weather.

I wish we had the addition of two rooms on the South side. They are absolutely necessary I think. If you have the kitchen up you will have more room, but still not enough. I think we might venture on the addition if I see a way to earn the cost of it this Winter or Fall by two or three months work. But we will discuss this when I get home.

You must look out for a hired girl, tho' I really don't know where we can all sleep unless I bring a tent and sleep out with the children like soldiers. How would Freddy & Willie like that.

You will excuse me writing any more; it is so oppressively hot and I really cannot think of anything. I should like Jane to tell me how the sign, that I painted, looks. Did Baker pay the balance—the whole is $4.87½. If he has not I will settle with him when I come home.

I shall perhaps have something more interesting next time. With best love to you all,

I am yours affectly,
WmHBradbury

Nashville
July 31st 1865
My dear wife,

I received yours of the 25th in about three days after its date.

I have finished my court-martial reporting for the present. This is the last day of this court until it re-assembles on the 4th Sept. next when there may be two or three days work. There is another court about to be convened in perhaps a few days which will probably give me employment for 10 days.

I expect to make about $200 out of this. I shall make out my bill tomorrow. I shall do the best I can until towards the end of August when I shall come home.

I am afraid we shall have much difficulty in getting a girl or woman or anybody to wait upon you. I wish we had room for a darkey woman.

I shall stir the children up with a long pole when I come home and bring good boys and girls something pretty.

My health is very good and the weather is cool and pleasant just now. The nights have been quite cool lately. We shall have it hot again bye & bye.

We have peaches, pears, apples & melons. I would send you some peaches if I thought they would keep four days, perhaps longer.

Maj. Thruston is going home this week & wishes to have me in charge of the office. I still sleep at the Hotel de Cumberland and board elsewhere.

It is quite time we had another letter from Charles. That rascal of a Fred has never written again. I think I might as well send him another $50 as keep it doing nothing.

Look out for the Atlantic telegraph—we must soon hear of its completion.[16]

I can't think of any more to say this time. I send my best love to you all. What is Jane doing? I don't hear anything from her.

I am your affectionate husband,

WmHBradbury

Nashville
August 3rd 1865
My dear wife,

I enclose you express receipt for a box of peaches. The charges are all paid. You ought to get them in a day or two after the receipt of this. They will keep two or three days after you get them. I suppose you require no directions as to their use.

I received today $200 for my services as short-hand writer. I expect to get another case tomorrow. Maj. Thruston wishes me to remain here doing his absence & to be on hand to report the balance of the Col. Crane's trial which re-convenes on the 4th Sept. Probably my services could be dispensed with until the 10th. I am inclined to leave here for home about the 20th & start back about the 7th Sept. It would be near $100 in my pocket to be here during the balance of the court trial.

The editor of the *Cincinnati Gazette* wishes me to make a report of the case which will be worth about $50. You see my services are in demand.

In addition to this, Genl. Fisk[17] who has charge of the Freedmen & Refugees throughout this part of the South, wishes me to be his private secretary & to accompany him on a tour through the South and remain with him when he gets back to Nashville. How can I do these things & attend to my family? That's what's the matter.

At the same [time] it would be a nice thing to have a few hundred dollars laid by. I enclose you $30. If I did not intend coming home soon, I would send it all by express.

I have written a letter to Gen. Fisk at his request enclosing a strong letter of recommendation from Maj. Thruston who has just gone home.

The weather is rainy & sultry and mosquitoes are very troublesome. The stink and dirt about Nashville are intolerable and it seems almost impossible to avoid disease this summer.

Unless I am required to report Capt. Smith's case tomorrow, I shall begin my account for the *Cincinnati Gazette* of Col. Crane's trial. If nothing of great necessity intervenes, I shall start for home on the 20th.

I hope you will spare no expense in getting somebody to wait upon you. You should look out in time.

I see gold is advancing in price and articles of food will advance with it. It will soon to be time to receive the box of clothing from Charles. I have heard nothing from Fred.

If I come home, I shall not start back until they telegraph for me. I wish I could find something at home as profitable as here. I do dislike being away so much at a time when the children require attention. We will talk it all over when I get home.

I expect to receive a letter from you tomorrow. I will write again in a few days.

I am now in the office all alone. I have a room here now and have left the "Hotel de Cumberland" which is full of bugs. The night is damp there and sweaty & very disagreeable.

Having nothing more to say, I send my best love to you all. The peaches are for good children.

I am your affectionate husband,
WmHBradbury

Nashville
August 9th 1865
My dear wife,

I am still here doing nothing of much account, but superintending Maj. Thruston's business a little, and writing a report of Col. Crane's trial for the *Cincinnati Gazette.* If nothing more profitable offers, I think of starting for home about the 20th by which the business of the office will not be of much importance. I shall bring the tent with me and the children can sleep out of doors soldier fashion. I shall bring another blanket also. We shall want three long sticks to fix it.

Gen. Fisk wants me to come to his office & will pay me $150 per month if he can arrange it with his Quartermaster. I told him I could not possibly come before the middle of next September.

On the 8th I reported two speeches at the colored convention delivered by Gen. Fisk & a colored preacher. They occupied nearly two columns. I will send you the paper if I can find it. I staid writing them out until 2 o' clock in the morning.

The weather is very sultry and close. The evenings are warm & mosquitoes abound. I hope you have it more pleasant.

I have heard no more from Fred. The box of clothes from Charles will be here inside of another month probably.

I think 10 feet by 12 is too small for the kitchen. I should have made it the whole width.

I enclose you $20 which leaves me about $90. I expect to get about $40 for what I have already done for the *Cincinnati Gazette.*

I don't know that I have anything more to say this time.

I send my best love to you all. My health is pretty good considering the weather. I board now at a bully good place.

The night is very warm & close & still and dark.

I am,
Your affectionate husband,
WmHBradbury

Nashville
August 15th 1865
My dear wife,

I duly received your letter of the 7th August. Taking into consideration the uncertainty of the event & the fact that I had nothing here to do that was profitable, I engaged with Gen. Fisk today at $150 per month. In addition to this, I hope to pick up a few dollars by corresponding with the Nashville paper with which I am well acquainted.

I commence tomorrow my duties with Gen. Fisk and on Thursday next I shall accompany him on his tour through Northern Alabama & East Tennessee. I hope you will spare no pain & expense to make yourself & the children quite comfortable. I should have been glad to have come home & helped all I could, but my staying, too, will save at least $100 and that sum, tho it will not compensate for my absence, will procure many indulgences. If I thought you would not make use of it in that way, I would certainly come home & ease you of some of the drudgery.

Gen. Fisk gives me permission to finish Col. Crane's trial, which will amount to about $70 or perhaps $100, besides $50 which I shall get from the *Cincinnati Gazette* for my report of the case, of which I have already written more than one half.

It will be sometime in October before I can be at home and am sure I regret it very much for I want to see you & the children. It seems as if I had been away from you a very long time.

When I do come I will bring the tent and the children can play soldier & sleep outdoors. If I were to come now I should be required back about the 4th Sept by which time the event might not have taken place. If I did not come back I should lose considerable. I do entreat you to make use of the money I send & procure all the comfort you can. If you want me to come, I will come if possible.

I received a short letter from Charles. He says he will send the box of clothing, &c. I think we may look out for it about the latter part of September. I have heard nothing from Frederic since.

I have now $180. I think of sending a $50 bill to Frederic by this mail. I send you $20 which with what I have sent before will be sufficient for some time.

The weather looks cooler just now, but the wind dies away at night & the heat & the mosquitoes & the bugs are very bad. As soon as we get into East Tennessee I hope to find it better. I had a hard night last night.

I remain,
Your affectionate husband,
WmHBradbury

Nashville
Aug.18th 1865
My dear wife,

Your letter of the 14th came to hand yesterday. I am sorry the peaches were all spoiled. The man from whom I bought them said he would pick me some nice ones that would keep and the express agent said they would keep a week. They did not cost much and the man says he will give me another box. I shall know better next time. I thought there would be scarcely any peaches in Chicago by the time you got those. I am glad you made up the disappointment by treating the children.

My last letter will explain how much money I have sent Frederic —$50. I suppose I spend considerably less than anybody else in a similar position, $5 a week is the very lowest price for board in the whole city and at a place where Irish laborers, etc. take their meals.[18]

Private boarding houses charge from $7 to $12 a week. A lieutenant at our office says it costs him nearly $50 per month. The correspondent of the New York *Herald* gets his board & lodging as a favor at $15 per week. Everything is extremely dear here.

If I have spent anything out of the way, I have earned it by extra labor. It does not cost me anything for lodging, but I must spend the evening somewhere and I generally go to the *Press & Times* newspapers' office which is just as good as a reading room for they have all the papers & magazines. I buy a few drinks sometimes, but it cost me nothing to go to the theatre. I must spend the time some way. There is nobody left at the office but orderlies who have no intelligence. Editors of newspapers are good company and I write little things for them.

I send you $20 more which leaves me about $90. I am sorry Mrs. Neimire has disappointed you.[19] I think you ought to get an efficient person if it costs $2 per day. I should feel much better if I were sure that you were comfortable in that respect.

If I were sure the event would take place immediately, I would come home now and jet back before Col. Crane's trial was resumed. This will be about the 8th of Sept.

Gen. Fisk wants my services all the time I suppose. He is gone away for a fortnight and will expect me [to] be on hand when he comes back to take down testimony in shorthand and help generally in his office.

It appears to me that my best hold this Fall will be at Nashville or somewhere near there. I shall practice my shorthand and make myself competent to get good pay nearer home. A good short-hand writer can get a place in almost any large city.

I intend to come home as soon as I can, perhaps in September and stay a month. I could be spared better now than any time, but I ought to be back in the early part of next month. If you are likely to suffer or be inconvenienced much by my absence, I will come as soon as you send for me.[20]

My health has not been very good lately. The city is unwholesome and the weather is hot. The wind dies away at night & mosquitoes are numerous. We shall soon have it cooler.

The children must be very good and Father will remember them when he comes home. I send my best love to you all & wish I could be with & stay with you.

Your affectionate husband,

WmHBradbury

Can't you get the service of Mrs. Cutler?

I wrote to Charles the other day urging him to hold on to his cotton & wait for a rise of price.

Nashville
Aug. 26, 1865
My dear wife,

I duly received yours of the 19th. I send you another $20 as I know you can keep it better than I. I was much pleased with your letter. I am very glad you feel easy and comfortable and that you have a cool room to eat in. I should like to pop in some time & see you all seated round the table.

I have just agreed to sell the report of Crane's trial which I have already written to a Cincinnati paper for $30. I expect to get at least $20 for the balance of it. Gen. Fisk agreed to pay me $150 a month. At the end of this month I shall have made upwards of $300 since I left home last time. In September I shall make about $175 and then I shall endeavor to come home. Just take notice how much I send you from this time out.

I was kept awake until 2 o'clock this morning by mosquitoes & a fire in the city which burned quickly for about two hours. There were two steam fire engines playing upon it. The weather has been cool and bracing but it is now hot again. I shall get some oil of peppermint to keep off the mosquitoes.

I sleep in a room with all the windows and doors open on an iron bedstead with a corn husk mattress and a blanket for covering. The room is in the office & does not cost anything.

Gen. Fisk will not be back before the 7th of next month. My duties with him will be to take down testimony of colored people who make complaints. Their evidence is not admitted before the regular courts and the Freedmen's Bureau is established for their benefit and in case it appears that they have been wrong, the military authorities assist the Freedmen's court by carrying out its decrees. Otherwise a colored man could never collect a debt or have a wrong addressed unless he could procure a white witness on his side. The evidence of colored people is good against each other.

I will write you regularly about twice a week. I send my love to you and the children.

Your affectionate husband,
WmHBradbury

Head-Quarters Military Division of the Tennessee
August 30th 1865
My dear wife,

I duly received yours of the 23rd. Gen. Fisk finds that he cannot retain me. He is not authorized by law to do so. I was therefore relieved on Saturday from further duty & have nothing to do until Col. Crane's trial comes on the 4th Sept.

The trial will not last more than 10 days; and if nothing profitable presents itself, I shall start for home at its close and be with you very likely about the 20th.

I am glad to hear the children are so good. I shall certainly bring them something. I think of you all every day.

I think owing to the scarcity of wheat caused by the failure of the crops in many places that flour will be higher. You should buy a stock of it unless it has just risen in price. I know a merchant here who is holding seven thousand barrels for a rise.

I received the other day a letter from Fred. He says if I send him much more money, he will be owing me. He says his employers are very indulgent and he seems to have a nice place. He has been there about seven years.

The weather is more pleasant that it has been, but the nights are still and warm, and mosquitoes are very abundant & troublesome. They torment me for two or three hours every night until it becomes cool enough to keep covered up.

We have had no rain for a very long time and the trees are beginning to shed their leaves from dryness. The streets are dusty and hot, but we have a cool pleasant office where I attend to what there is to be done for Maj. Thruston & practice shorthand.

I frequently go to the newspaper office & read the *Press & Times* & other papers from all parts of the country.

I have heard nothing lately from Charles. I wrote him advising him to hold his cotton for a rise.

We ought to receive the box of clothing pretty soon. I wrote to Fred about it.

With my best love to you all,

I am your affect. husband,

WmHBradbury

I will write every few days.

15

"To Clasp You Once More in My Arms"

September 2, 1865–December 15, 1865

Mary Bradbury safely delivered their sixth child, to William's profound disappointment another son. While he had not expressed a gender preference during her pregnancy, now that the baby had arrived, William seemed deflated, if not depressed, over the news of another son. Perhaps to him, the prospect of another daughter meant that he would have a chance for another girl like Jane. He had shared so much with Jane; she was his little scholar as well as an adored daughter. Like her mother, Jane was also a hard worker.

When Bradbury suggested that his son be named Charles, it is hard to imagine that they had not already considered his elder brother's name for one of the other four sons. By naming the baby Charles, Bradbury seemed resigned rather than happy and speculated aloud, by pen, that they might come to love baby Charles over time. With such a beginning, the challenges in life "Charley" later faced are more understandable.[1]

Nearly two months would pass before Bradbury could get a furlough home, and by then he had warmed somewhat to the concept of another child in the house, even a boy. And in the weeks that passed, Bradbury seemed to regain his old self and was once again in a fervor to see his beloved Mary.

Change had arrived in England too. Since brother Charles Bradbury, a widower, was on their minds, when news of his second marriage came, it did not seem to be a great surprise. Marrying his sister-in-law, newly widowed,[2] was a source of positive news; now Charles's children would again have a mother.

As other court cases came and went, Champ Ferguson's execution papers, prepared by Bradbury for the court, were read on the convicted murderer's final day of life, October 20, 1865. The execution day had attracted members of the press from around the country, and the coverage given the event itself was, for the time, graphic and sensational. While the perceived imminence of John Hunt Morgan had caused Private Bradbury so much concern two years earlier, it was Ferguson, another guerrilla raider, whose prosecution and execution Bradbury would document for the court. Reflecting the mentality of the times, a member of the prosecution's team, Judge Advocate Major Blackman, spoke out with a surprising statement at the end of Ferguson's trial. He claimed that there was also an unchecked, unbridled power that helped create men like Champ Ferguson. His diatribe ended with some metaphoric finger-pointing directed at the women in the court and in the region: "It was that they [Confederate women] also by their smiles and frowns incited and drove the men of the South to deeds that would have shocked the world."[3] That women were responsible for or accessories to Champ Ferguson's murders and his horrific methods was a stretch of the imagination. Ferguson owned up to most, not all, of the murders charged to him and indicated that there were likely others that never made it to the list. When he swung on the gallows, two Confederate females, not known to have incited him to murder and who had stayed in the background of his life at their home near Sparta, Tennessee, were there to witness that fateful day. His wife, Martha, and sixteen-year-old daughter, Ann, said their last goodbyes to "poor, dear Papa."[4]

Bradbury would not see that other troublesome case, the Crane court-martial trial, completed while he worked for the courts. A variety of political officials were concerned with continuing the case and making it public.

Tennessee's state comptroller, Joseph Smith Fowler, alerted his political ally President Andrew Johnson that suppression of Crane's case could well serve the "friends" of the party and Johnson in particular:

> The part relating to the election . . . [was] known to many of the friends of the ticket. . . . Without commending the course pursued as the best for republican institutions, it is not now possible to change it. To recover now, this subject can do nothing but expose the friends of the government who greatly fear the result. If there is

> any case in which a trial should be suppressed, this appears to me to be one of them. Col. Crane relies very greatly on your good will and hopes not to be compelled to undergo a trial that will exhaust all his means whilst he is conscious of success and which he believes calculated to disparage him for the gratification of personal malice.[5]

Those remarks, both collegial and cautionary, to Johnson during the early days of his presidency were ironic in light of Fowler's future role. As U.S. Senator from 1866 to 1871, Fowler found much to dislike in President Johnson's administration, and he said so publicly. By 1867 Senator Fowler would have a personally and professionally painful task, perhaps the hardest of his lifetime—voting on the issue of impeachment of President Johnson.[6]

The closing days of Bradbury's service to the Judge Advocate seemed rushed, as he made decisions on where to live and how to support himself and his family. He was introduced to members of the Tennessee state legislature and continued to keep company in high social circles.

Bradbury had the good fortune of meeting American writer Artemus Ward. Ward would soon be in London for stage performances, but he would also become managing editor of *Punch,* quite an accomplishment for an American. But for Ward, considered a brilliant writer, London would be his undoing. Within two years, Ward would die in Hampshire, England, at the young age of thirty-three.[7]

The Christmas holiday was impending upon them as well. Yet Bradbury was beginning to separate from Major Thruston and other comrades of long-standing in spite of their pleas that he stay in Nashville. He did not indicate in his letters home that he wanted to stay there, nor did he want to move the family to Nashville. The decision must not have been difficult, but disengaging from his network of friends and supporters may have been very hard.

Getting home, though, would be the right start to getting on with the rest of his life. Time would have to take care of many things. Decisions about many of them had been suspended for years: career, public land acquisitions in Kansas and Nebraska, additions to the house, lawsuits, and of course distributing rewards for good deportment reports among the children.

He was not career army. It was all right to go home—others had. It was now time for Private Bradbury to face the final challenge—the return to civilian life chock-full of uncertainty. He could do it; he would do it. Bradbury just had to work up to it in his own way. Then he, too, would be heading home to Mary and their six children in Dwight, Illinois, and the prospect of more adventures on the prairie.

Nashville
Sept. 2nd 1865
My dear wife,

I have just received yours of the 26th and 30th. I am very glad to hear that you were safely delivered and that you are as well as could be expected. I have been thinking about you every day. I send my kindest love & sympathies to you & the dear little boy.[8] I wish it had been a girl.[9]

Circumstances have so turned that I shall come home as soon as I can collect what is due to me. Gen. Fisk was not authorized to retain me and I left on the 26th August. Col. Crane's trial is postponed for another month by direction of the President and order of the Secretary of War. These things together with your condition induced me to decide to come home. Gen. Fisk owes me $50, the Cincinnati *Commercial* $35. As I shall be home soon, I have not much to say now.

With regard to Petzer, I shall be guided by the best advice I can get when I reach home. At the rate he has been paying for the land, it will take nearly 20 years to clear it. If he would engage to pay the balance in four years, it would be worthwhile to consider the proposition. You did right to send him to Grant. I wrote to Grant twice but he never replied. Don't say anything more to Petzer.

I have read the letters from your mother. I feel very sorry for her. We must send her photographs of the children or some little present. It seems strange that she cannot agree with her daughter-in-law. I am sure I should take a pleasure in pleasing her. I always thought she was a very nice old lady. Old Mrs. Bedford could not agree with her daughter-in-law. I suppose it is quite common to have such difficulties.

The weather has changed and we are now having very heavy rains. I hope there will be no bridges washed away between me and my dear wife.[10] I think we shall have a spell of cooler weather now. I will not say any more now as I hope to be with you next week certainly.

I send my best & dearest love to you & all the children & kisses to the baby. I suppose we should call it Charles.[11]

Your very affectionate husband,

WmHBradbury

Nashville
Oct. 16th 1865
My dear wife,

I received this morning your letter of the 13th enclosing one from Charles. I am glad he has married Mrs. Sutcliffe & I shall write and tell him so. I suppose we may expect the box within two weeks.

I am sorry to hear that the children are still unwell & hope soon to be with you and share the trouble with you.

The President has again interfered in this trial and given Crane 30 more days to obtain testimony for his defense. The members of the court are highly indignant about it. The Judge Advocate would like me to stay and be on hand on thro' 13th November, but I really feel as if I was neglecting you at home. As it is, I think I can get home with $150.

I have to make up the report for the *Commercial* newspaper and perhaps write to Manchester and then I think I shall start for sweet home. If I find that I can ride for nothing on the cars, it might pay to come here again for a few days.

I meant to have written yesterday, but I was busy writing up the testimony of a long-winded witness—a Major General.

I suppose you want me to arrange about the hay and trim the stock, etc. and do all the chores and I feel as if I ought to come home & give you some relief in the work. I do so long to clasp you once more in my arms and to hear the prattle of the children. You need not write in answer to this until you hear from me again.

I think you had better get John Hetzel to write to Topeka about the taxes. It is uncertain whether I may go, but on second thought you had better wait until I get home as you will have no money to spare. I will write you again before I start.

I send my best & sweetest love to you & the children.

I am your ever affectionate husband,

WmHBradbury

Nashville
Oct. 20—1865
My dearest wife,

I shall start for home tomorrow night or Sunday morning. I received your letter this morning.

The court adjourned until the 13th of November & may not possibly meet then. I have nothing certain to keep me here tho' I think by pushing I could become reporter to the state house of Representatives which would be worth about $200 per month. My friends are going to see what can be done.

I want also to see about the trial against Petzer, to build a barn, etc. But the chief thing why I want to come home is to see you my dearest wife. I long to see you & the children, especially you. It will not cost me much to come home.

I promised Col. Thruston to come again if there was a probability of 10 days more trial. That will be $100 & a little besides from the newspapers. I received today $130 from the govt & expect $60 or $70 from the *Commercial.* This paper & the [Cincinnati] *Gazette* are having a high old quarrel over my report. I will tell you when I get home.

Col. Thruston wants me to come to Nashville to live. I will talk it all over when I get home. Get the children on their good behavior so that we can have a good time.

I shall be introduced tomorrow to some of the "honorable members" of the legislature. The *Cincinnati Commercial* will have about 12 columns of my report of the Crane trial in their paper of Saturday.

Champ Ferguson was hung today. He was found guilty of the charges & specifications I had prepared against him.

With best love to you all,
I am your faithful & affectionate husband,
WmHBradbury

Nashville
Nov. 20th 1865
My dear wife,

I wrote to you last Wednesday of my arrival here.[12]

The Crane trial still drags its slow length along. The testimony is through, but the speeches, &c & taking up of the record will occupy this coming week and I am inclined to think that my services will be required. At all events I will bet you twenty kisses that I bring back with me $100. Won't that be "bully"? Well, we won't count our chickens before they are hatched.

I may be employed after the conclusion of this case in reporting a murder trial where a respected citizen of Nashville shot his wife's paramour. The man himself wishes a full report to show the provocation he had in his wife's shameful incontinence.[13]

I will say nothing about the box of goods & letters as you will of course send me word.

The weather has been wet, but is now cleared off. I suppose you have had snow and sleet. I often think how you get along with the cows. I suppose the pigs are getting fat. By the way, what did you [do] with. . . [section missing]

Head-Quarters Military Division of the Tennessee
Nashville
December 10th 1865
My dear wife,

I received yours of December 4th two days ago. I wrote to Charles yesterday and am now preparing a letter to the *Manchester Guardian* which I intend to finish before the court begins which I expect will be tomorrow, Tuesday.

I mean to be at home with you next week but one [week]—that is—before Christmas day. I shall start as soon as ever the case is over. You want me to tell you everything. Well, you know I love you well enough to do so.

I intend to come home—let me see that I don't figure too high—but I shall come home with I don't know how much more than I brought with me. Now then, I took $30 with me & you sent me $50 that makes $80. Well, without counting that, if I have good luck, when I arrive at home I shall be $160 richer than when I started. That of course includes the blankets which cost me $50 & $30. I sent to Topeka for the taxes. Now this amount & few thousand kisses will be a nice Christmas gift, won't it?

I intend to buy a stove in Chicago. I shall scarcely have time to look up a carpet. I think of buying some of these dark grey soldiers blankets such as you have. I have two here. I think they will make good carpeting for kitchens & bedrooms. What do you think? You will have time to write and tell me. I shall be here ten days yet.

You speak of sitting up until 10 o'clock. I certainly sit up until past that time, but I have no work to do & have to spend the time as well as I can. I drove the letter to the *Manchester Guardian* so long that I was afraid to begin. I have begun & shall finish before the court meets. Now I shall admire the fruits of your industry!

In my letter to Charles, I gave some extracts from your last letter to please his wife & children.

I hope Freddy speaks his pieces distinctly so that anybody can tell what is meant. I suppose Jane will have some good composition to show me, and the little twins will remember Papa when he comes back from Nashville.

I have sent to Georgia for some peaches. I could not get any here. I shall be glad to hear if you receive the blankets. I will buy some more if you think we could sell them at a profit. They will not cost us a trifle more than $6 a pair delivered at Dwight.

I send my best & sweetest love to you all,
Your affectionate husband,
WmHBradbury

Nashville
Dec. 15th 1865
My dear wife,

I duly received yours of the 8th. The court-martial has not yet met. If I do not hear something definite about it soon, I shall give it up & come home. I have waited for it long enough.

The weather today & yesterday has been very cold. I suppose it has been a great deal worse with you. It makes me [worry] to think of you going out & milking. I think of you on all these occasions. I hope the children do their part without much talking to. There is every appearance of snow here.

I expected to have got a letter from you yesterday. I hope you received the blankets all safe.

I am glad to hear that baby is so good. I think we shall all love him as he grows older.[14]

If the trial comes on next Monday I shall get through as soon as possible so as to be with you on Christmas day.

I am writing another letter to the *Manchester Guardian* & shall furnish it tomorrow. I have much to say.

What do you think of those dark brown blankets for carpets? Some strips of different colors could be sewed up & down & across so as to improve the looks.

Col. Thruston will be back next Tuesday & married on Thursday. Artemus Ward will be here next week.[15] I shall be introduced to him.

I suppose you get the weekly paper I send you. I have subscribed for it & it will come regularly.

Having nothing more to say I conclude with my best & sweetest love to you all. I will write again on Sunday if I hear from you in the meantime.

Your affectionate husband,

WmHBradbury

The thermometer has been 12 degrees above zero. We think that pretty cold. I don't use an overcoat. I sent you $20 last time I wrote.

Afterword

"The Bradburys' Postwar Reconstruction" 1866–1900

"Ad Astra per Aspera"[1]
"O'er rugged rocks to starry sky;
By prickly paths to thrones on high;
Through Grief to Glory!—is the cry."

The Civil War was over, but its impact reverberated for generations. Picking up plows again, finding new places in society, and rejoining families were both challenging—and welcome—endeavors. Roles had changed—for men who had become experienced with the business of soldiering, and for women who had learned to take charge of daily life without their husbands and fathers.

The long-term costs of war included more than the lost lives and property. The lost opportunity costs from existing business affairs were surely high but hard to calculate. However, the costs of reconstructing families may have been the most challenging of computations; they came at a dear price, even for the Bradburys.

In spite of Captain Thruston's encouragement, the Bradburys never moved to Nashville, where William's career opportunities seemed so bright after the war. Instead, he returned to Dwight several months after his regimental comrades were discharged and resumed his personal and business activities: he practiced law, collected rents and mortgages, played characters in community theater,[2] wrote poetry, and speculated further in real estate in the American West.

Letters continued to fill the keepsake chests of the Bradbury women, particularly as Jane (later called "Jennie") went to college in Normal, Illinois. She was, as the eldest child, perhaps destined to become the teacher of the family. At a time when teachers were not required to attend college, Jennie Bradbury did. Already a practicing teacher, at age thirty Jennie continued studying advanced course work in biology and physical culture for her teaching in Shawnee County, Kansas.[3]

William H. Bradbury, the consummate scholar, no doubt longed to have at least one member of his family follow in his footsteps. Only Jennie inherited his scholarly tendencies. In her thirties, she married Emerson Grant,[4] a civil engineer for the Atchison Topeka Santa Fe Railway. They had two daughters, and they also raised from infancy one of her nieces as their own daughter.[5]

Eldest son Frederick Bradbury became a businessman in Kansas City and was known for his work in the metal industry. Fred was said to have crafted and installed the copper dome fitting atop the Kansas capitol in Topeka. After a successful career, Fred retired and spent his winters in Vista, California, and the summers in Spearsville, Kansas. He outlived all of his siblings.[6]

Will, or "Willie," operated a variety of businesses and was involved in many civic roles in Topeka[7] near the turn of the century. Married to Cora Metcalf in 1886, Will was perhaps best known for championship race horses and stock-breeding.[8] He died August 1, 1931.[9]

Of the twins, Edwin H. Bradbury's adult work life began with the Atchison Topeka Santa Fe Railway Company as a division engineer; later he worked in the construction department. He moved on to build his own business in Kansas City, where he was a general contractor and graded many of the street lines for the city. He had a son, Gilbert, and a daughter, Dorothy. Edwin died in 1928.[10]

Elwood, or "Ellie," maintained a brotherly correspondence with Jennie for many years, although little is known about his adult life. Elwood S. Bradbury died in 1932.[11]

The youngest son, Charles, the "little stranger," who might have been missing from the list of Bradbury children had Mary followed her husband's advice, struggled with his place in the family. "Charley" never rose to the positions in life nor gained the personal peace that came more easily for Jennie and his brothers. Ironically, coming from Dwight, a town that later became known for Dr. Leslie Keeley's[12] notorious gold "cures" for alcohol addiction, Charley seemed a lost soul in his adult years, struggling with alcoholism.[13] Charley died in 1908, the first of William H. and Mary Bradbury's children to die.[14]

The Bradburys' postwar letters reflect a lively era that encompassed many trends and subjects, including reconstruction, continued immigration and westward expansion, the challenges of weather on prairie lands when they were converted to ranches and farms, railroad growth, corporate trusts and monopolies, economic recession and depression, the loneliness of prairie women, and eruptions of war around the world.

As with many veterans, perhaps the best years of William H. Bradbury's life were the years spent in the Union Army—as he had predicted in the *Guardian*.[15] The years after the war were hard for the Bradbury family. At times they seemed consumed with seizing the opportunities before them. Yet these years were bittersweet, too, as the dreams of youth increasingly faded for William. He faced the realistic limits of his station in life, socially and economically.

For Mary, having her husband home again must have been a blessed relief. Yet in spite of his promise never to leave her again, in 1873 William sent Mary, Fred, Willie, Elwood, Edwin, and Charles by covered wagon to claim their new home in Topeka, Kansas. Mary and their sons worked hard to build a dairy business and watched the wild prairies of Kansas become fenced in around them.

It took William another seven years to satisfactorily disengage from his affairs in Illinois and rejoin his family. Before he moved to Kansas, Bradbury and other Livingston County residents surely enjoyed the sweet refrains, "He remains an Englishman. . . ." from the comic opera, *HMS Pinafore,* when it was commissioned locally for a special performance.[16] A verse from a poem that he wrote and read on the occasion of a Dwight community affair, "Dwight in 1928," afforded "Brad," as he was sometimes called, a forum for humorous predictions and pokes at his neighbors and friends.[17] Based on the nostalgia of his final years in Illinois, as reflected in the poem, it seems that leaving Dwight was harder than Bradbury expected.

William participated in many Grand Army of the Republic (G.A.R.),[18] veteran-related affairs, in Illinois and in Kansas, particularly when an occasion for a poetic recitation presented itself. Many of his poems were published by local literary journals; the most popular postwar poem attributed to him was the "Tide of Bloom."[19]

Mary Bradbury surely felt estranged from the familiarity of husband, daughter, extended family, friends, and the Illinois town that for twenty years she had helped build. For the more than a quarter of a century that followed, her extensive letters written from Kansas to Jennie and other family members back in Illinois would close with wistful messages and endearments to the "friends"—the ladies like Mrs. Eldredge and Mrs. Hetzel who stood by her, helped deliver her children, and helped see her through the rough years as an Englishwoman learning about life on the Illinois prairie.

Implementer of William's dreams, Mary began to confide in Jennie, when she reached adulthood, about the challenges of her own life. From mother to daughter, we see more of the life of one immigrant family who bore the burdens of the Civil War—on the homefront. The Bradburys had tried valiantly to make a "go of it" in opening the West that seemed "boundless," just as the advertisements had declared years before.[20] But life often unfolded differently among individual lives. Mary wrote candidly to Jennie: "If you take my advice you will take what enjoyment you can as you [go] through life without waiting for the future, it may never come."[21]

The burdens on a woman like Mary Brown Bradbury cannot go unnoticed. Having a husband return alive from a war that claimed nearly a million souls could have been sufficient solace. But men like William who had wandered the country and tasted the excitement of war, rubbed elbows with highly influential and powerful men of history, and had the opportunities for some prestige and status sometimes made poor settlers when they returned home. Mary needed a lot of help, but it appears unlikely that she got very much of it from her husband.

William did not keep Mary's letters sent to him during the war. A charitable explanation might be that it was difficult to store them and move them about as a soldier on the march. However, since Bradbury's baggage rode with that of the officers, and he could track a jar of jam across four states with an eagle's eye, it is more likely that Mary's crudely written letters were less valuable to him as mementos to save. Regardless, Mary could not match her husband's prolific writing. While father was away, he had considerable free time on his hands, an unknown luxury in Mary's Civil War years.

A precise count of Mary Bradbury's letters is impossible to determine in the absence of their complete preservation. If she was a reluctant writer, it may have been that William's critiques of her letters, just like those directed toward the children, were grating to her. At a minimum, Mary's time was so occupied with six children and running their business affairs per his extensive instructions that she likely had little time to write.

Bradbury made at least one lengthy trip back to England after the war, a working trip in 1872 to help his cousins Abel and Nathaniel Buckley with their election campaigns for seats in Parliament. William wrote broadsheets,[22] slogans, and essays which were distributed. Returning home to England was likely therapeutic in many ways. Living in Charles's mansion, rekindling old ties with friends, and feeling a part of the old "machinery" once more—the privileged and powerful upper class—was no doubt energizing.

William surely compared their outcomes in life. As Charles Bradbury's enterprises expanded, his financial empire grew accordingly. Yet Charles's wealth from business would contrast starkly to the personal losses he suffered in the years that followed. Unlike William, each of Charles's children died young, and both of his wives predeceased him, leaving a sorrowful man who rattled about the old mansion alone.[23]

Charles did not have William's scholarly education, but he was greatly influenced by the interests of his daughter, Kate Bradbury Griffith. Kate,[24] her husband, Francis Llewelyn Griffith, and her best friend, author Amelia Edwards,[25] devoted themselves to the evolving scholarly discipline of Egyptology, an interest which Charles supported financially.[26]

Having seen so much of the world and society and so many opportunities and social changes, William H. Bradbury's later years seem much less earnest than the war years, when the family was young and he was far away from them. What more could a Saddleworth lawyer on the Kansas prairie hope for than to perform his trade as duty and status required while occasionally transcending into the world of verse, that Victorian refuge throughout his life. As one of his acquaintances near Saddleworth, England wrote,

> Only a Poet, what moor do yo' crave,
> To sweeten life's journey fro' th' cradle to th' grave?[27]

However, through the newspaper clippings carefully placed in his scrapbooks, we can also see that Bradbury continued to concern himself with U.S. relations with England. It would not be surprising if "Brad" wondered whether he had become an American or would forever remain an Englishman living in America.[28]

A postwar writer contended that the large United States was far easier to understand, in spite of its vast internal differences, than was Great Britain, where "utter failure of England to govern or pacify Ireland lies in the fact that moods and ways of the one country are almost hopelessly unintelligible to the other."[29] One of Bradbury's scrapbooks containing clippings, now amber with age, was particularly noteworthy for its underlinings and asterisks, probably by his hand. Some remarks in these articles may have been quite close to the heart of the issue as he saw it:

> For two or three years past the English press has teemed with articles on the attitude and temper of America, and the question whether America hates or loves England; yet so far as we have observed the question is no nearer solution now that it was at first . . . two nations of the same blood, both fond of money and land, both adventurous and combative, and both having a profound belief in themselves.[30]

When he finally arrived in Kansas, Bradbury took a position with the Land Department of the Atchison Topeka Santa Fe Railway. Bradbury's paperwork helped to help bring about the laying of hundreds of miles of track in the 1880's. When the railroad and the country suffered economic depression in the early 1890's, Bradbury retired from the Atchison Topeka Santa Fe to manage his own loan brokerage business. The tediousness of the accounting of his own land and mortgage business continued for many years, as he collected interest on notes and sought higher-earning investments. His writing during the mid-1890's evolved to tackle timely and controversial subjects.[31]

Frederic Bradbury, one of his brother's longtime investors, finally seemed to have enough of business matters, perhaps content to spend his life seeking creature comforts while traveling in his golden years.[32] Frederic encouraged his brother William to relieve himself of his business cares, much as Frederic had done, especially those with their prosperous brother, Charles.

Yet William held out hopes, making trip after trip to Arkansas City, Kansas, probably hungering for the land he hoped to acquire when the Oklahoma Territory was opened.[33] Driven by personality, self-determination, ancestral history, and perhaps fate, Bradbury hungered for land from his childhood days. His best dreams were of land in the West, including those elusive acres that would never be his.

In bringing the Civil War–era legacy of the Bradburys to a close, two exceptional letters, one each from William and Mary to Jennie, are included at the end of this chapter (edited). They best reflect the heart and mind of each of them, in the middle of life, in 1880. These letters help frame a family's postwar reconstruction.

Of special interest is William's use of language, replete with scientific and foreign vocabulary, reflecting the exclusionary and erudite relationship he had with Jennie. By contrast, Mary's earthbound discussion of slaughtering and salting hogs did not require fanciful detail. Therein lay the world of differences between Jennie's parents. These two letters are representative of the numerous postwar letters of William and Mary.[34] Each parent consistently wrote to her separately, not on behalf of the other nor as a parental unit.

Topeka
Feby 18 (Wednesday)/80
My dear daughter,

> Your two letters were duly recd—one during my absence in South-Eastern Kansas.[35] Mother wrote you last week but I thought it best to write also. . . .
>
> Willie is about selling the milk route to Mr. Myers for $125 including cans. The cows are separate. Pasture is becoming scarce for the ensuing Summer & Willie is tired of peddling milk day after day & month after month.
>
> Mother has a head-ache this morning but she was up shortly after six. I got up before 6 when the boys did. Fred usually gets up first & makes the fires. He has steady occupation & seems bright & in good spirits & is taking care of his money. Edwin is learning phonography under my instructions & is progressing very well. Ellie [Elwood] writes to his Iowa girl & goes to dances as usual. It is funny to see him executing a pas de seule [solo dance] at odd & unexpected moments in the barn.
>
> Charley looks well & lively. He likes to win at cards. He is very punctual & precise about his work & frequently refers to the clock. Sometimes he gives orders to Ellie & even Willie.
>
> Willie wants to buy the 14 acres of land east of the fairgrounds & north of the land belonging to Handy & Campbell. The price is said to be $100 per acre. By clubbing together & borrowing a little we might raise $1400. His plan is then to build a stone house so that the family can "swarm" like bees when they become too numerous for the hive. The land which includes "the orchard" seems cheap enough. Some of us think it would be preferable to buy this than to build on to the present house or erect a small house elsewhere on the farm. Mother & Willie—who like to be acquiring property—are in favor of it.[36]

It looks to me like a big undertaking involving much present sacrifice. It would be foolish unless the road went through & there was a bridge to the fair grounds which would then give two fronts to the land—the North boundary of which is the classic Shuganaunga—the East boundary being the few acres owned by Ward & Noble.

It was very cold this morning. Venus looked very pale & pinched up just before sunrise.[37] The pump at the well was frozen, but we obtained water at the barn which was quite warm with 35 head of stock in it & the doors closed. . . . Ben Curtis' partner—Chas. Spencer—goes round delivering temperance lectures—particularly on the constitutional prohibition which it is proposed to introduce. This con catenation of ideas (catena—Latin for "chain") suggests Hargreaves.[38] He still owes me about $33-$35. I left the note with Watkins at the Exchange Bank.

Where is Hargreaves & what is he doing? He would rather spend $5 on good dinners & cigars than pay $2 on account of his debts. "Of such is the kingdom of—"

Charley has just appeared to warn me that the cattle are out & need watching. He wears a wampus [furry animal skin] with collar at the neck. This makes a dark calix [cavity] to his fair carolla [complexion]. His ears hanging like petioles [stems of leaves] only slightly sessile [stalkless]. . .

There is a remarkable book recently published in England—"Is Life worth living?" is the title.[39] I have read some of it. It is well written & very suggestive.

We all join in love.
Your affect. father,
WmHBradbury

Topeka, Kansas
March 21, 1880
My dear Jennie,

I received your long letter and as I do not feel entitled to a letter from you oftener than once in two weeks, I did not answer it last week. I knew Ed wrote to you also Father and that you would have an idea how we were prospering from what they wrote. . . .

I am also glad that your health is good. I often think that our associations have great influence over us. It is not so much the food we eat but cheer that helps us in good health, fullness and good nature combined.

My motive for ask if you was contented, where you are was this, when things do not go on all right here, I wondered in what way it would affect you if you was here.

I am not going to make any complaints nor find fault with any one only just mention a few things as they appear to me. In the first place I do not think Father is very contented and what matter [is] I do not know. What he does on the farm ammounts to very little. He goes to town most every day but I do not think he ever tries to get anything to do. He of course attends to his loan business and says he has made sixty dollars since he has been here which is very good and if he can get any more money to loan, he will perhaps make something more. But that is not sufficient to help him [keep] busy and without a fair ammount of a profitable employment, no one can enjoy life as they ought to do.

The next thing is Father expected when he came, he would be able to get some job to do in town and so did the boys think so. Hitherto we have been dissapointed. Will cannot do with him interfering with matters on the farm.[40]

I have been thinking things over as well as can and have come to the conclusion that we have to let things have their own way although it requires an effort of the mind to feel contented at all times and I know that if I am not cheerful it affects the whole family.

Now I am something like the woman who said her husband wiped [whipped] her if she did not do every thing to his liking. She was not quite sure whether she ought to complain or not.[41]

I must confess that I am not always contented. I work from morning till night, no stoping, no variation unless at the expence of the children and unless Father gets something to do, it never will be other wise.[42]

I am sure the farm will not support a hired girl, even if it would, we have not the room.[43] I am trying to bring my mind to take up the real or imaginary cross and do it cheerfuly and perhaps hope may revive. The children are good to me and Father is willing to do anything he can to help when he feels like it. I often think I am to blame because I should do the work more willing if I felt that Father was taking an active part in life like other men.

An idea came in my mind the other day that Mrs. Eldredge would do well with a Kindergarden school in Topeka.[44] I have not heard of there being anything of the kind and I think it would take well. Topeka takes pride in the education of all classes. We claim to have nearly fifteen thousand inhabitants and out of that number there would certainly be quite a number that would let their children attend if properly conducted. I am sure Topeka is by far a better place to live in than Dwight.

At the present time if people are not doing well, it is their own fault. I mean to say, that if they cannot find one thing to do, try something else. . . .

We killed four pigs last week. It's Will that cuts them up and Will and Mother that salts them. I should not know what to do without him. He has that restless disposition unless he [thinks] things are going on all right, is not satisfied.

I have mentioned these things that you may be aware how we are going on. I feel better the least few days and am in better spirits. At one time I did think you had better stay where you are for I could not bear to have you here and things not go on all right but I have now made up my mind to let things take their course.

There is two acres and a half of land to be sold just north of us, would you be willing to pay one hundred dollars an acre for it.[45] We have one hundred of your money. I like it because there are trees on it and it is that much nearer town. Father does not like it for a place to build a house on. I know that Mr. Gray lived there. Perhaps you remember the place.

You may under the bearing of my remarks thought I know the wording is dismoteled. The idea I wish to convey is that things are just about so and it depends upon ourselves whether we take things as they [are, and] make the best of them. I know other people have their troubles worse than we have. Though I did think at one time that is, Miss Hargreave's school in Dwight next year you would be better off to remain there also now I have determined to let things take their course and not trouble.

Much love to you and all,
your mother Mary Bradbury

Mary Brown Bradbury died on June 27, 1898. Her epitaph was "She hath done what she could," probably selected by William. Mary's friends and relatives had lost the soul, perhaps the fibrous ties that held the shadow box of her family's life together—one both brimming full of zest and vigor and with its ribbons of sorrow as well.

Determined to see the start of a new century, William survived Mary's death by just two years, dying on November 3, 1900. Within two short months of his death, the primary vestige of the Victorian Era was officially over as well; Queen Victoria died in early 1901. The "Prince on the Prairie," for whom Bradbury and the Dwight choir had once sung, the Prince of Wales who had been waiting so long to ascend to the throne, finally had his brief and tumultuous reign as King Edward VII.[46]

William spent his final weeks with Jennie Bradbury Grant's family in their home in Las Vegas Hot Springs, New Mexico.[47] Until his death, Bradbury continued writing frequently to his children, grandchildren, brothers Charles and Frederic, as well as negotiating complex business affairs. He remained as prolific a poet and essayist[48] in the wane of life as he had been a letter writer to Mary, the children, and newspapers so many years before. While we cannot know if or how William summed up his experiences "on the mesa of his life," a poem by that title written a few months before he died may reveal the feelings—and, perhaps, regrets—behind that reflective mind.[49]

William's brother Frederic Bradbury, a bachelor, outlived both William and Charles. William's children looked to Uncle Frederic to choose the inscription for their father's tombstone. Frederic selected a phrase from the ancient odes of Horace: "Integer Vitae Scelerisque Purus ["A man of blameless life and free of stain"], Wm. H. Bradbury, of England."[50]

The land that William mentioned purchasing in Topeka in his letter of February 18, 1880, was eventually purchased along with other land. Kept in the family through daughter Jennie Bradbury Grant and descending through the next generation, the land[51] was subsequently donated in 1976 by Mary A. Grant[52] and Dorothy Bradbury,[53] two of William and Mary's grandchildren, as a permanent open park for the people of Topeka, Kansas. The roughly eighty-acre parcel, known locally as the "Grant-Bradbury Park," remains in use with the tributaries of the Shunganunga still flowing nearby.[54]

As the fields and streams still engage the young of heart and hope, may they be associated with the quest of Civil War veteran William H. Bradbury, an immigrant attorney with a poetic heart, who left behind a unique perspective of the Civil War by his prolific writings. Along with Mary, his partner in the journey of life, the Bradburys helped shape the face of the country.

Land speculators like William and Mary Bradbury, influenced by immigration, the U.S. Civil War, and industrial changes, plowed the prairies and the plains as they crept westward. They laid the rails of the future, across the land of long-held dreams. Imagining the development of the United States frontier without them seems incomprehensible.[55]

William H. Bradbury, born an Englishman, was a kind of character destined for the future of the United States—a country that wanted and needed immigrants, entrepreneurs, poets, attorneys, soldiers, clerks, husbands, and fathers who would pen keen insights for us all.

Appendix

What became of some of Private Bradbury's comrades after the war? While there is no indication that Bradbury maintained many of his closest war-era relationships in civilian life, military and government records constitute a valuable paper trail to many of their postwar lives. A few veterans were selected as a way of representing the diverse community of Private Bradbury's comrades.

Lieutenant Colonel Gates Phillips Thruston was breveted Brigadier General for gallant service at the battles of Stone's River and Chickamauga at the end of the war on request of Major General George H. Thomas. General Thruston made Nashville his permanent home and married Ida Hamilton, a local woman from a strong Confederate background. He became successful in the insurance business and civic affairs, and in collecting historic artifacts. His interest led him in helping reorganize the Tennessee Historical Society in 1875, as its vice president for twenty years, and in authoring a lengthy book on Tennessee archaeology, *The Antiquities of Tennessee,* in 1890. Leaving behind extensive collections, as did Bradbury, General Thruston died in 1912 and was buried in Nashville's historic Mount Olivet Cemetery near other Civil War generals—both Confederate and Union.[1]

Major Reuben C. Kise of Indiana was seriously sick with dysentery throughout the war but would not resign. When he returned to Boone County, Indiana, he married his sweetheart, Adelia Shannon; their one child, Willie, was born in 1869. The persisting effects of war-contracted illness resulted in Major Kise's death only four years later.[2]

One of Bradbury's couriers to Mary, Private James Butterworth, was badly wounded at Bean's Station, Tennessee, in December 1863. A bugler under Captain John H. Colvin and normally responsible for the mail, Private Butterworth was called to the guns, whereupon he was hit. After the bullet was removed from his left ear, Butterworth remained deaf for the rest of his life.[3]

Captain Samuel T. Walkley, ever in pursuit of retrieving the elusive

Private Bradbury to the regiment, farmed in Kansas for three years after the war ended. Walkley became a clerk to the agent for the Comanche, Kiowa, and Apache Indians near Fort Cobb for a while. His final home was in Florida, where he died in 1900.[4]

Colonel Henry Case, whose children had played with Bradbury's before they relocated to Chicago, was breveted to Brigadier General by the end of the war. Case died in Norwich, Connecticut, in 1884 at age 61.[5]

Lieutenant George W. Gilchrist was in charge of bridge construction and maintenance of the Chicago & Alton Railroad before the war. During the 1864 campaigns, Gilchrist was promoted to the position of pioneer officer of the 1st brigade, 3rd division of the 20th Corps, and was made aide-de-camp to Colonel Benjamin Harrison.[6] In 1870, Gilchrist moved with his wife and children to Wakonda, South Dakota; he died in 1898.[7]

Lieutenant Elihu Chilcott relocated after the war and lived near Louisville, Kansas, with his wife Mary until her death in 1885. Their children settled in Guthrie, Oklahoma, and owned a land and loan company. Chilcott spent his final weeks in the National Home for Disabled Soldiers near Leavenworth, Kansas, where he died in 1911.[8]

Sergeant Major Curtis J. Judd became a financially successful partner in the Leslie E. Keeley Company in the 1890's and attended many of the 129th Illinois Infantry reunion meetings of the G.A.R.[9] Judd married Estelle Dow, and they were proprietors of a sanitarium for several years.[10] He died of pneumonia in Greenwich, Connecticut, in 1927, outliving most of his comrades.

Major William H. Bailhache returned to the family newspaper business. As Bradbury searched for meaningful work after the war, Bailhache's connections could have proved helpful. When the Bradburys were moving to Kansas, though, Bailhache and family[11] were heading further west. His final home was San Diego, California. There he managed the *Daily Bee* and also served as deputy tax collector and as the U.S. Customs Chinese inspector on Coronado Island.[12]

Lieutenant Colonel Andrew J. Cropsey of the 129th Illinois Infantry resigned in early 1864 due to poor health that started during the assignment at Gallatin, Tennessee. Years later, he and his wife Emma moved to Terrell, Texas. After his death, a special act of Congress was required to resolve his widow's pension claim.[13]

Finally, what became of the organizer of the 129th Illinois Infantry Volunteer Regiment, Colonel George P. Smith? His war-era medical history suggests that a more sympathetic view of Smith may be merited. Smith was likely misunderstood at the time, because he was quite ill. The angry and odd behavior that many witnessed was likely beyond his control, due to the suffering he was experiencing. Colonel Smith was so ill during the early months of the regiment's formation that he called for his wife, Margaret, and his brother, a doctor,[14] to take care of him in Tennessee.

After a four-day chase for guerrilla raiders, his health deteriorated further. The colonel suffered from the dreaded erysipelas,[15] onset in his face, an often-deadly disease that caused excruciating pain, disfigurement, and delirium. Two of his nurses contracted the disease and died from it. Colonel Smith was discharged on medical grounds. By then, early 1863, his performance had grown erratic, and his behavior seemed so hostile to troops and civilians alike that many were happy to see him leave.

After the war, Smith became managing editor of a newspaper in Jacksonville, Illinois. In 1869, he, too, moved to Kansas, where he struggled with outbreaks of erysipelas for the rest of his life.[16]

In 2001, the Tennessee Historical Commission erected historical marker 3B74 near Mitchellville, Tennessee, to recognize the site of the 129th Illinois Infantry's "Fort Smith," and historical marker 3B76 to recognize the Union fortifications at Buck Lodge, Tennessee.[17]

Notes

Abbreviations

a.u.	Author unknown
CMSR	Compiled Military Service Records
CSA	Confederate States of America
CTB	Charles Timothy Bradbury
FB	Frederic Bradbury
FHS	Filson Historical Society
HDS	Historical Data Systems, Inc., "Civil War Research & Genealogy Database"
IHS	Indiana Historical Society
ISHL	Illinois State Historical Library
KSHS	Kansas State Historical Society
LC	Library of Congress, Manuscript Division, William H. Bradbury Collection, Box 3098
MB	Mary Bradbury
NARA	National Archives & Records Administration, Washington, D.C.
n.d.	No date
n.p.	No publisher provided
PR	Pension Record
RG	Record Group 94
OR	*The War of the Rebellion: A Compilation of the Official Records of the Union and Confederate Armies*
SRL	University of Kansas, Spencer Research Library, the Kansas Collection, Grant-Bradbury Collection, MS 299 (B = Box, F = Folder)
WHB	William Henry Bradbury
WKU	Special Collections, Western Kentucky University, Bowling Green, Kentucky

Acknowledgments

1. Mary A. Grant's donations of her grandfather's Civil War letters were completed through a series of six donations from January 9, 1975, to December 30, 1976, as described in correspondence with the staff of the Manuscript Division of the Library of Congress. In SRL, B7, F33.

2. The letters of 129th Illinois Infantry comrades Alburtus and Laforest Dunham were particularly useful for clarifying and corroborating WHB's Civil War letters. Arthur H. DeRosier Jr., ed. *Through the South with a Union Soldier* (Johnson City: East Tennessee State University, 1969).

3. Leslie W. Dunlap, ed., "*Your Affectionate Husband, J. F. Culver*" (Iowa City: Friends of the University of Iowa Libraries, 1978).

Introduction

1. See WHB's letter of January 7, 1863. LC.

2. WHB was born on February 17, 1829, in Delph. He and his older brother, Charles Timothy (born September 22, 1827), were first educated at the Wharmton School. British Vital Records, FHL #1484390, for the years 1780–1851.

3. W.A. Phillips, "The American Land Question," *The Kansas Magazine*, Vol. 2 (November 1872): 412.

4. In J.W. Bradbury's August 31, 1833, letter from New York to his uncle, he indicated that six deaths had taken place on board during his Atlantic crossing. Saddleworth Historical Society Archives, H/HOW/35.

5. Letter written in 1835 by Charles Clifton on behalf of Mr. Broadbent to Timothy Bradbury, SRL, B2, F22.

6. Letter by Timothy Bradbury, Delph, England, dated December 15, 1821, to Mr. and Mrs. Benjamin Bradbury. SRL, B2, F3.

7. Letter dated December 29, 1835, from James Bradbury to his brother Timothy Bradbury. SRL, B2, F24.

8. Ibid.

9. Timothy Bradbury's letter (no month or day) to Charles Clifton, SRL, B2, F23.

10. Timothy Bradbury was born October 28, 1781, baptized at Friarmere Chapel, recorded by O. Buckley, and died February 22, 1839. A black-bordered death announcement card among the collection indicated, "My dear Father was interred on Thursday, the 28th of February at Heights Chapel." SRL, B2, F7.

11. WHB, "Reminiscences of an English Schoolboy, II," *Western School Journal*: 141–42. SRL, B1, F8.

12. WHB, "Reminiscences of an English Schoolboy, III," *Western School Journal*: 163–65. SRL, B1, F8.

13. "W. H. Bradbury Dead, Pioneer Land Office Man of the Santa Fe," *Dwight Star & Herald*, November 17, 1900.

14. Alfred Baker, *The Life of Sir Isaac Pitman* (London: Sir Isaac Pitman & Sons, L.T.D.,1930), 55.

15. Family genealogical papers in the Grant-Bradbury collection at SRL suggest that James Smith Buckley was a first cousin to Jane Buckley Bradbury, William's mother.

16. Timothy Bradbury's first wife's name was Hannah Gartside, which raises the possibility that it was his former father-in-law or brother-in-law who assumed the responsibility of arranging William's legal education and apprenticeship. However, information in the file suggests that the birth mother of the three sons was Jane Buckley Bradbury and not Hannah Gartside Bradbury. SRL, B3, F2.

17. "Articles of Agreement," dated 1845 between Jane Buckley Bradbury of Delph and James Smith Buckley (executrix and executor named in the "Last Will and Testament of Timothy Bradbury") and William Henry Bradbury and Henry Gartside. SRL, B3, F1.

18. Some of the many letters that support the premise that Frederic Bradbury's share (among brothers) from their parents' estate, administered by brother Charles, was inequitable include: November 4, 1900, to nephew William Bradbury (SRL, B5, F4); Octo-

ber 10, 1907, to Jennie Bradbury Grant (SRL, B7, F12); February 22, 1908, to Jennie Bradbury Grant (SRL, B5, F2); and letter by Frederic's nephew-in-law Francis Llewelyn Griffith, dated April 7, 1912, to Jennie Bradbury Grant (SRL, B7, F11).

19. Mr. Tomlin was CTB's father-in-law.

20. Letter dated October 27, 1852, from William H. Bradbury to Charles T. Bradbury. SRL, B7, F1.

21. Paul Wallace Gates, "The Role of the Land Speculator in Western Development," *The Pennsylvania Magazine of History and Biography* 66, No. 3 (October 1942): 317.

22. CTB was involved in the building of the Manchester Ship Canal and was a leader in the Calico Printers Association as a mill owner. CTB held a seat on the stock exchange and was well known as a colorful personality of the day. William Haslam Mills, *Grey Pastures* (London: Chatto and Windus, 1924), 116–24.

23. Letter dated January 7, 1853, from WHB to CTB. SRL, B7, F1.

24. Glenda Riley, *The Female Frontier: A Comparative View of Women on the Prairie and the Plains* (Lawrence: University Press of Kansas, 1988), 12.

25. Ibid., 63.

26. David L. Cohn, *The Life and Times of King Cotton* (New York: Oxford University Press, 1956), 101.

27. Gates, 327.

28. *History of Grundy County, Illinois* (Chicago: O. L. Baskin & Co., 1882), 42, 55.

29. Born September 1, 1825, John Brown was a farmer until 1867, when he moved to Morris, Illinois. There he acquired a drugstore business, which he operated until 1884. SRL, B3, F21.

30. Ann Brown (maiden name unknown unless it was also 'Brown') was born at Barton-under-Needwood in Staffordshire, England, November 23, 1826. She married John Brown on August 27, 1850; they had nine children. Ann Brown died in January 1903. Obituary clipping from unspecified newspaper (n.d.). SRL, B3, F24.

31. Letter dated April 27, 1849, from John Brown to his sister Mary Brown. SRL, B3, F24.

32. "A Brief History of John Brown," typed from notes taken during a 1905 oral interview. SRL, B3, F21. John Brown died two years after the death of his wife in 1905 at age eighty. SRL, B3, F24.

33. Theodora Penny Martin, *The Sound of Our Own Voices* (Boston: Beacon Press, 1987), 28.

34. Ibid.

35. Thomas H. O'Connor, *Lords of the Loom, The Cotton Whigs and the Coming of the Civil War* (New York: Charles Scribner's Sons, 1968), 162.

36. William G. Dustin, comp., *The History of Dwight, Illinois* (Dwight: Dustin and Wassell, 1894), 60.

37. The 1860 population of Pontiac, Illinois, was 733; in spite of this, at least 350 men enlisted in the Union Army, obviously an enormous portion of the population. HDS, "Town Data."

38. Susan Rubinow Gorsky, *Femininity to Feminism: Women and Literature in the Nineteenth Century* (New York: Twayne Publishers, 1992), 25.

39. Martin, 26.

40. Poem by William H. Bradbury, circa 1864, on the reverse side of a letter to daughter Jane. ISHL, "New Acquisitions: Grant-Bradbury," an unprocessed collection.

1. "My Dear Wife and Children"

1. Dustin, 14.

2. An adjutant was the chief staff officer; orders were issued by and received for the general commanding officer through this position.

3. Riley, 32–33, 46–47.

4. Private Samuel Starling enlisted at Frankfort, Kentucky, Co. G of the 1st KY Inf. A promotion to rank of 2nd lieutenant quickly followed, and by December 6, 1862, he was commissioned captain of the 8th KY Cav. HDS, "Soldier History." While he may have thought of himself as a major, army records do not reflect this at this time. When Bradbury wrote about meeting Starling, he referred to his rank as lieutenant.

5. Letter from S.M. Starling to his daughters, March 20, 1863. WKU, MSS 38, B8, F2.

6. Philip D. Plattenburg of Pontiac enlisted on September 8, 1862, as adjutant of the 129th IL Inf., although illness prevented him from joining the men for some time. NARA, CMSR.

7. Colonel George P. Smith was fifty years old when he was first commissioned as Major of the 69th Illinois Infantry from June 14, 1862, until mid-September. According to his postwar records, he moved from Virginia due to his anti-slavery sentiments and speeches. Smith, married to Margaret, practiced medicine in adjacent Grundy County, Illinois, for several years prior to the war and was also the editor of a newspaper, *The Republican.* NARA, PR.

8. David McWilliams opened the first store in Dwight in 1855. Dustin, 487.

9. Andrew J. Cropsey was a Methodist minister from Fairbury when he enlisted. Ibid., 349.

10. Thirty-eight-year-old Henry Case, originally from Norwich, Connecticut, enlisted at Winchester, Illinois. Early in the war with the 14th IL Inf. he was a 1st lieutenant, later a captain; as major of the 7th IL Cav. Case would serve the 129th IL Inf. as lieutenant colonel and acting colonel during Col. Smith's continuing absences until fully appointed to that position in May 1863. Frederick H. Dyer, *A Compendium of the War of the Rebellion,* Vol. 1 (New York: Thomas Yoseloff, 1959), 459; HDS, "Officer Directory."

11. Manning Smith, a merchant, was born in Ipswich, Massachusetts, and was twenty-six years old when he enlisted in Co. B of the 129th IL Inf. NARA, PR.

12. Curtis Judson Judd, twenty-three years old, was a comrade in Co. B with Bradbury. Judd was born in Otis, Massachusetts. NARA, PR. Eugene R. Stevens was also a private in the company. HDS, "Soldier History."

13. This letter is not part of the collection. It probably either miscarried or was not kept for some reason. LC.

14. Confederate General Braxton Bragg was expected to descend upon Louisville at any time; the city was largely evacuated of civilians.

15. "Secesh" was short way of referring to a person who supported the secession of the Confederate States from the United States.

16. Kentucky's Treasurer James William Garrard was in the middle of his fourth term when Private Bradbury encountered his wife (unable to locate name). Garrard was also the grandson of Kentucky's second governor, James Garrard. Misc. files of the Kentucky Department for Libraries & Archives; *200 Years of the Kentucky Treasury.*

17. Samuel T. Walkley (elsewhere "Walkly") enlisted in Co. B at the same time as Bradbury. While Captain Walkley helped organize the enlistment of Co. B and no doubt was well acquainted with the Bradburys, Private Bradbury did not consider Walkley fair in business affairs. This may be explained by WHB's persistent frustration with a business deal with an "L.N. Walkley," who was probably a relative of Samuel. In 1851, Captain Walkley was married to Sarah J. Calkins Currier, a widow, in Beloit, Wisconsin. He had divorced Adelia Walkley several months earlier in Ohio. NARA, PR.

18. A frequent complaint of officers was that they had to use their own funds to keep up the appearances of their positions.

19. Forty-eight-year-old Mexican War veteran General Ebenezer Dumont, lawyer,

legislator, and banker from Versailles, Indiana, was particularly annoyed with CSA General Morgan's raids upon Indiana's river towns such as his own. Mark M. Boatner III, *The Civil War Dictionary* (New York: David McKay Company, 1959), 208; NARA, CMSR.

20. Colonel Marshall W. Chapin of Detroit, Michigan, was thirty-three years old when he became the 38th Brigade's commander of the 10th Division, which included the 23rd Michigan, the 102nd and 111th Ohio, and the 129th Illinois Infantry at this time. Dyer, Vol. 1, 433; HDS, "Regiment History."

21. WHB omitted the purpose of this excursion; the 129th IL Inf. was in pursuit of CSA General John Hunt Morgan and guerrilla raiders. James A. Ramage, *Rebel Raider* (Lexington: University Press of Kentucky, 1986), 104; DeRosier, 28.

22. At age forty-seven, Union General Crittenden of Kentucky was the son of U.S. Senator John Jordan Crittenden. Boatner, 208.

23. General Robert Seaman Granger of Ohio was a graduate of West Point and had served during the Mexican War. He was breveted brigadier-general for action at Lawrenceburg, Kentucky, on October 9, 1862. Stewart Sifakis, *Who Was Who in the Union*, Vol. 1 (New York: Facts on File, Inc., 1988), 159–160. General Granger's command at this time included: 17th KY Inf., 1st Middle TN Inf., 3rd TN Cav., 4th TN Cav., 12th IN Battery, 20th IN Battery and the post at Gallatin, which included the 129th IL Inf., 106th OH Inf., 13th IN Battery, 50th OH Inf., and the 71st OH Inf. Dyer, Vol. 1, 452.

24. A friend of Bradbury's, Lt. Joseph Franklin Culver of Pontiac would become a captain in 1864. A businessman back home, Culver was married to Mary Murphy less than a year before he left for soldiering. Well-educated, having attended Dickinson College in Carlisle, Pennsylvania, he had also taught and served as principal of schools before the war. Culver's published letter collection to his wife Mary is referenced throughout this text. As Bradbury's duties took him further away from the regiment he started with, Culver's book provides more information about the men from Livingston County in the 129th. Culver did not mention in a letter to his wife of the same date that he was sick. The two comrades had likely discussed Culver's worries for his family in Carlisle, which would soon be under Confederate occupation. Dunlap, 20–22, 89.

25. This is the first of many mentions of a man by the name of Keyt who in some way failed to keep his end of a business agreement with WHB. In spite of research, no further information on Keyt was found.

26. Captain James Hughes Stokes was born in Hagerstown, Maryland, in 1815. He was a graduate of West Point and commander of the Board of Trade Light Artillery Battery. Organized in Chicago on August 1, 1862, their troops saw extensive duty under the Armies of the Ohio and the Cumberland and the Military Division of the Mississippi. Stokes was breveted brigadier-general near the end of the war. Ezra J. Warner, *Generals in Blue* (Baton Rouge: Louisiana State University Press, 1992), 478.

27. The *Pontiac Sentinel* was WHB's local newspaper. This is the first occasion in which WHB suggested that he had sufficient knowledge of regimental circumstances to write to a newspaper.

28. This letter was written at a significant turning point for WHB. From this time until early 1864, WHB would be detached to headquarters, separated from his friends and comrades in the 129th IL Inf. NARA, PR; Regimental Letter, Endorsement, Order, Index, and Misc. Book, E112–115, 1–17, Vol. 3 of 6; and "Special Order No. 24, December 3, 1862."

29. William Gagan (elsewhere "Gagen") became editor of the *Pontiac Sentinel* in 1858. Gagan also traveled to and from the troops carrying packages and mail, conducting some subtler trading as well as gathering newsworthy items for people to read back home during the early months of the war. However, by August 1863, Gagan gave it up and moved to Oakland, California, where he published the *Oakland Daily News*; Will-

iam LeBaron Jr., *The History of Livingston County, Illinois* (Chicago: Self published, 1878), 318; Dunlap, 125.

30. Identifying the correct "Morgan" is speculation; however, R.P. Morgan was considered the founder of Dwight, its original land owner, and its railroad engineer. Dustin, 3.

31. CTB maintained frequent communications with the family in Illinois. While WHB was in the army, CTB's letters were routed by MB; sometimes mail was lost due to railroad vandalism by guerrilla raiders.

32. WHB worried about his eight-year-old daughter's dreams, considering them indicators of unhappiness or of poor health, particularly mental health. "A Chapter on Dreams," *Harper's New Monthly Magazine* 2, No. 12 (May 1851): 768–74. Perhaps a more accurate word would be "nightmares," which many children whose fathers had gone off to war may have experienced. Yet WHB was typically much more concerned with Jane's state of mind and activities than with the other children. Perhaps WHB was reading and staying abreast of then-current theories about daughters and dreams:

> . . . we know that something is the matter and a power is at work upon them and not mainly for good, not mainly according to the lessons of the home, the school, and the church. Our daughters, as being the most sensitive, may sooner indicate the tendency of their dispositions, and interpret to us the code of the social arbiter that claims homage.

Samuel Osgood, "Mental Health," *Harper's New Monthly Magazine* 28, No. 166 (March 1864): 496.

33. The troops were very enthusiastic with General William Starke Rosecran's replacement of General Buell. Jennifer Cain Bohrnstedt, ed., *Soldiering with Sherman: The Civil War Letters of George F. Cram* (DeKalb: Northern Illinois University Press, 2000), 59.

34. WHB likely continued to participate in some form of business affairs with his brother's mill works, Chapel Hill Mill. In the early 1860's, CTB first introduced power-loom weaving to the factory. In 1886, the John Henry Gartside Company took over Chapel Hill Mill, which might explain the continuing involvement of Gartside surname in Bradbury's letters. *Dukinfield Cotton Mills,* Ian Haynes (Manchester, England: Neil Richardson Publications, 1993), 38-40.

35. An old British term of endearment, especially towards small children.

36. Private William H. Borin would be discharged for disability on March 13, 1863. NARA, CMSR.

37. One consequence of being apart from the regiment was that WHB might not be able to generate as much income from newspaper writing.

38. WHB's concerns about the Kansas land are continuing themes in his directions to MB.

2. *"If We Go to England. . ."*

1. "Diary of Josie Underwood," also known as the "Nazro Diary," WKU, Manuscript Division.

2. The tone of the opening of this letter was a bit rough for a pregnant woman left with all the responsibilities of children, home, and business. In light of this example, we are left to wonder if MB welcomed all of her husband's letters home.

3. As business conditions grew unpredictable and frustrating, dreams of returning to Droylsden provided a ray of hope for the Bradburys. Yet the officials of towns of his youth—Ashton, Oldham, and Stalybridge—were (literally) reading the Riot Act (a piece

of British legislation from 1715 that was read to unruly crowds who congregated to put them on notice to disperse) to angry out-of-work mill workers who were suffering due to reduced imports of cotton during the U.S. Civil War. Many mill owners demanded that the British government officially recognize the Confederacy in order to save the economy and their own personal wealth. So while the proverbial grass looked greener to the Bradburys, they would not have found their former English villages and towns in better conditions. Samuel Hill, *Bygone Stalybridge* (Leeds: M.T.D. Rigg Publications, 1987), 86–99; Ian Haynes, *Dukinfield Cotton Mills* (Manchester: Neil Richardson, 1993), 27–31.

4. WHB probably was referring to Joseph D. McDonald, formerly a corporal in the 129th IL Inf. who was discharged. Dustin, 25.

5. There are two plausible "John Browns" here—this is either a droll remark referencing the famous John Brown whose 1857 raid on the arsenal at Harper's Ferry, Virginia, created such uproar or his wife's brother, John Brown, of Grundy County, Illinois, who was not as ambitious in all business matters as WHB. The meaning is ambiguous; either inference makes sense in the context of his frustration.

6. During a bleak moment, WHB only saw two options—return to the old, established family back in England or throw their full effort into becoming American settlers and farmers.

7. Mitchellville, Tennessee, was in the heart of the homeland of Confederate guerrilla raiders. Walter T. Durham, *Rebellion Revisited* (Franklin: Hillsboro Press, 1999), 108–12. Mitchellville was also important for its proximity to the Louisville & Nashville Railroad, which by this time was closely guarded by Union forces yet still experienced the frequent threat of guerrilla attacks. For the next seven months, the 129th Illinois Infantry would remain in this region (Buck's Lodge, Fountainhead, Richland Station, and South Tunnel) while it officially organized camp at Gallatin, the county seat. NARA, RG94, AG, 129 Illinois Infantry Order Book E112–115.

8. Private Eli Lower, Co. B, enlisted with WHB. He and his wife are frequently mentioned in WHB's letters suggesting a friendship prior to the war. NARA, CMSR.

9. Lt. George W. Gilchrist, of Dwight, Illinois, was a friend as well as comrade in Co. B. NARA, CMSR & PR. Gilchrist was probably WHB's source of information about the status of the regiment and Union forces in the region.

10. Elihu Chilcott, of Dwight, Illinois, enlisted in Co. B and was commissioned 2nd Lieutenant of Co. B. In spite of rumors Mary may have heard on the homefront, Chilcott was still present among the troops. NARA, CMSR.

11. Sergeant Northrup Riggs enlisted in Co. B along with WHB. NARA, CMSR. It was curious that Riggs wanted to write to WHB's wife unless he was not receiving mail from home.

12. MB must have sent him a previously used although uncancelled stamp or train ticket, which WHB, in a moment of sternness and "high moral ground," felt obligated to disparage. A small, even feeble gesture of assistance by his wife, even if wrong, did not go unnoticed.

13. Captain John B. Perry, of Co. C, 129th IL Inf., was from Rook's Creek, Illinois. HDS, "Soldier History." There were six Perrys in this regiment, all of whom joined on September 8, 1862, suggesting an extended family enlistment. HDS, "Regiment Experience."

14. Lt. Stephen H. Kyle, Co. C, 129th IL Inf., died of disease at Bowling Green, Kentucky, on December 1, 1862. Dustin, 30. Private Alburtus Dunham wrote on November 18, 1862, that he had stayed with Lt. Kyle at Bowling Green: "I am tonight in a better place than common—at a private mansion ½ [mile] from camp, sitting up with Lieut. Kyle. He has been very sick with the Tiphoid Fever." Within a month or so, Lt.

Kyle's caretaker, Private Dunham, would also die—of "brain fever"—at Fountain Head, Tennessee. DeRosier, 45–51.

15. Frederic (FB), sometimes spelled with the *k,* was WHB's brother, who lived in New York.

16. The reference to Poughkeepsie could have been New York, an area richly settled by British immigrants, many from the same town as Bradbury. Perhaps they stayed there for a while before making their way to Illinois, some possibly with FB. Maurice Dennett, ed., *The Cherry Valley Chronicles: Letters from Thomas Buckley and family to Ralph Buckley and family, 1845–1875* (Uppermill: Saddleworth Historical Society, 1991), 89–106. However, Poughkeepsie, New York, would have been considerably out of the way for a furlough home to Illinois, which raises the question of an alternative—Poughkeepsie, Indiana, a town that they also could have encountered as they made their way to Illinois several years earlier and that would have been much closer. While a postal destination existed in Poughkeepsie, Indiana, until 1856, it is unlikely that there was a court there, which suggests that the legal dispute in question was taken to the Allen County, Indiana, courthouse at Fort Wayne. J. David Baker, *The Postal History of Indiana* (Louisville: Leonard Hartmann, Philatelic Bibliophile, 1976), 1011.

17. Mrs. Eldredge's company was likely intended as midwife to the impending birth of their child.

18. The draw to Droylsden lingered like a siren's song. As WHB's conditions worsened, the more attractive a return to Droylsden seemed.

19. An old expression that meant that he seemed like a person in a high position, such as a parliamentarian, a lawyer, or a judge—that is, someone who wore black robes.

20. It is interesting that WHB wrote of an impending railroad raid that morning. Too far away for him to hear, CSA Gen. John Hunt Morgan selected December 7, 1862, for his raid on vulnerable Union forces at Hartsville, Tennessee, claiming a total victory, costing many lives, and shaming Union officers, many of whom were from Illinois. Ramage, 128–133; Dyer, Vol. 2, 850.

21. A reference to his comrade Manning Smith of Co. B, who had left his assignment with Regimental Quartermaster McWilliams for higher duty under the Division Commissary. MB would likely be interested to hear about promotions like this among their friends and neighbors. NARA, CMSR. The Commissary of Subsistence (CS) had extensive regulations for the purchasing, storing, preparation, and feeding of troops. Because there was potential for abuse and non-compliance, a major at CS wrote, "Who has ever heard of quartermaster and commissaries as anything but rogues?" H.C. Symonds, *Report of a Commissary of Subsistence 1861–85* (Sing Sing: Vireun School, n.d.), 199.

22. Try as he would to nudge her to write more frequently, MB generally disappointed WHB's optimism for correspondence.

23. A reference to the battle of Hartsville, Tennessee, east of Nashville. There the brigade leadership was overtaken by Col. Absalom Moore of Ottawa County, Illinois, and the 104th IL Inf. OR, Series 1, Vol. 20, Part 2, Chapter 32, 45–59.

24. Bradbury had a great capacity to distance himself from his comrades. One might think he would wish them well under inspection, but he privately hoped for some comeuppance instead. He may have been looking for a bit of revenge because he did not get the commission he wanted and felt that less competent men were in leadership roles that should have been offered to him.

25. When Colonel Smith arrived at Buck Lodge, Tennessee, in mid-December, he dispatched General Rosecrans about the appallingly low number of effective troops and the lack of fortifications. OR, Series 1, Vol. 20, Part 2, Chapter 32, 214.

26. Either because MB had not been handling these matters well enough or because she would soon give birth, WHB took the added measure of a power of attorney to

handle their affairs. Nevertheless, this would not be the last she would hear about Keyt, the farm, the rents, or the Kansas land.

27. Patrick Fuge was a comrade in Co. B. HDS, "Soldier History."

28. Sergeant Earl H. Henyon was from Dwight, Illinois; he would die early in January 1863 at Fountain Head, Tennessee. HDS, "Soldier History."

29. General Mahlon Dickerson Manson, or "old rugged" as WHB referred to him, had seen considerable fighting in his life before arriving in Bowling Green. Sifakis, 263.

30. Years later, regimental comrade Captain W.B. Fyffe of Co. G would write about character and the morality of soldiers away from home:

> There is no better place than in a camp to see a man's natural character. He is away from home, family, friends, and the endearments of female society; he is thrown back on himself and what is good or bad in him very soon shows itself. . . . I do not think our best men would encourage a fond mother to send her darling boy into the army for the purpose of developing his moral or religious nature or to fit him for the pulpit!

W.B. Fyffe, "Memories of the War, Chapter 10" (Pontiac: *Pontiac Sentinel,* n.d.). In WHB's scrapbook, SRL, 89–08–64, B2, F5.

31. This remark suggests that MB was either not pleased about some aspect of WHB's paying to have his clothes cleaned or that the price was too high.

32. WHB was trying out a drastic idea on his wife, one that he never carried out.

33. Capt. Walkley back at the regiment was clearly peeved that he could not exert control over one of his healthy men, Private Bradbury. Yet the latter calculated correctly that upon such demands commanding officers at headquarters would keep WHB at their sides instead.

34. Hetzel (elsewhere "Hetzell") was born in Bavaria in 1833. He was another storekeeper in Dwight and well-known to the Bradbury family. Dustin, 22. In fact, his wife was a close companion of MB's, and in the years to come, their daughters, both named Jennie, were lifelong friends as well. LeBaron, 671.

35. Christian soldiers commonly protested that the military did not respect Sunday as Sabbath.

36. This remark reflects the belief, prevalent during the era, that the moon's cycle played a determining role in important events like childbirth.

37. WHB does not mention whether or not he processed the soldier's papers, although in future letters it seems that he did—for $50.

38. Her "trial," or delivery date, was rapidly approaching.

39. As a native of England, WHB may have overstated the ultimate impact of Europe's distress over the U.S. Civil War. Letters to and from his brothers and other relatives in England may have emphasized the concern over their potential involvement.

40. Harper's publications were quite popular during this time. For men with little to do, these were surely a delight to find.

41. Similar words, even uttered by WHB, would be heard during and after the war—that the war was "good" (financially) for someone.

3. "Stand on Your Dignity!"

1. Pointing out the painful course that lay ahead, Congressman Robert Hatton of Lebanon, Tennessee, an area that would become a stronghold of Confederate sympathy (near the site of the Battle of Hartsville), spoke eloquently on the House floor that the country would suffer terribly by the unfolding secession movement:

> Can nothing be done to stay this revolution? If not, it will sweep us all to a common ruin . . . our fair land scourged and blighted as by the hand of any angry

> God will be divided into fragments. . . . Sir, Tennesseans cannot be driven. . . . "Tennessee will never be coerced by men North or South." She will do what she believes best to comport with her dignity and honor. . . . I am determined not to be driven from the faithful performance of what I conceive my duty, by the mad cry of crazy enthusiasts. . . . If on account of our wicked perverseness and want of patriotism, our country is not saved, and revolution and civil war ensue; when the youth of the country shall have been cut down like grass, our cities and villages burned, and our fields laid waste . . . we will be pointed at by our fellow citizens, who will say, as in shame we avert their faces, "He was member of the Thirty-Sixth Congress!"

"Speech of Hon. Robert Hatton, ofTennessee, in the House of Representatives February 8, 1861," the *Congressional Globe*, Government Publication. Congressman, Colonel, and finally C.S.A. Brigadier General Hatton would not face any shame after the war. He was killed at the battle of Seven Pines, Virginia, on May 31, 1861, less than four months after his powerful speech in Washington. James Vaulx Drake, *Life of General Robert Hatton* (Nashville: Marshall & Bruce, Pub., 1867), 418–26; U.S. Congressional Documents and Debates, 1774–1873, the *Congressional Globe*, Appendix, House of Representatives, 36th Congress, 2nd Session, pp. 170-173.

2. NARA, RG94 Records of the AG's Office, 129th IL Inf., Order Book, Co. A, E 112–115, Vol. 4 of 6, January 4, 1863.

3. NARA, RG94 Records of the AG's Office, 129th IL Inf., Regimental Letter, Endorsement, Order, Index and Misc. Book E112–115, PI–17, Vol. 3 of 6, February 9, 1863.

4. Ibid.

5. Ibid.

6. Colonel George P. Smith resigned on May 8, 1863. NARA, PR & CMSR.

7. Private Leander Morgan's role in the lives of the Bradburys is subtle and understated in light of WHB's insistence on high moral conduct. In future letters, we can conclude that WHB moved Morgan's papers to the top of the stack at headquarters in exchange for cash and Morgan's help with chores back home for MB.

8. This incident also revealed the inner turmoil of the 129th IL Inf. regiment. It was colorfully described by Private Charles Laforest Dunham of Co. C who participated in it:

> We run on to a nest of rebels of about a 100, thay was riden long the railroad. They tore up one rail and cut both of the telegraph wires. Thare aim was to captur a train of horses that was a going down. . . . We ordered him [the Confederate] to stop and he put spurs to his horse and lunged into the bushes. . . . He was drest in our close [clothes]. In a few minuts thare was about a dozen came in plane lite but our commander did not order us to fire. . . . About that time thay all broke and run . . . that let 8 prisoners go that thay had taken, too of our men and 6 sitizens. We had the range write throug the timbres shouting, the snow flew for surtain. Thare wasnt but too shots fired. They were fired at the lieutenant [who commanded], but thay did not hit him.

DeRosier, 55.

9. While trying to add comforting words to his wife, now saddled with twins as well, WHB's remarks seemed somewhat condescending, implying—"if others can do it, you can too."

10. It was a "venture," or a gamble, of sorts to send cash through the mail as it might be stolen along the way.

11. While the county had public aid programs for soldiers' families, WHB was determined to keep his family's name off the list.

12. The existence of an "unexpected source" suggests that WHB may have taken cash bribes from soldiers who wanted their papers brought to the top of the stack (for example, Leander Morgan) or that he was performing some writing tasks for pay for other clerks who were behind in their work.

13. Balancing trade between two local merchants who were also friends of the Bradburys must have resulted in some awkward moments.

14. Since Dwight was a temperance town, WHB's recommendation that his wife get a supply of ale suggests that he thought it was for medicinal purposes and would have been socially acceptable for that reason. Dustin, 36–38.

15. "Fancy women" may have been a euphemism for prostitutes.

16. Ann Brown, MB's sister-in-law, came to help with the delivery and care of the new babies and the other children. The length of Ann's visit is unknown.

17. Leander Morgan was now at home in Dwight, where he helped with hauling the Bradburys' coal, a troublesome chore with which MB had previously struggled.

18. This moment seems to be the beginning of WHB's relent that his family would receive some public assistance.

19. By "examination," what may be meant is Mary's prior attendance for a court deposition regarding the unspecified incident in Poughkeepsie mentioned earlier.

20. This comment referred to their cows.

21. General Henry Moses Judah replaced General Manson in command; WHB mentioned him by name in subsequent letters.

22. This is possibly the most angry letter WHB wrote during the war.

23. Lt. Reuben C. Kise, of Lebanon, Indiana, enlisted the 10th IN Inf. in 1861; he was promoted to the rank of captain and assistant adjutant general. NARA, PR & CMSR.

24. Sergeant K.F. Petticord enlisted on October 11, 1861, at Glasgow, Kentucky, as a private in Co. C, 2nd KY Cav., joining John Hunt Morgan, the chief of CSA guerrilla raiders. According to Colonel Smith, Petticord was said to have committed the unforgivable offense of dressing entire squads of his men in Federal uniforms while robbing houses and plundering the local area in disguise. When Mrs. Petticord told Colonel Smith that she would rather see them "rot" before asking her husband to stop his raids, the agitated colonel seemed to implode with anger. NARA, 129th IL Inf. Regimental Letter Book, February 7, 1863, to and from General Manson's headquarters in Bowling Green.

25. The emergence of new and more rigid leadership under General Judah was a significant change for WHB. Judah's background may help explain his style. Born in 1821 on the eastern shore of Maryland, Henry M. Judah was the son of an Episcopal minister and graduated from West Point in 1843. During the Winter of 1862–63, General Judah served as acting inspector general of the Army of the Ohio. Warner, 255–56.

26. Assuming this is the same Mrs. Jones referenced earlier (December 2, 1862), the nature of that court trial may have been a domestic dispute or divorce.

27. A rare playful exchange between the couple.

28. Years later, a comrade wrote a contrasting view of this incident, in which five men of the 129th IL Inf. were briefly captured by General Morgan and his men not far from the Louisville & Nashville Railroad station at Buck Lodge, Tennessee. W.B. Fyffe, "Memories of the War, Chapter 10" (Pontiac: *Pontiac Sentinel,* n.d.), SRL, 89–08–64, B2, F5.

29. SRL, B7, F13.

30. Ann Brown's maiden name is not known. However, according to undated sources published at the time of her death (n.d., n.p., 1903), she was born at Barton-under-Needwood, Staffordshire, England in 1826. Her children with Mary's brother, John Brown, included Fannie, Mrs. Henry June, Thomas, Mrs. Darius Miller, Joseph, Mrs. Harry Cherrier, William, Jennie Knox, and Albert. SRL, B3, F24.

31. A fever among five children at home during the winter could become an outbreak overnight. Both MB and WHB were very observant of health factors which would be expected coming from England, where their own childhood memories likely recalled that for every person who died from old age or violence, eight died of disease. Nearly one infant in three in 1840 England failed to see the age of five. Edwin Chadwick, *Report on the Sanitary Condition of the Labouring Population of Great Britain*, 1842; and http://landow.stg.brown.edu/victorian/health/health10.html.

32. Likely a description of the diphtheria which was rampant during this time.

33. MB is referencing WHB's letter of complaint and his refusal of their neighbors' efforts to help her and the children while he was away. As WHB likely wrote with the anger that he expressed to her, this letter probably became a subject of much gossip around town.

4. *"Chief of the Topographical Engineers"*

1. James A.B. Scherer, *Cotton as a World Power* (New York: Frederick A. Stokes Company, 1916), 264.

2. Cohn, 25–26.

3. Remarks by British Parliamentarians on October 11, 1864, reflect this concern: "You can best tell whether the Government at Washington look to unite our provinces to their own Northern Dominion [Canada]. But if they do, they must look to a fight with us." William Devereux Jones, "The British Conservative and the American Civil War," *The American Historical Review* 58, No. 3 (April 1953): 540–41.

4. Ibid., 529.

5. Scherer, 278.

6. Cohn, 131.

7. A. Sellew Roberts, "The Federal Government and Confederate Cotton," *The American Historical Review* 32, No. 3 (1927): 262.

8. Cohn, 132.

9. Ibid., 138.

10. Ralph Earle to Prime Minister Disraeli. Jones, 532.

11. [Anonymous] *A Letter to an English Friend on the American War* (New York: Anson D.F. Randolph, July 1863), 19.

12. The mystery of WHB's map remains unsolved. Someone else may have taken the credit for his work or the publication of other like maps by army engineers may have superceded his work. The map that comes closest to fitting his description is "Map of Bowling Green, Ky., Showing its Approaches and Defenses," surveyed and drawn under authority of Major J.H. Simpson, Chief Engineer, Department of the Ohio, by Lieut. N.S. Andrews, 6th MI Battery, 1863. It accompanied Simpson's report and is shown on page 769 of Series I, Vol. 39, Part 3, of the OR. A search of the Map Division of the Library of Congress did not produce any maps of the period credited to Bradbury.

13. Private John K. Ketcham [or Ketchum] of Dwight, Illinois, enlisted in Co. B. He was one of the few men from the small town who would have the sad fate of dying during the war. He died in Chattanooga on June 26, 1864. HDS, "Soldier History."

14. James Strong was one of the elected members of Dwight's town board. Dustin, 37.

15. While more discussion of WHB's map will follow in subsequent notes, it is worth noting that regimental comrade George H. Blakeslee, of Co. G, submitted many maps similar to the one WHB described. Of course, WHB and Blakeslee could have independently created similar maps at roughly the same time. Blakeslee's maps, however, endured and have often been reprinted in publications over the last century. They reside in

the Map Division of the Library of Congress: G3961.S5 1863, #389.7, B6 vault. Blakeslee, who became the regimental historian, lived in Lomax, Nebraska, years after the war. Newspaper clipping, n.p., n.d. [likely the *Pontiac Sentinel*], in WHB's scrapbook, SRL, 89–08–64, B2, F5.

16. It was curious that WHB deferred the naming of his sons to the neighbors, especially since the names "Edwin" and "Elwood" are not found among his ancestry. It had been customary among the Bradbury and Buckley families to use ancestors' names. This was perhaps the adoption of a more American practice—another sign of WHB's break from the traditions of his past.

17. Indiana native General Ambrose Burnside was a graduate of West Point. He reluctantly accepted President Lincoln's call for leadership at a critical time in the Union army's push south. T. Harry Williams, *Lincoln and His Generals* (New York: Alfred A. Knopf, 1952), 180–82.

18. General Jeremiah Tilford Boyle was born in Mercer County, Kentucky, in 1818. He was educated at Princeton as a lawyer. In May 1862, Secretary of War Edward M. Stanton directed General Boyle to take command of Union forces in Kentucky. Warner, 40.

19. Lt. Colonel Gilbert E. Pratt was 28 years old when he enlisted as a private at St. Johns, Michigan, on August 12, 1861. He was promoted rapidly and was commissioned in Co. B of 8th MI Inf. in September 1861. Taken prisoner in June 1862, he was later released and returned to lead the 23rd MI Inf. in their movements south. His earnest rise in rank and heroic experiences as a soldier did not spare him a cruel end. NARA, PR & CMSR.

20. It seems that someone was counteracting WHB's efforts without his knowledge. Why a soldier as competent as WHB was not granted a commission remains a mystery.

21. U.S. Army Brigadier General Alfred Washington Ellett commanded the Mississippi Marine Brigade at this time. Boatner, 262. The flagship *Autocrat* constituted Ellett's headquarters, from which, on the request of Admiral Farragut, he directed the *Switzerland* and the *Lancaster* to ram Confederate batteries above Vicksburg in March 1863. Their duties were deadly, in sharp contrast to the comfortable camp assignments WHB imagined them to be enjoying. OR, Series 1, Vol. 24, Part I, Chapter 36, 473–75.

22. Mayall was not officially listed on the regimental roster; the term "Hon. Member" suggests that he may have been a citizen-soldier (perhaps a politician) from Illinois who came to pitch in while the company was short a captain, but was never technically part of the army. Further information on Mayall was not found. HDS, "Regimental Experience."

23. Of his children, WHB was undoubtedly closest to Jane and was very preoccupied with her moods, education, and development as a young lady. His brother, FB, recognized their close bond in many letters.

24. A tongue-in-cheek remark—WHB did not in fact hold the "Hon. Member" in high esteem.

25. Without precise details it is difficult to be certain, but it seemed that MB may have visited her husband in or near camp. How the children would have been cared for in her absence is a mystery.

26. Confederate soldier Owsley may or may not have held the rank of Major. Curiously, earlier that month a man by the name of M.H. Owsley of Burkesville, Kentucky, registered for a visit at the nearby Mammoth Caves. WKU "Typed Register of Visitors to Mammoth Caves," 25. An H.M. Owsley served in the CSA 2nd KY Cav. and enlisted at Hartsville, Tennessee. HDS, "Soldier History."

27. Capt. Kise was commissioned Assistant Adjutant General by General Manson

for "assisting and arranging the troops on the field and communicating my orders." OR, Series I, Vol. 7, Part 1, Chapter 86.

28. Having been home to see them in person, the twins were less abstract in WHB's writing from this point forward.

5. "More Compliments than Coppers"

1. William Elsey Connelley, *Quantrill & The Border Wars* (New York: Konecky & Konecky, 1909), 284–395.

2. This expression meant that WHB reaped praise fairly easily, but getting paid for his efforts was more difficult.

3. General George Lucas Hartsuff of New York was an 1852 graduate of West Point, appointed from Michigan. After recovering from serious wounds at Antietam, he took the command of the 23rd Corps in Kentucky and East Tennessee in mid-1863. Sifakis, 182; Warner, 212–13. Hartsuff received word at Glasgow on July 3, 1863, from General Judah, who was based outside Tompkinsville, Kentucky, just twenty miles away. Dispatches between Major James R. Hough, the commanding officer in Tompkinsville and Capt. Kise (who WHB immediately served) describing the occupying forces nearby were as follows:

> Returned scouts report, rebels at Turkey Neck Bend commenced moving yesterday afternoon and the remainder left this morning. Large portion took the Burkesville road; portion went in the direction of Martinsville [burg]. Whole rebel force estimated from 2,000 to 10,000 [a considerable range] . . . think force which left Turkey Neck Bend cannot re-enforce those at Burkesville, who have made an attack on General Hobson. He [General Manson] will send cavalry to make a diversion at Mud Camp and hold the main force for further orders.

OR, Series 1, Vol. 23, Part 2, Chapter 35, 681. Examples of such dispatches indicate that Glasgow was not nearly as boring a place as WHB had expected when he first arrived.

4. WHB seemed very confident that he could control his own destiny by defying assignments both requested and ordered.

5. At least one of Bradbury's friends, James Butterworth from Wapella, Illinois, was a member of the 107th IL Inf., which may explain WHB's request for assignment to this regiment. See HDS, "Soldier History," and http://www.rootsweb.com/~usgenweb/il/dewitt/census/1860/0747.gif. If these refer to the same "Mr. Butterworth," there is a possibility that they had known each other back in England; as such, this could explain why Bradbury entrusted him to carry money back to Mary on his behalf. NARA, PR & CMSR.

6. Spite aside, WHB seemed genuinely depressed about leaving the more central operations in Bowling Green and remaining so distant from his old regiment.

7. Hardtack was army bread in the form of a flat, square-shaped hard cracker that traveled well and lasted a long time. Soaked in coffee or water, hardtack would swell in size. http://www.us-civilwar.com

8. The 5th IN Cav. was organized in Indianapolis under Colonel Felix Graham. It spent considerable time scouting the border counties of Indiana and Kentucky until it was moved to Glasgow in March 1863. They joined the search for Morgan's raiders throughout Kentucky and middle Tennessee. That spring, they burned the town of Celina, Tennessee, where they took many prisoners mentioned in WHB's letters. The cavalry regiment would be among the first Union troops to enter Knoxville in September. *The Union Army, A History of Military Affairs in the Loyal States 1861–65*, Vol. 3 (Madison: Federal Publishing, 1908), 168.

9. General Judah's continuous pursuit of John Hunt Morgan came at some personal

cost—both to his health and to his career. Judah's critics considered his judgment poor and rash: "A Commander, so eager was his impulse to pitch at the enemy, even when the odds were greatly against him." The Plattsburgh [NY] *Republican*, January 20, 1866. Judah would not live to see the first anniversary of the end of the war. Warner, 256.

10. Judge Jacob Safford was a member of the first board of directors of the Atchison and Topeka Railroad Company, the forerunner of the Atchison Topeka Santa Fe Railway. Glenn D. Bradley, *The Story of the Santa Fe* (Palmdale, California: Omni Publications, 1995), 29–30. WHB was a land speculator in Kansas and Judge Safford was both an advisor to WHB and a promoter of these lands for future railway development. Keith L. Bryant Jr., *History of the Atchison, Topeka and Santa Fe Railway* (New York: Macmillan Publishing, 1974), 8–12.

11. It is not clear how this accounting and exchange of goods for services was accomplished, but it may have been in an informal—if not illegal—way to enhance the low pay of certain soldiers. Whether it was misappropriation or not, it is ironically the kind of behavior for which WHB would have chastised MB. Yet it also helps explain the motivation of some war-weary southerners and border-state residents to sympathize with the Confederacy. Permitting Union clerks and officers to board in their homes in this manner provided civilians access to goods and supplies that were impossible to obtain otherwise.

12. The Commissary Department was responsible for "the good and sufficient storehouses, sheds, [tar]paulins, or other proper and adequate means of covering and protecting subsistence supplies. . . . Care must be taken to keep the storerooms dry and well ventilated." *Regulations for the Subsistence Department of the Army of the United States* (Washington, D.C.: Government Printing Office, 1863), 9–10.

13. WHB may not have known it, but Basil Duke was more than just one of Morgan's comrads; he was also Morgan's brother-in-law and trusted adviser. Ramage, 50.

14. That a slave sale could have been held at this time (after the Emancipation Proclamation) and place, under Union occupation of the region, seems incongruous; it is not described in other comrades' letters home.

15. This is a description of desiccated vegetables, a drying and preservation method that remains in use today.

16. WHB seems to have had ambitious expectations for Jane, asking her to perform quite complex calculations at the age of 10. A ration was the U.S. Army's algorithm of essential daily food allowances and included the following for one person:

> Twelve ounces of pork or bacon, or, one pound and four ounces of salted or fresh beef; one pound and six ounces of soft bread or flour, or, one pound of hard bread, or, one pound and four ounces of corn meal; and to every one hundred rations, fifteen pounds of beans or peas, and ten pounds of rice or hominy; ten pounds of green coffee, or, eight pounds of roasted and ground coffee, or, one pound and eight ounces of tea; fifteen pounds of sugar, four quarts of vinegar; one pound and four ounces of adamantine or star candles; four pounds of soap; three pounds and twelve ounces of salt; four ounces of pepper; thirty pounds of potatoes, when practicable, and one quart of molasses.

Regulations for the Subsistence Department of the Army (Washington, D.C.: Government Printing Office, 1863), 9–12.

17. Despite an extensive search, the author of this clever passage for recalling the proper use of collective nouns could not be identified.

6. *"Bully for Us!"*

1. Dyer, Vol. 2, 864–65.

2. WHB, "The Campaign in East Tennessee: Brig. Gen. Julius White's Command," *Chicago Tribune*, February 4, 1864.

3. OR, Series 1, Vol. 30, Part 3, Chapter 42, 333.

4. Gerald L. Augustus, *The Loudon County Area of East Tennessee in the War 1861–1865* (Paducah: Turner Publishing, 2000), 15–22.

5. Charles F. Bryan Jr., "Tories' Amidst Rebels: Confederate Occupation of East Tennessee, 1861–63," *The East Tennessee Historical Society's Publications*, No. 60 (1988), 21–22.

6. Born in South Carolina and raised in Alabama, CSA General James Longstreet, General Lee's "war horse," was another West Point graduate. Stewart Sifakis, *Who Was Who in the Confederacy*, Vol. 2 (New York: Facts on File, Inc., 1988), 175–76.

7. General Orlando Bolivar Willcox was born in Detroit, Michigan, in 1823 and was an 1847 graduate of West Point. Also educated as a lawyer, he participated with the Army of the Potomac in many of the eastern battles throughout 1861 and 1862, and was taken prisoner in the summer of 1862. He served in the Army and Department of Ohio in eastern Tennessee until March 16, 1864, and was then returned to the Army of the Potomac for the balance of the war. Sifakis, Vol. 1, 454.

8. Daniel E. Sutherland, ed., *A Very Violent Rebel* (Knoxville: University of Tennessee Press, 1996), 217. The property still stands and has been recognized by the National Register of Historic Places as the Mabry-Hazen House & Museum. More information is available from the Hazen Historical Museum Foundation. Born in Massachusetts, Samuel H. Lunt lived in Iowa, where he enlisted on May 4, 1861. *Roster of Iowa Soldiers*, Vol. 1; HDS, "Soldier History."

9. Sutherland, xxi, 41, 45, 82.

10. Ibid., 41, 46–47

11. The Kain family lived next door to Ellen Renshaw House. William Calib Kain organized Kain's Light Artillery Company and subsequently the Mabry Artillery. Ibid., 207; OR, Series 1, Vol. 16, Part 2, Chapter 28, 716–18.

12. OR, Series 1, Vol. 16, Part 2, Chapter 28, 716, 722.

13. Sutherland, 208–51.

14. Stephen V. Ash, ed., *Secessionists and Other Scoundrels* (Baton Rouge: Louisiana State University Press, 1999), 44–51.

15. Sutherland, 39–41.

16. WHB letter May 30, 1864, in which the historic storming of Ft. Sanders was recalled.

17. William P. Sanders was born in Frankfort, Kentucky, in 1833 and was a member of the West Point class of 1856. Sanders was commissioned colonel of the 5th KY Cav. in March 1863 and was commissioned brigadier-general on October 18, 1863. Just one month later, General Sanders was mortally wounded. HDS, "Officer Directory."

18. Benjamin was chief of artillery of the 9th Army Corps. Just 24 years old, he had graduated from West Point in 1861. His apprenticeship was spent in a succession of campaigns: Bull Run, Yorktown, Malvern Hill, Manassas, Antietam, Vicksburg, and Fredericksburg. MOLLUS (Military Order of the Loyal League of the United States), Commandery of the District of Columbia, War Paper 65, "Raising the Siege of Knoxville," by Gilbert C. Kniffen, November 7, 1906, 13. (Kniffen, a native of Paris, Kentucky, was a commissary officer during the Civil War and retired as chief of the Pension Bureau in 1909.) MOLLUS membership information for Kniffen courtesy of HDS.

19. It is now the Confederate Memorial Hall.

20. Jack Renfro, "Remnants of Civil War Knoxville," *Civil War Times Illustrated* (May/June 1994), 52.

21. Ibid., 52.

22. Sutherland, 45.

23. Renfro, 53.

24. In the space of only a few minutes, General Longstreet suffered the following

casualties: 129 dead, 458 wounded, and 226 missing in action. *The Union Army,* Vol. 6; Kniffen, 15–16.

25. Kniffen, 16–20.

26. Sutherland, 57.

27. Those who failed to furnish the Union Army with oaths of allegiance and loyalty were placed on trains and wagons headed for Georgia and points southward.

28. Quite an understatement—this was one of the briefest and least structured letters that WHB wrote.

29. A wounded area of tissue that failed to heal properly. Joseph G. Richardson, M.D., *Health and Longevity* (Philadelphia: Home Health Society, 1914), 998, 1217.

30. The "Railroad men" of Dwight included James G. Spencer, who relocated from New York and was a descendant of the first governor of New York. He owned 1200 acres and was one of the early engineers of the Chicago, Alton & St. Louis line. The Prince of Wales resided in Spencer's home during the former's famous hunting expedition to Dwight in 1860. The other two "Railroad men" were Henry Gardner and R.P. Morgan, both civil engineers. LeBaron, 481.

31. The movements of certain CSA guerrilla troops, which included Champ Ferguson, across the various crossing points of the Cumberland River (Mud Camp, Smith's Ferry) and through the already terrorized and barren villages, are described in great detail in OR, Series 1, Vol. 30, Part 2, Chapter 41, 576–580.

32. Charles T. Bradbury, William's brother in England.

33. Shortly after this, conditions became different than WHB's exaltations might have predicted. General Halleck ordered General Burnside to move his troops to aid General Rosecrans. Burnside, however, felt Knoxville was too vulnerable and that any great evacuation of East Tennessee would be unwise. On September 27, 1863, President Lincoln intervened with a compromise: "Hold your present positions and send Rosecrans what you can spare in the quickest and safest way. . . . East Tennessee can be no more than temporarily lost so long as Chattanooga is firmly held." OR, Series 1, Vol. 30, Part 3, Chapter 42, 667–68, 904–05.

34. William Henry Bailhache was born at Chillicothe, Ohio, on August 14, 1826. He moved with his father, a newspaper owner named John Bailhache, to Alton, Illinois, in 1836. Before the Civil War, William H. Bailhache was one of the owners and managers of the *State Journal* in Springfield, Illinois. President Lincoln appointed him Captain and Assistant Quartermaster, which suggests that they were acquainted. The Bailhache family moved in high social and political circles in south-central Illinois. NARA, CMSR & PR; ISHL, Bailhache-Brayman Collection; *Dwight Star and Herald,* November 17, 1900.

35. While we can't know what MB was writing him about, WHB's response seemed insulting.

36. A euphemistic way of saying that they were taking what they could from anyone who had anything.

37. Mrs. Bradbury's penmanship was not as precise as her husband's.

38. Mr. O.F. Pearre was the principal of Dwight's school from 1861 to 1863. Dustin, 116.

39. Always hanging over WHB's head was the threat of being demanded back at his regiment by Captain Walkley, Co. B, 129th IL Inf.

40. It is unclear whether this would have served to comfort WHB as an endearing reminder of his wife or if he wanted to critique her sewing.

41. WHB's letters home during the time of the Knoxville battle are either missing or never existed. Bradbury may not have had either the luxury to write as he had earlier nor the assurance that mail would get through. More than fifty officers' reports tell the Union's tale of the dark days of November and December 1863. OR Series 1, Vol. 31,

Part 1, Chapter 43, 256–257. Yet Bradbury reflected on the terrible battles of Knoxville some months later, which documents that he was in Knoxville during the battles (cf. his letter of May 30, 1864). The deafening sounds, the deprivations of personal movement and shipment of goods, and the faces of captured Confederate troops are possibly nowhere better documented than in Ellen Renshaw House's diary. Sutherland, 38-77.

7. *"After the Loaves and the Fishes"*

1. Estimated length of furlough based on dating of letters and his remark in letter of February 6, "imagine six weeks of washing."

2. Concern for smallpox was well founded. An outbreak of the disease was thinning the ranks in Nashville during the first three months of 1864. Bohrnstedt, 64.

3. "The Situation at Knoxville and Vicinity, Special Correspondence of the Chicago Tribune, Feb. 11, 1864," by William H. Bradbury, published in the *Chicago Tribune*, February 17, 1864.

4. Sutherland, 86.

5. Ibid.

6. Ibid., 112.

7. "From our special Correspondent, W.H.B., Knoxville, Tenn., Feby, 16, 1864," published in the *Chicago Tribune*, February 29, 1864. This article was WHB's retrospective report, written as though the timing was still prior to the siege of Knoxville.

8. "Dateline Knoxville, TN, Feb. 24, 1864," *Chicago Tribune*, published March 3, 1864, signed WHB. The language from Isaiah 61:3 is included in this excerpt.

9. Kain is the correct spelling.

10. Baize was a coarse woolen cloth often used for tablecloths and other domestic goods.

11. The pen was likely a Christmas present.

12. Given the amount of military intelligence that WHB revealed to the newspapers in the middle of a still-unfolding war, it is only amazing that Private Bradbury used his true initials, WHB, at the end of the article.

13. While soldiers typically requested ginger for medicinal use to cure dyspepsia and diarrhea at the front, ginger beer, an aerated drink similar to ale, was also commonly consumed for many years.

14. WHB had been separated from the 129th IL Inf. and his neighbors from Livingston County, Illinois, since the winter of 1862–63 in Bowling Green.

15. Since WHB had been apart from the regiment for so long and his route to Lookout Valley was via Knoxville rather than via Nashville with the regiment, he missed the journey that his comrade Charles Laforest Dunham described in a letter dated March 14, 1864:

> I tell you what we had a ruff old time a comeing over the mountains out of our train. Thare was thirty or forty mules died so you can guess what kind of a time we had, and thare is know telling how many wageons smashed down.... The roads are strewd with dead mules. It beats any thing I ever hurd tell of. If I could see you I could tell you of my great sights but it would take me a month of sundays to wright it.

DeRosier, 107–08.

16. SRL, B5, F3.

17. FB's fond remembrance of his brother's early poetry was likely a delightful bit of nostalgia for Jane, who surely missed her father greatly by this time.

18. SRL, B5, F6.

19. The brigade included the 105th IL Inf., 102nd IL Inf., 70th IN Inf., and the 79th OH Inf. in addition to the 129th IL Inf. Dyer, 455, 459.

20. SRL, B5, F3.

21. A more comprehensive view of WHB's active land speculation business. By this time, only public lands in Kansas and Nebraska were still widely available for purchase that were similar to the Grundy County, Illinois, lands where WHB first settled. Paul Wallace Gates, "Frontier Landlords and Pioneer Tenants," *Journal of the Illinois State Historical Society* 38, No. 1 (March 1945): 179–183.

22. This probably refers to either his cousin James Buckley or his brother-in-law James Brown.

23. The settlement referred to here could be either the estate of his parents or the sale of WHB's interests in the mill business in England.

24. He was not just correcting the children's papers, but his wife's letters too.

25. ISHL, Bailhache-Brayman Collection, B2, F7. WHB's comrade Lt. Culver also wrote that night to his wife about the way he spent the evening in a three-hour singing session with WHB, Col. Benjamin Harrison, and Alf. Huetson. Dunlap, 249.

8. *"I Don't Like This Field Work"*

1. *Chicago Tribune*, written March 24, 1864, printed March 31, 1864.

2. Article 57 reads: "Whosoever shall be convicted of holding correspondence with, or giving intelligence to the enemy, either directly or indirectly, shall suffer death, or such other punishment as shall be ordered by the sentence of a court-martial." Louis LeGrand, M.D., *The Military Handbook and Soldier's Manual of Information* (New York: Beadle and Company, 1861), 16.

3. James G. Randall, "The Newspaper Problem in Its Bearing Upon Military Secrecy During the Civil War," *The American Historical Review* 23, No. 2 (January 1918): 311–17.

4. Jacob D. Cox, *Campaigns of the Civil War: Atlanta*, Vol. 9 (New York: Charles Scribner's Sons, 1882), 59–62.

5. DeRosier, 122.

6. Dunlap, 262–84.

7. Letter by Benjamin Harrison to his wife, Caroline, dated July 21, 1864, from "Howell's Mill, 4 miles from Atlanta." W. H. Smith Memorial Library, Indiana Historical Society, Collection M132 B1F9.

8. Harvey Green, *The Light of the Home: An Intimate View of the Lives of Women in Victorian America* (New York: Pantheon Books, 1983), 86.

9. Ibid., 87.

10. Patricia Branca, *Silent Sisterhood: Middle Class Women in the Victorian Home* (Pittsburgh: Carnegie-Mellon University Press, 1975), 14.

11. Ibid., 88–91.

12. As the owner of a cotton mill in England, CTB's view of the rebellion was driven by economic motives.

13. Cartes de visite were small photographs of the period, approximately 2.25" by 3.75". They were often mounted on a thick material similar to cardboard so they would last longer.

14. In his efforts to persuade MB to go to Chicago for photographs, WHB may have overlooked the logistical challenges of traveling with five children, two of whom were twin babies.

15. WHB's reasoning here was that low rooms could cause poor air quality and, indirectly, sickness.

16. The only time in which his initials are in reverse order as "BHW". Perhaps WHB thought that this would sufficiently conceal his identity.

17. What the "scandal" was is not known. It may have been about WHB's newspaper writing.

18. In this context, "the Review" was a formal review of the troops by the commanding officers with full uniform, arms, and accouterment. In anticipation of the upcoming Atlanta campaign, the Review would serve to emphasize the importance of the troops' attention to detail and obedience. While dreaded by the average soldier, such reviews also served to build esprit du corps among the men and confidence in their senior officers.

19. Brigadier General William Thomas Ward of Kentucky was fifty-six years old at the time. Sifakis, Vol. 1, 437. WHB, Lt. Culver, and other soldiers were not happy with General Ward's command. Bohrnstedt, 112–14; Dunlap, 264, 265n.

20. On April 3, 1864, Comrade Charles Laforest Dunham wrote home that "we have preaching now evry sabath when the wether will admit. You see our church is a large one all out dores." DeRosier, 113. In his letter of May 1, 1864, he noted that the church activities had increased: "We ar haveing quite a revival in our Regt. We went to work and put up a church—it is about the size of our house." Ibid., 116.

21. There is no record of Bradbury getting into trouble for any controversy his articles might have caused at home or at Lookout Valley. NARA, PR & CMSR.

22. There is no explanation of Frances's identity.

23. General Daniel Butterfield, born in Utica, New York, in 1831, was a college graduate working as a merchant at the start of the war. His military career began as Colonel of the 12th NY Militia, but he rose quickly through army ranks. Warner, 62. Major General Butterfield commanded the 3rd Division of the 20th Army Corps from April 14 to June 29, 1864. Dyer, Vol. 1, 459.

24. While only a few days earlier, WHB had resolved to suspend writing rather than risk getting into trouble, now that he was in the employ and good graces of General Butterfield—the possibility of writing again for the newspapers seemed irresistible.

25. Mr. C. Roadnight, from "the chalky cliffs of old England," settled near Dwight in 1857. He was known for his fine education and was frequently called "Sir Charles." Roadnight was the freight agent of the Chicago, Alton & St. Louis Railroad for many years. Dustin, 5.

26. General Hugh Judson Kilpatrick, a West Point graduate who commanded the cavalry, was just twenty-eight years old at the start of the Atlanta Campaign. General William D. Whipple, thirty-eight years old and also a West Point graduate, was a native New Yorker. General George Henry Thomas, at age forty-eight years old and a West Point graduate, led critical assignments for Generals Grant and Sherman. Sufakis, Vol. 1, 222, 449, 410.

27. WHB's diary was not with his letters and has not been located. Odd as it seems, we can infer from his remarks that WHB felt justified in writing articles as long as he worked from "his" diary, rather than General Butterfield's.

28. Dan's identity is not known, but he may have been a freedman or former slave.

29. Gates Phillips Thruston (elsewhere "Thurston") was a 26-year-old lawyer born in Dayton, Ohio. The nephew of Union Brigadier General Charles M. Thruston and the grandson of Buckner Thruston (U.S. Senator, Kentucky, 1804–1809), he was commissioned captain of Co. C, 1st OH Inf. in August 1861. Steady promotions followed—major in September 1863 and lt. colonel by June 1864. WHB and Thruston apparently got along very well, perhaps because of their British roots or their legal background. Unlike many officers, WHB did not have harsh words for Thruston. NARA, PR & CMSR.

30. MB must have taken on sewing jobs to earn extra income.

31. The Bartholics were long-standing members of the Dwight community. Dustin, 40, 52.

32. The genus of the "sensitive plant," or littleleaf sensitive-briar, is Mimosa microphylla, often called by Schrankia microphylla. Wilbur Duncan and Marion Duncan, *Wildflowers of the Eastern United States* (Athens: University of Georgia Press, 1999). It is a non-native plant to U.S. soil and invades and spreads easily. Georgia Natural Heritage Program and the Center for Aquatic and Invasive Plants, University of Florida.

Furthermore, William was concerned with Jane's sensitivity; knowing that Jane may have known the popular children's story, "My Schoolmates: The Sensitive Plant," by Abbie (from the *Youth's Companion,* July 9, 1846, 37–38), this might explain her father's reasons for sending her a specimen.

33. Timothy seed was a type of grass used as fodder for livestock.

34. George Flagler was one of the early settlers and town leaders of Dwight, Illinois. Dustin, 89, 101.

35. Tonsil infection.

36. Characterizing guns as "pesky" was probably WHB's way of putting his wife's mind at rest that he was not particularly in harm's way.

9. "Let It Go to Thunder!"

1. OR, Series 1, Vol. 38, Part II, Chapter 50, Report No. 73, 397.

2. General John Bell Hood, Kentucky native, was another West Point graduate. Sifakis, Vol. 2, 134–35.

3. General John Bell Hood's dispatch to General Sherman on September 12, 1843. William T. Sherman, *Sherman's Memoirs* (New York: The Great Commander Series, 1994), 422–34.

4. Ibid., 426.

5. WHB was uncharacteristically short-tempered with MB here.

6. A wafer was a small, pasted seal used to secure letters.

7. WHB's handwriting appeared on different occasions as both "Petzer" and "Pitzer." The Illinois Public Domain Land Tract Sales Database and the 1860 Census of Livingston County, Illinois, list both Petzer and Pitzer as surnames, one of which could refer to the individual with whom he had unsatisfactory business affairs.

8. The reference is to John Brown, Mary's brother in Morris, Illinois.

9. WHB's model of a receipt for MB to use with Harford was kept with the letter. SRL, B7, F1.

10. Judge Advocate Thruston had joined the 14th A.C. near Atlanta and carried many military orders between generals. FHS, Gates Phillips Thruston Collection, 685; Letter to Mother, Sept. 4, 1864.

11. The description seems consistent with poison oak or ivy.

12. WHB was residing at a fine home near the north side of Atlanta.

13. Captain William W. Webber of Morris, Illinois, began service with the 4th IL Cav. in September 1861. HDS, "Soldier History."

14. Scurvy could become a serious disorder. It was caused by dietary deficiency of ascorbic acid, and many soldiers and sailors suffered from it. A diet including pickles, sauerkraut (cabbage), or citrus fruit would have helped prevent it. J.M. Da Costa, *Medical Diagnosis* (Philadelphia: J.B. Lippincott Company, 1890), 922–25.

10. "All I Live For"

1. Andersonville Prison existed from February 1864 to April 1865. Disease and death rates in all prisoner-of-war camps, including Andersonville, were high. Boatner, 15.

2. Isaiah 61:3 is incorporated in this poem. See Chapter 7, Note 8.

3. Among the men of the 129th IL Inf. who were killed during the Atlanta Campaign were J.L. Ketcham, Enos Morris, August Stahl, G.A. Sarvis, Jerry Randall, and William Hoffman. Dustin, 30–31.

4. No such ale appeared in research of historic ales of England, so either his handwriting or his memory may be to blame.

5. WHB may have used Epsom salts internally, diluted in water, which would produce a laxative effect. Dermatitis at that time was treated as a fundamental intestinal disorder, so they were likely trying to "cleanse" him of his skin disease—both inside and out. DaCosta, 922–25.

6. WHB used large, block printed letters instead of his normal cursive style of handwriting.

7. Thruston wrote to his family on the same day. "Chattanooga is a poor exchange for Atlanta but with all its mud and shabbiness, it is so much nearer home that I do not regret the change." FHS, Gates Phillip Thruston Collection, 685.

8. Thruston complained in a letter home that General Thomas seemed to be keeping them in Chattanooga, "away from temptation and communication." And, perhaps sharing WHB's sentiment, Thruston added: "If I am to lose the glory and excitement of field service, and am to be confined to office work, it would be some satisfaction at least to be where I could see something of society and have a good time." FHS, Letter to Mother, Nov. 26, 1864.

9. The colonel, who wrote home about this, would later become President Harrison. IHS, Nov. 27, 1864, letter to Caroline Harrison, M132, 31F9.

10. Root & Cady was a well-known publisher of song sheet music in Chicago. http://www.chicagohis.org.

11. SRL, B7, F13.

11. "Everybody has the Blues Sometimes"

1. Private Cornelius Smith, of Geneva, Wisconsin, was a member of Co. C of 22nd WI Infantry. NARA, CMSR, PR.

2. That is, troops had to travel north to obtain passage by ship in order to join their comrades, by then in the Carolinas to the south.

3. She may have been a resident with whom WHB boarded or perhaps his cook or laundrywoman.

4. Lt. Culver had gone home to Illinois. With the news of Sherman's movement to the seacoast, detached and furloughed men such as Culver had to make their way to New York for ship transport southward. Dunlap, 387–94.

5. James and Lucy Brown were MB's brother and sister-in-law who lived in England on the Isle of Man. SRL, B4, F11 & B7, F40.

6. Dr. Duponco's Golden Periodical Pills were used as a stimulant to induce miscarriage or prevention of a continued state of pregnancy.

7. Indeed, this extensive letter to the *Guardian,* his first published in Britain, was more than 2,400 words long.

8. It was interesting that he worried about the one child who was an avid scholar on her own. Dustin, 118.

9. After twelve years of marriage and five children, this may be the most romantic wartime paragraph that WHB wrote to his wife.

10. Newspaper writing was usually firsthand and spontaneous for WHB. As the high command moved on to the sea, Bradbury was left with bits and pieces of dispatches, rumors, and overheard discussions in order to create reports.

11. Noteworthy as an occasion in which he seemed to appreciate Mary's advice and planned to follow her suggestion.

12. According to genealogical files, Dr. William D. Dorris was born in 1802 in Robertson County, Tennessee. A veteran of the Mexican War, Dorris was a controversial person in Tennessee, where he lived prior to the Civil War, for his opposition to secession and slavery. When Kentucky announced its neutrality in 1861, Dr. Dorris moved his family to Tompkinsville, Kentucky. When the Union Army occupied Nashville, he returned at age 60 and volunteered his services as a citizen-soldier, serving as scout, guide, and sharpshooter. In his subsequent attempts to obtain a Civil War pension (they were denied), he claimed to have participated in 155 battles or skirmishes. He lived to the age of 90. Burnice Dorris Waggoner, "My Dorris Family Line," 48–66, February 7, 1980, unpublished manuscript of the Tennessee State Library and Archives and the Robertson County Archives.

13. The "expected change" would likely have been a terminated pregnancy if Mary had followed her husband's advice about taking Duponco's pills.

14. His remark that he's not "reproving" Mary seems to belie his true feeling that he held her responsible for this particular pregnancy.

15. When Thruston wrote to his sister Janet, on Jan. 16, 1865, he provided a colorful insight to this party, one that he was in charge of: "I shall never again wonder that there was a Ball at Brussells on the eve of the Battle of Waterloo. . . . I was dragooned into being chariman of the committee of arrangements for the party, by being placed there without my knowledge. . . . The supper cost a thousand dollars . . . so you see that with all our war scenes and mud scenes—rather an alarming state of gaiety exists here. . . . In my reflective moments, I am a little ashamed of my worldliness . . . but my sin does not create widows or orphans or break hearts." FHS, Gates Phillips Thruston Collection, 685.

16. It is hard to say if this simple remark was intended to be chastising and angry or jocular and teasing; more likely, it was the latter.

17. A charitable interpretation of this remark might have been, "I'm satisfied if you have accepted this pregnancy, although I still hope you are proven wrong about it; if the pregnancy was to come to an end, it would be all right with me."

18. If Mary was depressed, lonely, and pregnant with her sixth child, she may have been staying at home intentionally to avoid gossip about her "condition."

19. This remark seems insulting to MB, yet WHB likely meant that the ladies found it easy to associate among other active women in town and MB was somewhat reclusive then.

20. "Tableaux" refers to a practice of the day known as a "tableau vivant," an occasion in which a group of people, usually women, dressed in period attire and posed motionless to represent a scene, usually some dramatic and well-known moment from history or from a popular novel or play. *Oxford Universal Dictionary*. In addition, the "Ladies Loyal League" of Dwight, established in 1863, met in the Eldredges' house, where they sponsored fund-raising events to send support to the troops, such as a cow to the Springfield hospital for milk and butter for recovering soldiers. Their tablexaux were both social and fundraising events, often with oyster suppers following. Dustin, 29.

21. It is understandable that MB's spirits might have sunk that winter. MB may have been impervious to WHB's efforts to rally her spirits.

22. A "housewife" was a soldier's all-purpose kit for mending.

23. WHB is offering ideas for his birthday gifts to Jane, who wants to send him something.

24. Estimated due date for their next child.

25. Apparently the storekeeper Hetzel also served as the town postmaster, as rural

delivery to homes did not exist yet. Arthur Summerfield, *U.S. Mail, The Story of the United States Postal Service* (New York: Holt, Rinehart & Winston, 1960), 83–85.

26. Bradbury was teasing the children; Willie's appetite appeaared to be a subject of droll family humor.

27. WHB's first note of acceptance for the new little Bradbury who would join their family.

28. Jane was apparently doing her part for the soldiers by making homemade envelopes for their use.

29. Jane Bradbury surely treasured Smith's letter as it was kept among the Civil War letters. LC.

30. The missing word was "baby."

31. Apparently WHB often corrected letters and compositions of family members, including MB's, and returned them for instructive value.

12. "The Federals in the Southwest"

1. *Manchester Guardian,* March 27, 1865.

2. Ibid.

3. Ibid.

4. MB's use of this tonic could have contributed to what today is termed fetal alcohol syndrome in the baby. See http://www.mwac.nps.gov/bottle_glass/hostetter.html

5. Presumably the Hetzels had another child of their own or perhaps a grandchild.

6. A remarkable insight, from a great distance no less, for a nineteenth-century father to be concerned with his daughter's self-esteem, a social construct that would not become popularized for a few more decades.

7. At a time when the country had undergone great carnage, WHB saw the opportunity for personal gain.

8. Kate Bradbury, WHB's niece, was very young in 1865, but she would leave a profound legacy as a patron of archaeology and Egyptology. Margaret S. Drower, *Flinders Petrie: A Life in Archaeology* (London: Victor Gollancz, Ltd., 1985), 199, 206, 222–23, 283–84.

9. This was, it seems, one of the most heartfelt, autobiographical statements in his letters to the *Guardian*—how the war had personally affected him.

10. Thruston wanted to stay in Nashville at least in part because of personal affairs as he wrote to Mother, March 3, 1865: "I find my business requires so much of my time that I will either have to slight it (no) or back square out of my social engagements. . . . The state of society here is rather curious. The young men are either killed off or in the Southern army . . . but the young ladies are all still here and after playing the part of nuns and being true to their Southern lovers and allegiances through three long, lonely years—they are all beginning to be subjugated. . . . They dance to Yankee Doodle without grumbling and are always ready for a flirtation or even something more serious." FHS, Gates Phillips Thruston Collection, 685.

11. "In like sixty" was an expression meaning "to flood-like proportions" or "with exuberance."

12. SRL, B7, F1 (repository of CTB's letters).

13. Most likely due to his social status, brother CTB was acquainted with the *Guardian*'s editor, Charles Prestwich Scott. See http://www.manchester2002-uk.com/celebs/authors2.html for more information about Scott.

14. The quote, one of bluster and bravado, was a paraphrase of a line from Act 3, Scene 2 of Shakespeare's *Hamlet.* The original line is "Let the galled jade wince, our withers are unwrung."

15. "Merrill's Horse" referred to Colonel Lewis Merrill's command, ultimately com-

posed of cavalry troops from the 2nd Missouri (of which there was a Michigan Battalion) and 1st New York, and infantry troops from Illinois (23rd, 37th, 42nd, and 44th), 70th New York, and 47th Ohio. See http://modoc1873.com/7thcavmajbre.html and http://www.geocities.com/~micivilwar/cavalry/merrill.htm.

16. Their children's other cousin in England was Emma Bradbury, the youngest child of CTB.

17. Sergeant Frank Angle, Co. B, 129th IL Inf., was killed on March 16, 1865, at Taylor's Hole, North Carolina. Private Charles M. Rawlings, also of Co. B, was taken prisoner of war, as WHB had heard. NARA, CMSR.

18. Unlike most soldiers, WHB expressed little anguish or concern over President Lincoln's assassination. As WHB was not a native American, he did not seem to feel the loss as much as fellow soldiers like his friend Lt. Culver, who wrote home: "I never saw so much sadness manifested. The whole army is silent as the grave." Dunlap, 434–35.

19. This is a line from Act 3, Scene 1 of Shakespeare's *Julius Caesar.*

13. "Headquarters of the Cumberland"

1. WKU, Champ Ferguson file.

2. Thurman Sensing, *Champ Ferguson: Confederate Guerrilla* (Nashville: Vanderbilt University, 1942), 33.

3. CSA Lt. Walter F. "Champ" Ferguson enlisted in the 2nd KY Inf. in July 1861. After being taken prisoner-of-war in February 1862, he escaped and joined General John Morgan's 2nd KY Cav. Called a notorious outlaw by some, Ferguson's deep commitment to and ferocity in killing rather than taking Union troops prisoner was well known. A good deal of the notoriety associated with Morgan might be appropriately attributed to outliers like Ferguson, whose atrocities even upset Morgan's right-hand man, Basil Duke. Ramage, 85, 101, 143. Ferguson was captured in May 1865 by Union officers. OR, Series 1, Vol. 49, Part 2, 931.

4. Sensing, 34-36.

5. WKU, Champ Ferguson file.

6. WHB liberally adapted a verse from Sir Walter Scott, *Pibroch of Donald Dhu,* that in its correct form would have read: "Come as the winds come when the forests are rended; Come as the waves come when navies are stranded."

7. Colonel James F. Jacques, of Quincy, Illinois, led the 73rd IL Inf. into numerous battles, including Perryville, Stone's River, Chickamauga, Missionary Ridge, Atlanta, and Nashville. HDS, "Soldier History" and "Regiment History."

8. Edward Perronet. See http://www.cyberhymnal.org/bio/p/e/perronet_e.htm

9. "Pie-plant" or "pieplant" is also known as rhubarb.

10. Apparently WHB had gotten a furlough, as he had been hoping.

11. WHB was working every angle to get home before the baby arrived.

12. This must have been around the advent of balloons as children's toys.

13. The only "Lacey" that can be identified is Private Henry Lacy McFee of Co. B. HDS, "Soldier History."

14. WHB took part in a momentous occasion in history by covering the first convention of the Freedmen and Refugee Bureau in August 1865. As the complex social issues began to unfold after the war, African Americans began to ask tough questions, primarily seeking equal participation in the legislative processes that affected their lives—work, property, education, and legal matters. John Cimprich, *Slavery's End in Tennessee, 1861–65* (Tuscaloosa: University of Alabama Press, 1985), 126–31.

14. "General Fisk and the Freedmen's Bureau"

1. OR, Series 3, Vol. 5, 532.

2. NARA, RG94, Court-martial records of John C. Crane.

3. Letter of July 17, 1865, to President Andrew Johnson from G.O. Grannis, NARA, Court-martial records of John C. Crane. In addition, just a few months before, then Vice President Johnson extolled Col. Crane's administrative efficiency during a speech in Nashville. Leroy P. Graf, ed., *The Papers of Andrew Johnson*, Vol. 7, 1864–1865 (Knoxville: University of Tennessee Press, 1986), 269.

4. Lunt died July 28, 1865. NARA, PR & CMSR.

5. OR, Series 3, Vol. 5, 533–34.

6. Ibid., 48.

7. Paul David Phillips, "A History of the Freedmen's Bureau in Tennessee" (Ph.D. diss., Vanderbilt University, 1964), 57.

8. Ibid.

9. Ibid., 67.

10. A bold declaration for the era about the irrelevance of skin color to intelligence.

11. This was not merely idle banter for his letter; CTB was apparently awaiting word before speculating in cotton futures, as later letters show.

12. While WHB had counted on the *Tribune*'s use of his account of the Crane case, when they did not use it, he may have let the Cincinnati newspaper have it out of spite. This may explain his remark in the previous letter of "fixing it [with the *Tribune*] bye & bye."

13. Thruston wrote to his mother, too, about the Crane trial: "It is important that I should 'leave no stone unturned' in my efforts to prosecute the case." FHS, Gates Phillips Thruston Collection, 685; Letter July 16, 1865.

14. Foolscap is a type of coarse paper often used for drawing or wrapping.

15. Likely a relative of comrade Charles Kochlein in Co. B, 129th IL Inf. WHB probably wanted to hire her as a housekeeper or midwife. HDS, "Regiment Personnel Listing."

16. Following the progress of The Atlantic Telegraph was especially important for the Bradbury family, as the brothers could communicate more efficiently about their business affairs with each other. It began as an American enterprise and was capitalized by British businessmen during the U.S. Civil War. Ships began to lay the cable in July 1865, but due to a break in the line, the cable would not fully span the Atlantic until 1866. See http://www.canadahistory.com/atlanticcable1866.htm.

17. General Clinton Bowen Fisk was born in New York in 1828. His military career began as Colonel of the 33rd MO Inf. His assignment to the Freedmen & Refugee Bureau allowed him to travel and witness firsthand the conditions and challenges of African Americans struggling to piece new lives together after the war. Fisk's role in Nashville combined two of his greatest interests later in life—education and opportunities for African Americans. Cimprich, 127; Sifakis, Vol. 1, 137; William S. McFeely, *Yankee Stepfather: General O.O. Howard and the Freedmen* (New York: W.W. Norton & Company, 1968), 67, 117–20.

18. With his upper-class English roots, the notion of boarding with Irish workers was probably dreadful to WHB.

19. Once again, Mary failed to obtain a woman who suited her or would stay in the job. This surname does not appear in other local resources.

20. Given his erudition and intelligence, WHB's obliviousness that his wife needed help to care for six children and manage complex business affairs is in many ways baffling.

15. "To Clasp You Once More in My Arms"

1. Several letters in the collection refer to Charley's lack of focus and limited education as a child, his alcoholism, depression, and his indebtedness as an adult. Sister Jane (later, "Jennie") wrote Charley's obituary in January 1908, pointing out to the newspaper obituary writer her role in Charley's life:

"Please mention that his care in early life was by his only sister Jennie." SRL, MS 299.

2. Charles's new wife, a Mrs. Sutcliffe, was likely his late wife's sister-in-law.

3. The court proceedings are also quoted in Sensing, 246.

4. Ibid., 250.

5. Letter dated July 8, 1865, from Joseph S. Fowler on letterhead of the State of Tennessee Comptroller's Office to President Andrew Johnson. NARA, Court-martial records of John C. Crane.

6. Walter Durham, "How Say You Senator Fowler?" *Tennessee Historical Quarterly* 42, No. 1 (Spring 1983): 52–54; NARA, Crane court-martial file.

7. Melville D. Langdon, ed., *The Complete Works of Artemus Ward* (New York: A.L. Burt Company, 1898), 22–26.

8. Notice that the phrasing makes it seem as if the child had died.

9. This is the first time WHB mentioned his preference for a daughter.

10. This remark has a ring of trepidation to it, as if he was wondering how their life together would be.

11. Noticeably absent is the correct pronoun, "him"—instead he writes "it."

12. WHB had apparently obtained a short furlough to go home.

13. A more common term for what he meant was marital infidelity.

14. While an odd remark, extensive family letters indicate that WHB had a loving relationship with the youngest child, Charles. SRL, MS 299.

15. The circumstances of WHB's encounter with Artemus Ward, pseudonym for Charles Browne, are not included in the collection.

Afterword

1. "Ad Astra per Aspera," included in volume, *Poems,* by Wm. H. Bradbury, Topeka, Kansas, 1886. Kansas State Historical Society, Kansas History Center, Topeka, Kansas. "Ad Astra per Aspera" is the Kansas state motto, translated from Latin to mean "to the stars through difficulties."

2. Broadsheet for two performances at Kepplinger's Hall, Dwight, Illinois, September 17 [n.d., but after 1865] to raise money for sufferers of yellow fever. WHB played a role in the comedic play, "Mock Doctor!" SRL, MS 299.

3. Examinations which Jennie Bradbury completed on these subjects are in the collection. SRL, B8, F2.

4. Emerson Grant, born in Michigan in 1849, lived in Galesburg, Illinois, and his family tree included Ulysses S. Grant. SRL, B5, F16.

5. Emerson and Jennie Bradbury Grant's children were Edith and Mary Amelia. When Edwin Bradbury's first wife died after childbirth, Emerson and Jennie raised Edwin's daughter, Dorothy Bradbury, as their own child. SRL, MS 299.

6. Fred Bradbury died at age 81 in 1938. *Topeka State Journal* clipping in WHB's scrapbook (continued by granddaughter Mary Grant), March 2, 1938, SRL, MS 299.

7. William Bradbury represented Topeka at the International Good Roads Convention in St. Louis, April 27–29, 1903. *Transactions of the Kansas State Historical Society, 1903–1904,* Vol. 8 (Topeka: Geo. A. Clark, State Printer, 1904), 537.

8. Topeka newspaper clipping of young William's obituary (n.d.), SRL, MS 299. Cora Metcalf Bradbury died on January 15, 1930. Topeka Cemetery Association obituary clipping.

9. Topeka Cemetery Association records.

10. Edwin died at the age of 65, on January 6, 1928. His widow, Nellie Bradbury, was his second wife. Edwin was president of the Builders Association of Kansas City and an early member of the Meadow Lake Country Club. Obituary clipping from the *Topeka Journal,* January 7, 1928, SRL, MS 299.

11. Elwood was married to a woman named Mary. He died on December 12, 1932. Records of Topeka Cemetery Association; SRL, MS 299.

12. Further ironic because WHB was a friend of Dr. Keeley; the two corresponded for years. One example includes a letter from Dr. Keeley to WHB dated November 9, 1897, that mentioned a holiday to Gettysburg and Antietam. He closed his letter affectionately: "Please write me a good long letter, dear old comrade, one that will wake the house with the old enthusiasm of Capt. Bradbury." SRL, B7, F45.

13. There are references to Charley's alcoholism in numerous files of letters between family members beginning in the 1890's. He seems to have hit rock bottom in December 1898 when he was living in San Francisco under an assumed name (Walter Sandford). SRL, B4, F1.

14. Topeka Cemetery Association records for Charles H. Bradbury.

15. *Manchester Guardian,* May 20, 1865.

16. Dustin, 66.

17. A portion of the lengthy poem is included because of the recognizable characters WHB mentioned and the "air car" he envisioned by 1928. ("Oaklawn" was the cemetery.) Dustin, 61–62:

"Dwight in 1928"

. . . 'Well!' said guest, 'I once lived here, in times gone by, full fifty year,
Then I was young and spry, and gay, now I am old and turning gray. . .
Hetzel and Eldredge followed suit; plodding merchants of good repute.

About Dr. Keeley? The fact is, that he got rich on his country practice,
I knew him well! By the old stone mill he grew quite fat, and never was ill.'
'Enough of him!' said the stranger guest, 'Tell us something about the rest,
Judd and Parsons, Strong and Brad, Bakers and Thompsons and Kenyon and Cad.'
'Well, General Parsons of the millish, kept his command in good condish;
But he lost his life in a Commune riot, since he's been remarkably quiet.

Major Judd married a prim old maid who brushed his clothes & combed his head.
Of this State he was Adjutant General; all the troops went to his funeral.
Strong grew rich and jolly again, and died a stout old congressman.
Brad wrote poetry more and more, and got to be a terrible bore;
died of Astronomy on the brain—his loss was our eternal gain!

Postoffice Kenyon kept that place and always won the political race,
Cad went west for a change of air and died a Kansas millionaire.
Bakers and Thompsons spread all over, Grand-children thick as clover. . .
. . .Oaklawn Grounds were green and sweet, offering a calm and cool retreat.

Distance a mile from the city limits, time by the air car, just three minutes.
Rare slabs and obelisks pierced the air, former inhabitants all were there,
Sleeping beneath the solemn trees till God shall show them His mysteries!
Town Boards, school boards, supervisors, Profligate and stingy misers. . .
Mother and daughter, father and son, gathered together, one by one!
Epitaphs gave of the dead below a list of virtues set up for show.
Phonographs treasured precious tones of old John Smith and Young Bill Jones,
Photographs shown on each tomb glowing with the faces of life-like bloom.'
Said the guest, against his will 'The dead, the dead, are living still. . . .'

18. WHB was a member of Topeka's G.A.R. Lincoln Post #1. (a.u.) *Memorial Record, G.A.R. Lincoln Post #1,* Topeka, Kansas (n.d.).

19. "The Tide of Bloom"

From tropical climes, rich in boundless profusion
Of color and verdure and sweetest perfume,
Sweeps up toward the north with a welcome intrusion
The freshet of flowers,—the great tide of bloom!

Led on by the sun, like the waters of ocean,
It joyfully follows its god in its course;
Through the higher zones circling in fragrant devotion,
Now creeping with softness, now rolling in force.

Upward and onward, with colors all glowing,
The blooming tide tumbles o'er orchard and lea;
See! Out in advance is the dashing spray throwing
A roseate robe o'er the naked peach tree!

While northward, away! Are the early tints trending,
Here fuller and richer the young blossoms shine;
The almond-flowers clust'ring 'round slender boughs blending
With pale purple lilacs of fragrance divine!

The hyacinths, tulips and bleeding-hearts follow,
And drink from the current their own vivid hues;
While warmer streams shoot up each valley and hollow,
And purple and yellow and crimson diffuse.

As the sun beckons on, mounting higher and higher,
The floral tide deepens in color and tone,
'Till the laughing land, decked in her gorgeous attire,
Flames forth like the bride of the tropical zone!

Carnations and pansies, and lillies and roses,
Verbenas, sweet-williams and peonies red;
Steeped in the bloomy flood each flower discloses
Its beauty and fragrance, so soon to be shed!

The gay gladiolus with emerald sword waving,
And rich portulacas in carmine and gold,

In the high flood of summer their petals now laving,
Suffused with deep color, fresh brilliance unfold.

With the sun at his strongest, the tide at its turning,
Sweet-peas and tuberoses exhaling perfume,
And scarlet and crimson in dark bushes burning,
And gardens aflame mark the zenith of bloom!

But the ebbing tide tells towards the end of September
The tale of lost beauty, too soon on the wane;
Yet the chrysanthemums bid us remember
The glories of summer lamented in vain.

While the tide's at the flow let us seize on its treasure,
Enjoy its rare colors and richest perfume;
The beauty of nature was made for our pleasure,—
How thankful we are for the great Tide of Bloom!

—Wm. H.Bradbury, 1878

20. "The Public Domain of the United States is almost boundless. . . . We want yet more people to wake our sleeping wealth; strong-armed men to press to the front in our march of civilization, and conquest easy victories with the plowshare—to 'tickle our prairies with a hoe that they may laugh with a harvest.' We offer them the greatest boon on earth—Manhood and Independence. . . . Let the home founded by our emigrant fathers continue open in its many mansions of the emigrants of today." Frederick B. Goddard, *Where to Emigrate and Why: Homes and Fortunes in The Boundless West* (Chicago: The People's Publishing Company, 1869), 9, 13.

21. Letter dated September 19, 1879. SRL, B7, F8.

22. Signed "W.B.[WHB]" "Abel Buckley for Ashton!!" [broadsheet] (Ashton-under-Lyne: William Brown Printer, February 3, 1874). Saddleworth Historical Society, L324.1.

23. "C. T. Bradbury, 1827–1907, [Memorial] Address by Rev. E. Armitage, April 19, 1907." SRL, B7, F34.

24. Kate Bradbury Griffith died March 2, 1902. Manchester Central Archives.

25. Miss Amelia B. Edwards spoke to Boston audiences in 1889 on the "Art of the Novelist"; she was often accompanied by Kate Bradbury Griffith on her trips throughout the U.S. On the stage, Miss Edwards was presented by Mrs. Mary Livermore. SRL, B8, F5. When Edwards died, she left most of her estate to Kate Bradbury Griffith, who then established a chair of Egyptology at the University of London in honor of Miss Edwards.

26. The "Last Will and Testament of one Charles Timothy Bradbury, Esq., of Riversvale Hall" [dated Oct. 3, 1905] provided for bequests to the Albion New Church, Ashton-under-Lyne; the District Infirmary at Ashton-under-Lyne; to Abel Buckley and his children; his servants, gardeners, coachmen; various Griffith relatives; with the balance going to his son-in-law, Francis "Frank" Llewellyn Griffith, a renowned archaeologist and Egyptologist and by that time a widower. SRL, B8, 1. CTB died April 16, 1907. Manchester Central Archives. Frank Griffith died in 1934; his second wife used funds from his estate to build the Griffith Institute, which opened in January 1939 behind the Ashmolean Museum. See http://www.ashmol.ox.ac.uk/gri/1griffit.html. The Griffith Institute (named after Francis Llewellyn Griffith) at Oxford University was financially endowed by the estates of Kate Bradbury Griffith and her father, Charles T. Bradbury. [n.a.] Commonplace Book of Kate Bradbury Griffith's mother [n.d.], Manches-

ter Central Archives. Left without heirs, Charles bequeathed his estate to endow the study of Egyptology in the early twentieth century at Oxford University.

27. Samuel Laycock, known as the laureate of the cotton famine, wrote "Only a Poet," n.d. Hill, 327.

28. An appropriate remark of the time about this issue, although the British writer can be viewed as derogatory about the Irish: "I cannot help; being impressed by the dramatic skill with which the American Democrats have succeeded in inducing [even] the Irish citizens, almost to a man, to follow their banner. . . . Foreigners in England remain foreigners always. . . . The feeling with which Americans regard the flag of the Union is quite unknown in England." Justin McCarthy, "American Men and Englishmen," *The Galaxy* 9, No. 6 (June 1870): 762–64.

29. Ibid., 759.

30. *New York Evening Post,* August 18, 1877.

31. Tackling socialism and communism as intellectual topics were departures from WHB's reports and poems. William H. Bradbury, "Socialism," *The Agorá,* 4 (Topeka: Crane & Company, 1895), 292–302.

32. FB wrote to the extended family in Kansas as he traveled throughout Europe, the Caribbean Islands, Florida, and California. SRL, MS 299.

33. SRL, MS 299; William Willard Howard, "The Rush to Oklahoma," *Harper's Weekly* 33 (May 18, 1889): 391–94.

34. SRL, B7, F6.

35. William had just moved to Topeka from Illinois, after years of delay, when he began to visit Arkansas City, Kansas, to reconnoiter land opportunities that would soon arise in Oklahoma. Arkansas City was conveniently located on a railroad spur route of the Atchison Topeka Santa Fe Railway. SRL, MS 299.

36. It is hard to know if this remark was tongue-in-cheek or not. There is no indication that Mary and young Will were the driving forces behind land acquisition in this family.

37. Among the extensive holdings of the Grant-Bradbury collection are a series of astronomy periodicals that related the significance of varying stellar positions. WHB and brother FB both studied the stars.

38. The only Hargreaves mentioned in the *History of Dwight, Illinois* are a minister and F.B. Hargeaves, a lawyer. Dustin, 49.

39. The author, a philosopher and social theorist of his day, wrote about socialism (which may explain WHB's subsequent interest in the subject), war, and democracy. William Hurrell Mallock, *Is Life Worth Living?* (New York, G.P. Putnam's Sons, 1879).

40. "Will" was "Willie" in the Civil War letters, his father's namesake and third child of six. Will would have career successes other than in the dairy business, apparently his parents' idea. SRL, MS 299.

41. MB's insight and wit were fortunately articulated and preserved after the war.

42. Perhaps one of the most candid and heartfelt messages from MB to anyone about the plight of her daily life.

43. For more than twenty-five years, William had tried in vain to secure hired help for his wife. Even as she approached the age of 60, Mary was still protesting.

44. Mary's wonderful plan would have brought close two very dear to her—daughter Jennie to teach, and her old friend from Dwight.

45. At one point, it must have appeared that Jennie Bradbury would remain unmarried, and her mother seemed to want to gather the family together nearby. However, Jennie did marry Emerson W. Grant when she was about 34 years old, and her own life became quite full with adventures of its own. SRL, MS 299.

46. J. Castell Hopkins, *The Life of King Edward VII* (Toronto: W.E. Scrull, 1910), 311–20.

47. Las Vegas Hot Springs, New Mexico, was a work and home site for the family of Emerson Grant and Jennie Bradbury Grant for many years. Emerson was a civil engineer for the Atchison Topeka Santa Fe Railway. SRL, MS 299. The ATSFR was considered an economic boon to the region; Las Vegas Hot Springs, NM, developed rapidly as a summer resort community with many hotels and camps, including the Harvey House. "Advertising Sunshine," *The Santa Fe Magazine* (Chicago: n.p., October 1913), 47–48.

48. The following passage depicts the breadth of subjects that WHB tackled in print later in life: "A community well managed by a capable executive upheld by an obedient constituency, may secure material prosperity of a humble type by the sacrifice of individual liberty, privacy and intellectual development; but such sacrifices are abhorrent to the average American citizen. . . . In the opinion of the writer there is no panacea for the labor troubles or the social and industrial ills incident to our complex business arrangements, intense life and increasing population. We can only mitigate these evils. . . . The individual practice of the golden rule, or self-restraint, temperance, charity, and the rest of the Christian virtues will do more than any laws or government regulations that can be devised." William H. Bradbury, "Socialism," *The Agorá,* Vol. 4 (Topeka: Crane & Company, 1895), 292–302.

49. "On the Mesa"

Where mountain vistas greet the sight and rushing torrents strike the ear,
And canyons deep exclude the light, the Mesa's level tops appear.
Where Pike's Peak's ermin'd shoulders rise; listening hills in silence wait,
Gigantic monoliths surprise the trav'ler at God's garden gate.
Through dark and bright, from far and near, this "Garden of the Gods" is seen;
And gorgeous rocks grand portals rear to guard the entrances between.

Like statues of a bygone time, or frozen sentinels they stand—
Grim figures, stark, almost sublime—behind the Mesa's level land.
They filled me with a solemn awe, as, turning from the mountain's shrine,
With backward glance I shuddering saw them peeping o'er the Mesa's line.
No refuge from them could I find, though flying far from scenes so weird,
For ever as I looked behind, those strange and fearful shapes appeared.
Thus on the mesa of our life, the rude plateau of past events—
What startling images are rife, what specters there have pitched their tents.
Keen memories of wrong words spoken; of misspent time; unrighteous deeds;
Grim ghosts of resolutions broken; Sad disregard of sacred creeds.

Such forms our conscience conjures up to haunt the mind in later years,
We cannot turn aside the cup; in vain are our remorseful tears.

—Wm. H. Bradbury, December, 1899, Topeka, Kansas.

50. The Bradbury family plot is located on a knoll of the Topeka Cemetery overlooking the city of Topeka, Kansas.

51. The land located at 65th and Topeka Avenues was adopted by Mayor Bill McCormick and the Topeka Board of Commissioners on September 28, 1976, by Resolution No. 3073. Granddaughters Mary A. Grant and Dorothy Bradbury were recognized as Honorary Citizens of the City of Topeka on August 20, 1976. Correspondence in the Grant-Bradbury Park file of the Parks and Recreation Department of the City of Topeka, Kansas.

52. Professor Mary A. Grant's extraordinary forty-year career as a Classics scholar at the University of Kansas in Lawrence may have been influenced by her grandfather's classical education. Finishing her Ph.D. at the University of Wisconsin at the close of

World War I, Miss Grant spent her post-doctoral fellowship at the American Academy in Rome and wrote extensive letters to her family for many years. It is because of Miss Grant's preservation and donations that her grandparents' Civil War story remains. SRL, MS 299.

53. Dorothy Bradbury lived from February 2, 1899, to February 9, 1979. She shared a memorial marker in Topeka Cemetery with Mary Amelia Grant, her "sister"/cousin. Topeka Cemetery Association records.

54. Ibid.

55. Gates, 333.

Appendix

1. NARA, PR, FHS. Gates Phillips Thruston, *Ancestry of the Thruston-Phillips Families,* http://www.rootsweb.com/~usgenweb/special/family/thruston-phillips; W. Ridley Willis II, *A Walking Tour of Mt. Olivet Cemetery* (Nashville: Mt. Olivet Cemetery Co., 1993).

2. Major Kise died in Vincennes, Indiana, November 21, 1873. NARA, PR.

3. The Civil War pension file of James Butterworth includes an affidavit by William Armstrong, one of his former comrades, who wrote on his behalf February 3, 1906: "Being he was an Englishman, I used to be with him while in the army quite often." Butterworth was born in Rochdale, England, on August 18, 1838—not far from Bradbury's childhood home. He married Cecelia Spafford after the war and they had four children. In spite of his difficulties, James Butterworth outlived most of his comrades and was almost 100 years of age when he died in the care of his son in Los Angeles, California. NARA, PR.

4. NARA, PR.

5. NARA, CMSR, PR; HDS, "Officer History."

6. Colonel Harrison's November 27, 1864, letter home to his wife mentions Gilchrist. W.H. Smith Memorial Library, Indiana Historical Society, M132, B1F9.

7. NARA, PR.

8. Ibid.

9. *Dwight Star,* October 3, 1895 (clipping pasted in WHB's scrapbook), SRL, 89–08–64, B2, F5.

10. NARA, PR.

11. Bailhache's wife was named Adaline. Before he relocated to California, President Arthur appointed him Receiver of Public Moneys at Santa Fe, where they lived for four years. NARA, CMSR; see http://www.iltrails.org/miscbios1.htm.

12. NARA, PR.

13. Ibid.

14. Smith's brother was also editor of the *Republican,* a newspaper in Danville, Illinois, that supported President Lincoln. Ibid.

15. Erysipelas, caused by streptococcus pyogenes, manifested itself in odoriferous and pus-leaking lesions, fever, and/or chills; it killed many soldiers on both sides. Stewart Brooks, *Civil War Medicine* (Springfield: Charles C. Thomas Publisher, 1966), 81–83.

16. NARA, PR.

17. Col. Smith had the fortifications built in 1862. They are located near Highway 109 South and Old Brush Cemetery Road, Portland, Tennessee. More information is available from the Cumberland Valley Civil War Heritage Association and the Highland Rim Historical Society.

Bibliography

ARCHIVAL SOURCES

Illinois Historical Library and Archives, Manuscript Division, Bailhache-Brayman Collection, Box 2, October 19, 1864; unprocessed collection of Grant-Bradbury family.

Indiana Historical Society, Manuscripts and Archives Department, Benjamin Harrison Collection, 1853–1943, M0143, OM0325.

Kansas State Historical Society, Documents relating to the ATSFRR, 1890–93.

Library of Congress, Manuscript Division, The William H. Bradbury Collection

NARA, RG 94, PR, CMSR, Regimental Order and Letter Books, and Court Martial records.

Robertson County, Tennessee Archives

Saddleworth Historical Society Archives, H/HOW/35

Tameside Archives, Stalybridge: Broadsheets L324 (1870's)

Tennessee State Library and Archives. Waggoner, Burnice Dorris. "My Dorris Family Line," February 7, 1980.

City of Topeka, Kansas, Parks and Recreation Department Records.

Topeka Cemetery Association, Topeka, Kansas. Records of the internees of the Grant-Bradbury cemetery plots.

University of Kansas Libraries, Spencer Research Library, The Kansas Collection, The Grant-Bradbury Collection, RH MS 299, 89–08–64.

U.S. Army Military History Institute, Photographic Division, Carlisle, Pennsylvania.

Vanderbilt University, Nashville, Tennessee. Phillips, Paul David. "A History of the Freedmen's Bureau in Tennessee (Ph.D. Thesis)," 1964.

Western Kentucky University, Bowling Green, Kentucky, Department of Library Special Collections, Manuscripts & Folklife Archives:

Champ Ferguson, MS 1;

Lewis Starling Collection 1784–1970, MS38, B8, 4E;

"Mammoth Cave Hotel Registers," Vol. 2, MS66, B5.

PUBLISHED SOURCES

Periodicals

Chicago Tribune, extensive use of 1862–65.
Dwight Star, February 2, 1871.
Manchester Guardian, extensive use of 1865.
New York Evening Post, August 18, 1877
Pontiac Sentinel, extensive use, 1862–64.
Saddleworth Reporter, December 15, 1888.
Topeka Daily Capital, November 4, 1900.
Topeka Journal, July 1, 1925.

Articles and Books

[a.u.] "Advertising Sunshine." *The Santa Fe Magazine,* October 1913.
Angle, Paul M., ed., *Prairie State: Impressions of Illinois, 1673–1967 by Travelers and Other Observers.* Chicago: University of Chicago Press, 1968.
Ash, Stephen V., ed., *Secessionists and Other Scoundrels.* Baton Rouge: Louisiana State University Press, 1999.
Augustus, Gerald L. *The Loudon County Area of East Tennessee in the War 1861–1865.* Paducah: Turner Publishing Company, 2000.
Baines Directory. Saddleworth, 1823.
Baker, Alfred. *The Life of Sir Isaac Pitman.* London: Sir Isaac Pitman & Sons L.T.D., 1930.
Baker, David J. *The Postal History of Indiana.* Louisville: Leonard H. Hartmann, 1976.
Bartlett, John. *Bartlett's Familiar Quotations,* 10th ed. New York: Little, Brown & Company, 1919.
Boatner, III, Mark M. *The Civil War Dictionary.* New York: David McKay Company, Inc., 1959.
Bohrnstedt, Jennifer Cain, ed., *Soldiering with Sherman: The Civil War Letters of George F. Cram.* DeKalb: Northern Illinois University Press, 2000.
Bradbury, William H. *Poems* (pamphlet). Topeka: Hamilton Co., 1886.
Bradbury, William H. "Socialism." *The Agorá* 4, 1895.
Bradbury, William H. *Stedman Club Souvenir* (pamphlet). 1897.
Bradley, Glenn D. *The Story of the Santa Fe.* Palmdale, Calif.: Omni Publications, 1995.
Branca, Patricia. *Silent Sisterhood: Middle Class Women in the Victorian Home.* Pittsburgh: Carnegie-Mellon University Press, 1975.
Brierley, Morgan. *History of Saddleworth.* Oldham: Chronicle Printing Works, 1891.

Brooks, Stewart. *Civil War Medicine.* Springfield: Charles C. Thomas Publishers, 1966.

Bryan, Jr., Charles F. "Tories' Amidst Rebels: Confederate Occupation of East Tennessee, 1861–63." *East Tennessee Historical Society's Publications* 60, 1988.

Bryant, Jr., Keith L. *History of the Atchison, Topeka and Santa Fe Railway.* New York: Macmillan Publishing, 1974.

Chadwick, Sir Edwin. *Report on the Sanitary Condition of the Labouring Population of Great Britain.* London: W. Clowes & Sons, 1842.

Cimbala, Paul A. and Randall M. Miller, eds., *The Freedmen's Bureau and Reconstruction: Reconsiderations.* New York: Fordham University Press, 1999.

Cimprich, John. *Slavery's End in Tennessee 1861–1865.* Tuscaloosa: University of Alabama Press, 1985.

Circulars from the Commissary General of Subsistence. Washington, D.C.: Government Printing Office, 1865.

Cogan, Frances B. *All-American Girl: The Ideal of Real Womanhood in Mid-Nineteenth-Century America.* Athens: University of Georgia Press, 1989.

Cohn, David L. *The Life and Times of King Cotton.* New York: Oxford University Press, 1956.

Connelley, William Elsey. *Quantrill & The Border Wars.* New York: Konecky & Konecky, 1909.

Connelly, Thomas L. *Civil War Tennessee.* Knoxville: The University of Tennessee Press, 1979.

Corsan, W.C. *Two Months in the Confederate States: An Englishman's Travels Through the South.* Baton Rouge: Louisiana State University Press, 1996.

Cronin, Jill, comp., *Droylsden and Audenshaw: Images of England.* Gloucestershire: The Chalford Publishing Company, 1998.

Cutler, William G. *History of the State of Kansas.* Chicago: A.T. Andreas, 1883.

Da Costa, J.M. *Medical Diagnosis,* 7th ed. Philadelphia: J.B. Lippincott Co., 1890.

Davis, James E. *Frontier Illinois.* Bloomington: Indiana University Press, 1998.

Dennett, Maurice, ed., *The Cherry Valley Chronicles: Letters from Thomas Buckley and family to Ralph Buckley and family 1845–1875.* Uppermill: Saddleworth Historical Society, 1991.

DeRosier, Jr., Arthur H., ed., *Through the South with a Union Soldier.* Johnson City: East Tennessee State University, 1969.

Drake, James Vaulx. *Life of General Robert Hatton.* Nashville: Marshall & Bruce, Pub., 1867.

Drower, Margaret S. *Flinders Petrie: A Life in Archaeology.* London: Victor Gollancz Ltd., 1985.

Dunlap, Leslie W., ed., *"Your Affectionate Husband, J. F. Culver," Letters Written During the Civil War.* Iowa City: Friends of the University of Iowa Libraries, 1978.

Durham, Walter T. "How Say You, Senator Fowler?" *Tennessee Historical Quarterly* 42(1), Spring 1983.

Durham, Walter T. *Rebellion Revisited.* Franklin: Hillsboro Press, 1999.
Dustin, William G., comp., *The History of Dwight, Illinois.* Dwight: Dustin & Wassell, 1894.
Dyer, Frederick H. *A Compendium of the War of the Rebellion,* Vols. 1 & 2. New York: Thomas Yoseloff, 1959.
Fetterley, Judith, ed., *Provisions: A Reader from 19th Century American Women.* Bloomington: Indiana University Press, 1985.
Foster, George F. *Ashton-under-Lyne Centenary.* Rochdale: Grove Publishing Company, 1947.
Gates, Paul Wallace. "Frontier Landlords and Pioneer Tenants." *Journal of the Illinois State Historical Society* 38(1), March 1945.
Gates, Paul Wallace. "The Role of the Land Speculator in Western Development." *The Pennsylvania Magazine of History and Biography* 66(3), October 1942.
Gilbert, Sir William S. and Sir Arthur Sullivan. *H.M.S. Pinafore.* London: Opera-Comique, 1878.
Giles, F. W. *Thirty Years in Topeka.* n.p., reprinted 1960.
Goddard, Frederick B. *Where to Emigrate and Why: Homes and Fortune in The Boundless West.* Chicago: The People's Publishing Company, 1869.
Gorsky, Susan Rubinow. *Femininity to Feminism: Women and Literature in the Nineteenth Century.* New York: Twayne Publishers, 1992.
Gref, Leroy P., ed., *The Papers of Andrew Johnson,* Vol. 7, 1864–1865. Knoxville: University of Tennessee Press, 1986.
Green, Harvey. *The Light of the Home: An Intimate View of the Lives of Women in Victorian America.* New York: Pantheon Books, 1983.
Gurr, Duncan and Julian Hunt, eds. *The Cotton Mills of Oldham.* Oldham: Oldham Historical Society, 1979.
Haley, Bruce. *The Healthy Body and Victorian Culture.* Cambridge: Harvard University Press, 1978.
[a.u.] *Half a Century of Independency in Ashton-under-Lyne.* Ashton-under-Lyne: T. Cunningham and Son, Printers, 1868.
[a.u.] *Harper's New Monthly Magazine* 2(12), May 1851.
Harrison, Lowell H. *The Civil War in Kentucky.* Lexington: The University Press of Kentucky, 1975.
Hatton, Hon. Robert. "Speech in the House of Representatives, February 8, 1861." Washington: Congressional Globe.
Haynes, Ian. *Cotton in Ashton.* Tameside: Libraries and Arts Committee, 1987.
Haynes, Ian. *Dukinfield Cotton Mills.* Manchester: Neil Richardson, 1993.
Hill, Samuel. *Bygone Stalybridge.* Leeds: M.T.D. Rigg Publications, 1987 (first published 1907).
[a.u.] *History of Grundy County, Illinois.* Chicago: O.L. Baskin & Company, 1882.
[a.u.] *History of Livingston County, Illinois.* Chicago: Wm. LeBaron Jr., 1878.

Hopkins, J. Castell. *The Life of King Edward VII.* Toronto: W.E. Scrull, 1910.
Howard, William Willard. "The Rush to Oklahoma." *Harper's Weekly* 33, May 18, 1889.
Illinois Public Domain "Land Tract Sales Database," Illinois State Archives, http:/www.sos.state.il.us/depts/archives/data_lan.html.
Jones, William Devereux. "The British Conservative and the American Civil War." *The American Historical Review* 58(3), April 1953.
Journal of the Twentieth Annual Encampment of the Grand Army of the Republic, Department of Kansas. Topeka: W.Y. Morgan, Printer, 1901.
Kniffen, Gilbert C. *Raising the Siege of Knoxville.* Military Order of the Loyal Legion of the United States, Commandery of the District of Columbia, Vol. 3, War Paper 65, November 7, 1906.
Langdon, Melville D., ed., *The Complete Works of Artemus Ward.* New York: A.L. Burt Company, Publishers, 1898.
LeGrand, M.D., Louis. *The Military Handbook and Soldier's Manual of Information.* New York: Beadle and Company, 1861.
Lerner, Gerda. *The Female Experience: An American Documentary.* Indianapolis: Bobbs-Merrill Educational Publishing Company, Inc., 1977.
Lerner, Gerda. *The Woman in American History.* Menlo Park: Addison-Wesley Publishing Company, 1971.
[Anonymous] *A Letter to an English Friend on the American War.* New York: Anson D.F. Randolph, 1863.
McCarthy, Justin. "American Men and Englishmen." *The Galaxy* 9(6), June 1870.
McFeely, William S. *Yankee Stepfather: General O.O. Howard and the Freedmen.* New York: W.W. Norton & Company, Inc., 1968.
McPhillips, K. *Oldham: The Formative Years.* Manchester: Neil Richardson, 1997.
Mallock, William Hurrell. *Is Life Worth Living?* New York: G.P. Putnam's Sons, 1879.
Martin, Theodora Penny. *The Sound of Our Own Voices.* Boston: Beacon Press, 1987.
[a.u.] *Memorandum of the Annual Meeting of the Atchison Topeka Santa Fe Railway.* 1882.
Mills, William Haslam. *Grey Pastures: Sketches of Life in a Lancashire Town.* London: Chatto and Windus, 1924.
Neilson, William Allan, ed., *The Complete Works of William Shakespeare.* Cambridge: Houghton Mifflin Company, 1906.
Nieman, Donald G. *To Set the Law in Motion: The Freedmen's Bureau and the Legal Rights of Blacks, 1865–1868.* Millwood, N.Y.: KTO Press, 1979.
O'Connor, Thomas H. *Lords of the Loom, The Cotton Whigs and the Coming of the Civil War.* New York: Charles Scribner's Sons, 1968.
Osgood, Samuel. "Mental Health." *Harper's New Monthly Magazine* 28(166), March 1864.
Parry, Anne. *The Saddleworth American Connection.* Oldham: Saddleworth Historical Society, 1979.

Phillips, Paul T. *The Sectarian Spirit: Sectarianism, Society, and Politics in Victorian Cotton Towns.* Toronto: University of Toronto Press, 1982.

Phillips, W.A. "The American Land Question." *The Kansas Magazine,* Vol. 2, (July–December), 1872.

Piggott's Trade Directory. Delph, 1833.

Radges' 1885–1886 Directory of Topeka, Kansas.

Radges' 1888–1889 Directory of Topeka, Kansas.

Radges' 1899–1900 Directory of Topeka and Shawnee County.

Ramage, James A. *Rebel Raider, The Life of General John Hunt Morgan.* Lexington: University Press of Kentucky, 1986.

Randall, James G. "The Newspaper Problem in Its Bearing Upon Military Secrecy During the Civil War." *The American Historical Review* 23(2), January 1918.

Reach, Angus Bethune. "The Impact of Mechanisation in Saddleworth," from *The Morning Chronicle,* November 29, 1849.

———*Labour and the Poor in England and Wales 1849–1851,* Vol. 1. London: Frank Cass, 1983.

Rees, Joan. *Amelia Edwards: Traveller, Novelist & Egyptologist.* London: The Rubicon Press, 1998.

Regulations for the Subsistence Department of the Army of the United States. Washington: Government Printing Office (GPO), 1863.

Renfro, Jack. "Remnants of Civil War Knoxville." *Civil War Times Illustrated.* May/June 1994.

Richardson, Joseph G. *Health and Longevity.* Philadelphia: Home Health Society, 1914.

Riley, Glenda. *The Female Frontier: A Comparative View of Women on the Prarie and the Plains.* Lawrence: University Press of Kansas, 1988.

Roster of Iowa Soldiers, Vol. 1. Des Moines: Adjutant General, 1908.

Roster of the Members and Posts of the Grand Army of the Republic, Department of Kansas. Topeka: Frost Printer, 1894.

[a.u.] *The Saturday Night Literary Club 1883–1983.* Topeka (n.p.)

Scherer, James A.B. *Cotton as a World Power.* New York: Frederick A. Stokes Company, 1916.

Scott, Robert N. *The War of the Rebellion: A Compilation of the Official Records of the Union and Confederate Armies.* Washington: Government Printing Office, 1890.

Series 1, Vol. 7, Part 1, Ch. 17
Series 1, Vol. 16, Part 2, Ch. 28
Series 1, Vol. 20, Part 2, Ch. 32
Series 1, Vol. 23, Part 2, Ch. 35
Series 1, Vol. 24, Part 1, Ch. 36
Series 1, Vol. 30, Part 2, Ch. 42
Series 1, Vol. 30, Part 3, Chs. 42–43

Series 1, Vol. 31, Part 1, Ch. 43
Series 1, Vol. 32, Part 1, Ch. 44
Series 1, Vol. 38, Part 2, Ch. 50
Series 1, Vol. 39, Part 3
Series 1, Vol. 47, Part 1, Ch. 59
Series 1, Vol. 49, Part 2, Ch. 61
Series 3, Vol. 5

Sensing, Thurman. *Champ Ferguson:Confederate Guerilla.* Rev. ed. Nashville: Vanderbilt University Press, 1970.

Sheppley, Helen Edith. "Camp Butler in the Civil War Days." *Illinois State Historical Society Journal* 25, April 1932.

Sherman, William T. *Sherman's Memoirs.* New York: The Great Commander Series, 1994

Sifakis, Stewart. *Who Was Who in the Confederacy,* Vol. 2. New York: Facts on File, Inc., 1988.

Sifakis, Stewart. *Who Was Who in the Union,* Vol. 1. New York: Facts on File, Inc., 1988.

Slater's Trade Directory. Delph, 1843.

Speake, Robert and F.R. Witty. *A History of Droylsden.* Stockport: The Cloister Press, 1953.

Sutherland, Daniel E., ed., *A Very Violent Rebel: The Civil War Diary of Ellen Renshaw House.* Knoxville: University of Tennessee Press, 1996.

Symonds, H.C. *Report of a Commissary of Subsistence 1861–65.* Sing Sing: Vireun School, n.d.

Transactions of the Kansas State Historical Society, 1903–1904, Vol. 8. Topeka: Geo. A. Clark, State Printer, 1904.

Ward, James A. *Railroads and the Character of America, 1820–1887.* Knoxville: University of Tennessee Press, 1986.

Warner, Ezra J. *Generals in Blue.* Baton Rouge: Louisiana State University Press, 1992.

Wrigley, Ammon. *Songs of a Moorland Parish.* Saddleworth: Moore and Edwards Printers, 1912.

ADDITIONAL READING

Cole, Arthur Charles. *The Era of the Civil War, 1848–1870.* Urbana: University of Illinois Press, 1987.

Cone, William W. *Historical Sketch of Shawnee County, Kansas.* Topeka: Kansas Farmer Printing House, 1877.

[a.u.] "England's Neutrality." *Southern Literary Messenger* 37(12), December 1863.

[a.u.] *Farmer's Handbook and Immigrants' Guide to Northern Shawnee.* North Topeka: Root & Irwin, Times Printing House, 1879.

Fisher, Noel. "Definitions of Loyalty: Unionist Histories of the Civil War in East Tennessee." *The Journal of East Tennessee History* 67, 1995.

Fishwick, Henry. *A Genealogical Memorial of the Family of Buckley of Derby & Saddleworth.* Oldham, n.p., 1900.

Gates, Paul W., *Fifty Million Acres: Conflicts over Kansas Land Policy, 1854–1890.* Ithaca: Cornell University Press, 1954.

Gladstone, T.H. *The Englishman in Kansas.* Lincoln: University of Nebraska Press, 1971.

Hopkins, Alphonso A. *The Life of Clinton Bowen Fisk.* New York: Funk & Wagnalls, 1888.

King, James L., ed., *History of Shawnee County, Kansas and Representative Citizens.* Chicago: Richomond & Arnold, 1905.

Langsdorf, Edgar. "The First Hundred Years of the Kansas State Historical Society." *The Kansas Historical Quarterly* 41(3), Autumn 1975.

Lerner, Gerda. *The Female Experience: An American Documentary.* Indianapolis: Bobbs-Merrill, 1977.

Lerner, Gerda. *The Majority Finds Its Past: Placing Women in History.* New York: Oxford University Press, 1979.

[a.u.] *Literary Club of Topeka.* Topeka: Crane & Company, 1897.

Longmate, Norman. *Hungry Mills: The Story of the Lancashire Cotton Famine 1861–1865.* London: Temple Smith, 1978.

McDade, Arthur. "Tennessee Guerrilla Champ Ferguson. . ." *America's Civil War* 14(1), March 2001.

Mallock, William Hurrell. "Social Equality." *The Century* 25(2), December 1882.

Quaife, Milo Milton, ed., *A True Picture of Emigration.* Secaucus: Citadel Press, 1974.

Scott, Anne Firor. *The American Woman: Who Was She?* Englewood Cliffs: Prentice-Hall, 1971.

Scott, Anne Firor. *Making the Invisible Woman Visible.* Urbana: University of Illinois Press, 1984.

Scott, Anne Firor. *Women in American Life.* Boston: Houghton-Mifflin Company, 1970.

Seville, Sam. *With Ammon Wrigley in Saddleworth.* Oldham: Saddleworth Historical Society, 1984.

Shea, John C., comp. *Reminiscences of Quantrell's Raid upon the City of Lawrence, Kansas.* Kansas City: Isaac P. Moore, Printer, 1879.

Snell, Mark A., ed., *Dancing Along the Deadline.* Novato: Presidio Press, 1996.

Strasser, William A. "'A Terrible Calamity has Befallen Us': Unionist Women in Civil War East Tennessee." *The Journal of East Tennessee History* 71, 1999.

Stratton, Joanna L. *Pioneer Women: Voices from the Kansas Frontier.* New York: Simon and Schuster, 1981.

Wendt, Lloyd. *Chicago Tribune: The Rise of a Great American Newspaper.* Chicago: Rand McNally & Company, 1979.

Index

www.ingramcontent.com/pod-product-compliance
Lightning Source LLC
Chambersburg PA
CBHW020945310726
48980CB00001B/65

* 9 7 8 0 8 1 3 1 2 2 5 9 5 *